For Mileen
Stott

The Wild and Twisted World of RUBES®

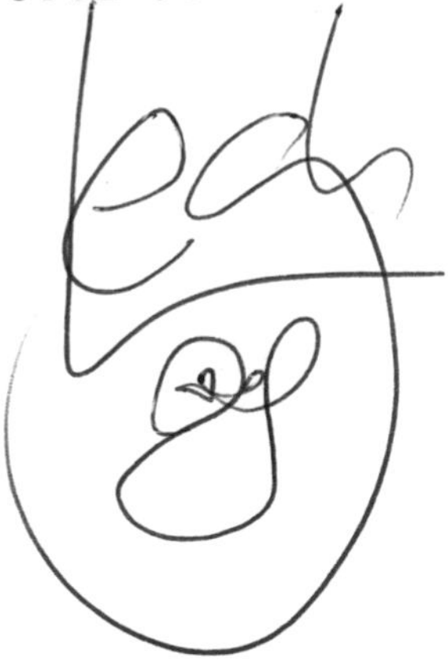

Other books by Leigh Rubin

The Wild Life of Cats

The Wild Life of Dogs

The Wild Life of Pets

The Wild Life of Cows

The Wild Life of Farm Animals

Rubes® Bible Cartoons

Rubes® Then and Now

Calves Can Be So Cruel

Rubes®

Notable Quotes

Encore!

Amusing Arrangements

Sharks are People Too!

The Wild Life of Love

The Wild and Twisted World of RUBES®

A Rubes® Cartoon Collection by Leigh Rubin

Andrews McMeel Publishing, LLC

Kansas City · Sydney · London

10 11 12 13 14 TEN 10 9 8 7 6 5 4 3 2 1

ISBN-13: 978-0-7407-9156-7
ISBN-10: 0-7407-9156-7

Library of Congress Control Number: 2009940827

Rubes® is distributed internationally by Creators Syndicate, Inc.

www.andrewsmcmeel.com

—— **ATTENTION: SCHOOLS AND BUSINESSES** ——

Andrews McMeel books are available at quantity discounts with bulk purchase for educational, business, or sales promotional use. For information, please write to: Special Sales Department, Andrews McMeel Publishing, LLC, 1130 Walnut Street, Kansas City, Missouri 64106.

For my wonderful parents, Stan and Natalie.
Thank you for a lifetime of love and encouragement.
This book wouldn't have been possible without you.

Special thanks to my brother Paull for some real gems.

Foreword

I have been asked a question that no parent should ever have to answer: "Which child of yours do you like the most?" That, in essence, is what I was asked to do for this book, only instead of picking just one favorite child, I had to select 240 . . . from a group of more than 9,000 kids. What's a parent to do?! While I am quite fond of all my "children," the constraints of a "Best of *Rubes*" collection has forced me to be extremely selective. That's the harsh reality of the situation; space is limited. I am not going to say the task of selecting the cartoons wasn't enjoyable. I haven't looked at some of the ones included in this collection in many years. Heck, it was actually a pretty fun few days. But in the end, there was only enough room for my very favorites. So, proud parent that I am, I happily present to you many of my most prized mental offspring from the past twenty-five years.

Enjoy!

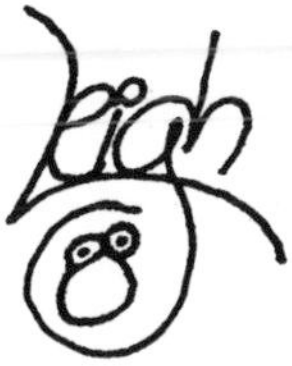

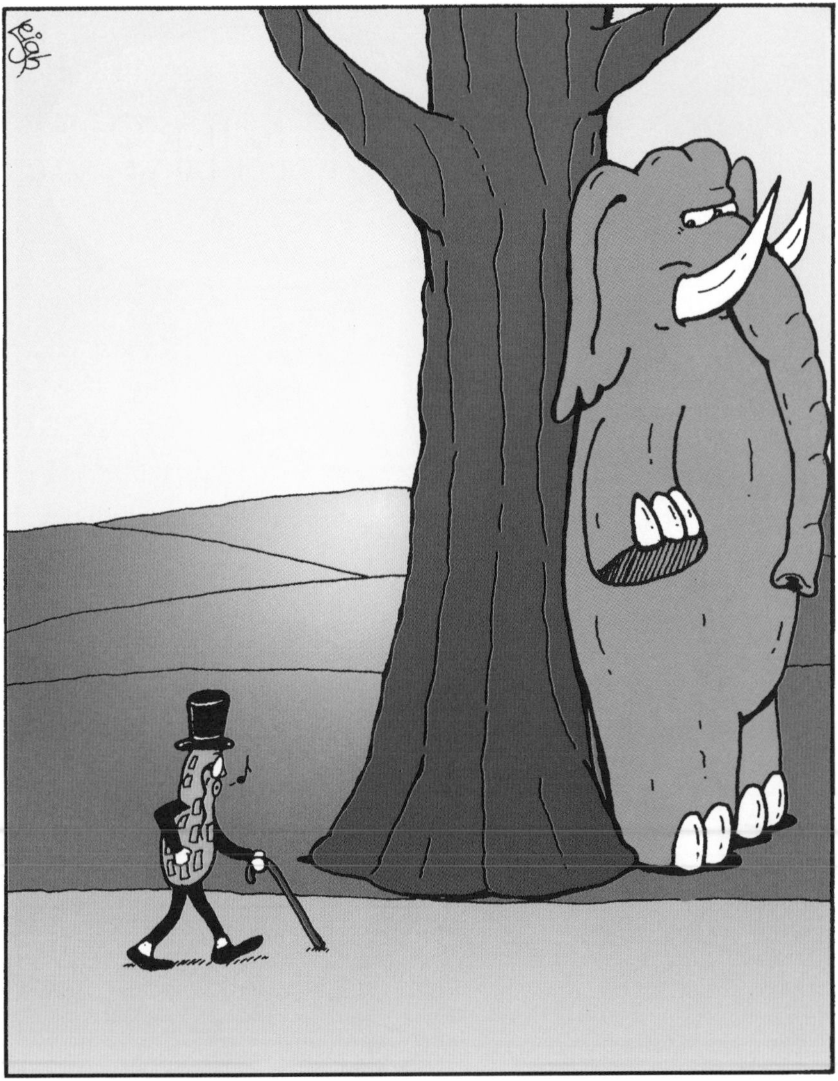

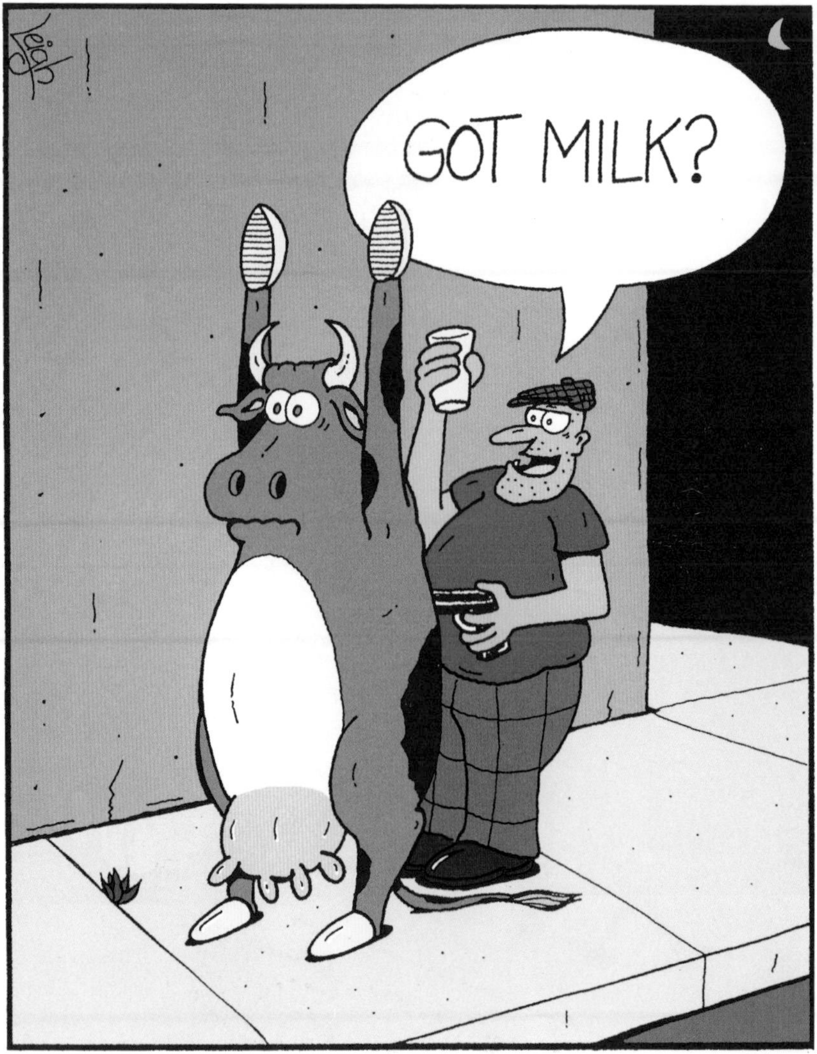
GOT MILK?

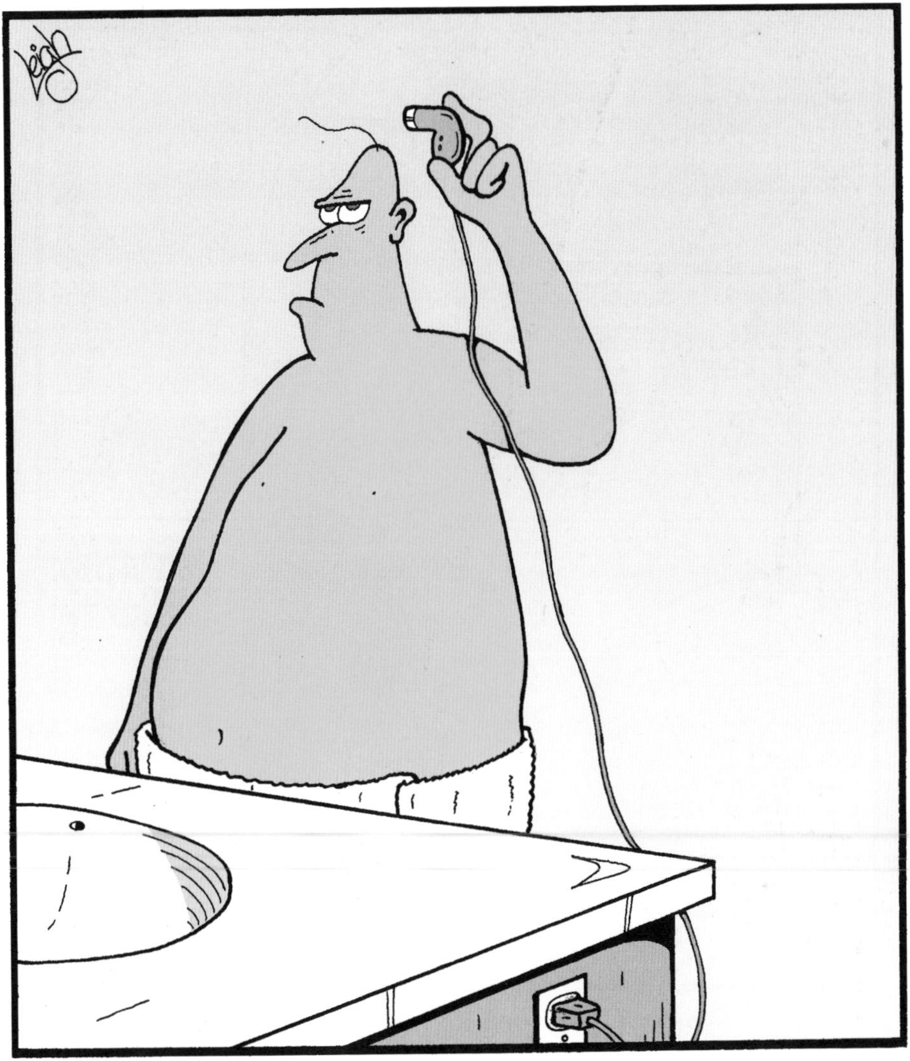

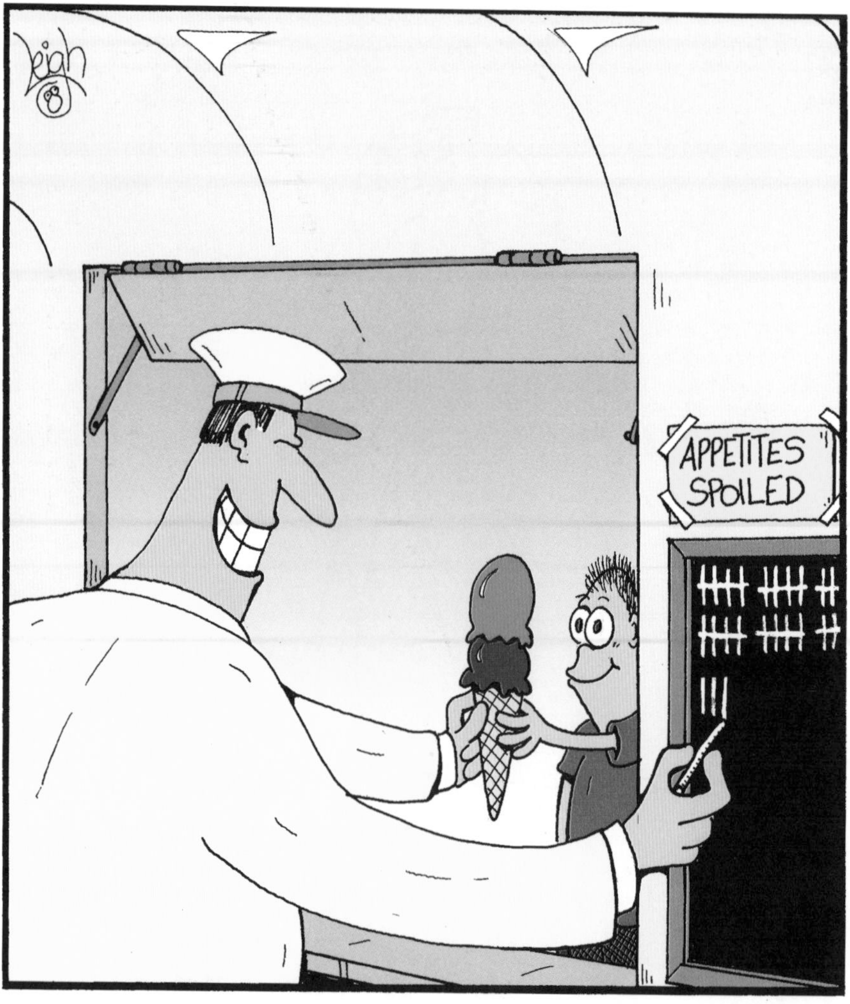
APPETITES SPOILED

Secret ice-cream man quotas

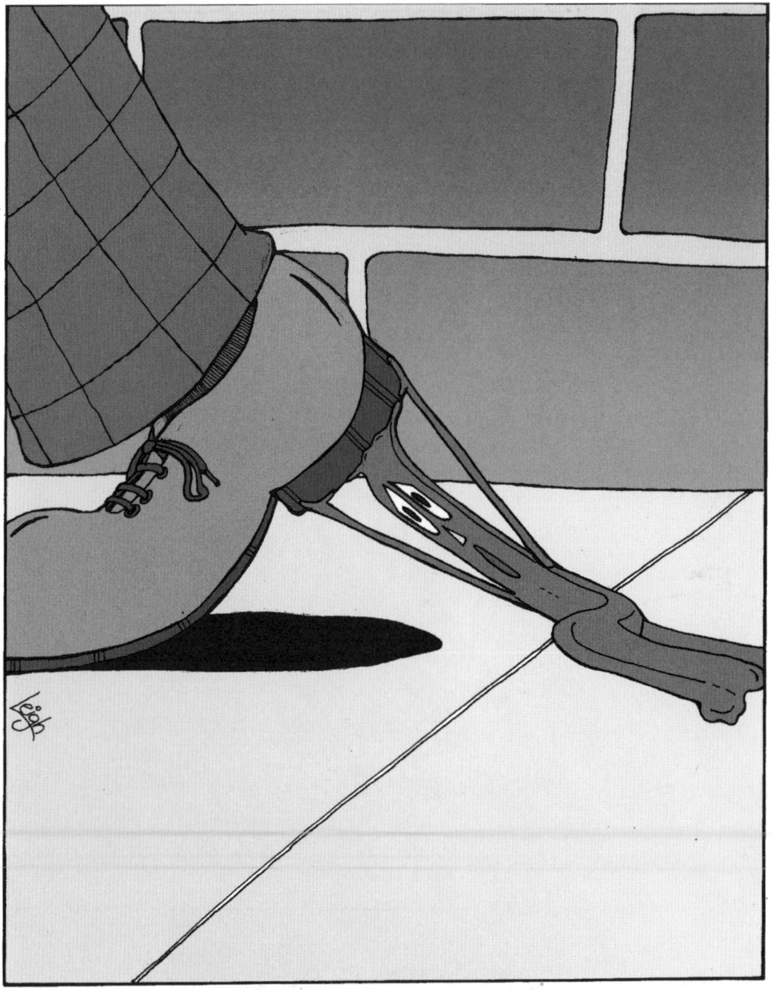
Leigh

Gumby's tragic demise

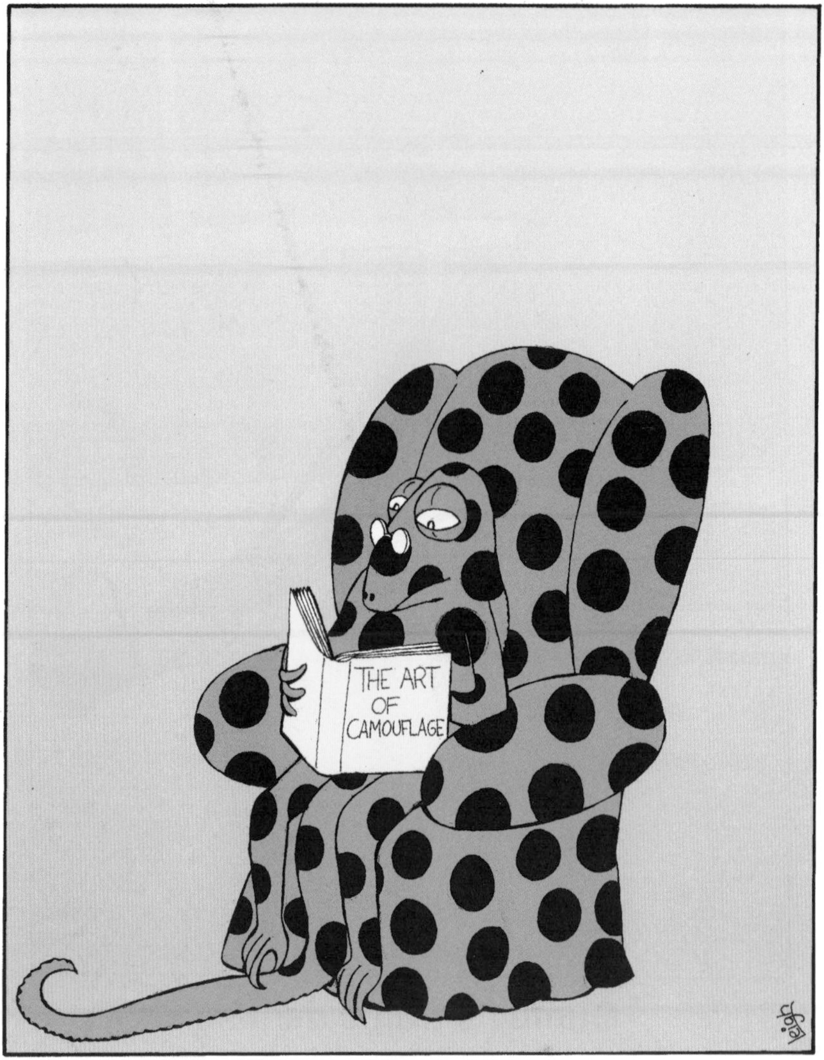
THE ART
OF
CAMOUFLAGE
leigh

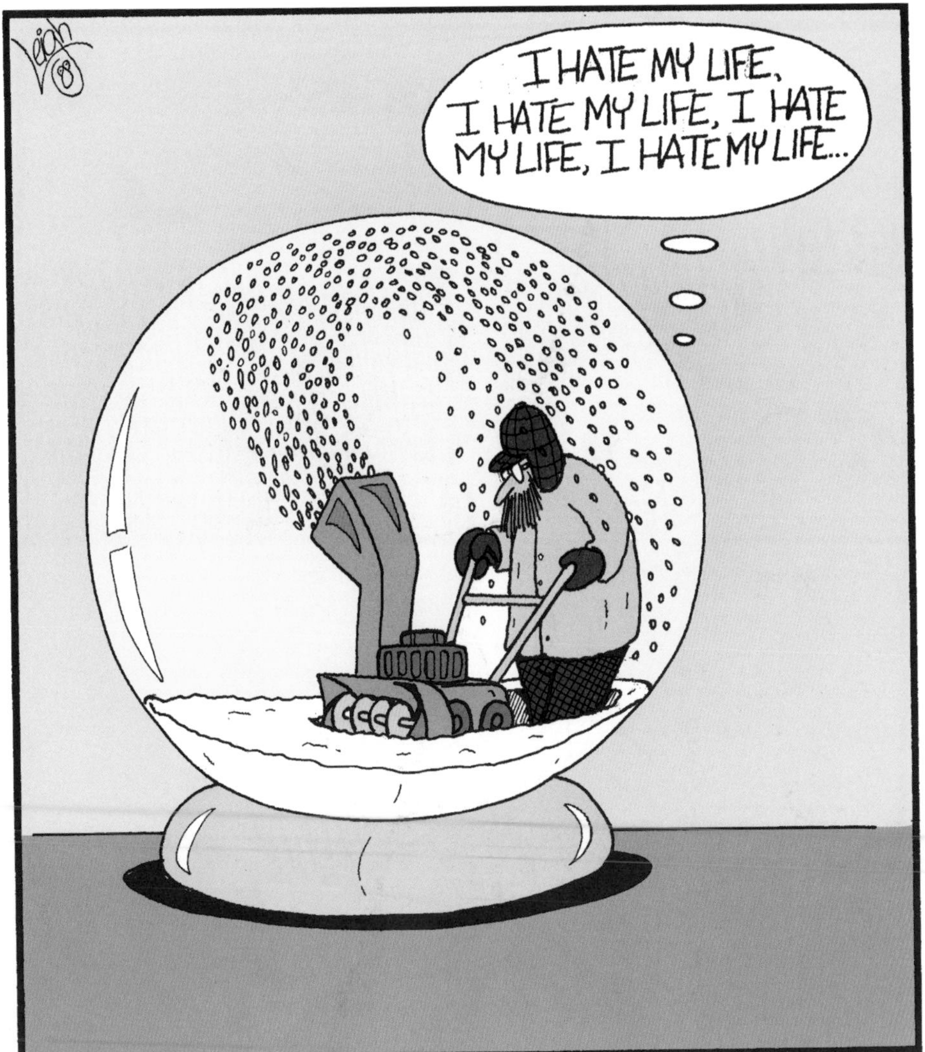
I HATE MY LIFE,
I HATE MY LIFE, I HATE
MY LIFE, I HATE MY LIFE...

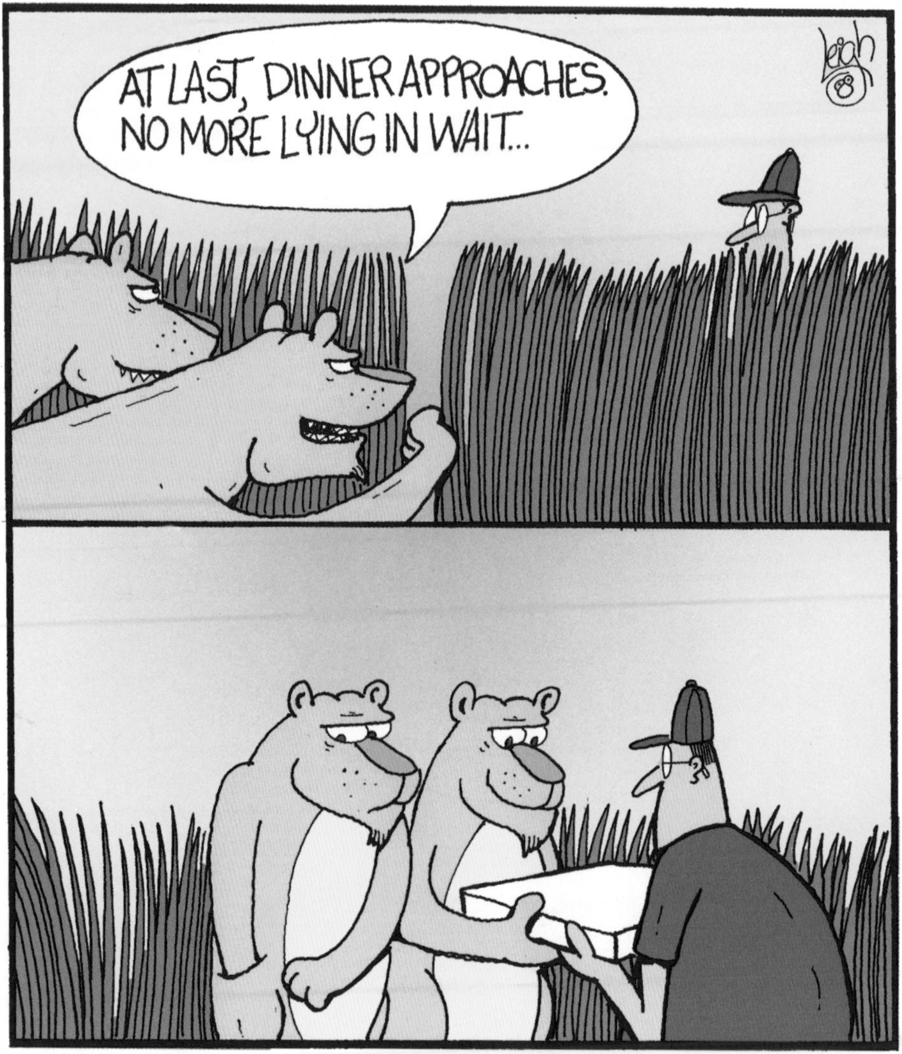
AT LAST, DINNER APPROACHES. NO MORE LYING IN WAIT...

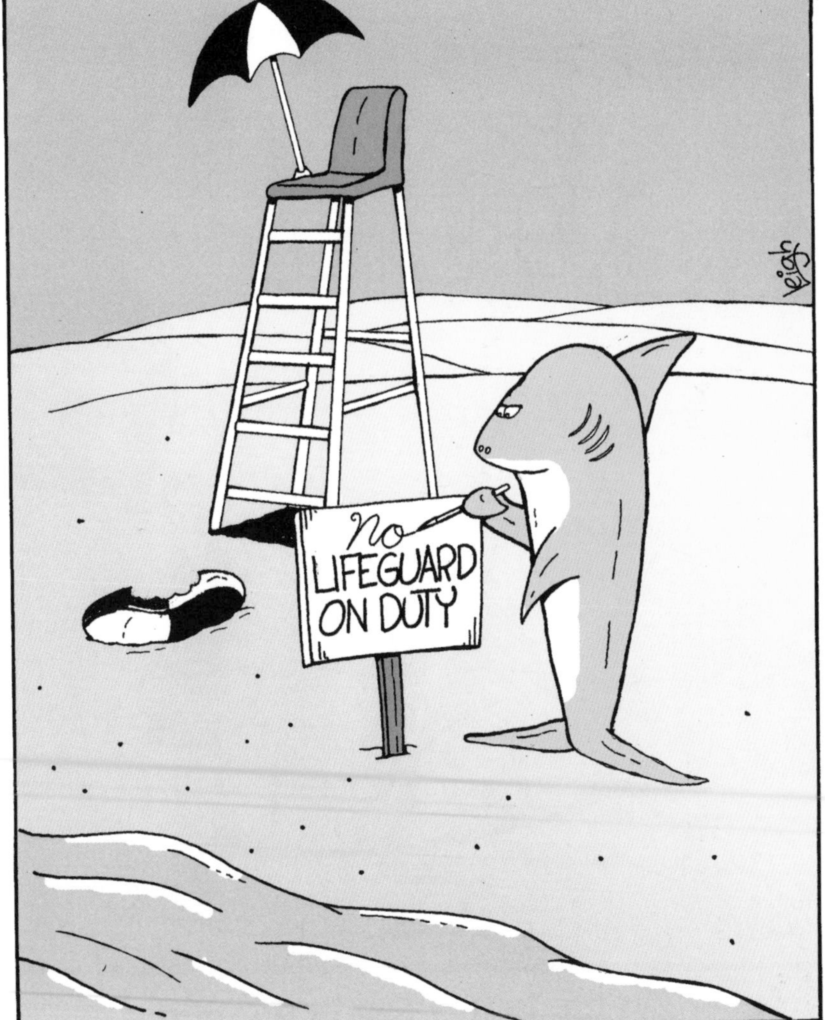
No
LIFEGUARD
ON DUTY
leigh

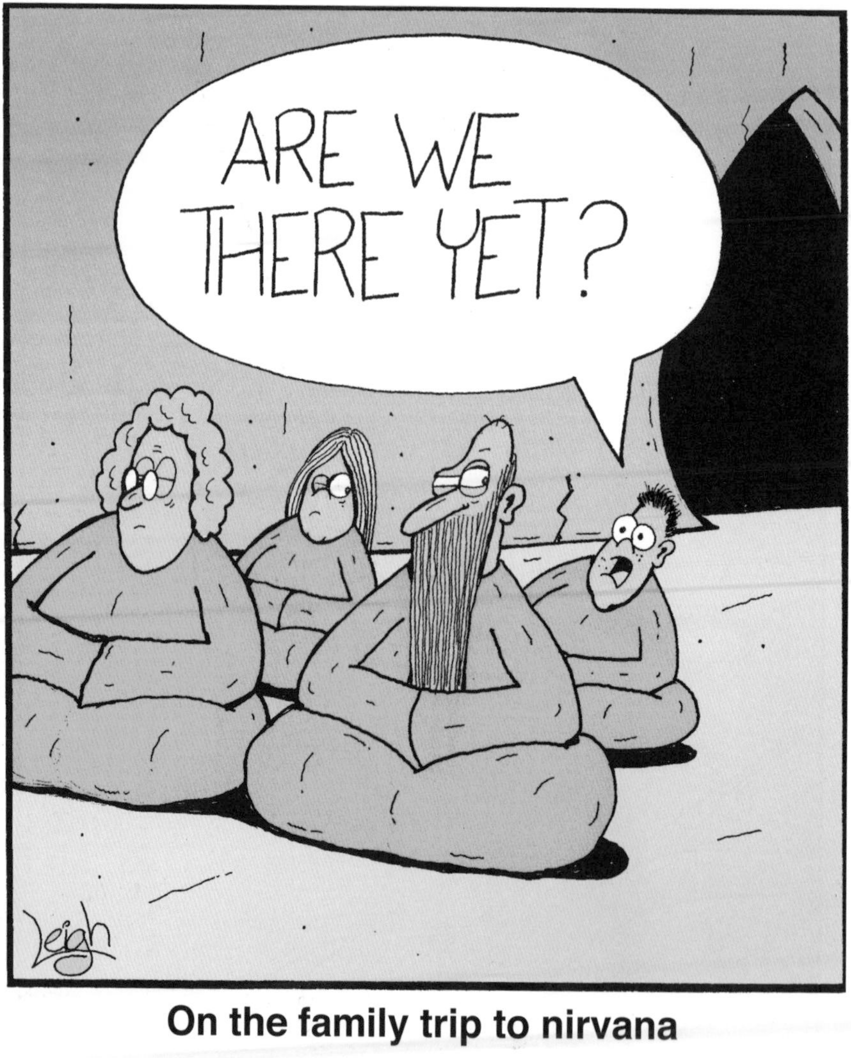
ARE WE THERE YET?
Leigh

On the family trip to nirvana

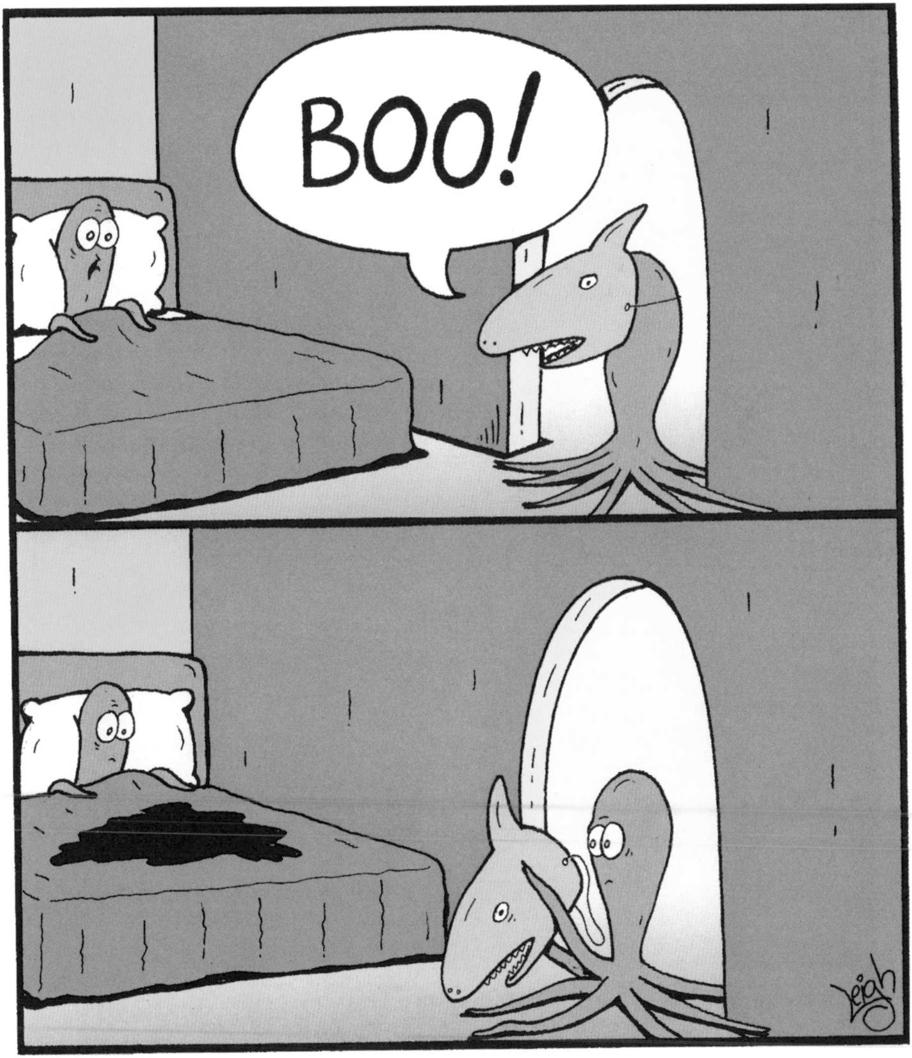
BOO!

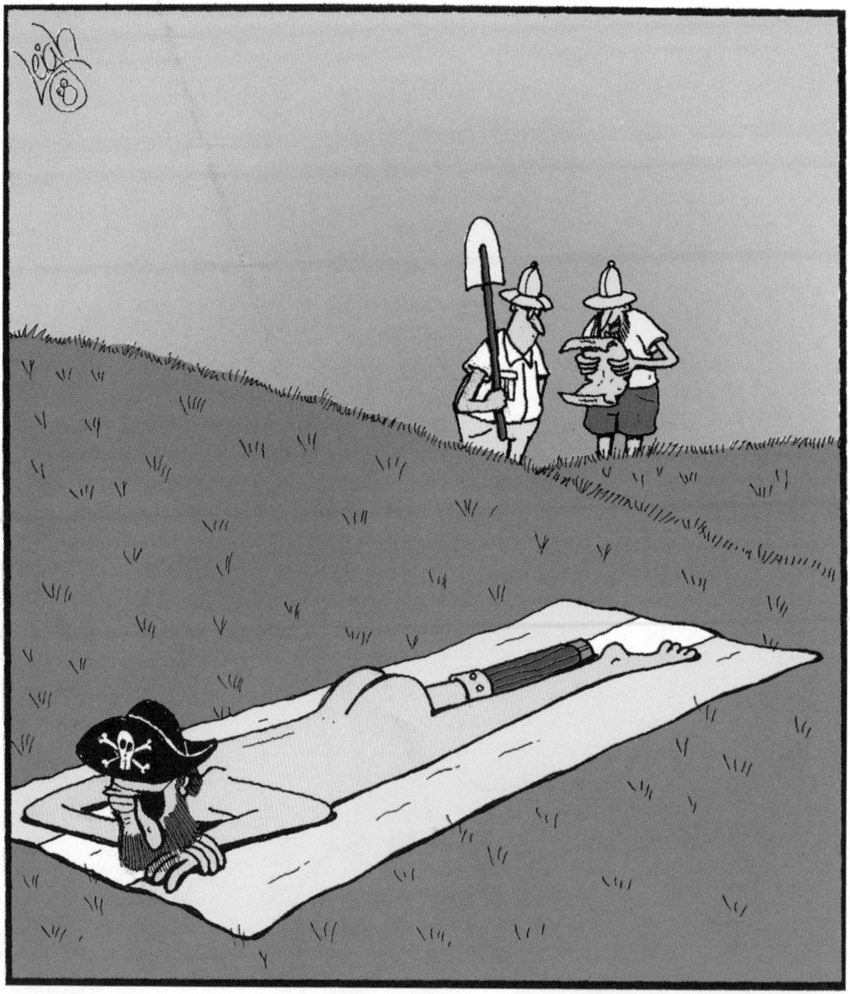

"According to this map, the pirate's booty lies just over the next hill."

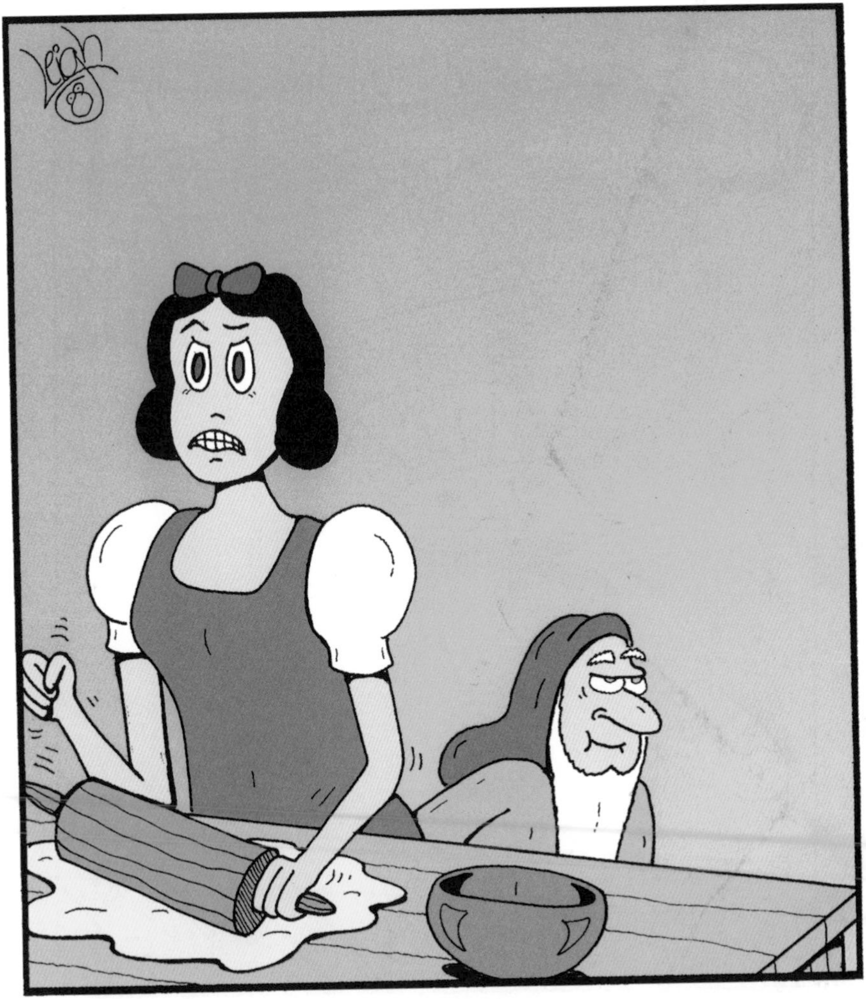

There would be a loud thud, and gone forever was the eighth and, undoubtedly, the most obnoxious dwarf, Gropey.

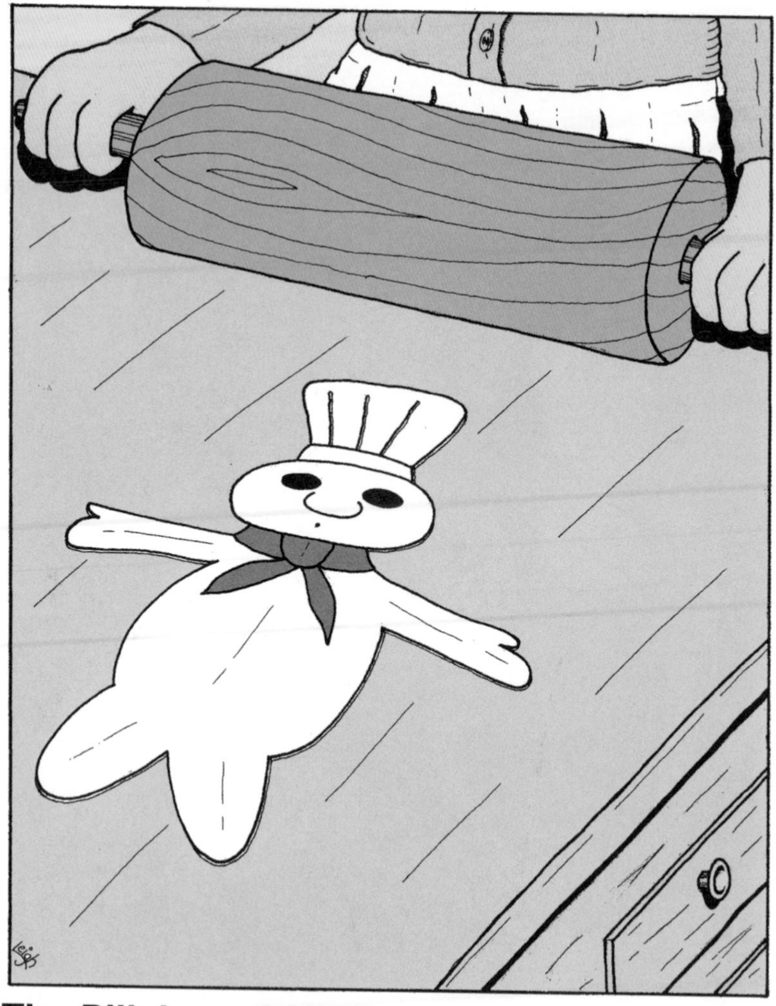
Leigh

The Pillsbury Doughboy meets his maker.

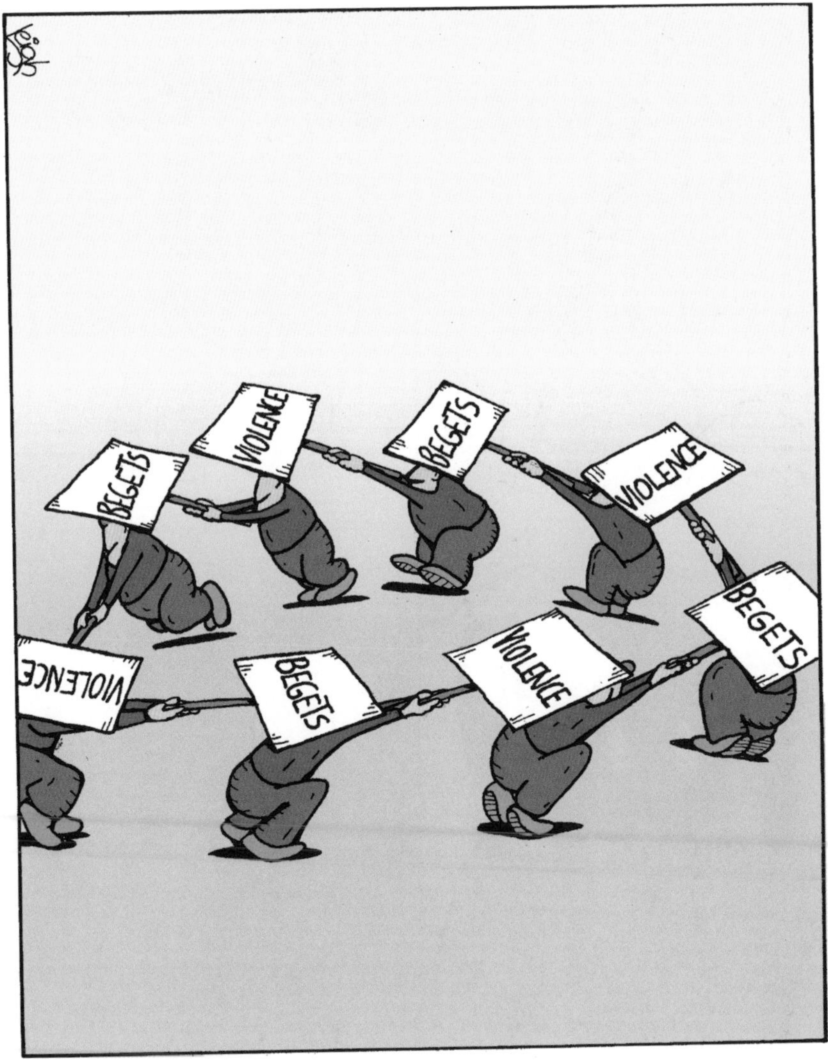
BEGETS
VIOLENCE
BEGETS
VIOLENCE
BEGETS
VIOLENCE
BEGETS
VIOLENCE

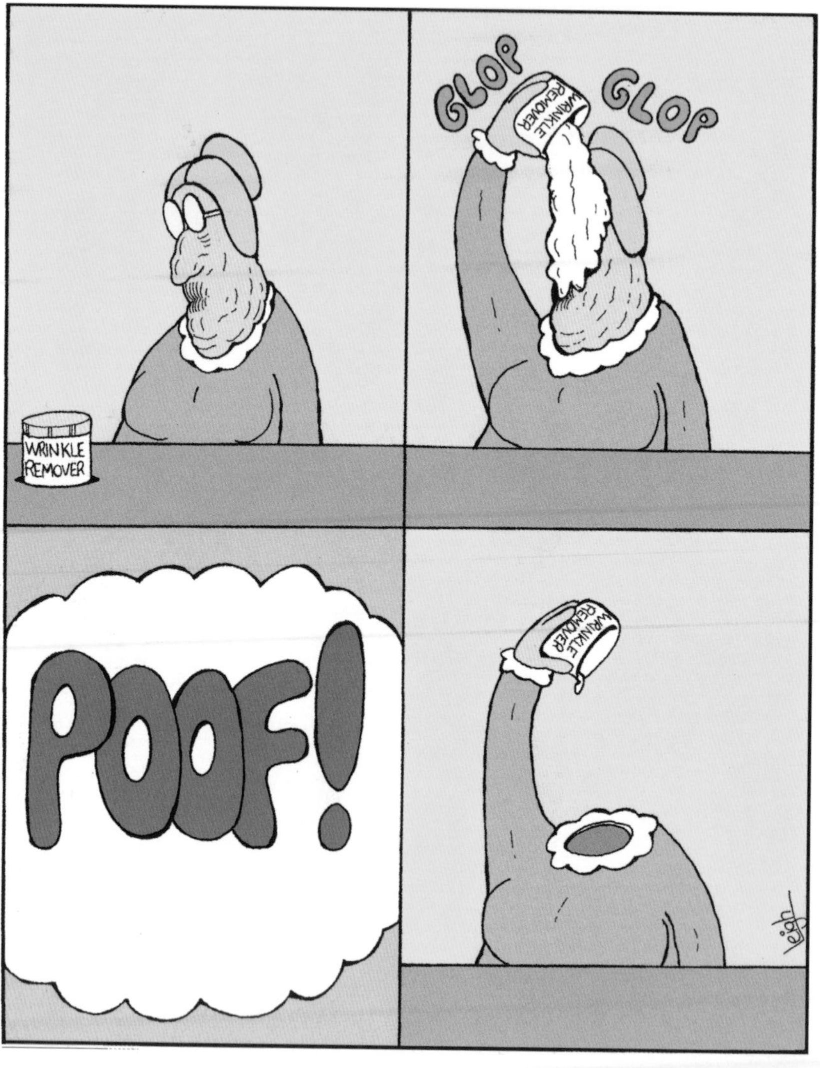
WRINKLE REMOVER
GLOP GLOP
WRINKLE REMOVER
POOF!
WRINKLE REMOVER
Leigh

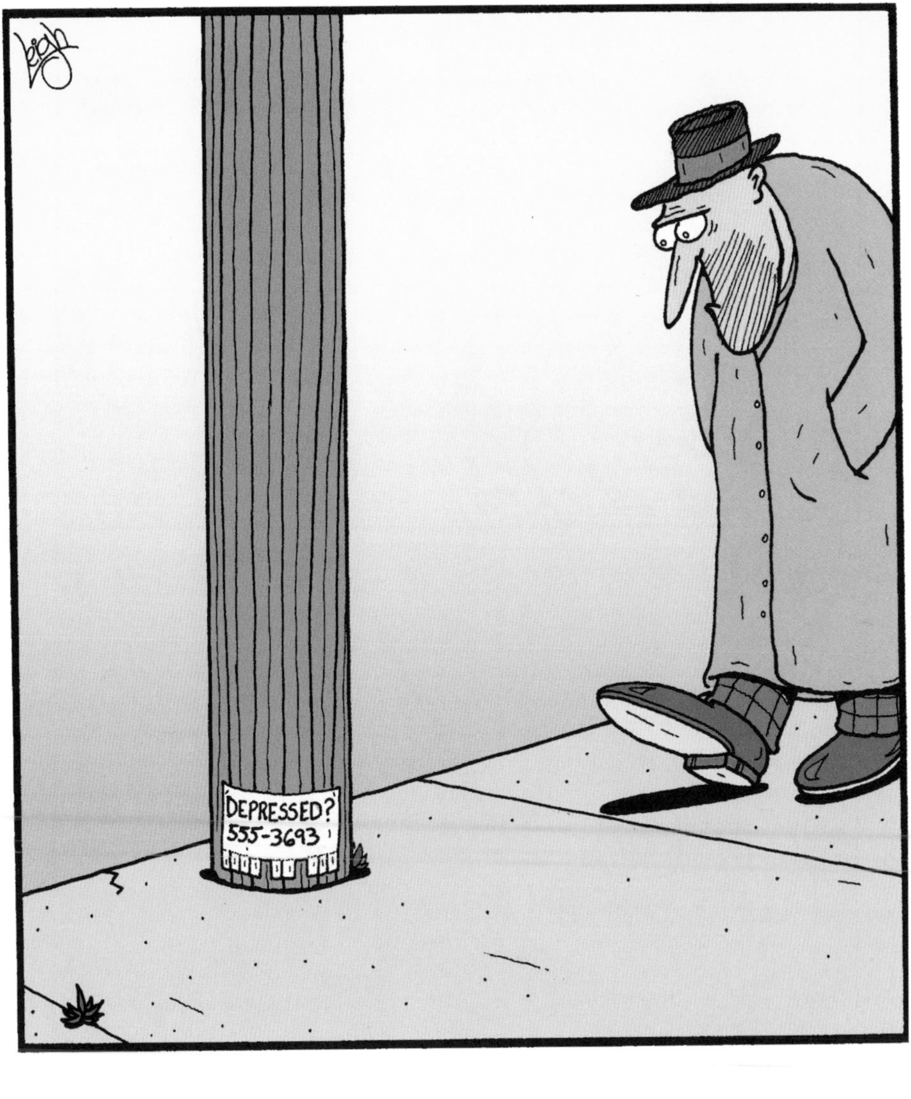
leigh
DEPRESSED?
555-3693

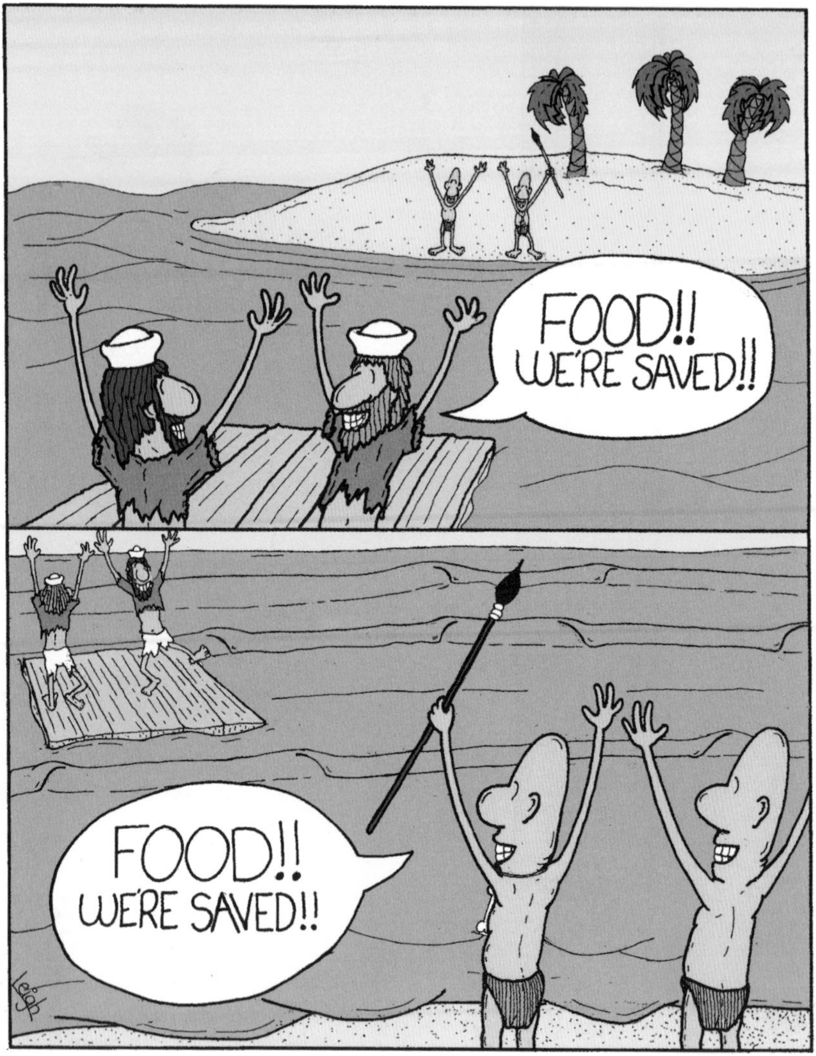
FOOD!!
WE'RE SAVED!!
FOOD!!
WE'RE SAVED!!
Leigh

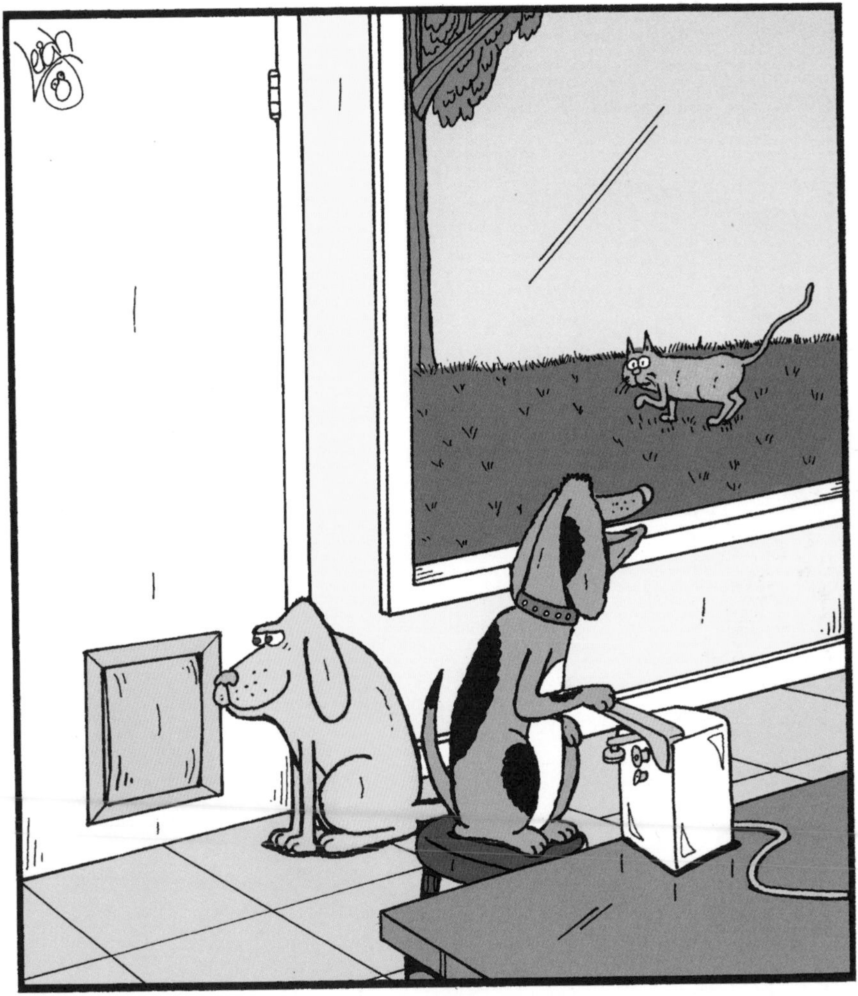

"Oh yeah, he heard it all right. Get ready . . ."

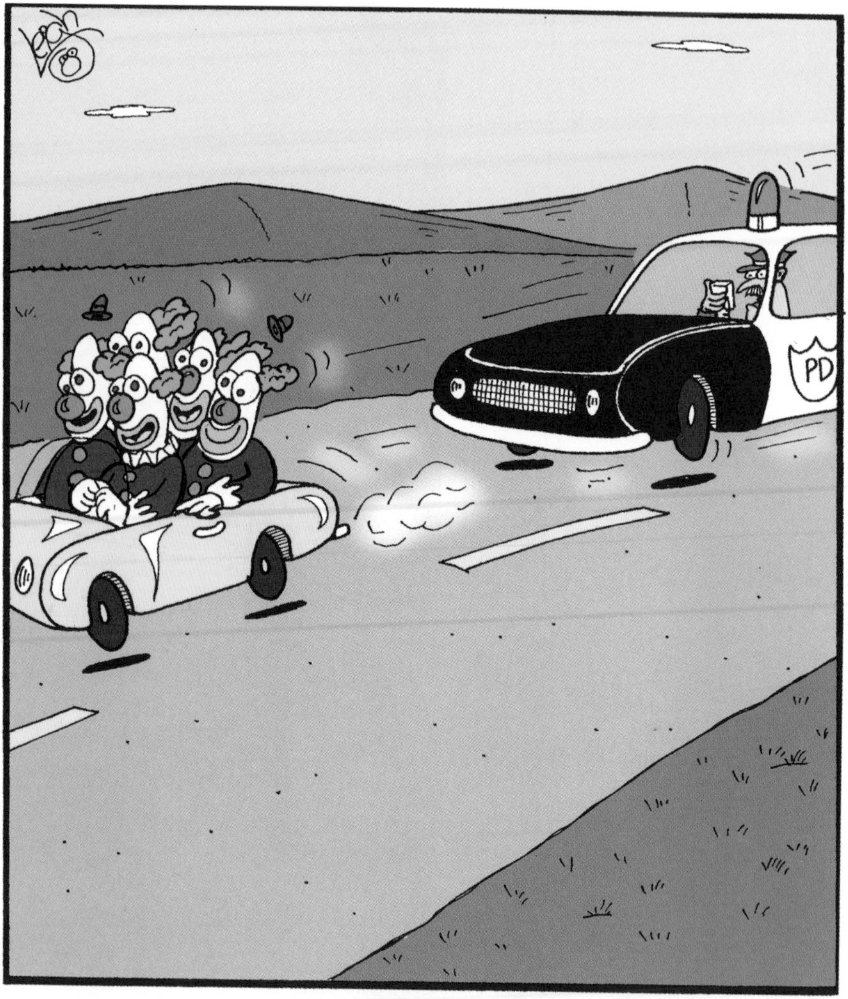
PD

"This is car seventeen . . . Am in pursuit of happiness . . . I repeat, am in pursuit of happiness . . ."

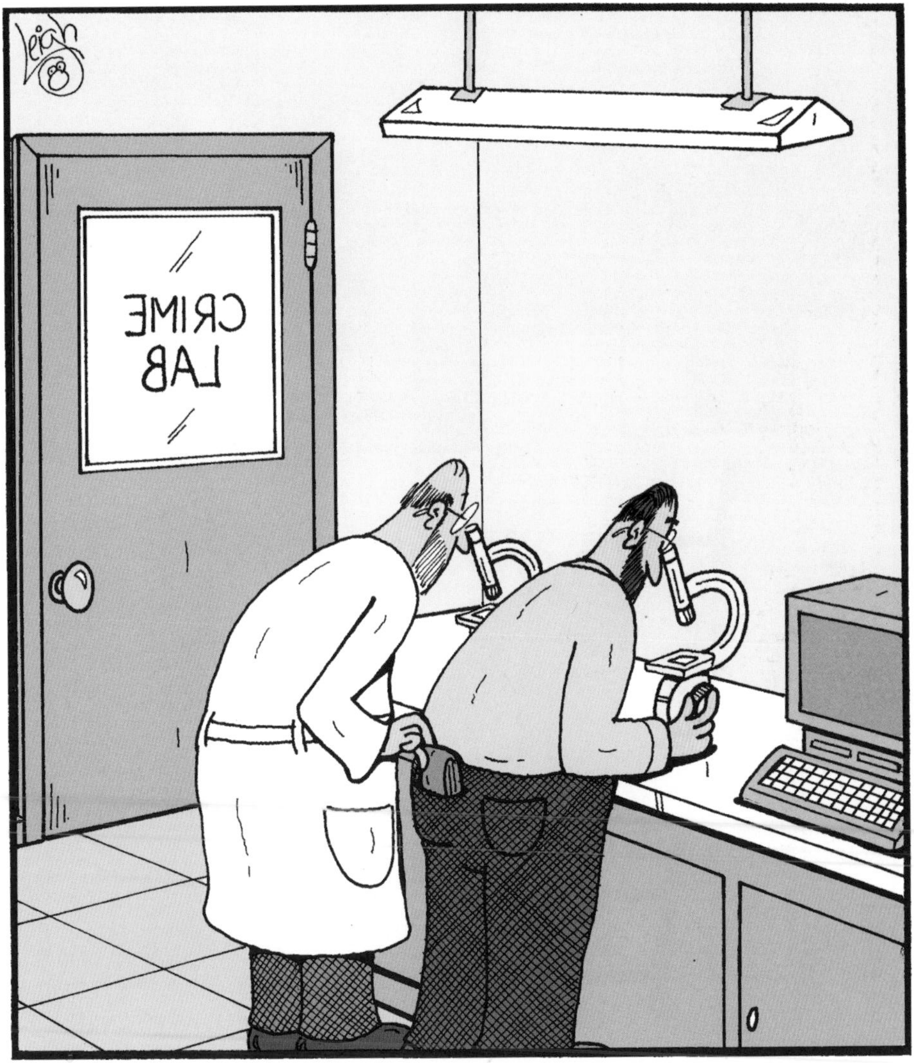
CRIME
LAB

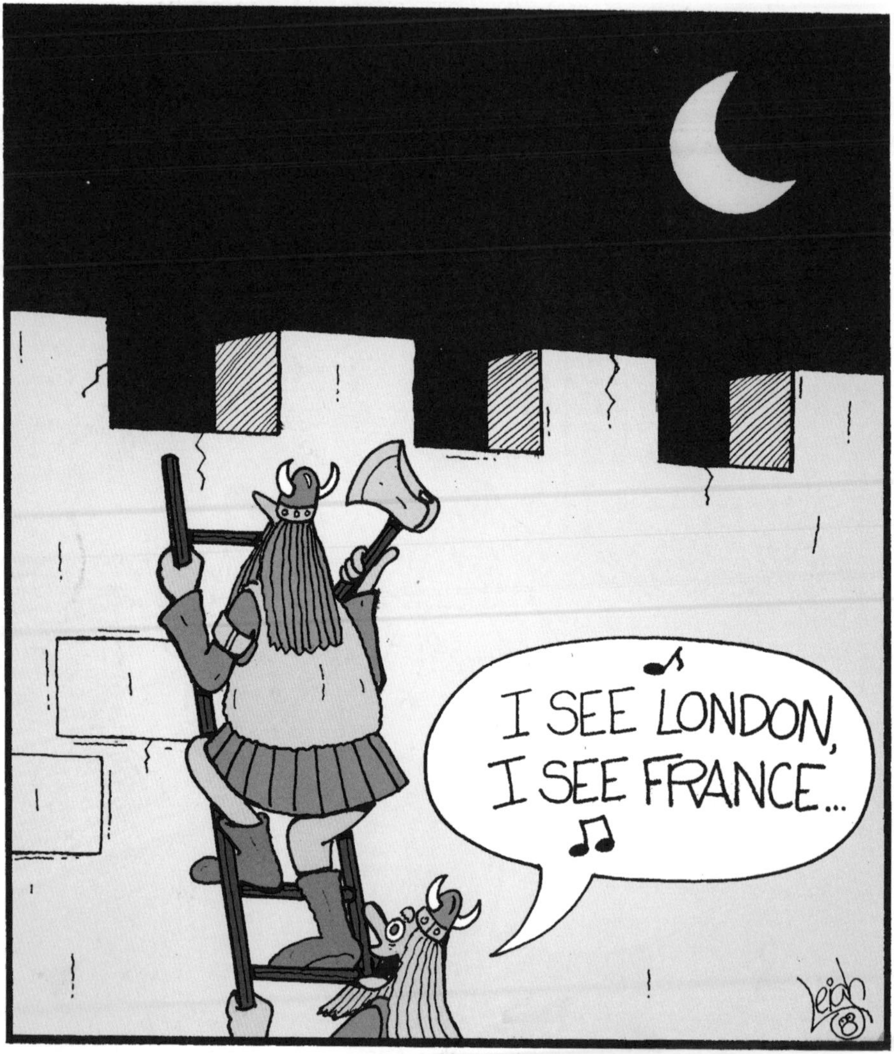
I SEE LONDON, I SEE FRANCE...
Leigh 88

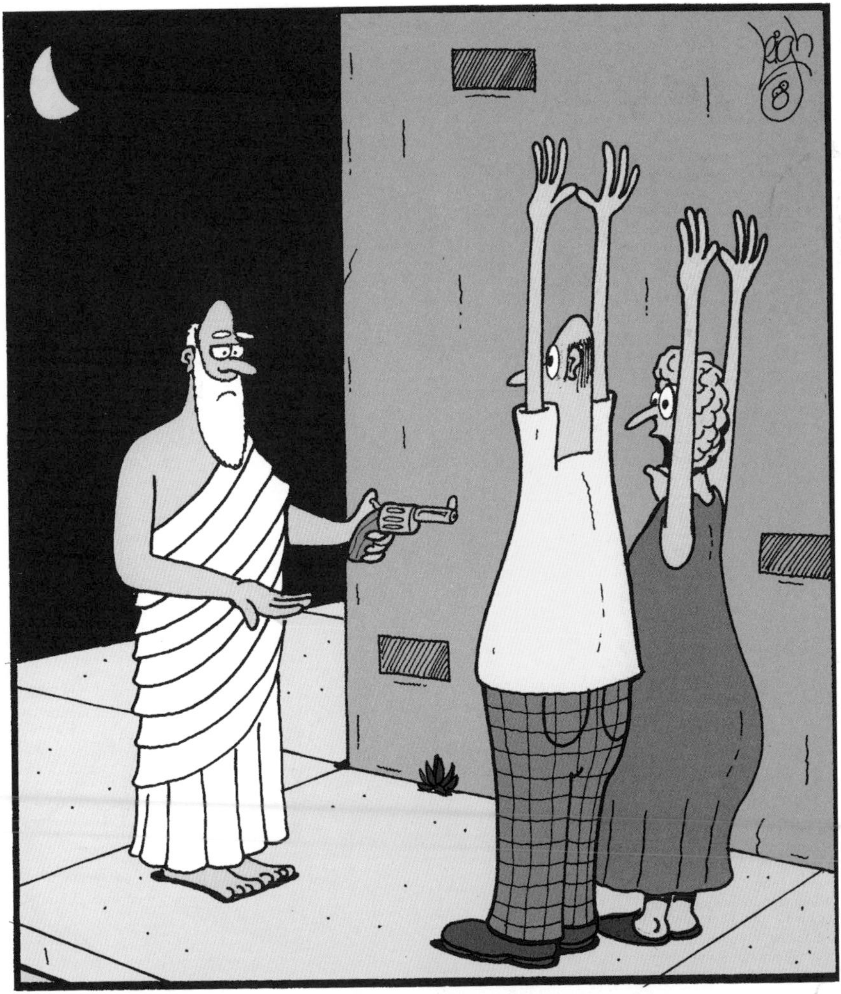

“For goodness’ sake, Harry, he’s a philosopher. Maybe you can reason with him!”

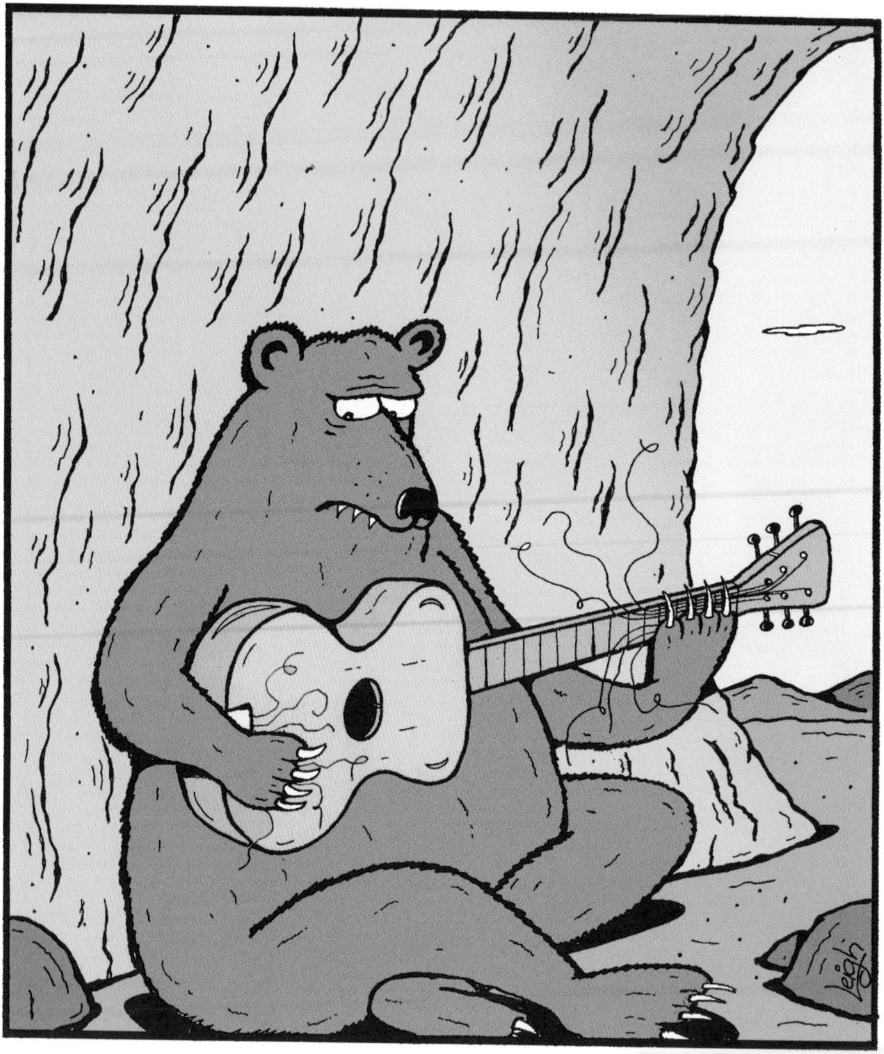

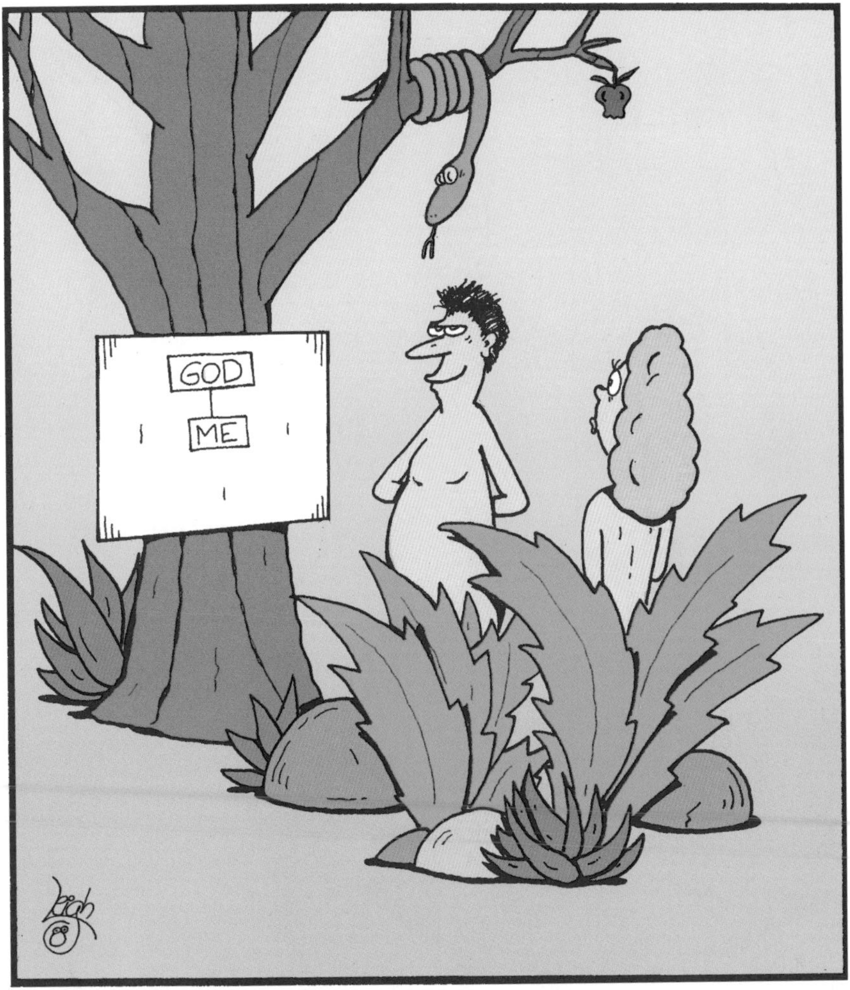
GOD
ME

In an attempt to impress the girl, Adam shows off his family tree.

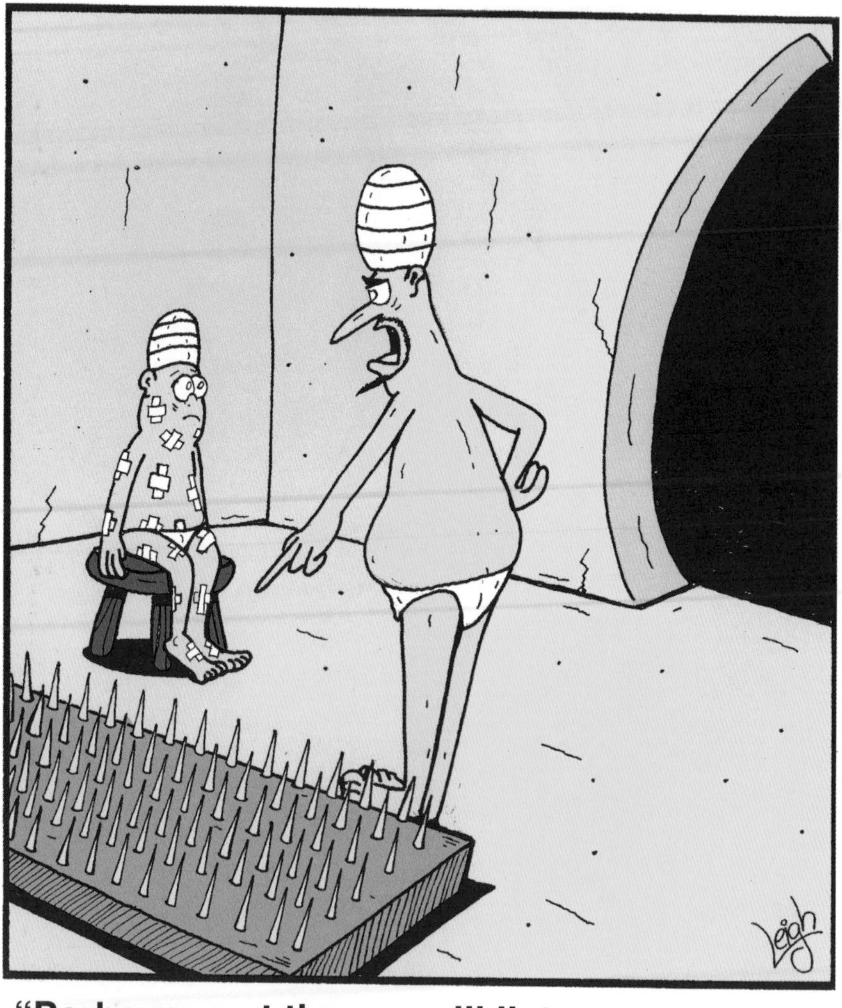
Leigh

"Perhaps next time, you'll listen to me when I tell you not to jump on your bed!"

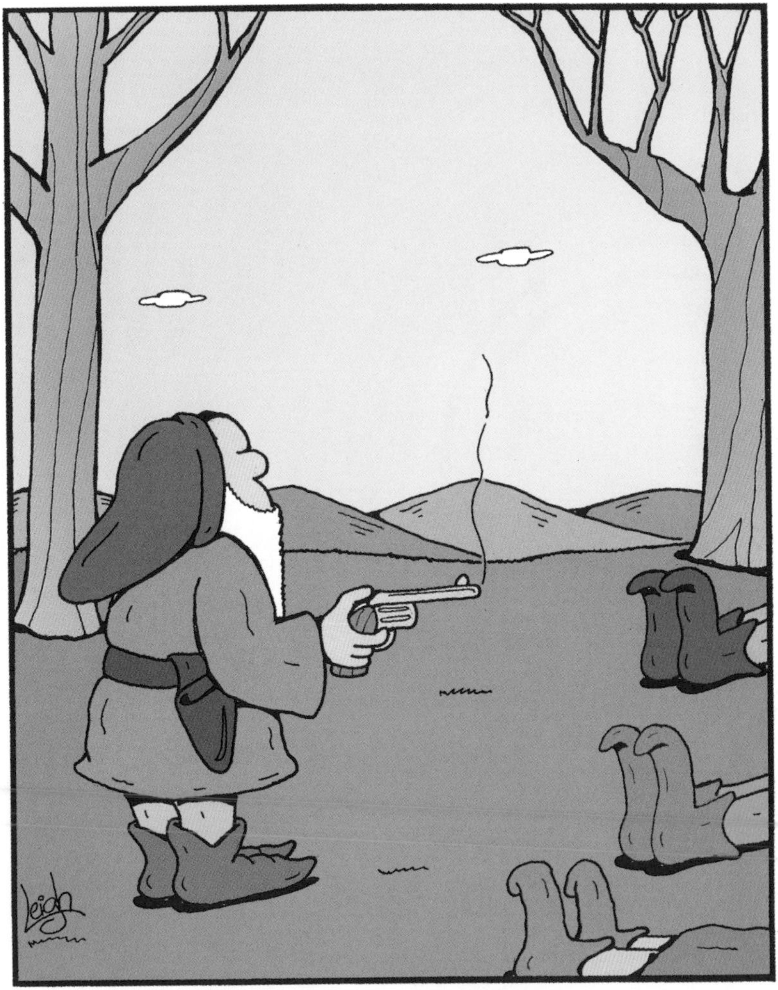
Leigh

Of all the dwarfs, the most volatile was Trigger Happy.

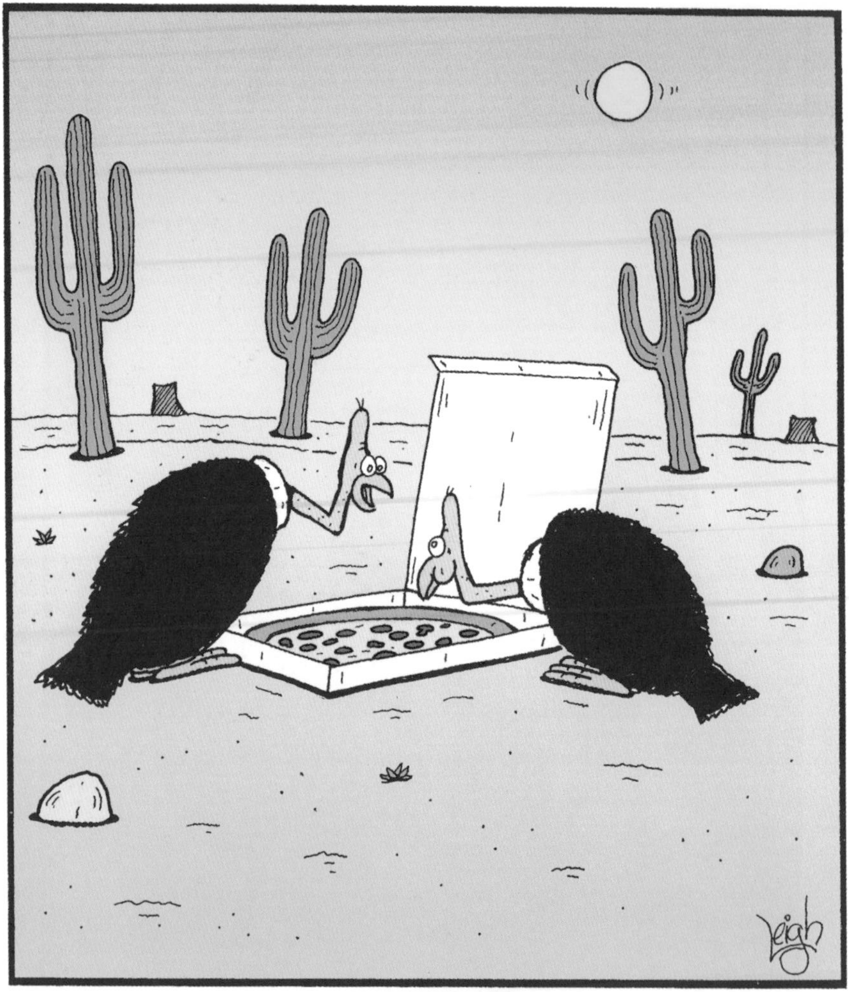
Leigh

"Isn't this marvelous? It's warm, gooey, and flat . . . Just like roadkill, but with all of your favorite toppings!"

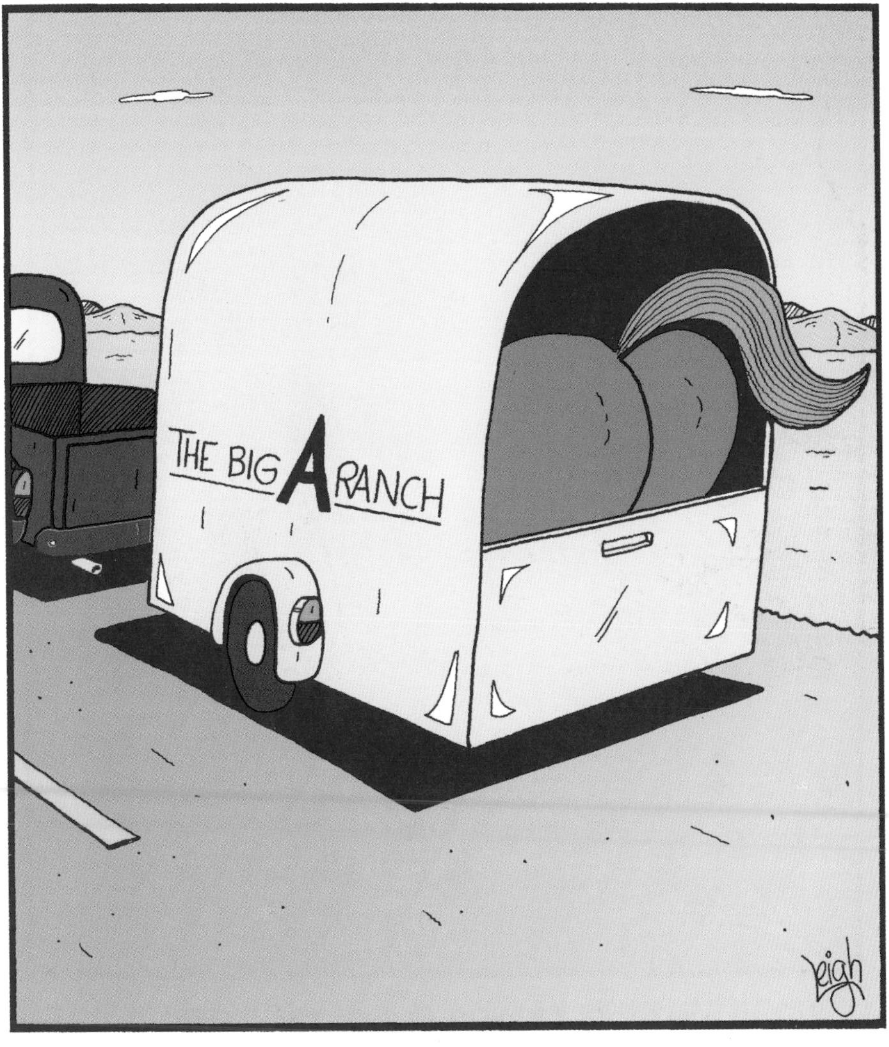
THE BIG A RANCH
leigh

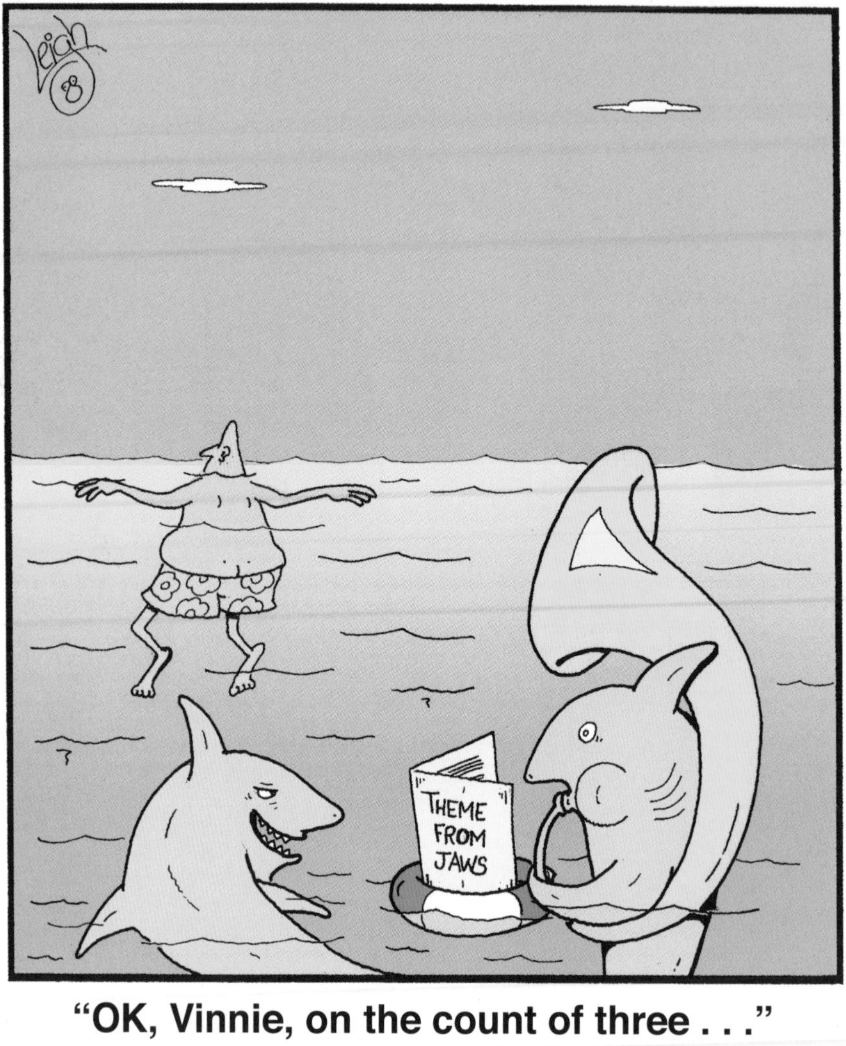
Leigh
THEME
FROM
JAWS

"OK, Vinnie, on the count of three . . ."

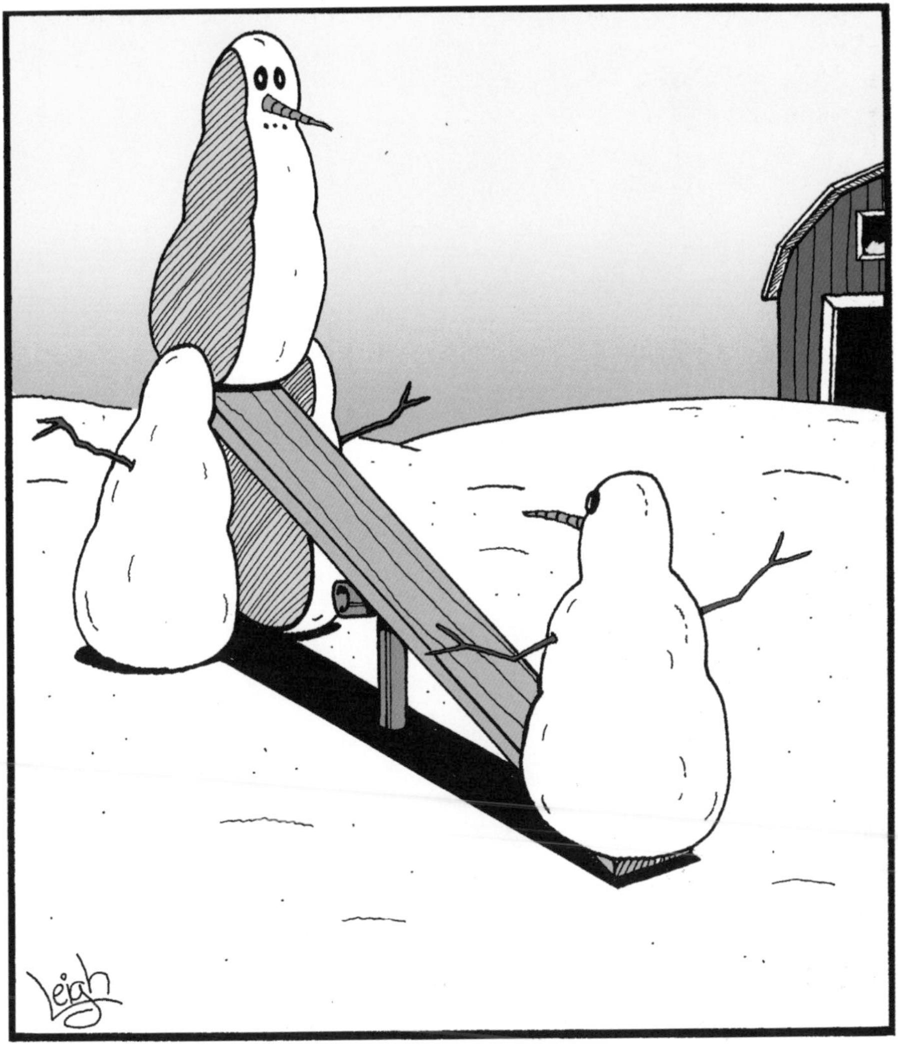
Leigh

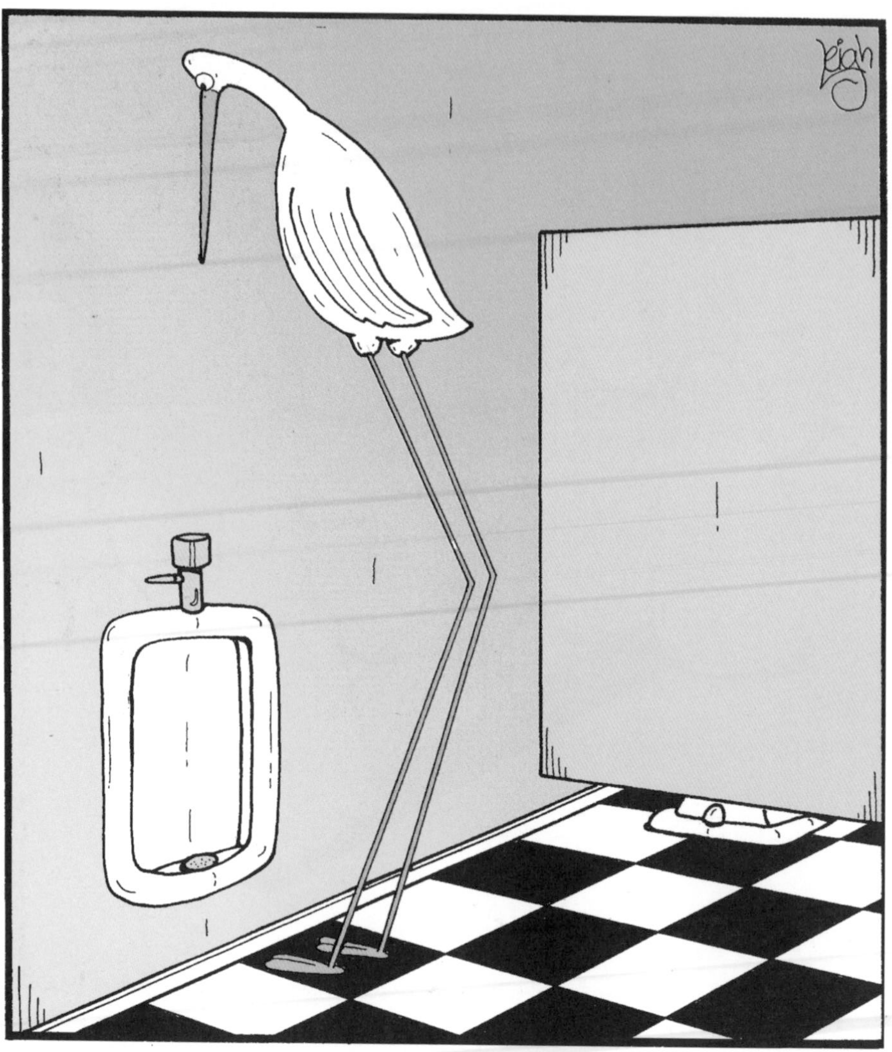
Leigh

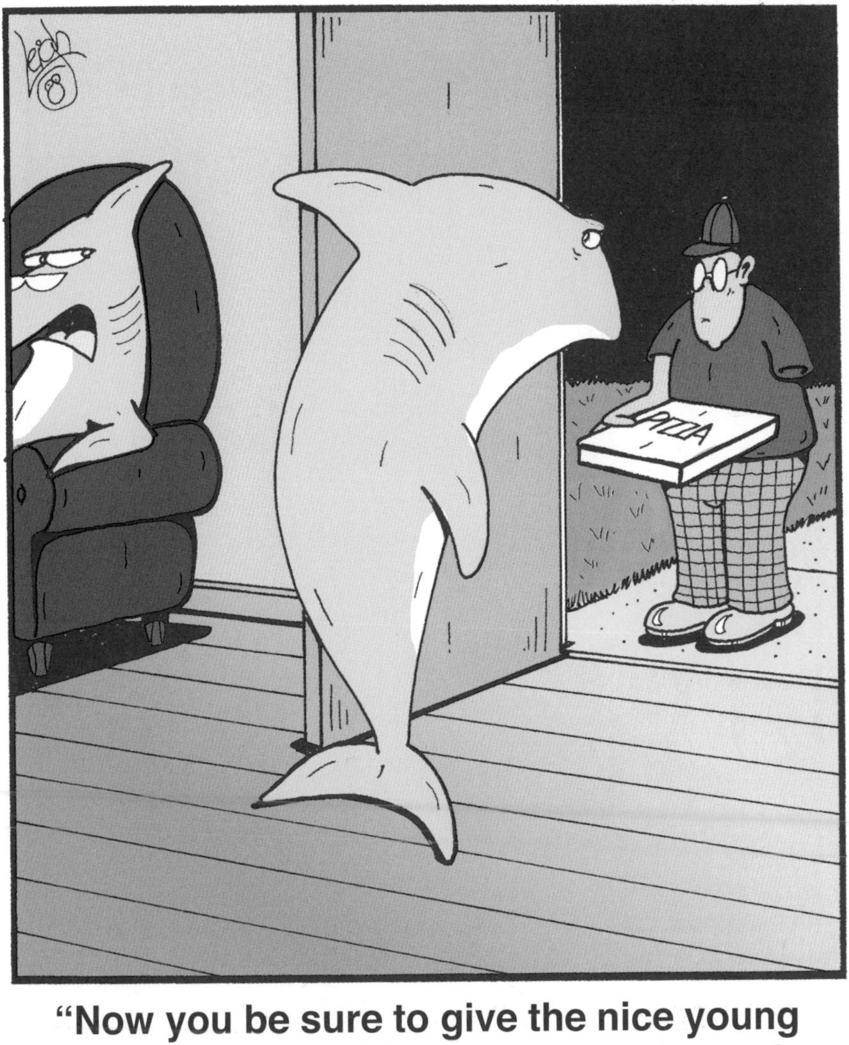
PIZZA

"Now you be sure to give the nice young man a little something extra to make up for last time."

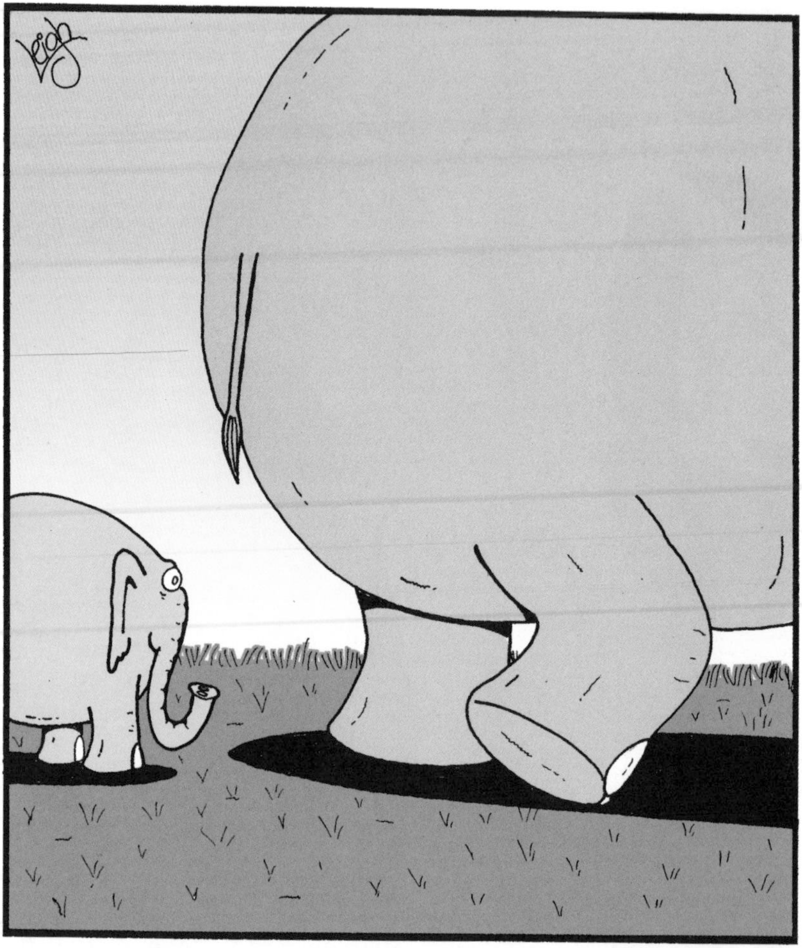
Leigh

That day, little Ethan would learn two valuable lessons: how elephants spread seeds and contribute to a diverse and healthy environment, and why he should never follow his mother too closely.

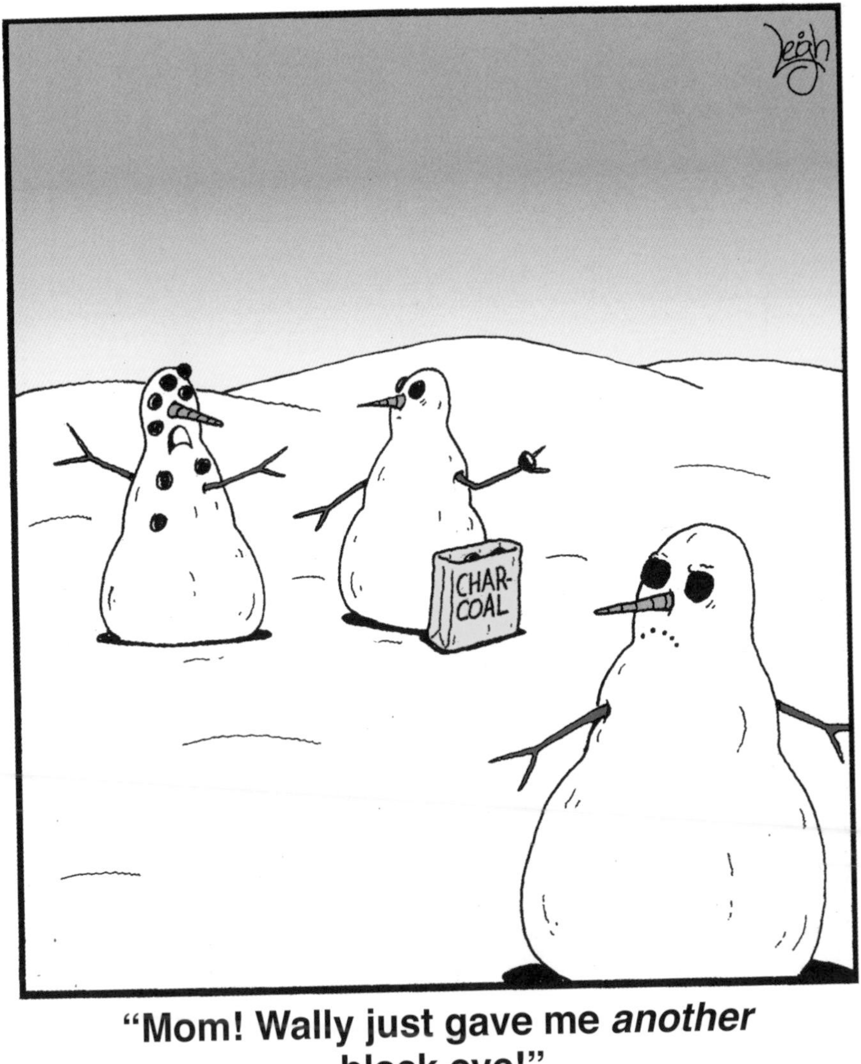
CHAR-
COAL

"Mom! Wally just gave me *another* black eye!"

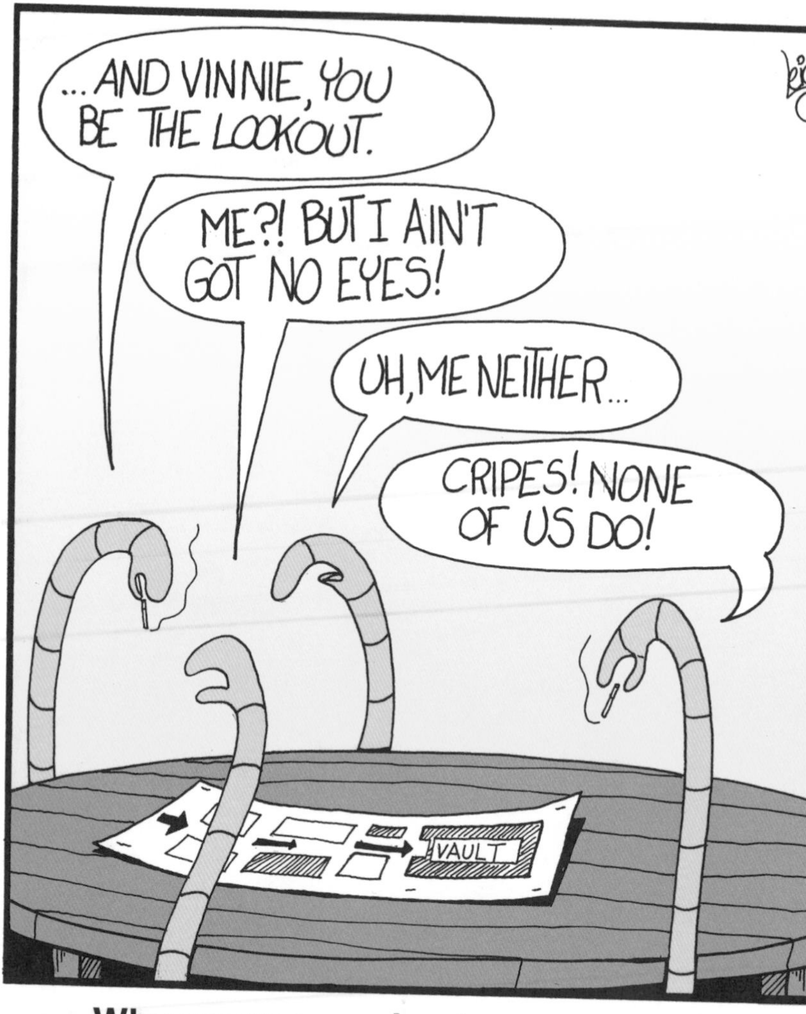
...AND VINNIE, YOU BE THE LOOKOUT.
ME?! BUT I AIN'T GOT NO EYES!
UH, ME NEITHER...
CRIPES! NONE OF US DO!
VAULT

Why worms rarely stage successful bank jobs

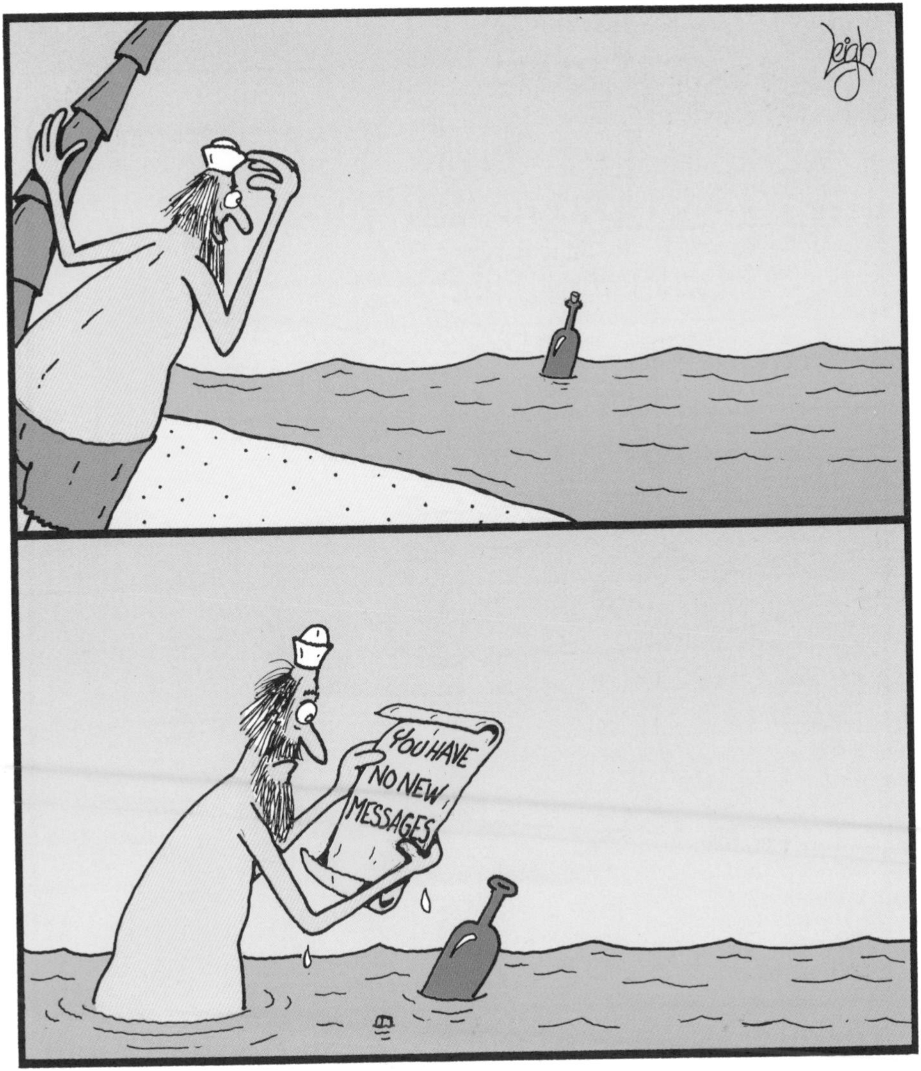
Leigh
YOU HAVE
NO NEW
MESSAGES

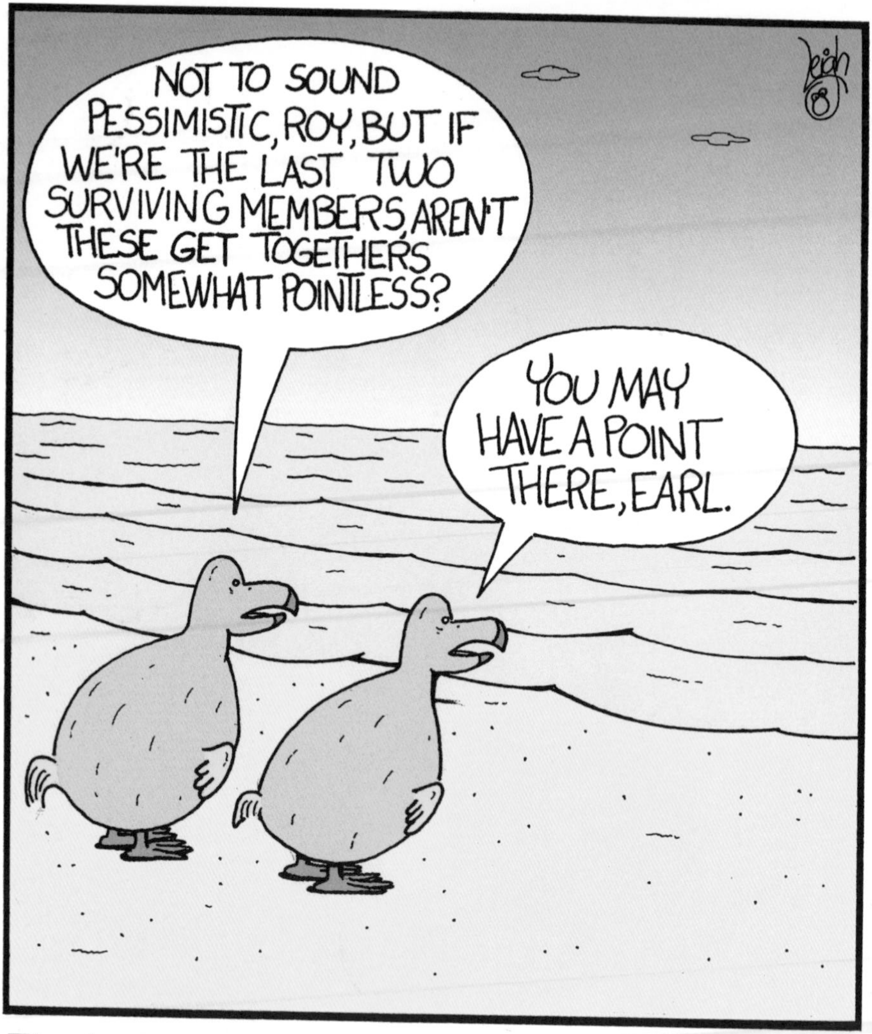
NOT TO SOUND PESSIMISTIC, ROY, BUT IF WE'RE THE LAST TWO SURVIVING MEMBERS AREN'T THESE GET TOGETHER'S SOMEWHAT POINTLESS?
YOU MAY HAVE A POINT THERE, EARL.
Leigh 08

The last meeting of the Save the Dodo Society

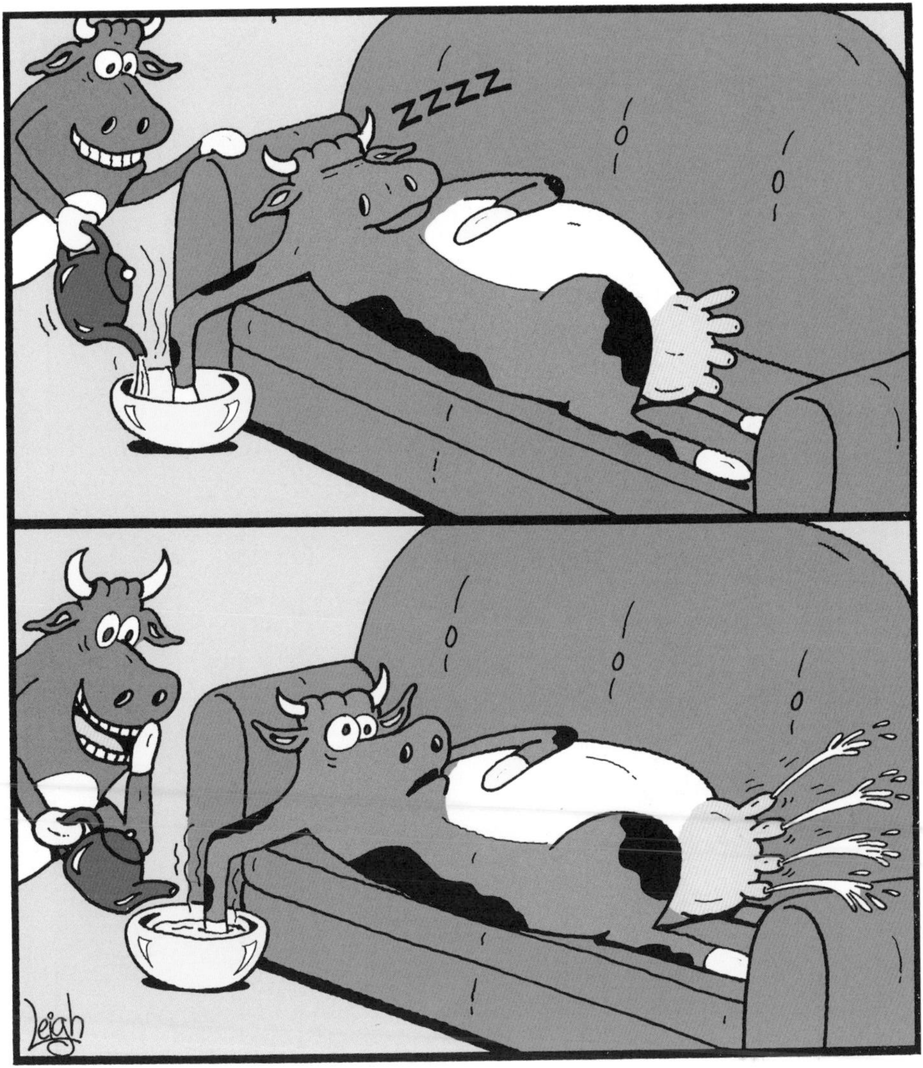
ZZZZ

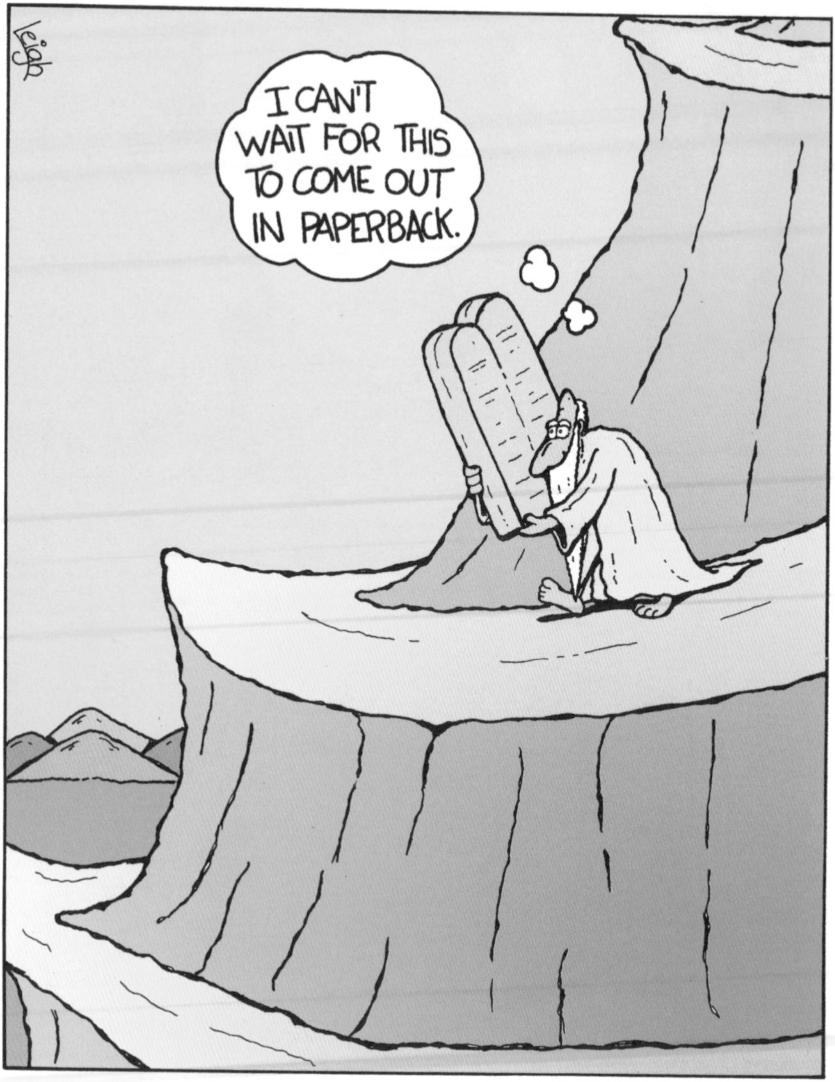
Leigh
I CAN'T WAIT FOR THIS TO COME OUT IN PAPERBACK.

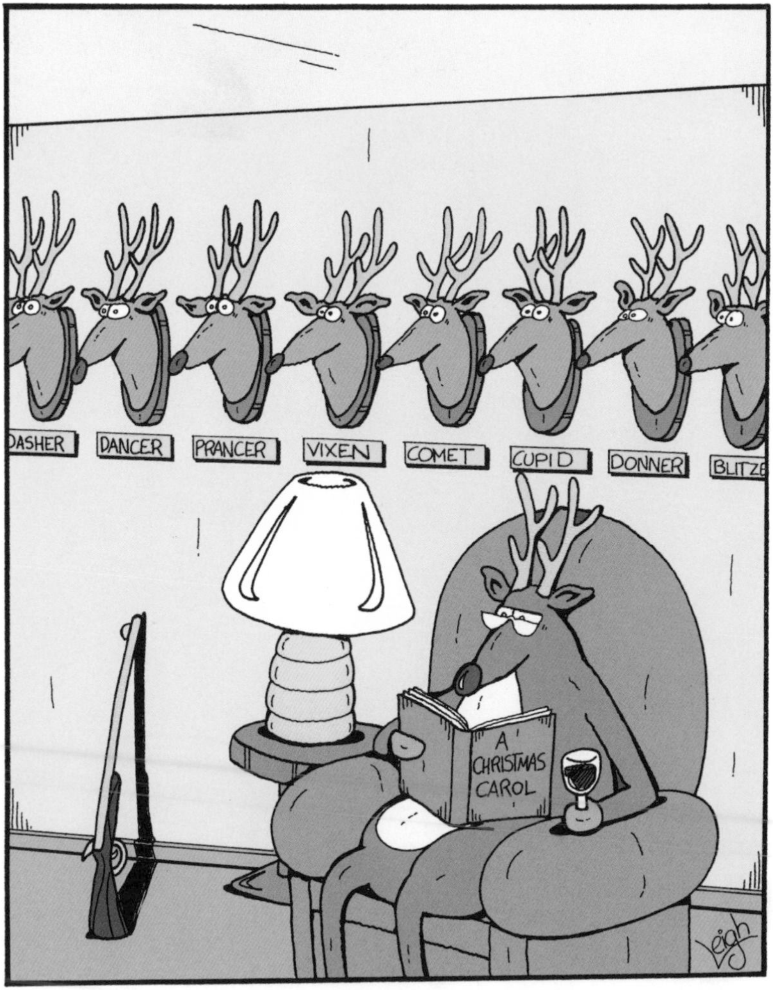
DASHER
DANCER
PRANCER
VIXEN
COMET
CUPID
DONNER
BLITZE
A CHRISTMAS CAROL
Leigh

All of the other reindeer *used* to laugh and call him names.

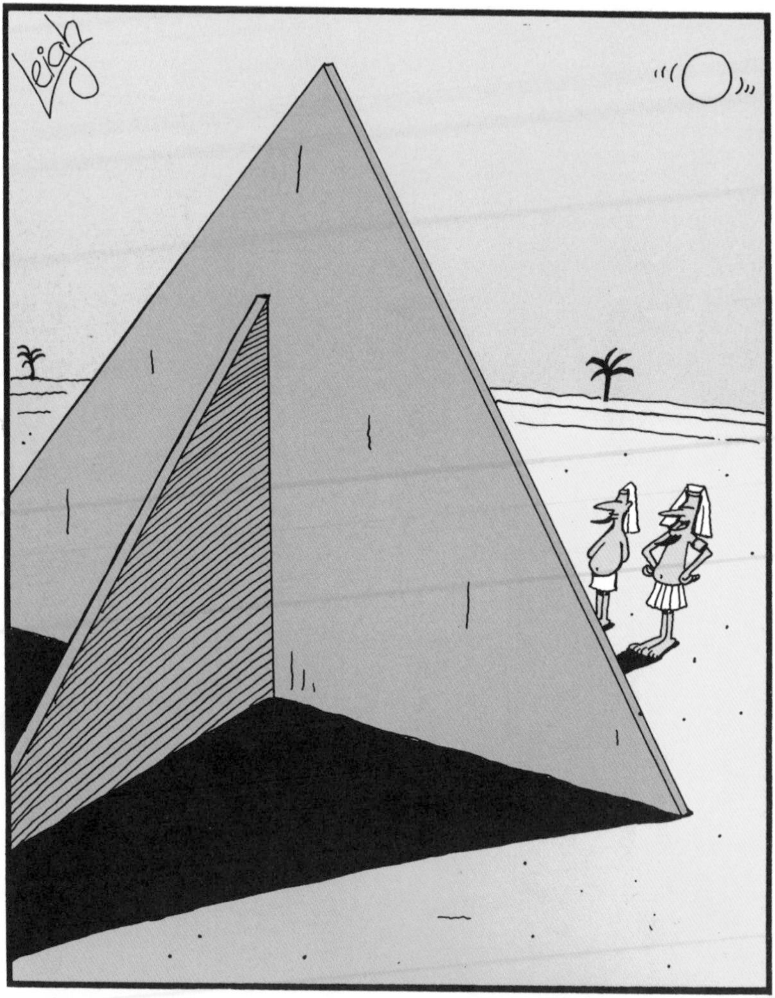
Leigh

"Excellent! Pharaoh will be quite pleased to learn that you've completed construction under budget and ahead of schedule."

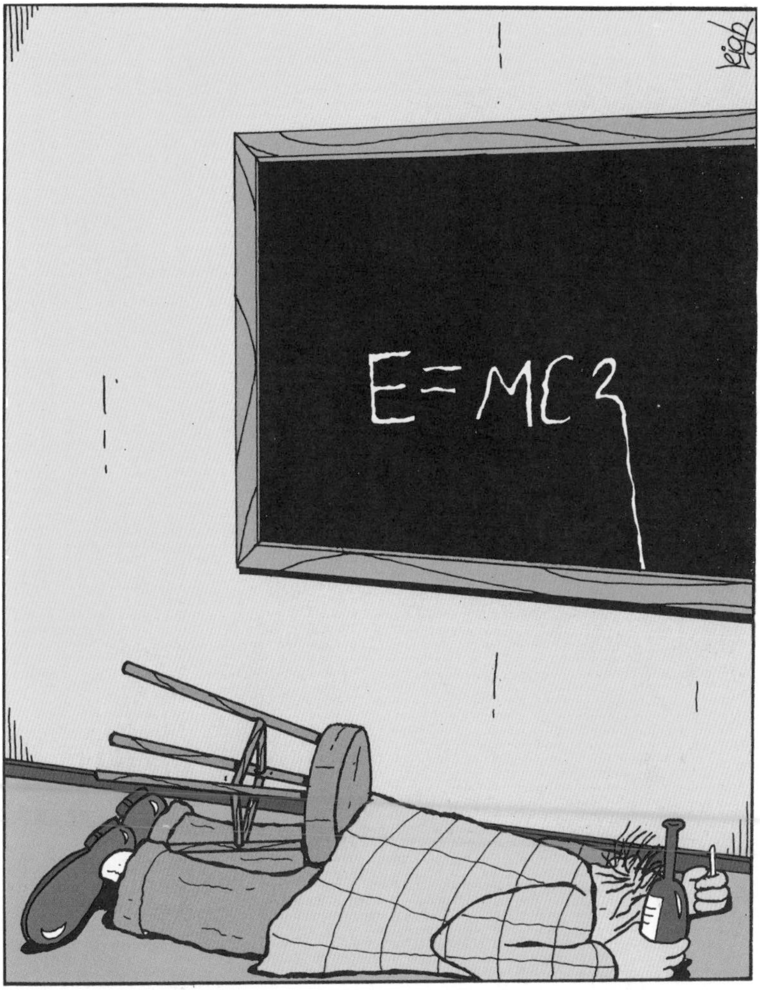
E=MC2

Early in his career, Einstein discovered the hazards of drinking and deriving.

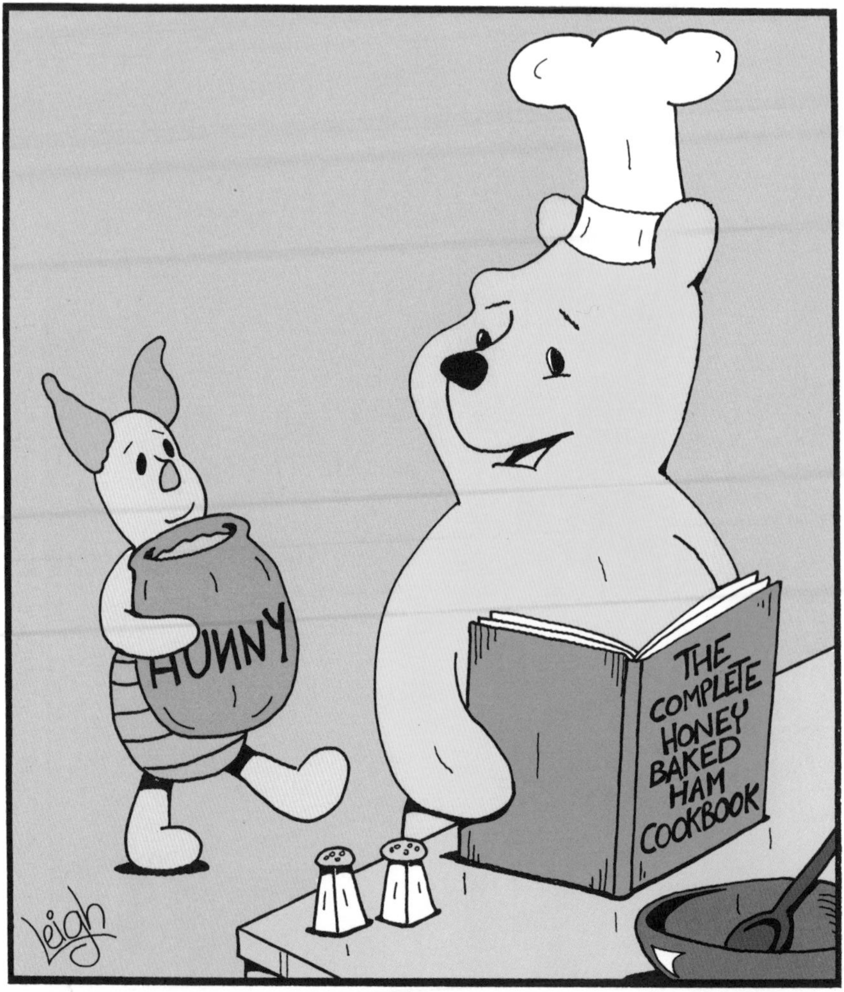
HUNNY
THE COMPLETE HONEY BAKED HAM COOKBOOK
Leigh

"Why, of course you can stay, Piglet. Without you, this dinner wouldn't be possible."

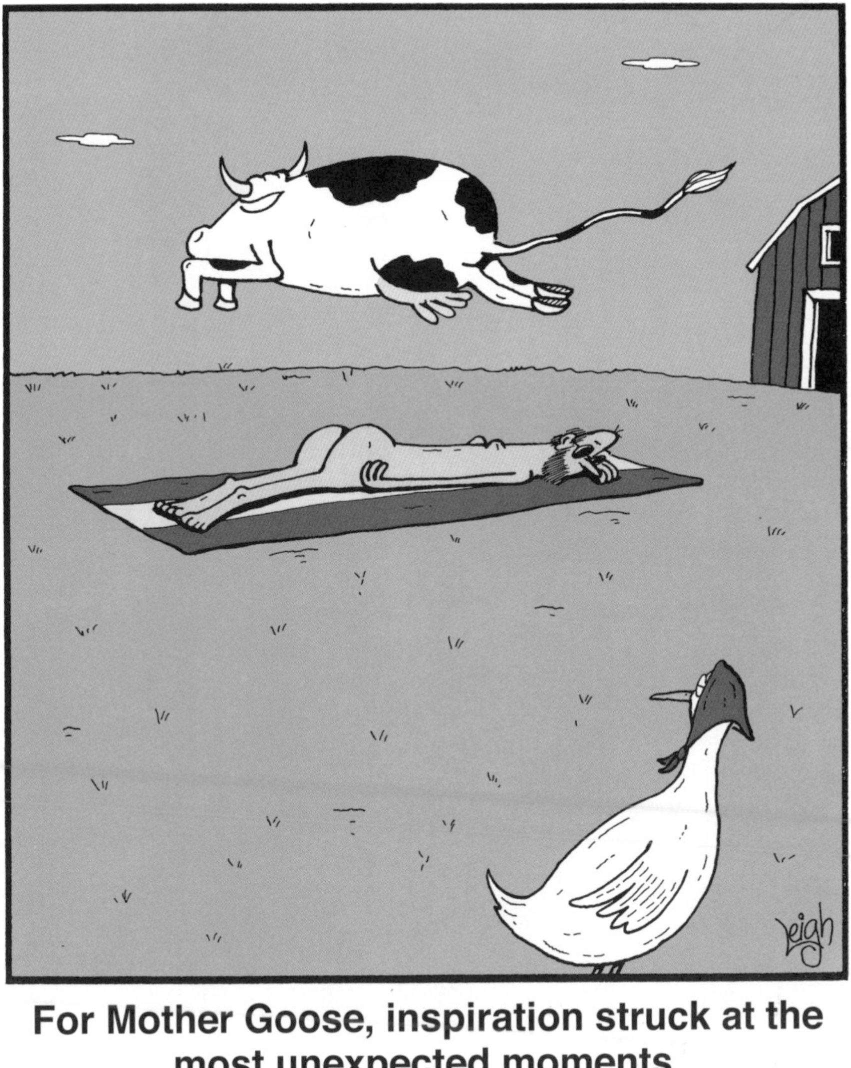
Leigh

For Mother Goose, inspiration struck at the most unexpected moments.

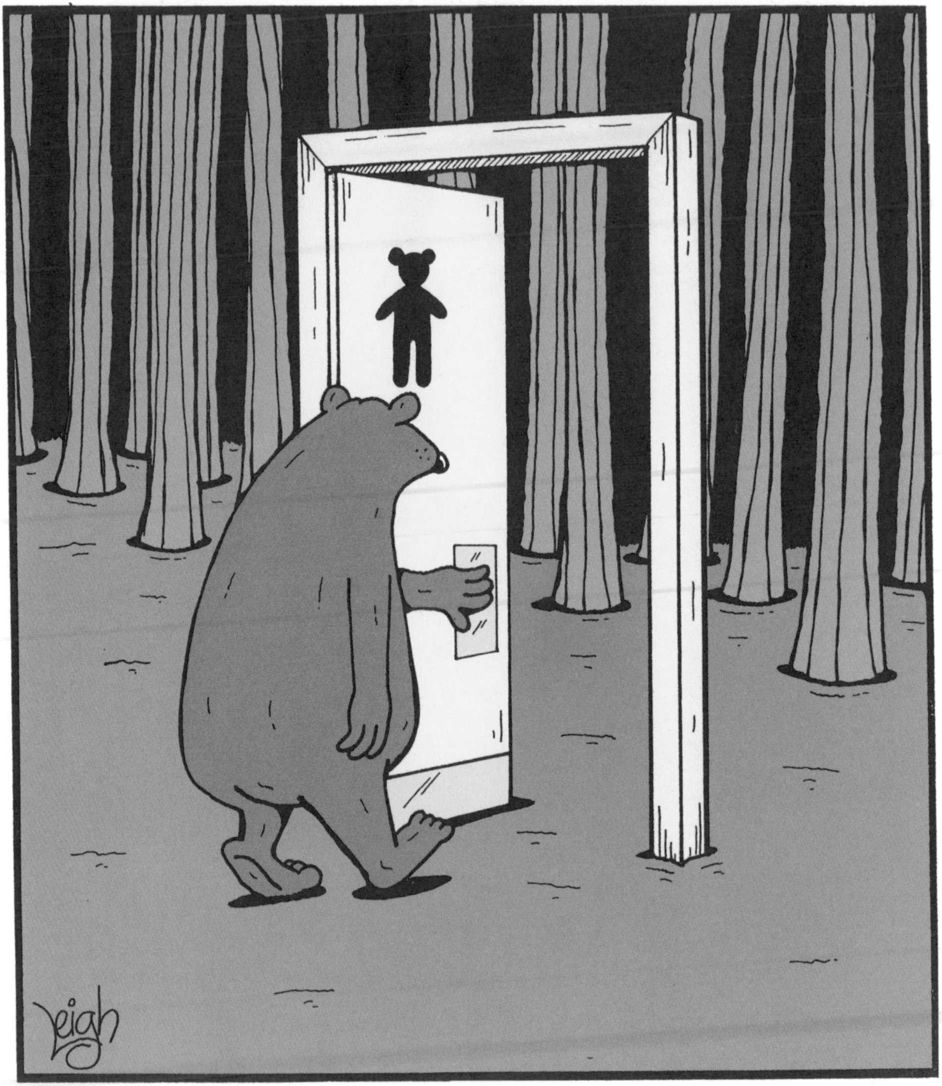
Leigh

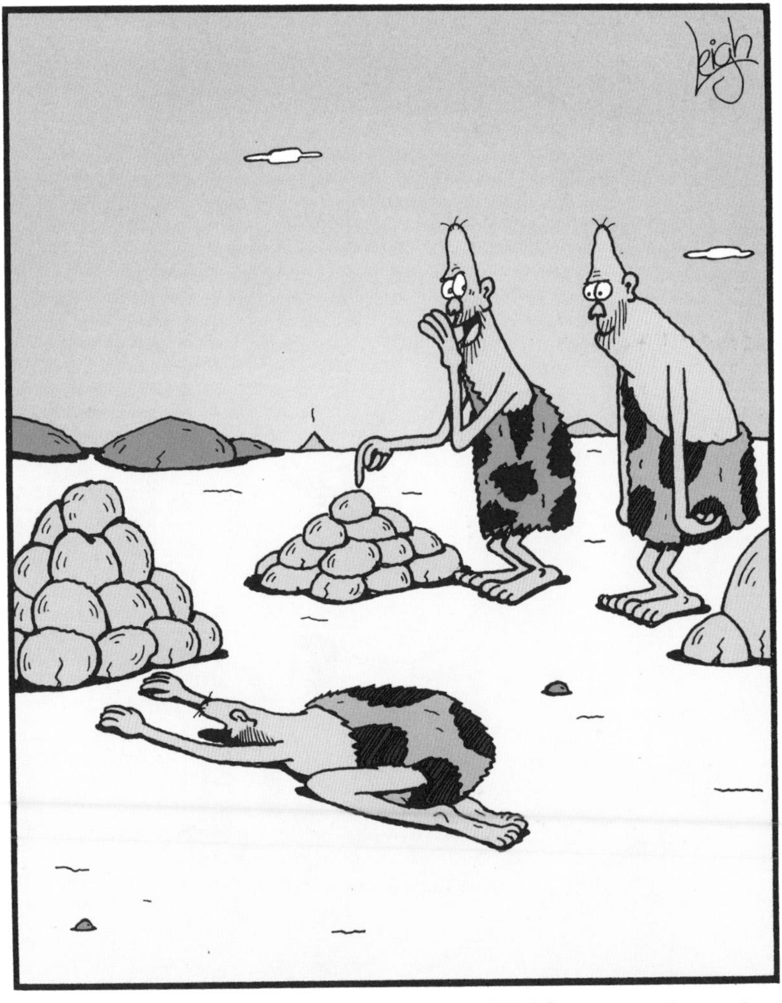
Leigh

"Doesn't Thog look silly?! He must not know that our pile of rocks is the *real* god!"

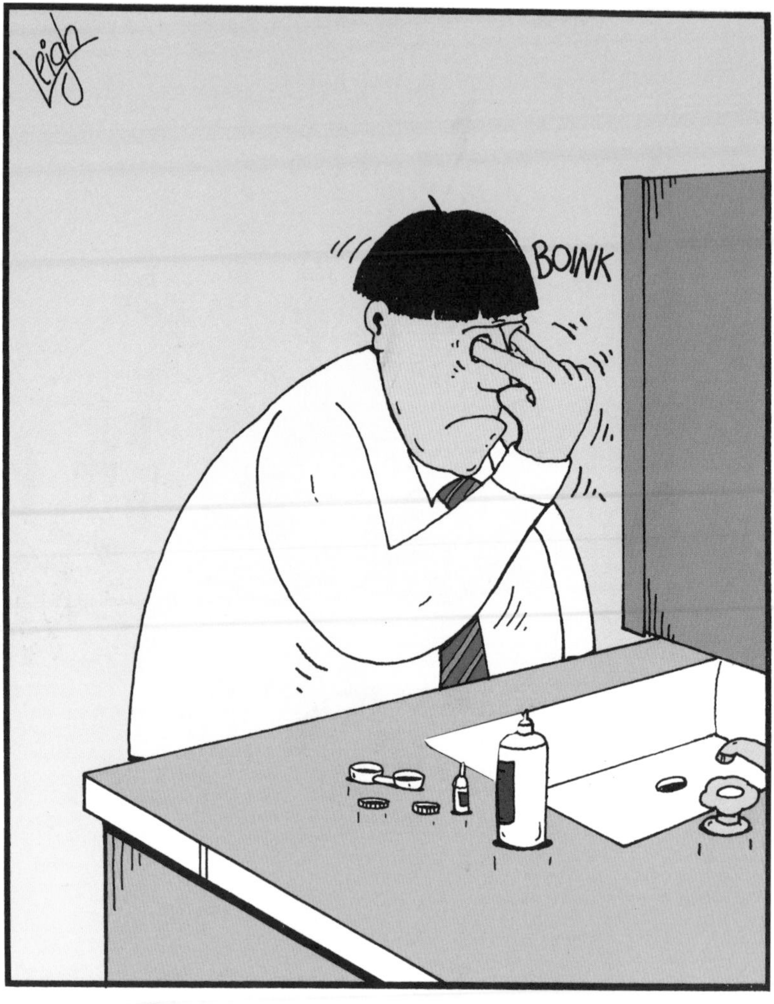
Leigh
BOINK

Moe puts on his contacts.

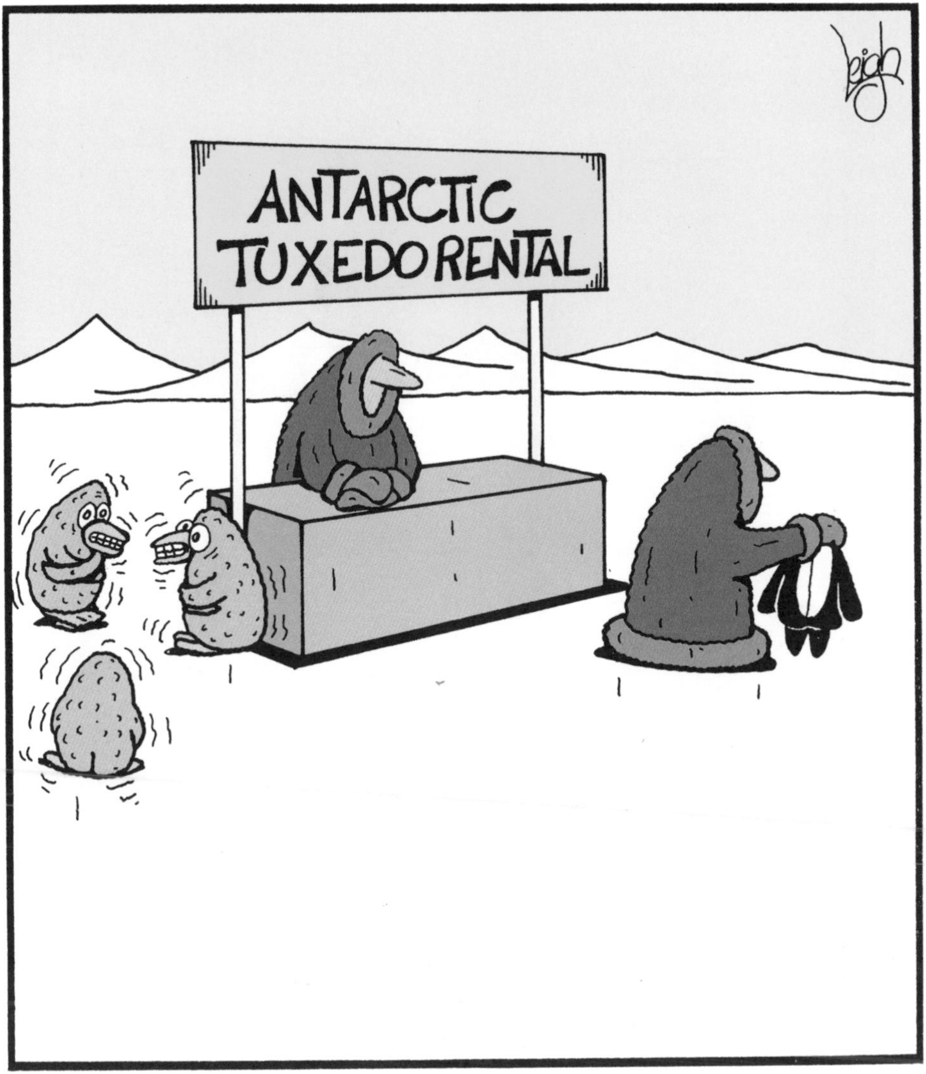
ANTARCTIC
TUXEDO RENTAL

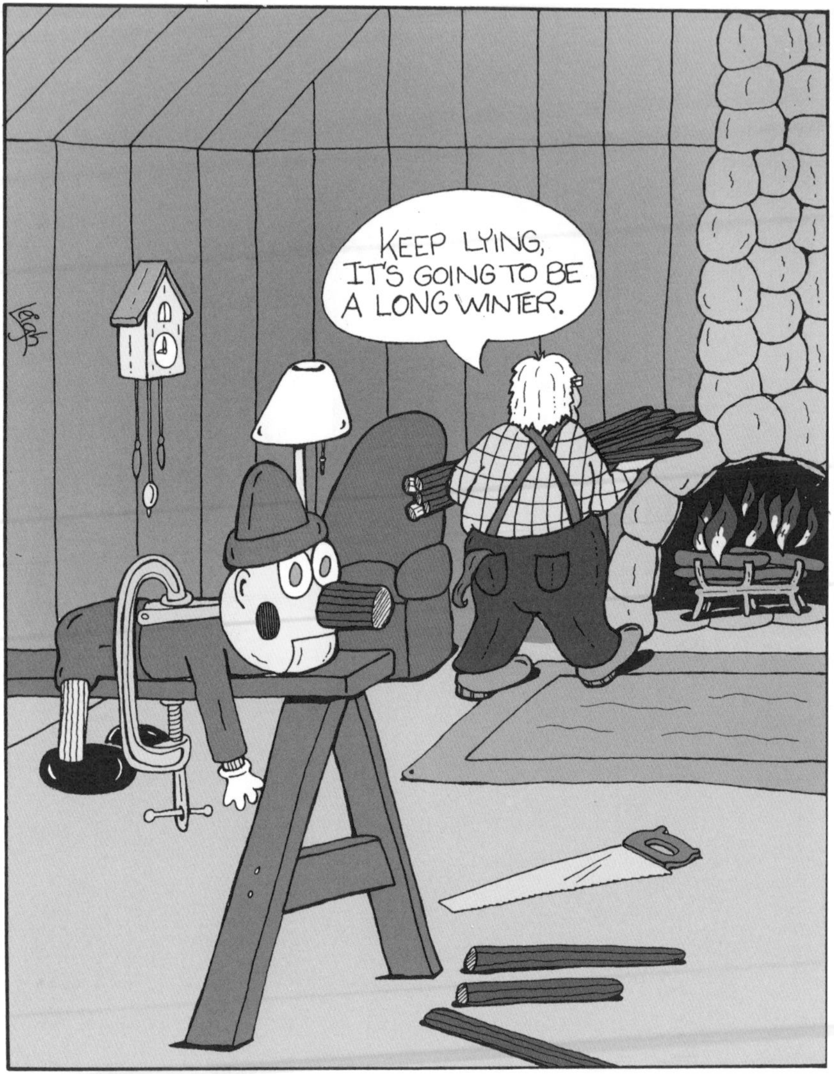
KEEP LYING, IT'S GOING TO BE A LONG WINTER.
Leigh

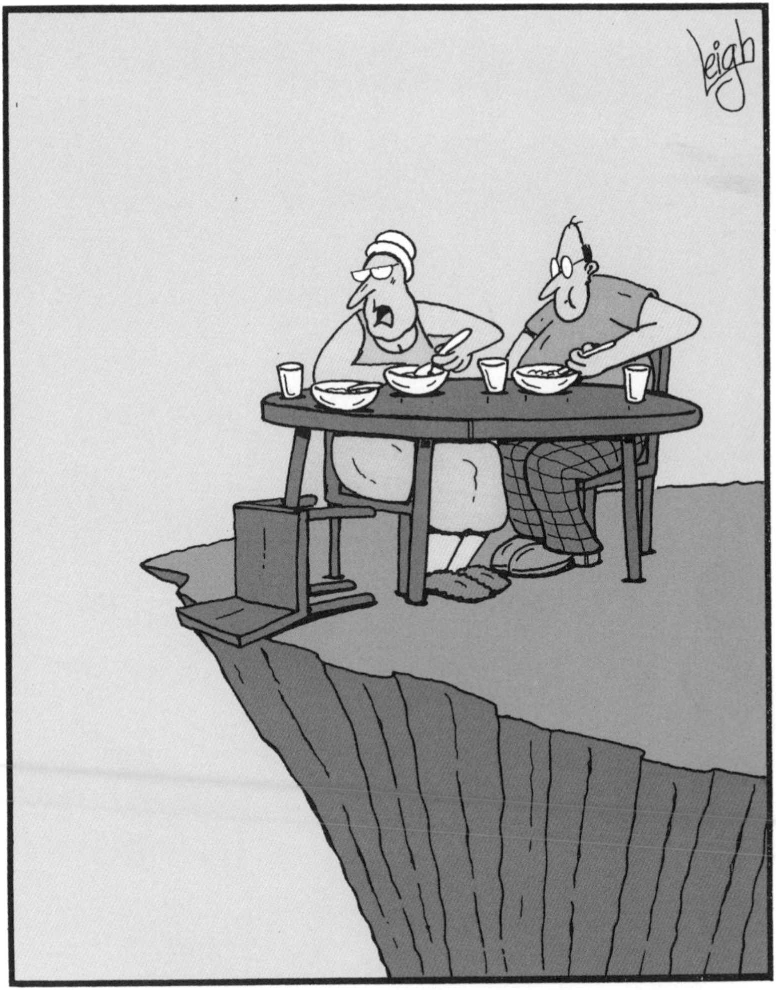
leigh

"It serves him right. I don't know how many times I told Junior not to tip his chair at the table."

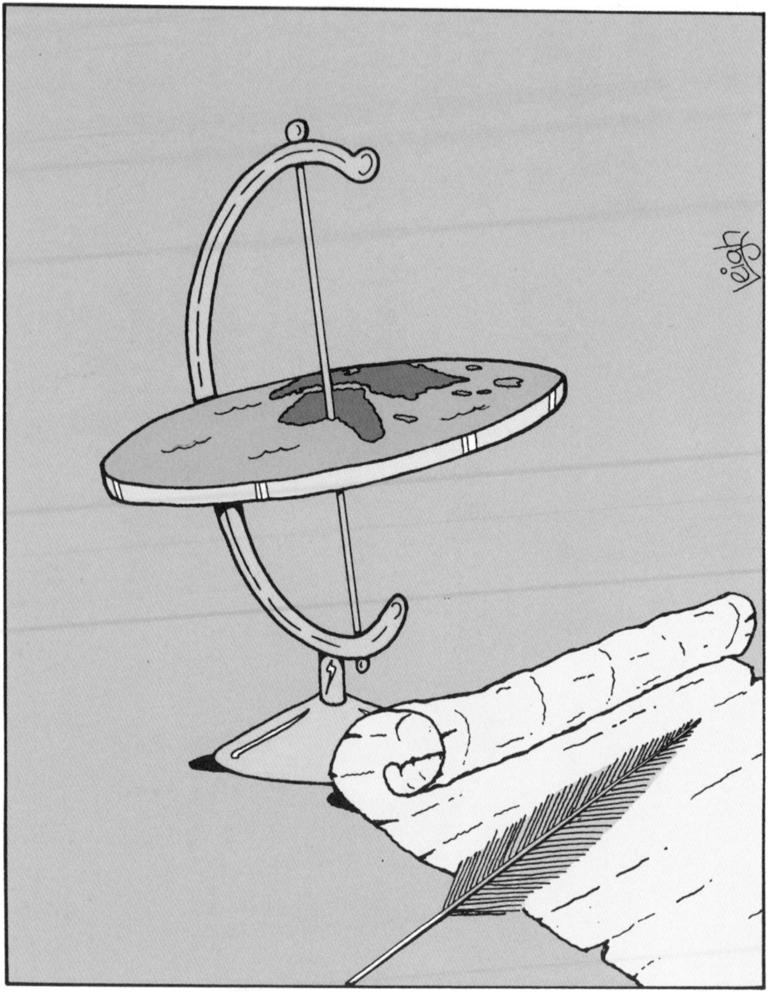
Leigh

Columbus' first globe

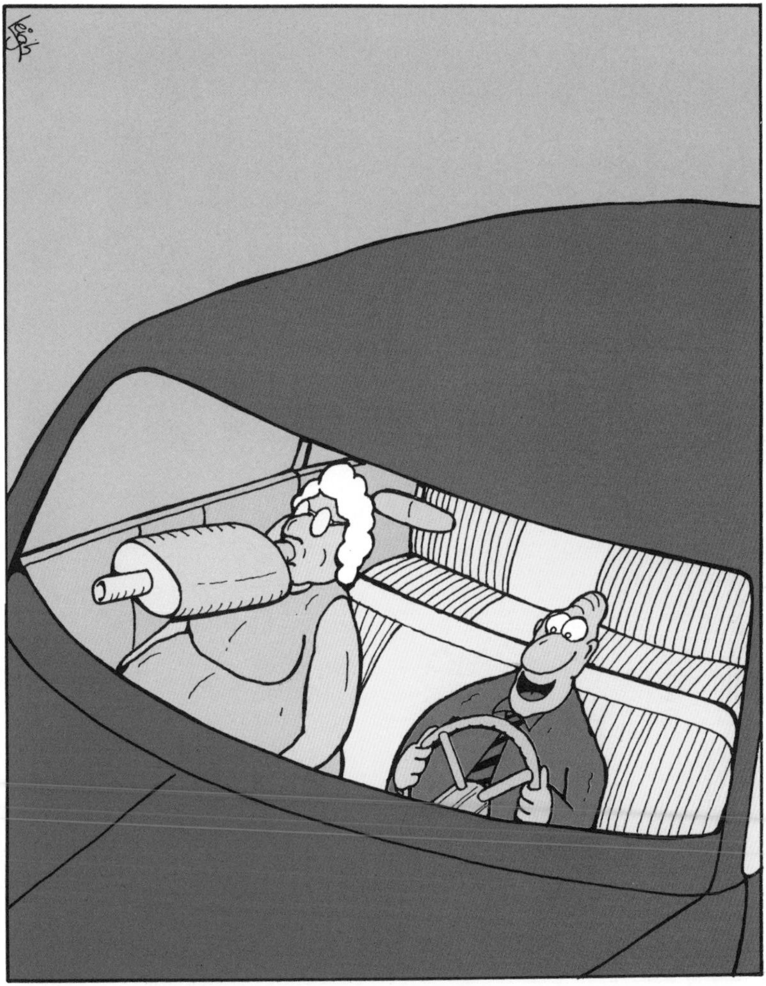
Leigh

"New muffler really keeps the car quiet, eh, honey?"

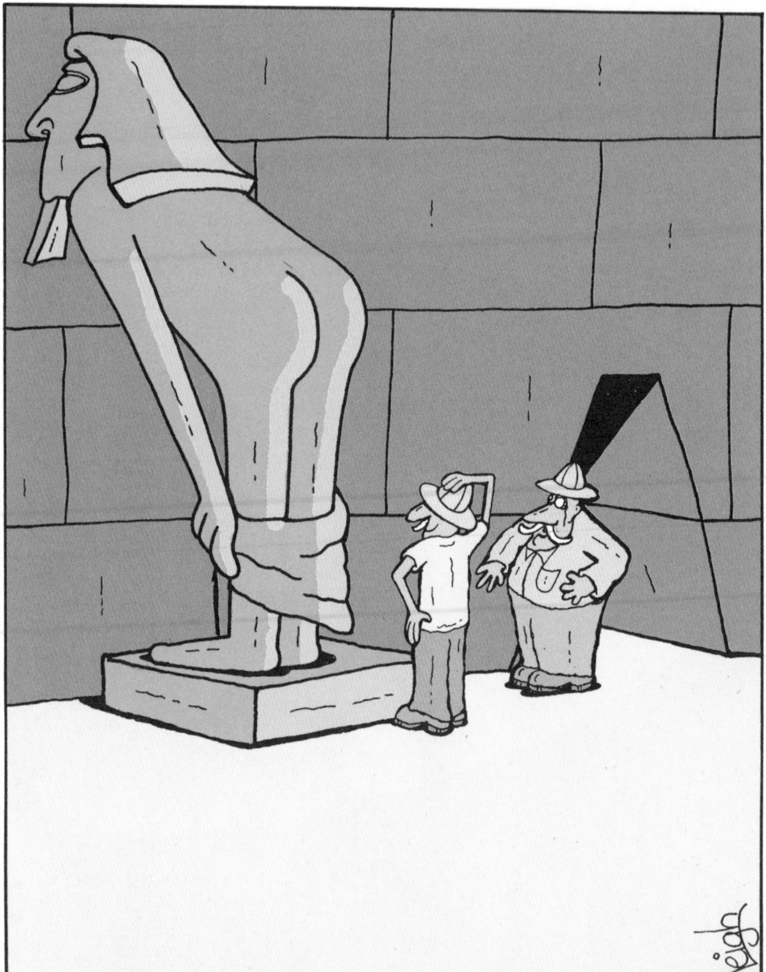

"Watson! Pinch me so I know I'm not dreaming! We've discovered the legendary temple of the moon god!"

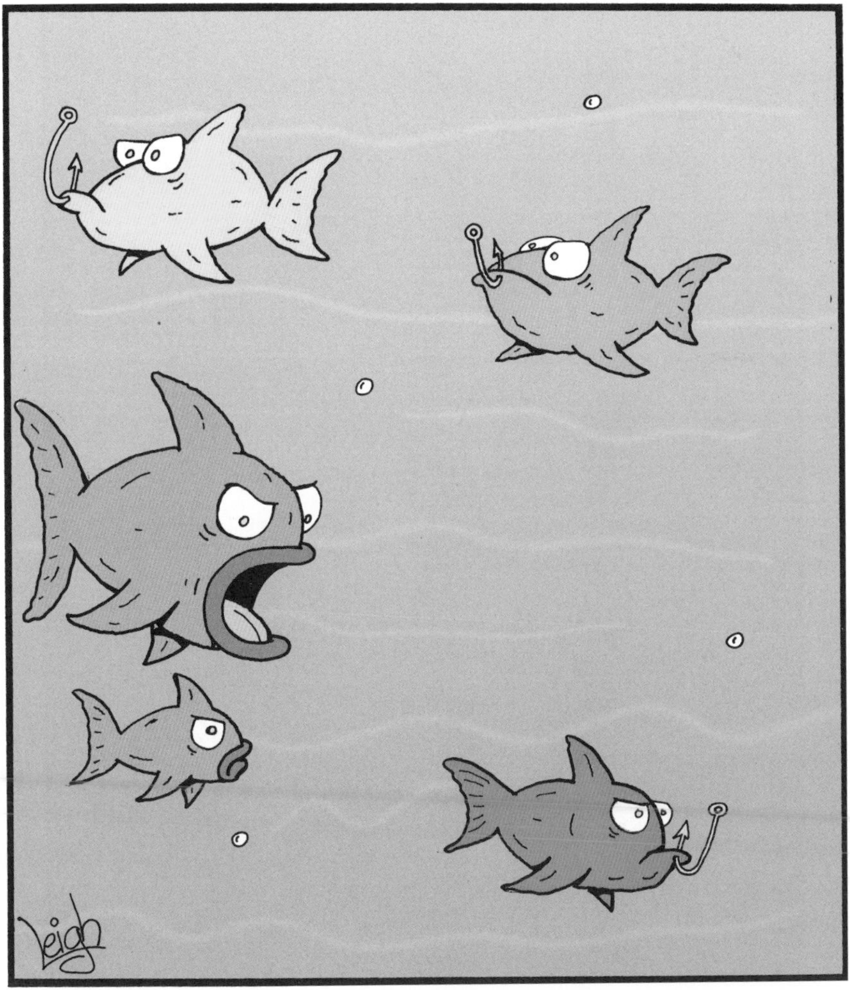
Leigh

"I don't care what all the other kids are doing, you're *not* getting your lip pierced."

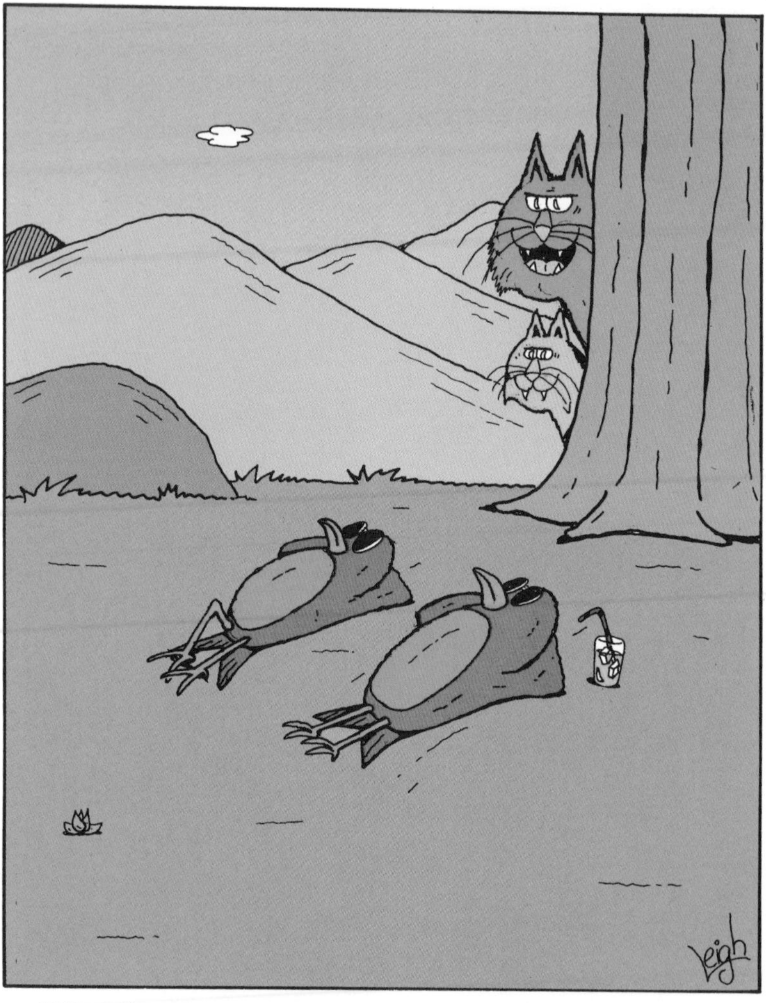
Leigh

"I'm in the mood for a little treat, Son. How'd you like some baskin' robins?"

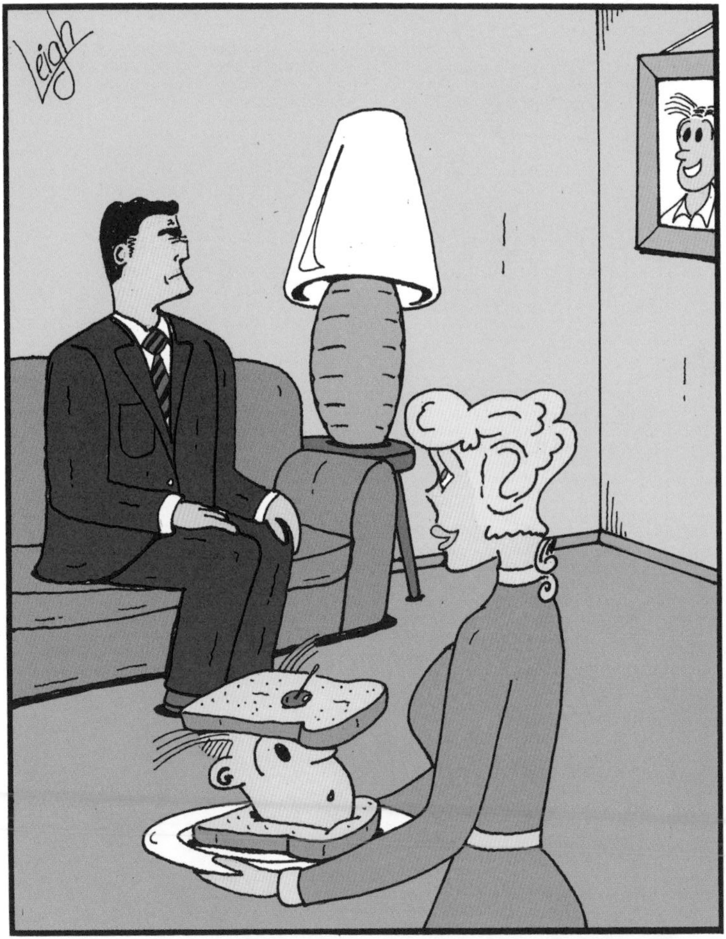
Leigh

"You must have worked up quite an appetite looking for my husband, Detective. Why don't you relax for a while and enjoy this nice, big Dagwood, er, sandwich I've prepared for you."

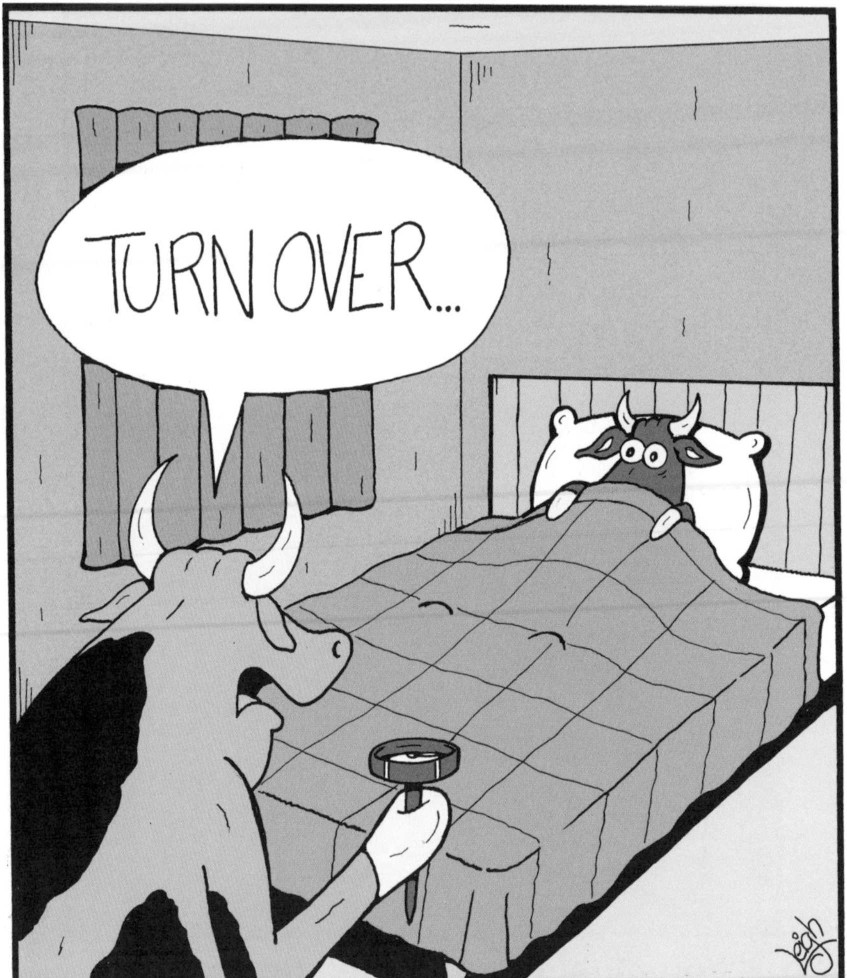
TURN OVER...

Just one look at his mother's meat thermometer and Clyde miraculously felt well enough to go to school.

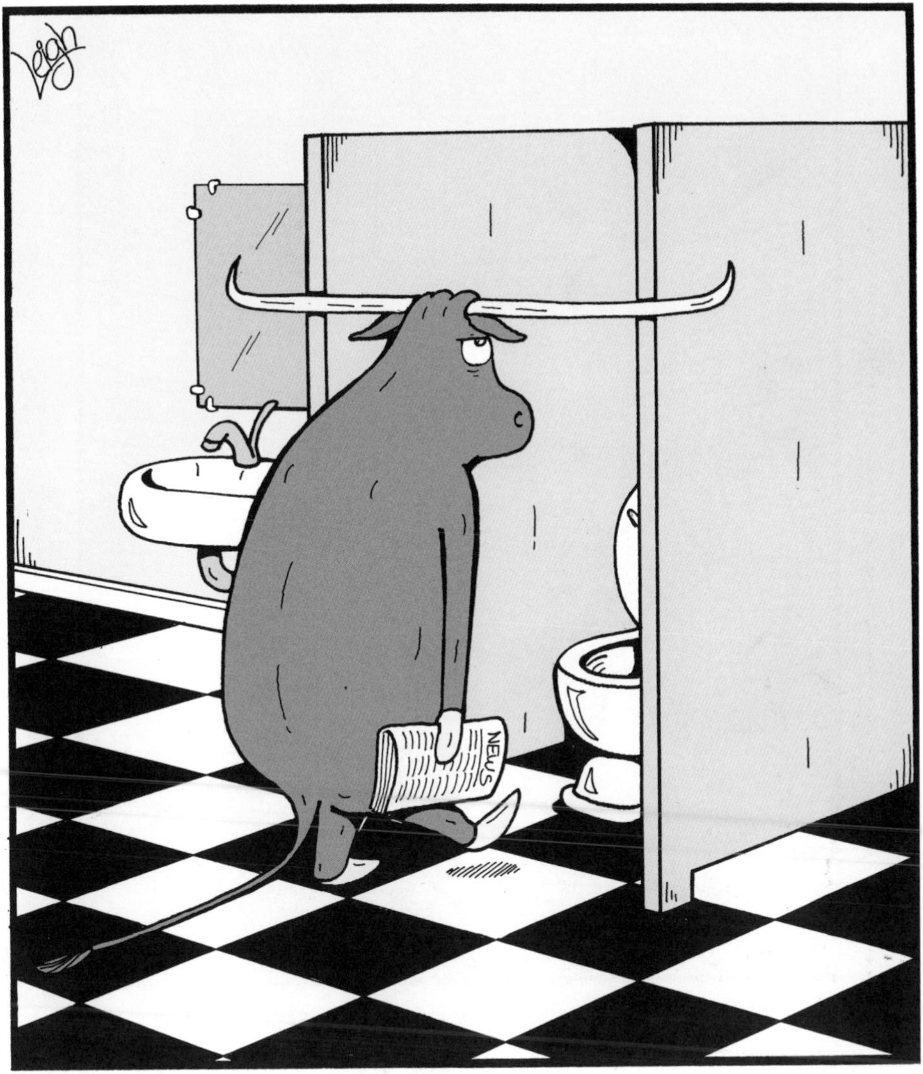
Leigh
NEWS

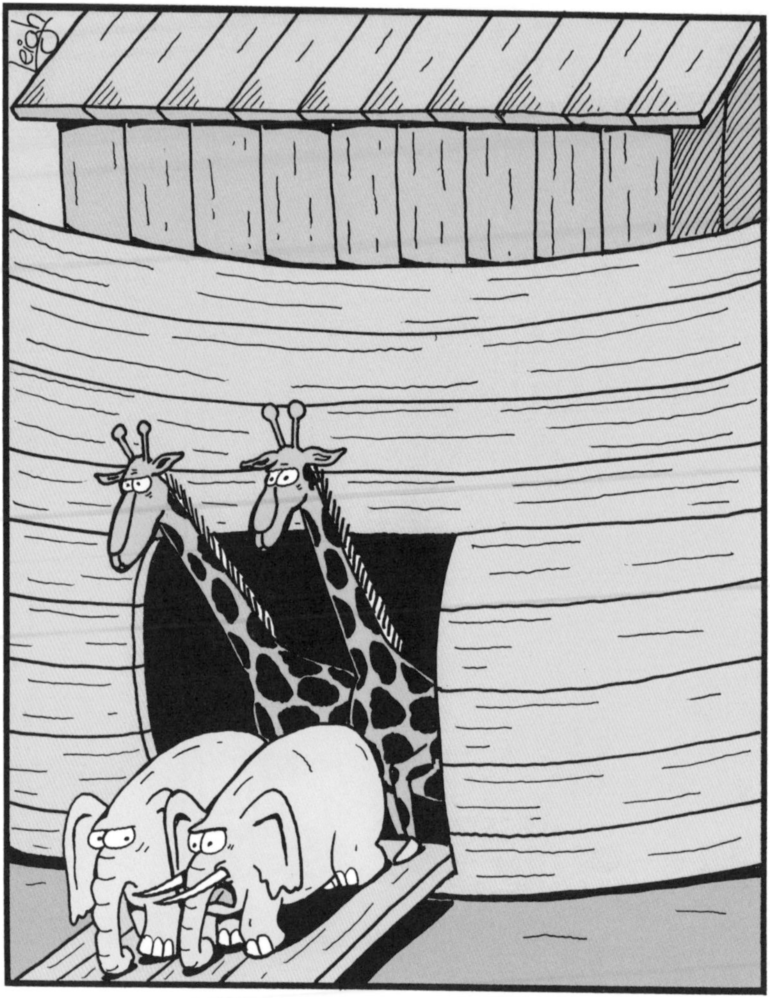
Leigh

"What a lousy trip . . . It rained the *whole* time!"

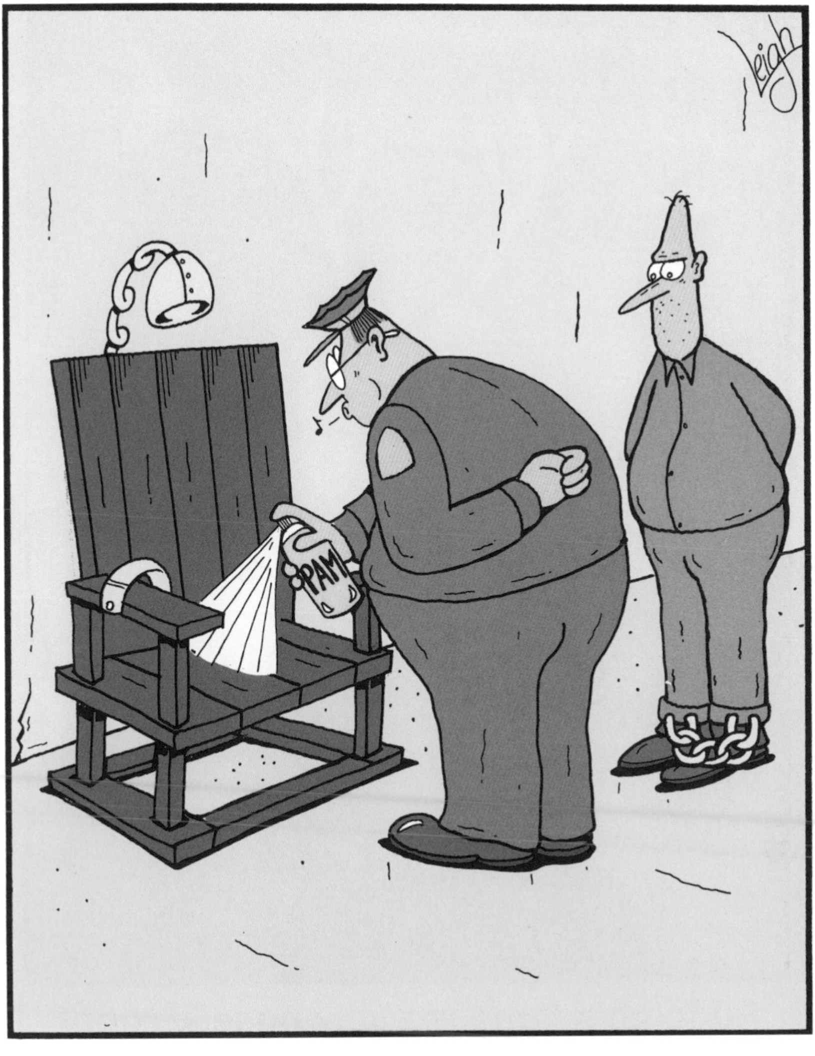
PAM
Leigh

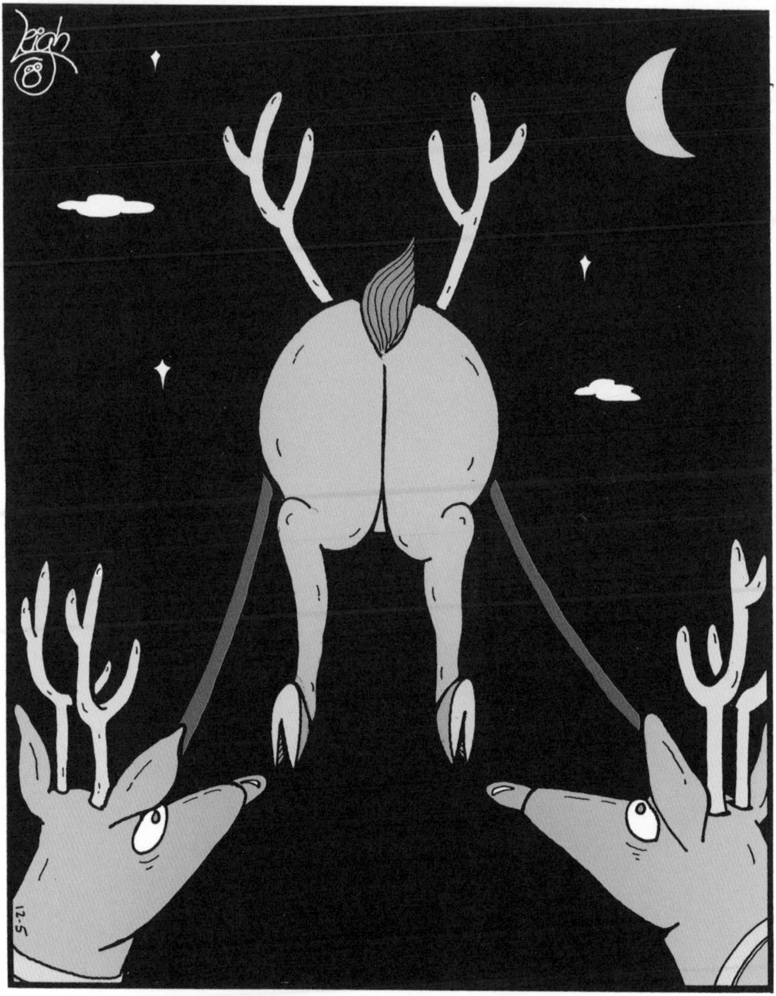
Leigh
12-5

Rudolph's famous shiny nose was not a view frequently enjoyed by his peers.

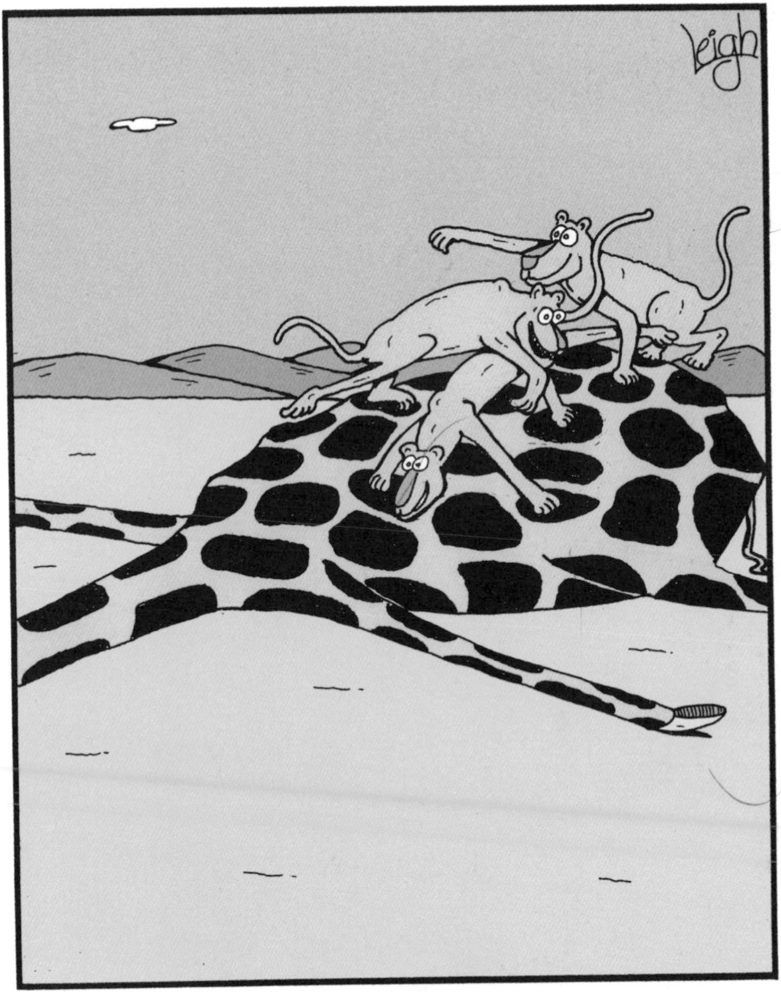
leigh

Lion Twister

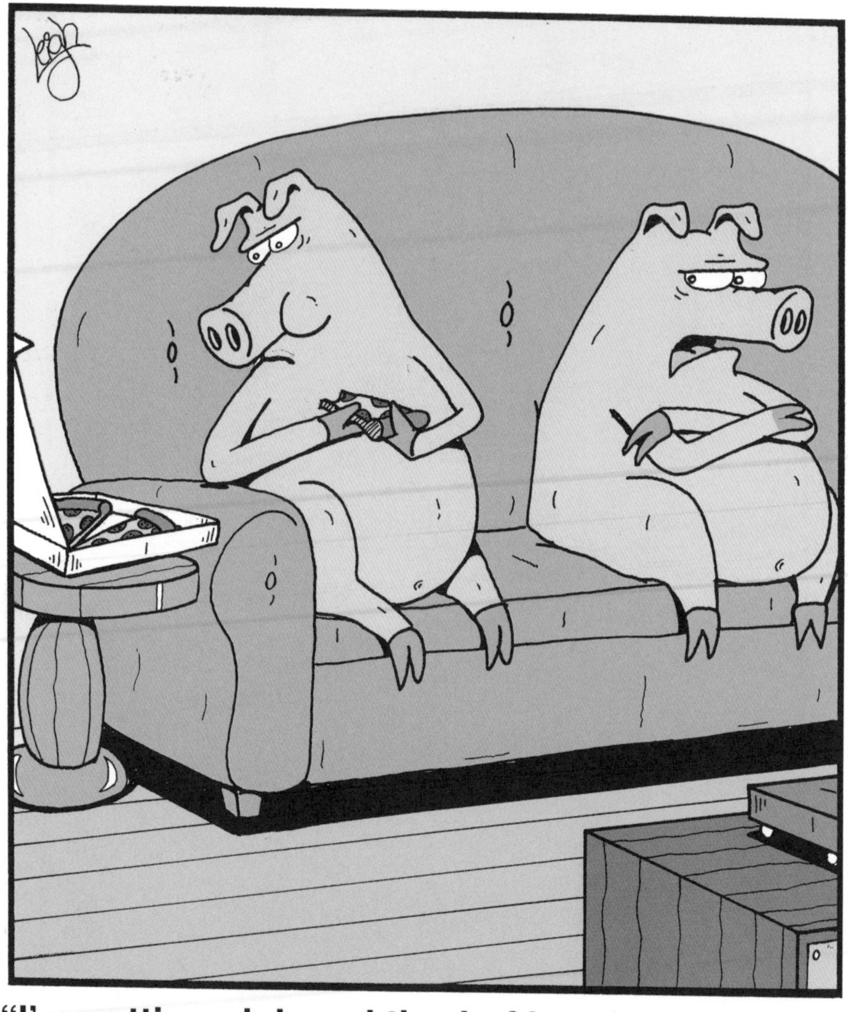

"I'm getting sick and tired of hearing you complain about my mother. If you dislike her that much then just pick off the *@#!%& pepperoni!"

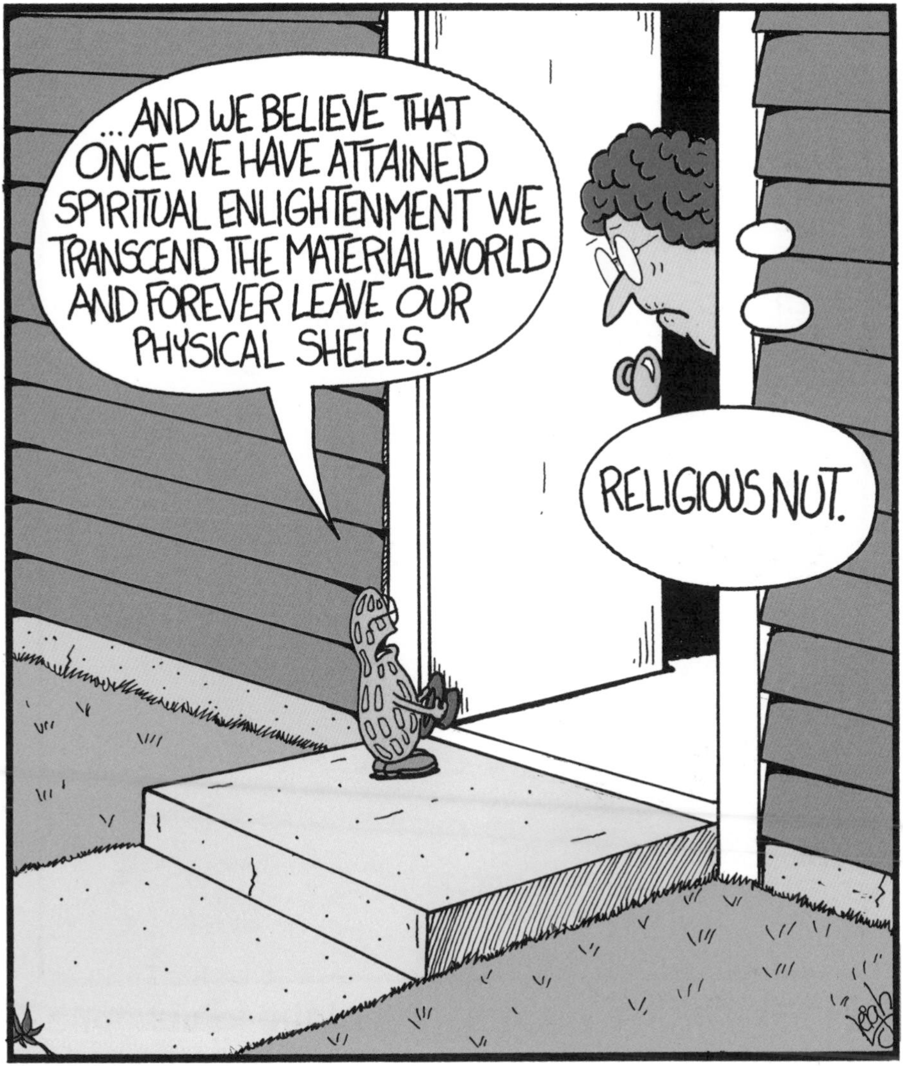
...AND WE BELIEVE THAT ONCE WE HAVE ATTAINED SPIRITUAL ENLIGHTENMENT WE TRANSCEND THE MATERIAL WORLD AND FOREVER LEAVE OUR PHYSICAL SHELLS.
RELIGIOUS NUT.

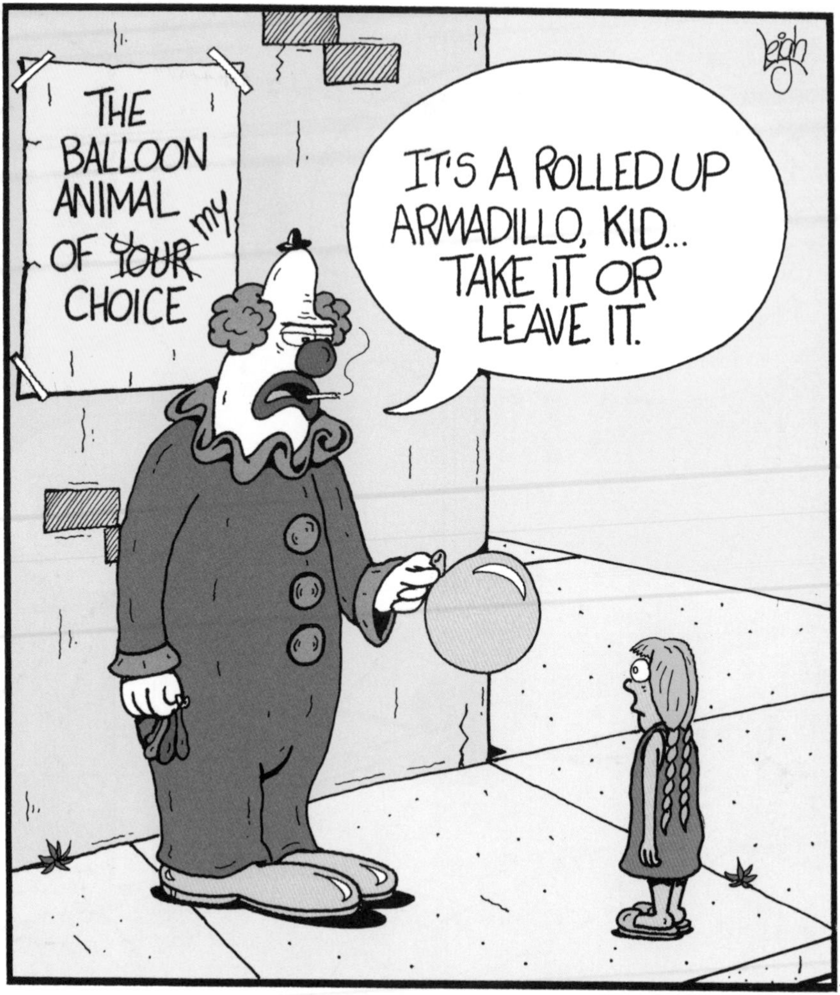
THE BALLOON ANIMAL OF ~~YOUR~~ my CHOICE
IT'S A ROLLED UP ARMADILLO, KID... TAKE IT OR LEAVE IT.

When it's obvious the thrill of the job is gone

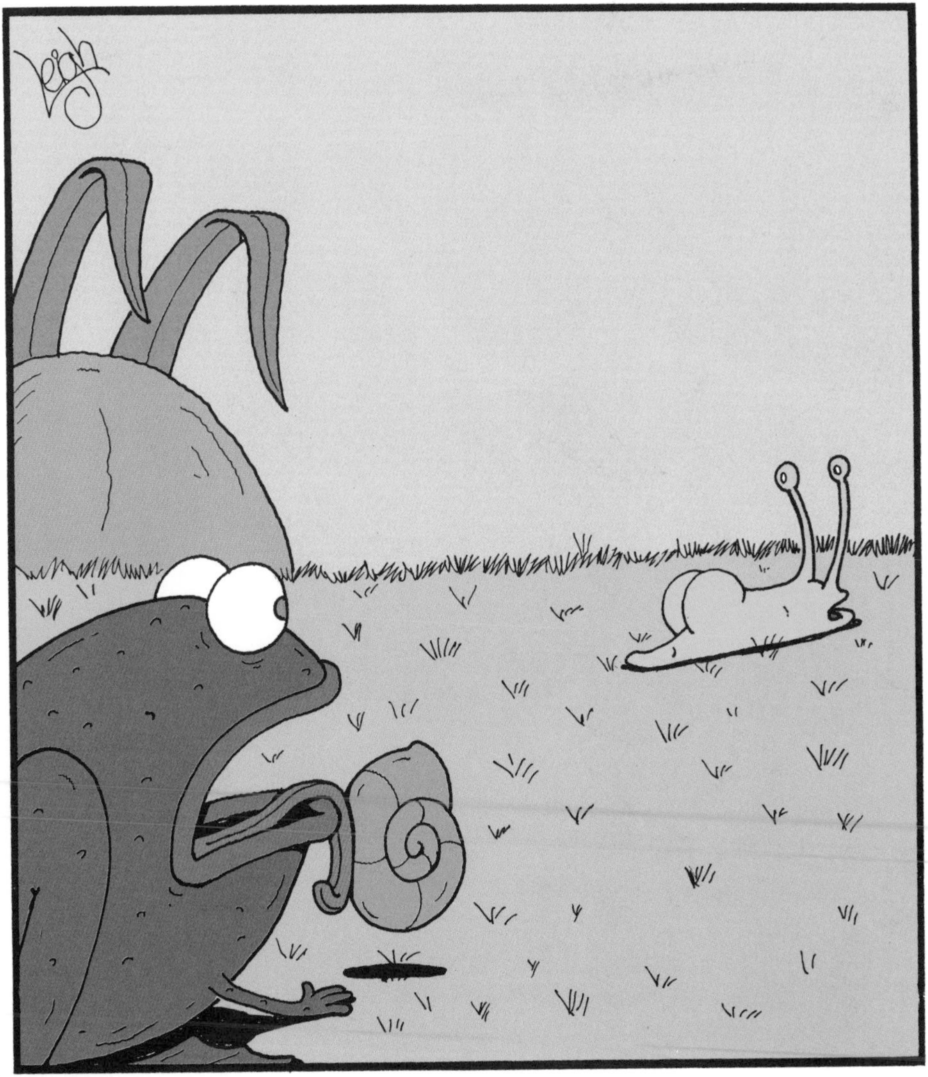

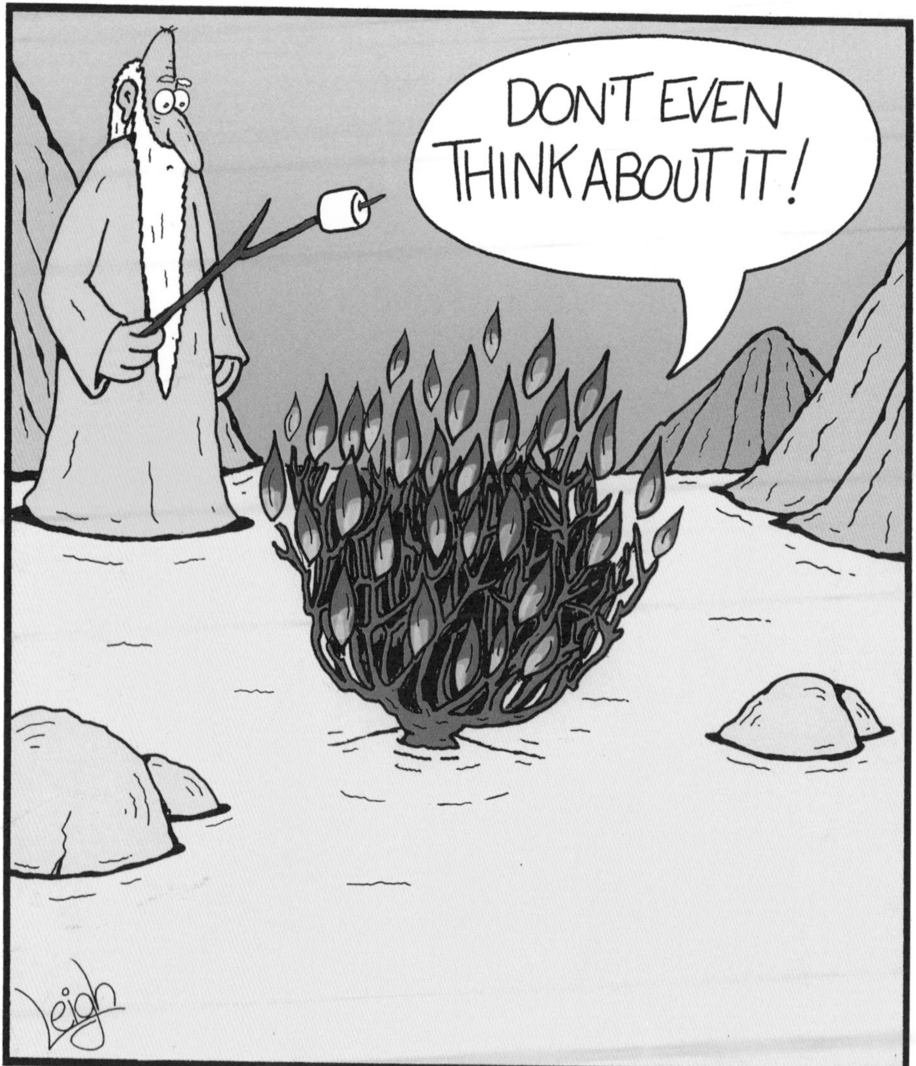
DON'T EVEN THINK ABOUT IT!
Leigh

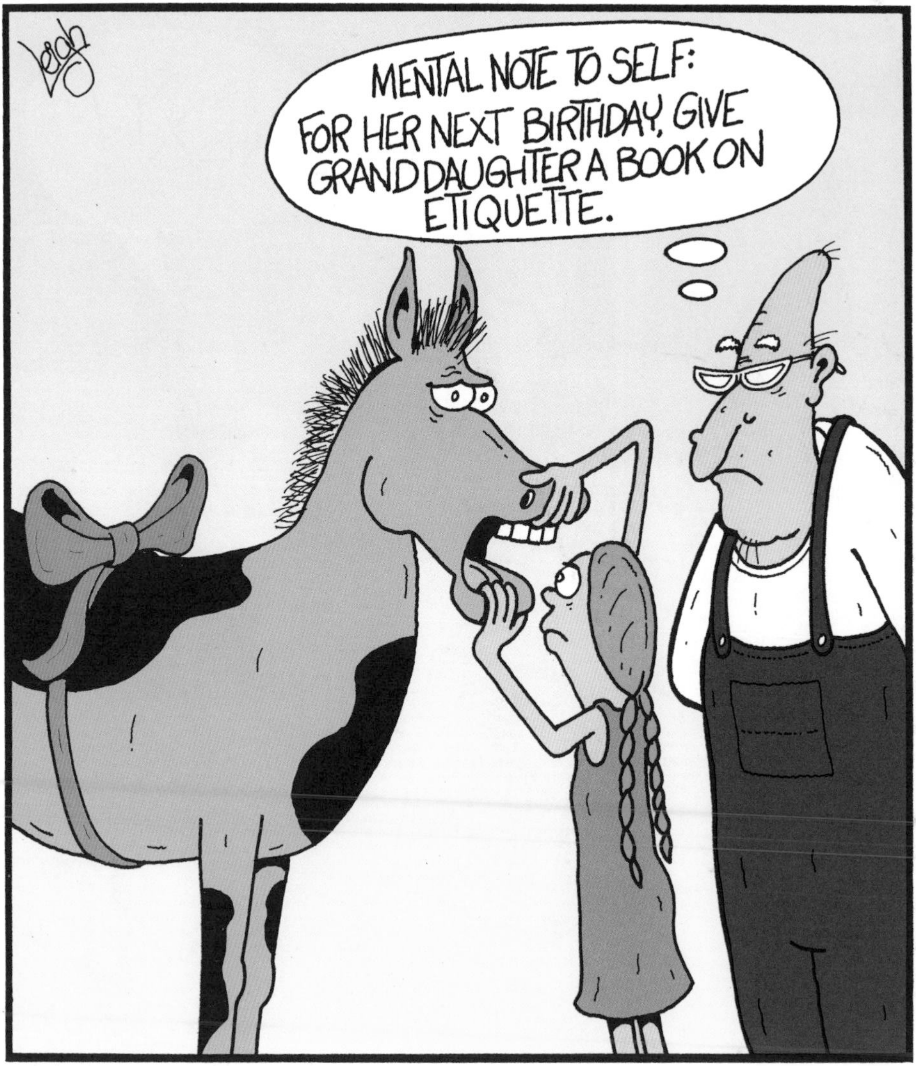
MENTAL NOTE TO SELF:
FOR HER NEXT BIRTHDAY, GIVE GRANDDAUGHTER A BOOK ON ETIQUETTE.

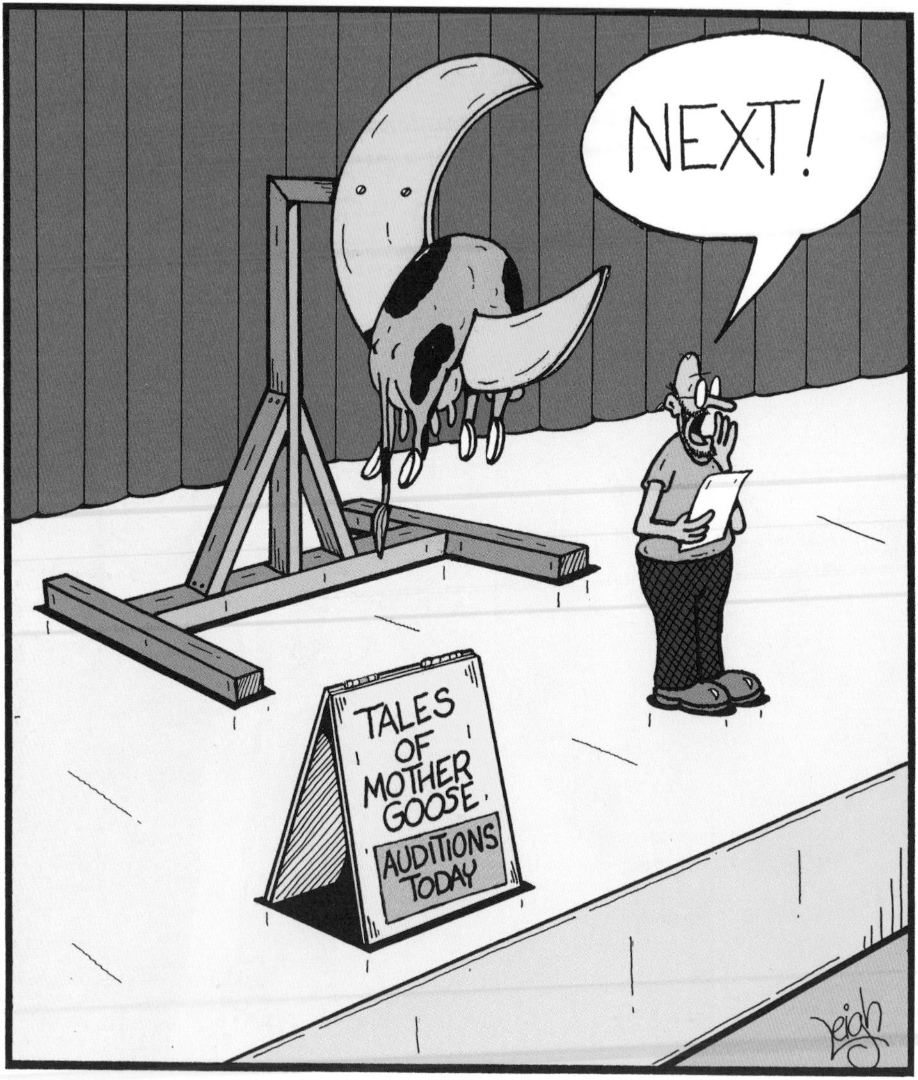
NEXT!
TALES OF MOTHER GOOSE
AUDITIONS TODAY
Leigh

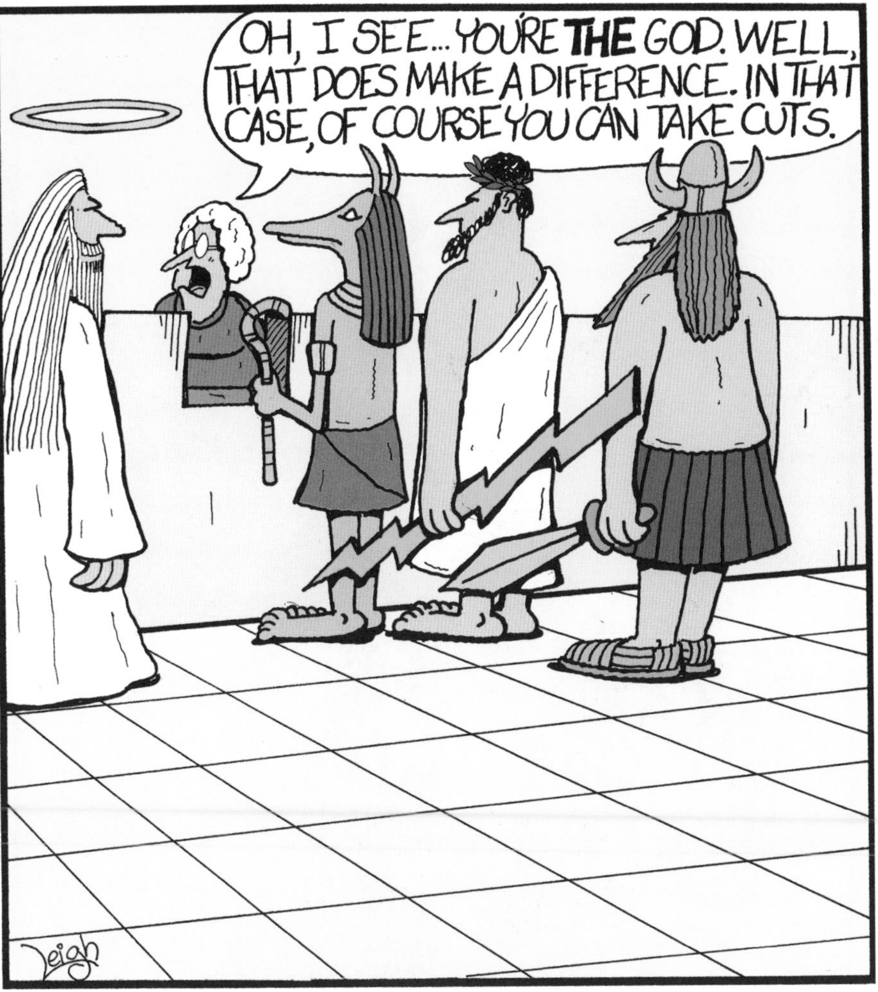
OH, I SEE... YOU'RE THE GOD. WELL, THAT DOES MAKE A DIFFERENCE. IN THAT CASE, OF COURSE YOU CAN TAKE CUTS.
Leigh

Taking full advantage of the First Commandment

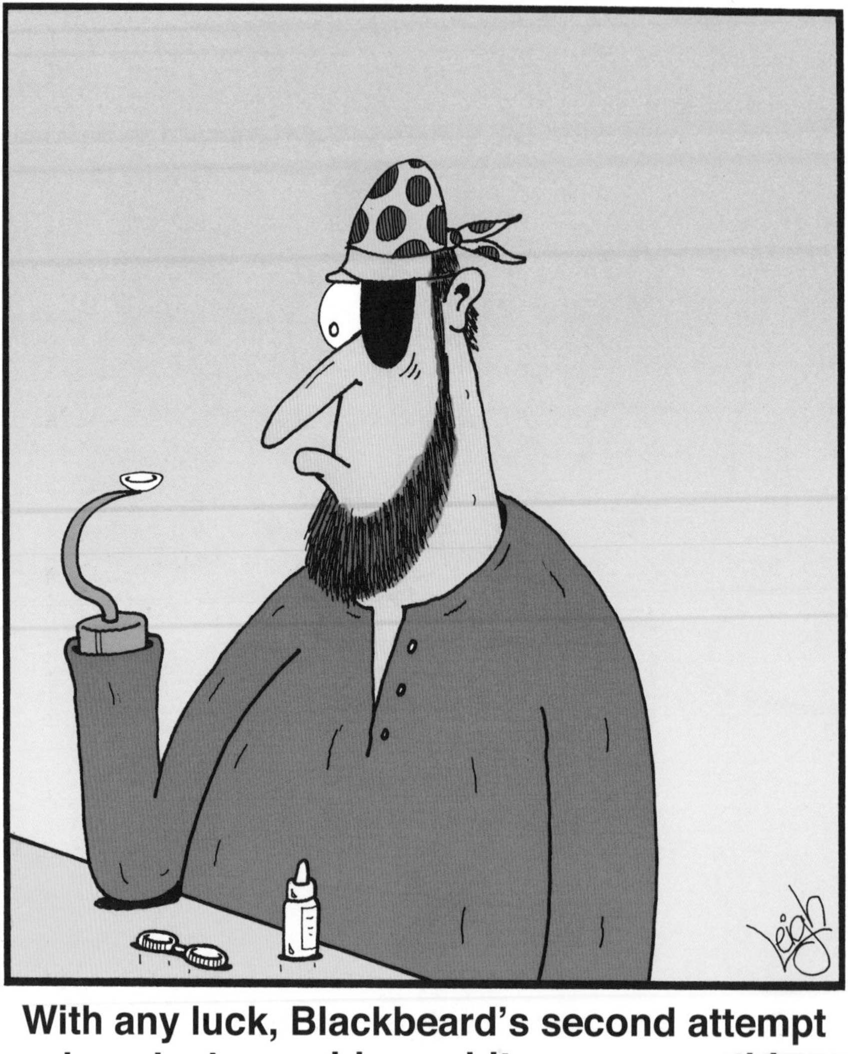

leigh

With any luck, Blackbeard's second attempt at contacts would go a bit more smoothly.

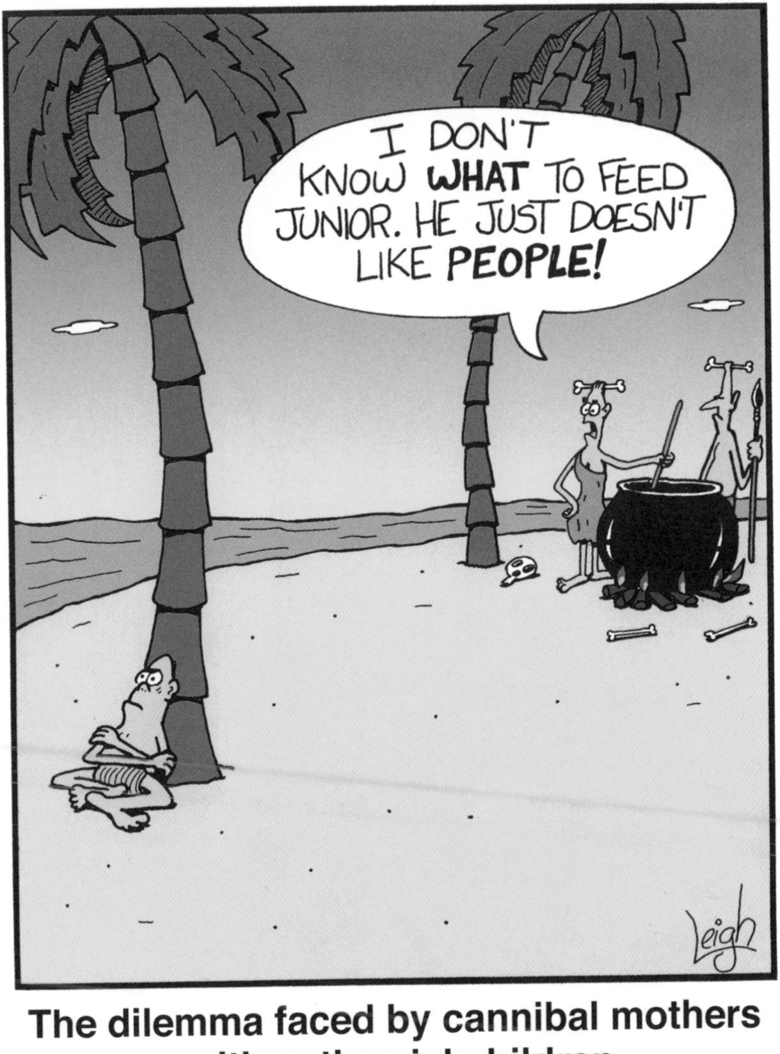
I DON'T KNOW **WHAT** TO FEED JUNIOR. HE JUST DOESN'T LIKE **PEOPLE**!
Leigh

The dilemma faced by cannibal mothers with antisocial children

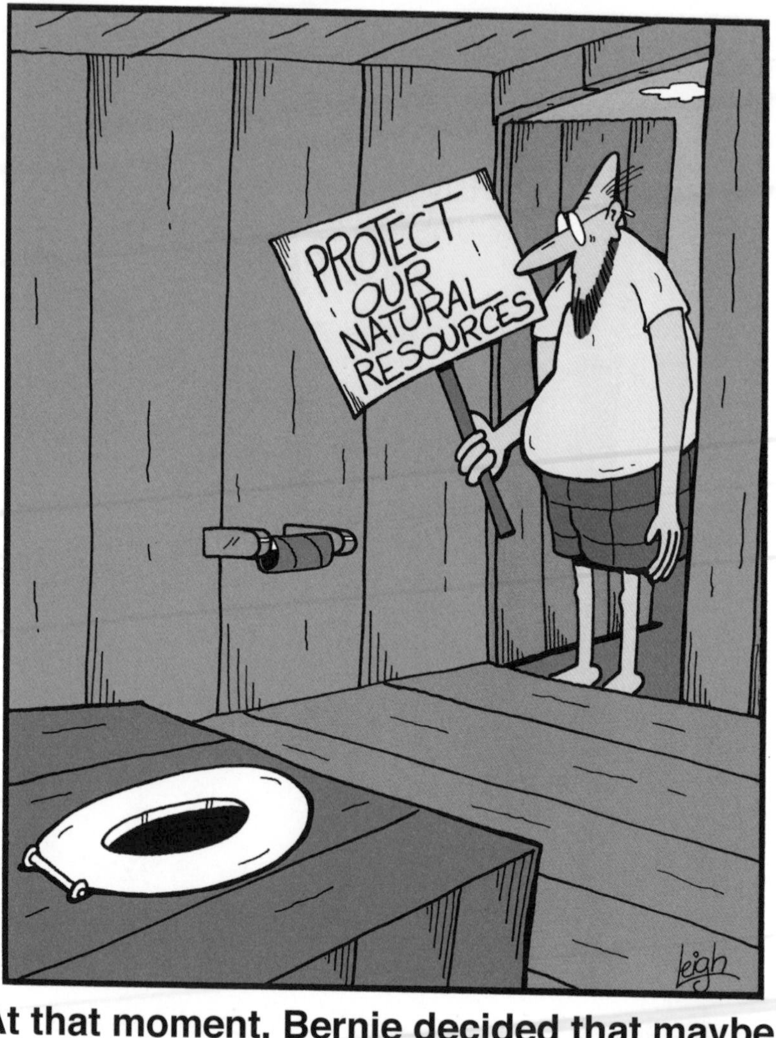
PROTECT OUR NATURAL RESOURCES
Leigh

At that moment, Bernie decided that maybe, just maybe, they didn't need to save *all* the trees.

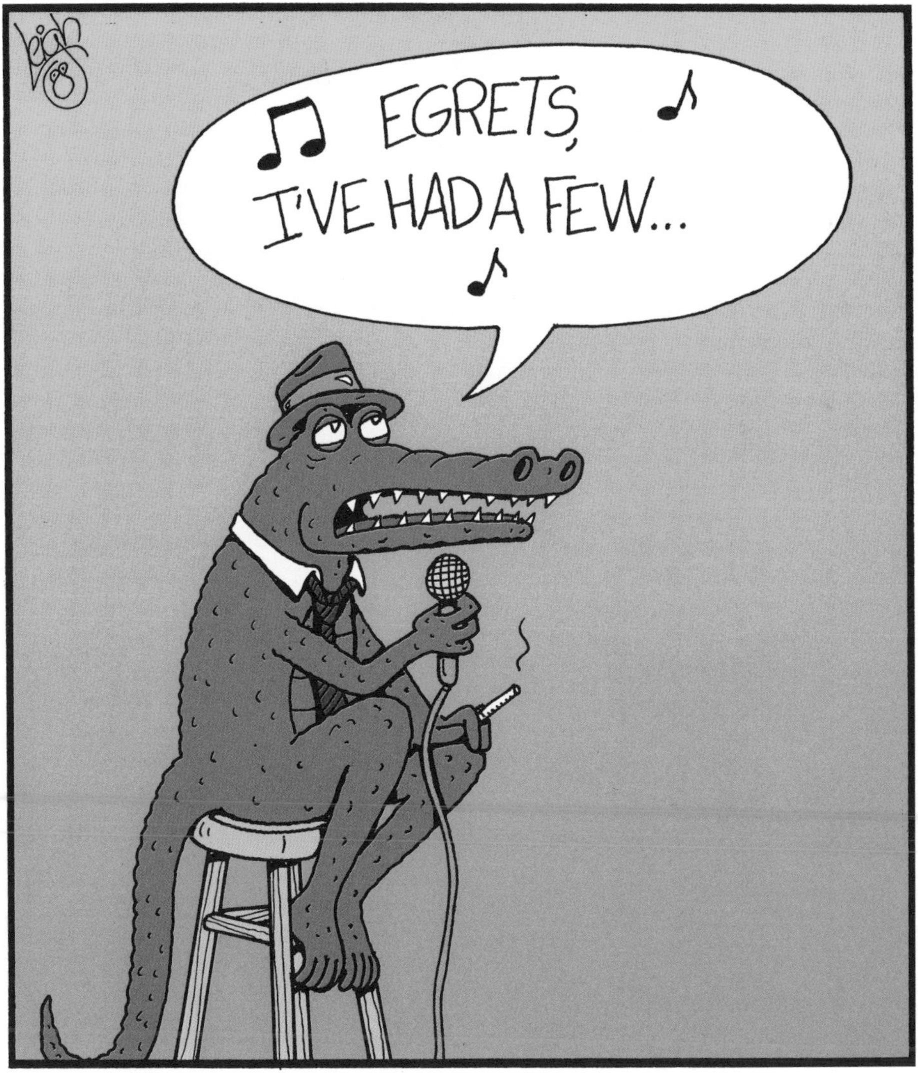
EGRETS,
I'VE HAD A FEW...

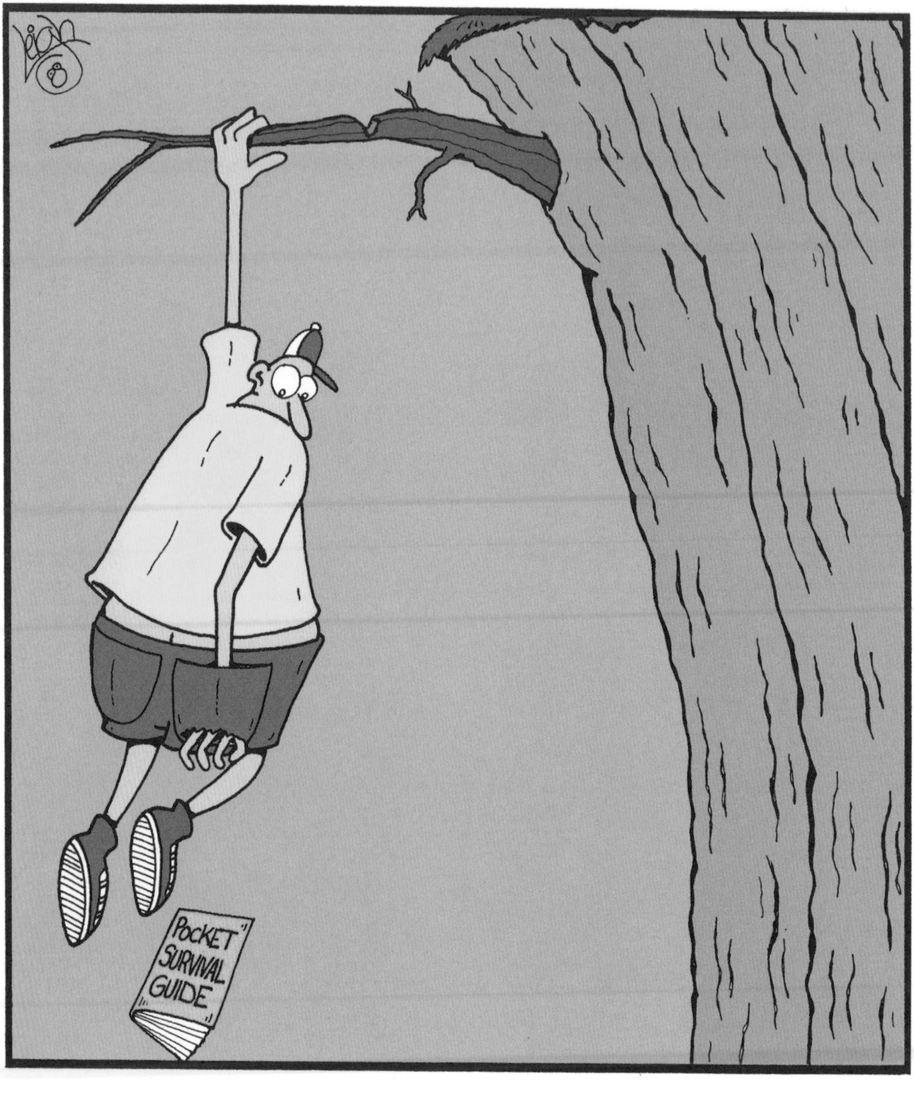
POCKET SURVIVAL GUIDE

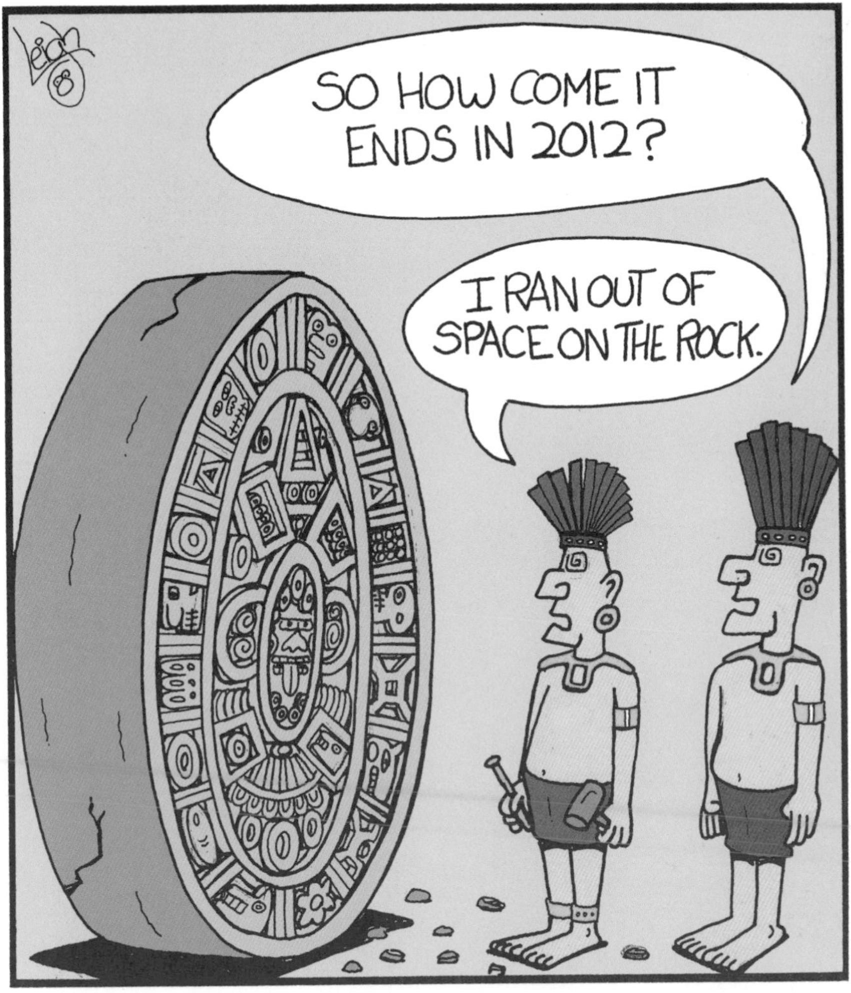
SO HOW COME IT ENDS IN 2012?
I RAN OUT OF SPACE ON THE ROCK.

At last, the mystery of the Mayan calendar revealed

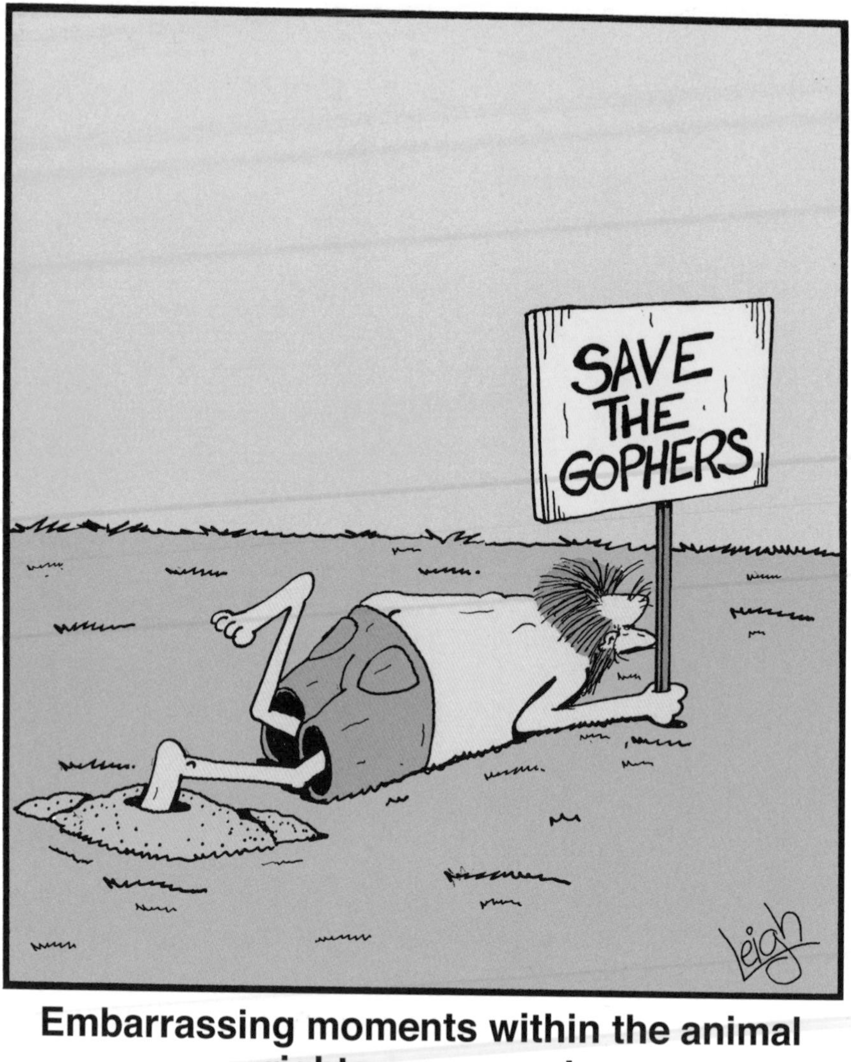
SAVE THE GOPHERS
Leigh

Embarrassing moments within the animal rights movement

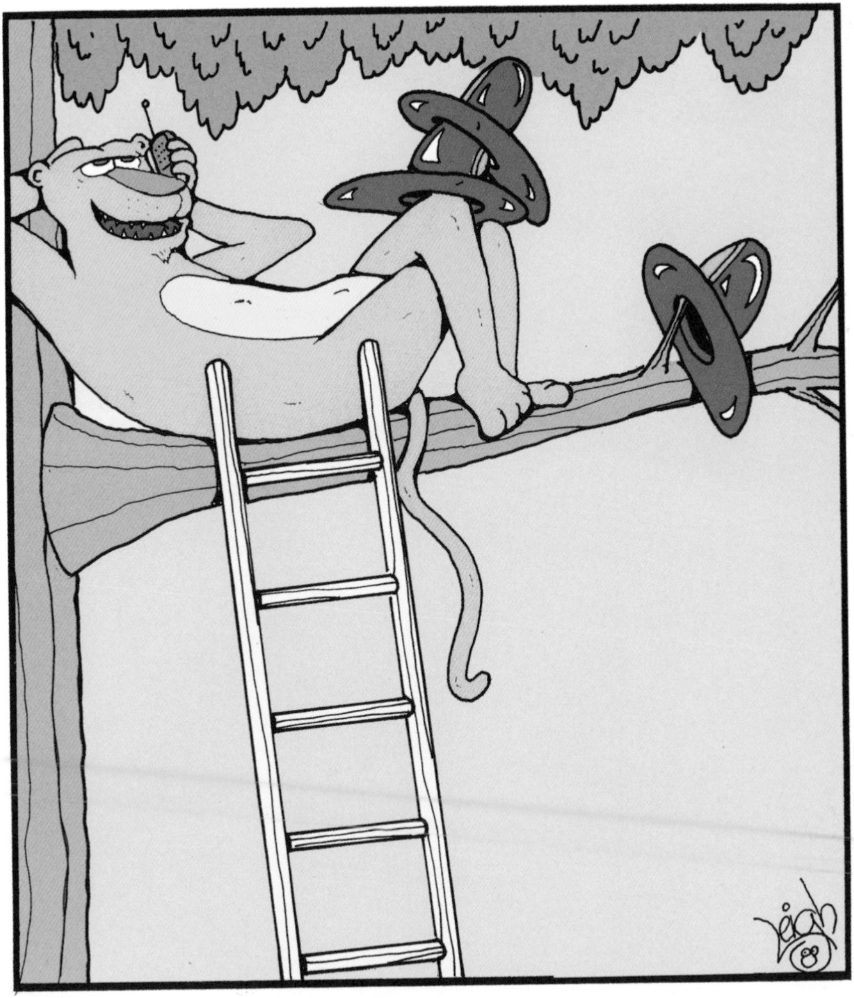

"I'd like to report a rather large cat stuck up a tree."

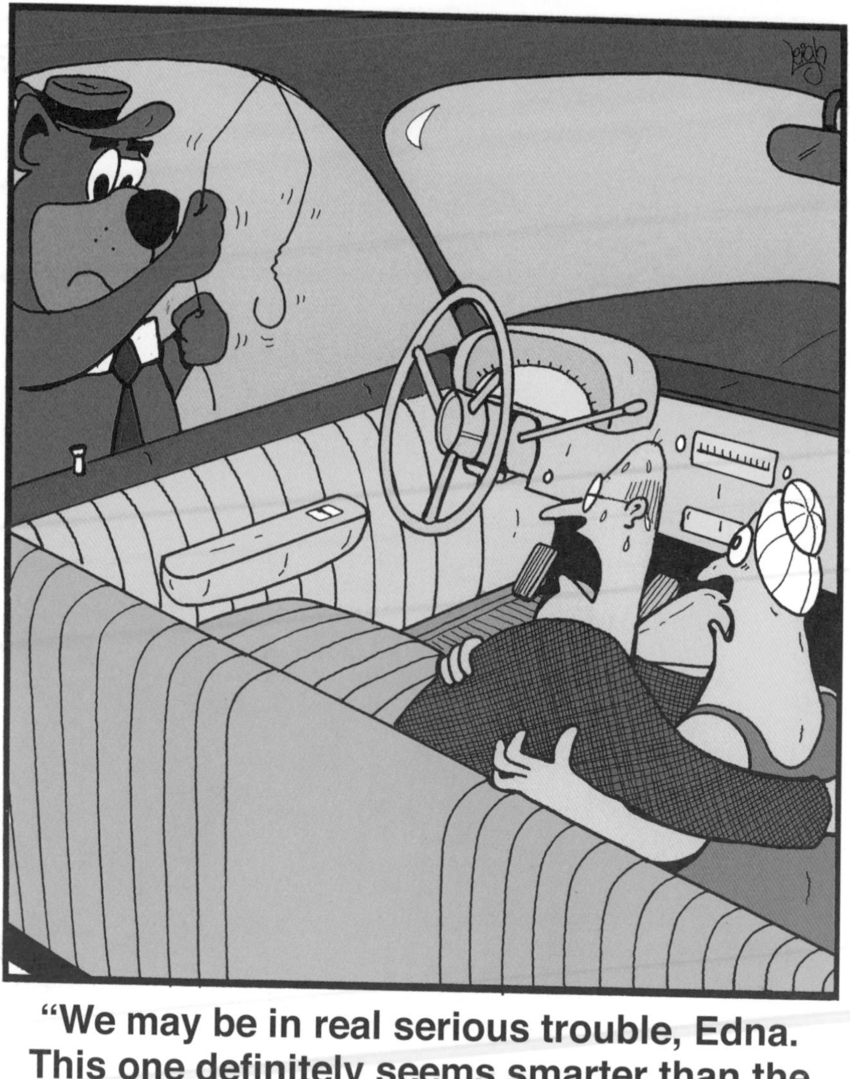

"We may be in real serious trouble, Edna. This one definitely seems smarter than the average bear!"

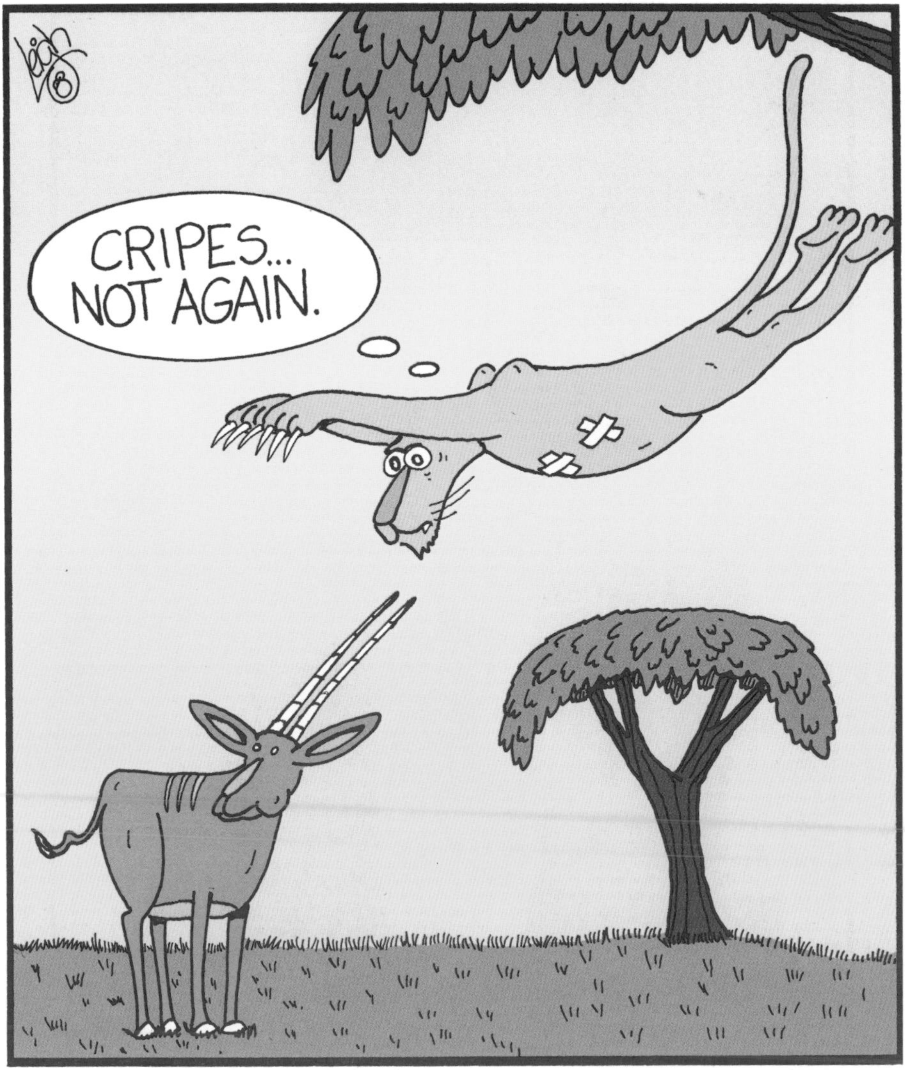
CRIPES...
NOT AGAIN.

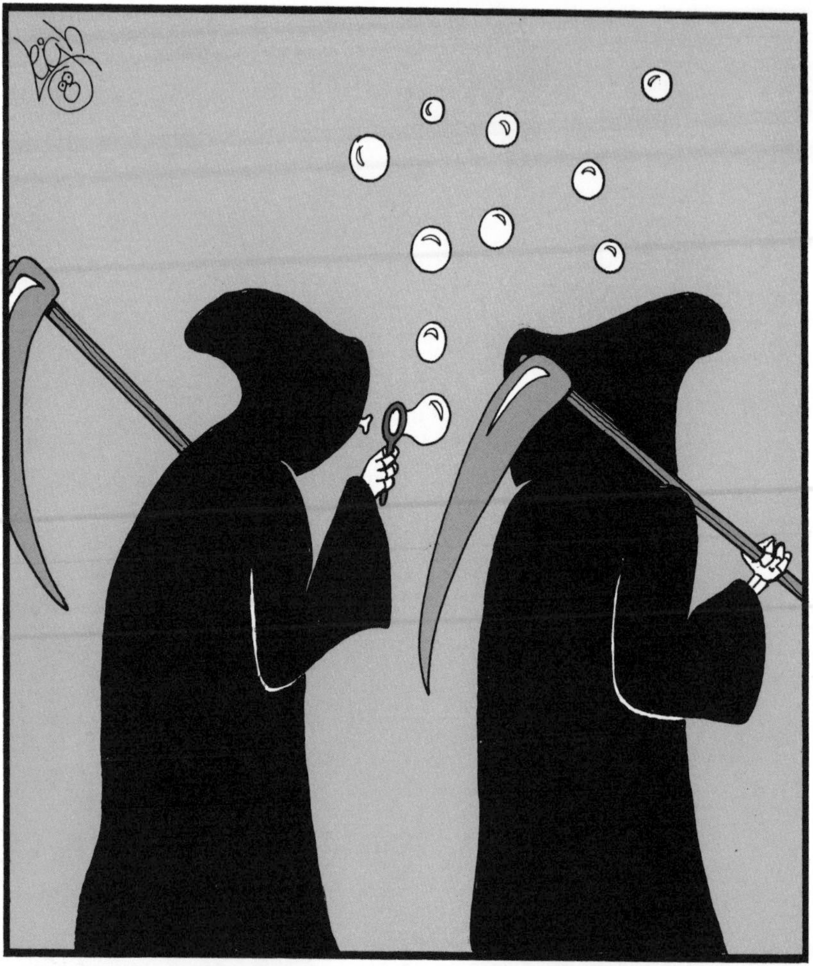

"Seriously, dude, what you do on your own time is none of my business, but when we're out and about there's a certain public image we need to maintain."

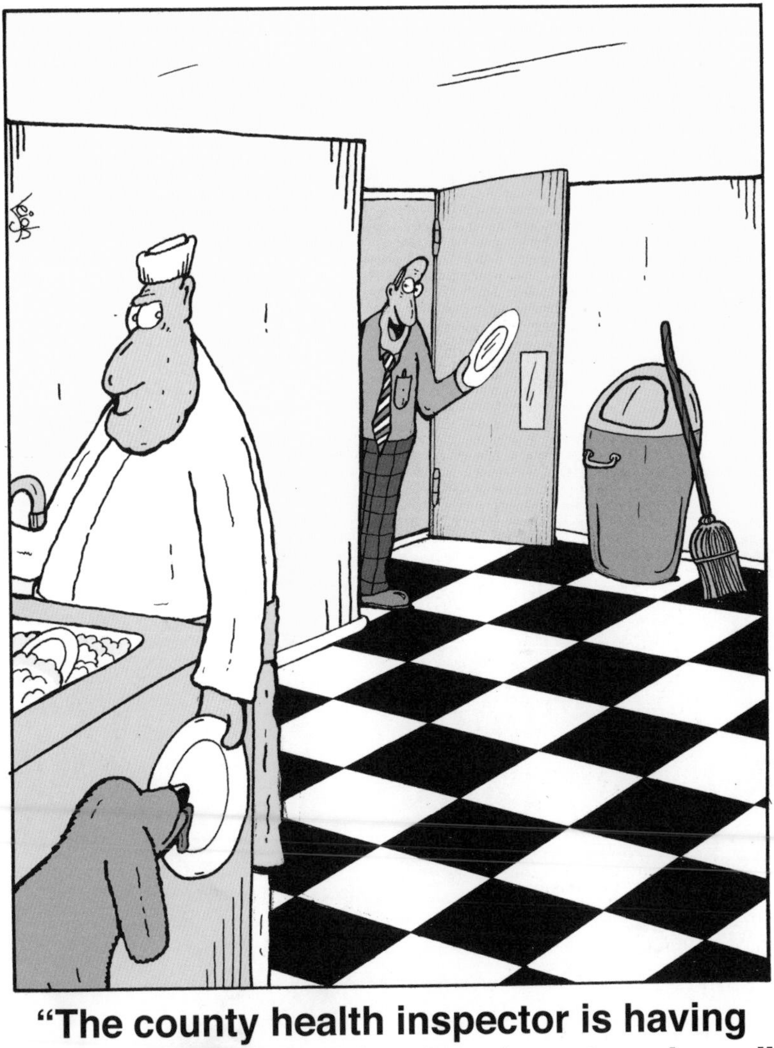
Leigh

"The county health inspector is having lunch. Make sure his plate is extra clean."

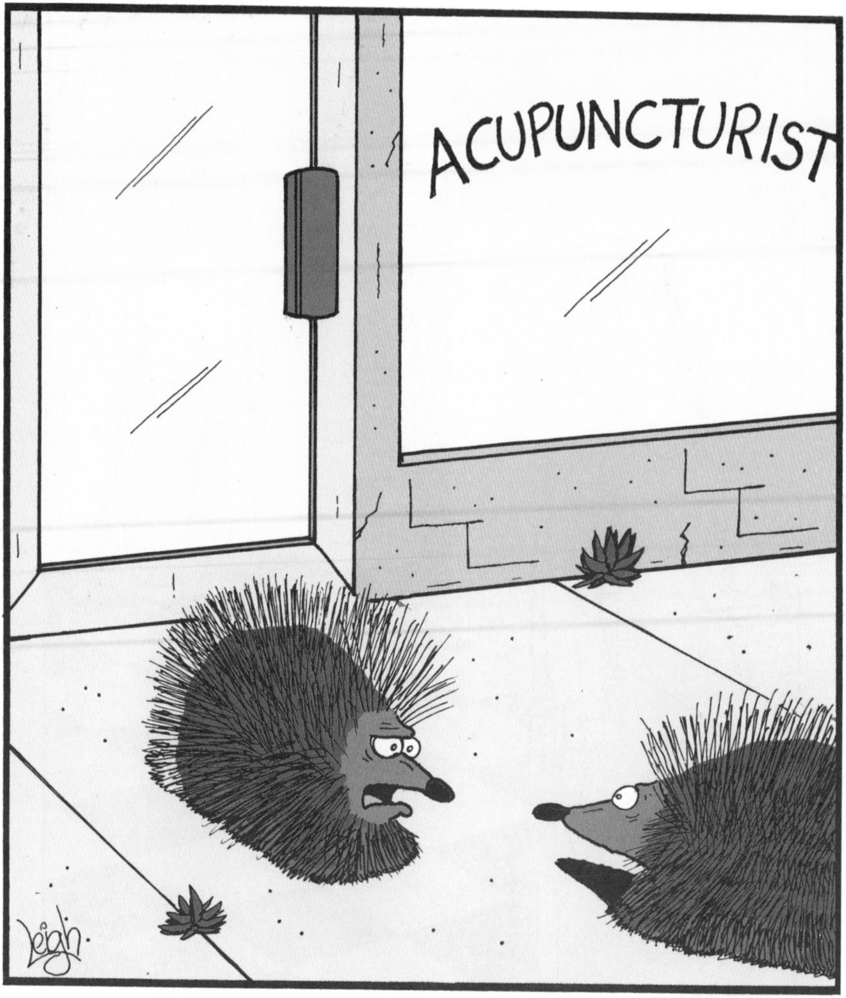
ACUPUNCTURIST
Leigh

"No, it didn't work, and now he's in pain, too."

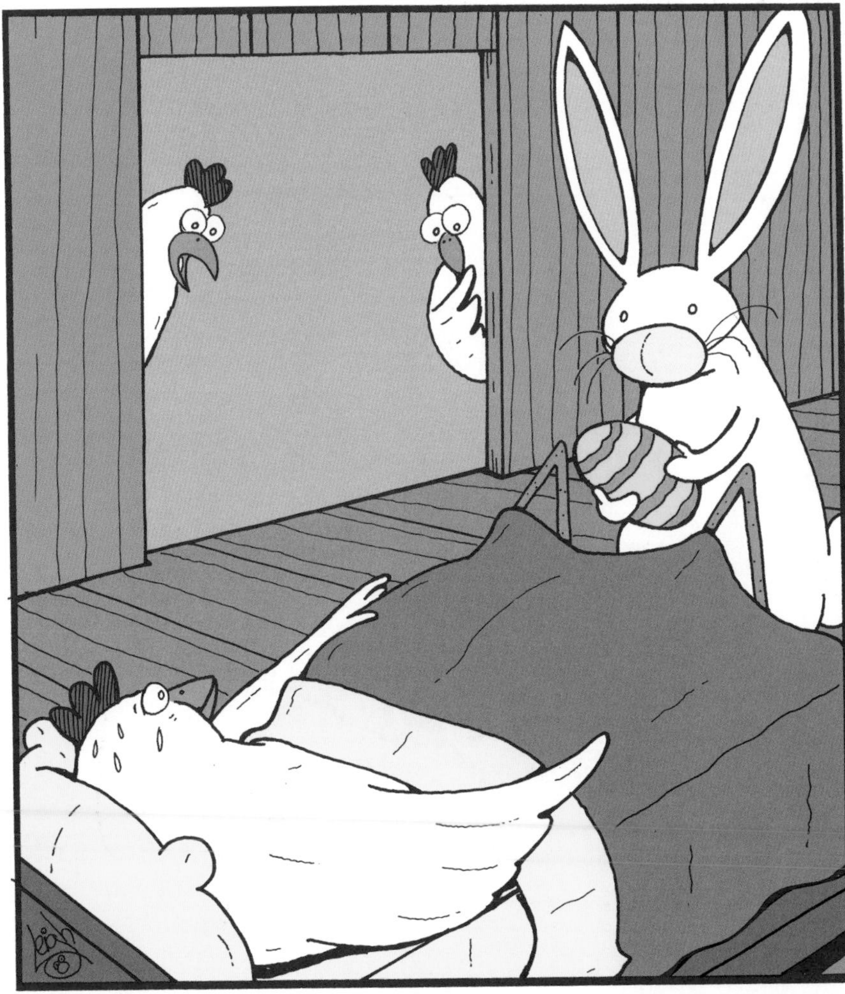
Larson

"Well, I'll be . . . He really does deliver 'em!"

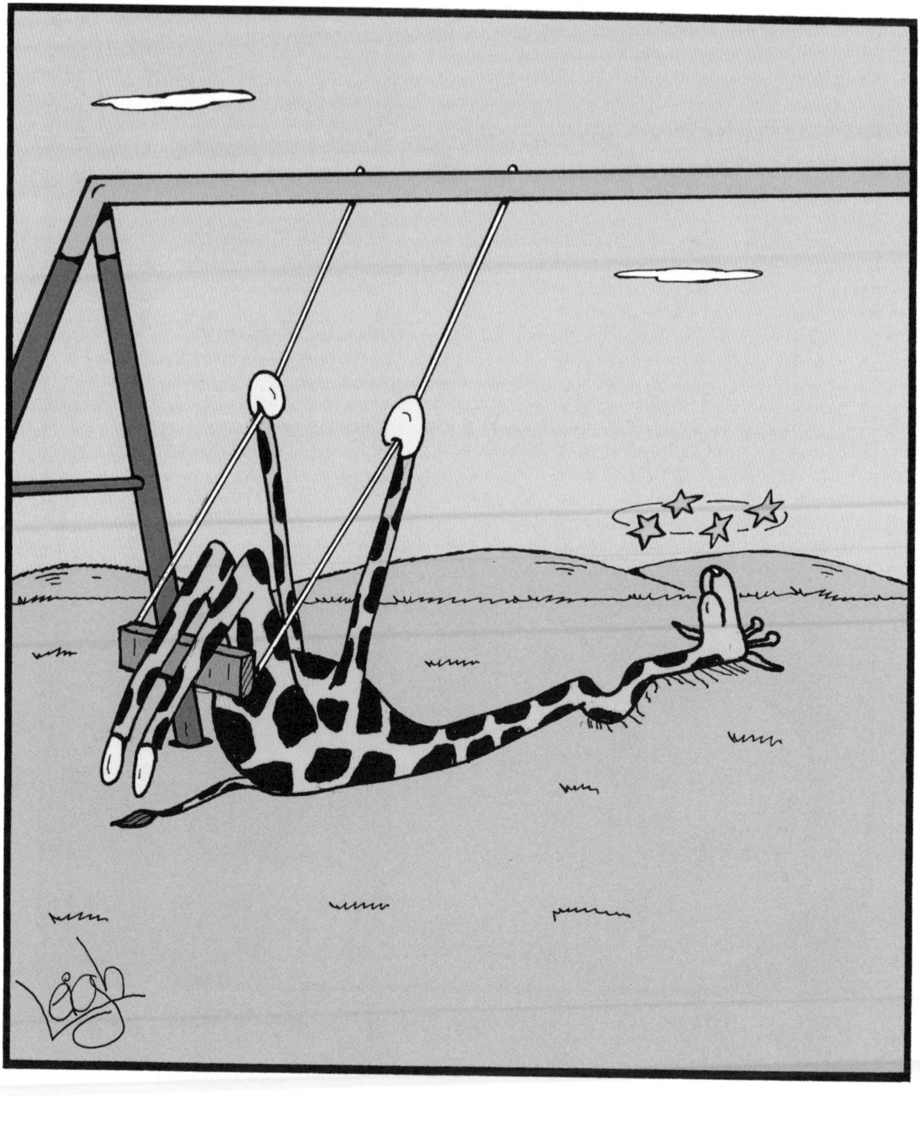

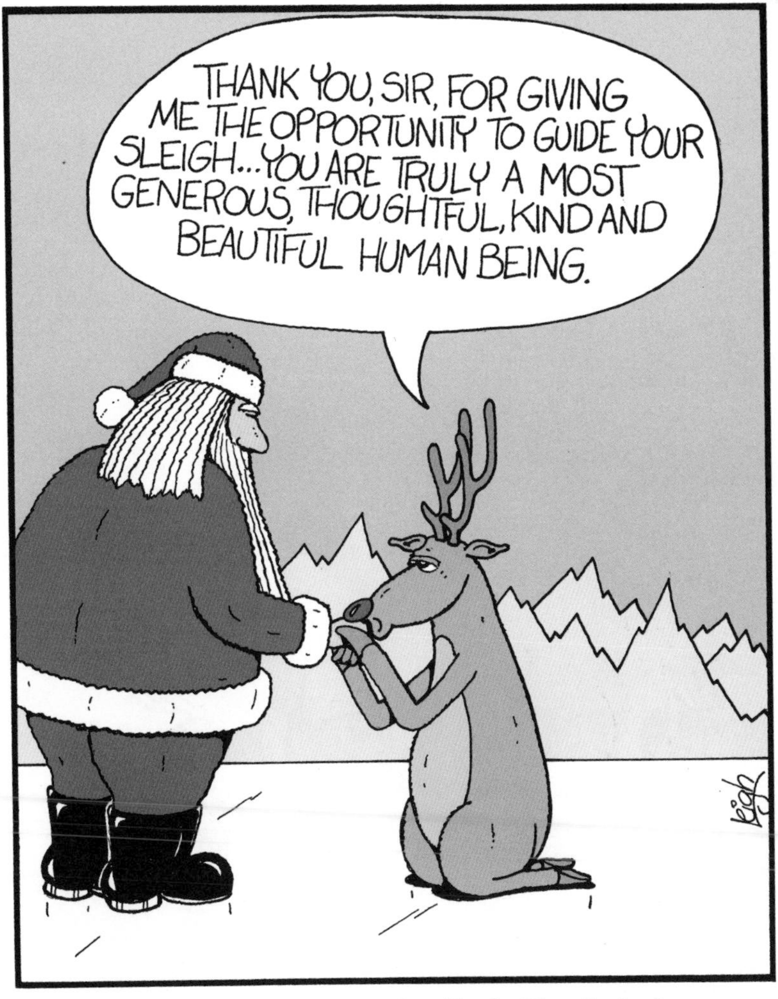
THANK YOU, SIR, FOR GIVING ME THE OPPORTUNITY TO GUIDE YOUR SLEIGH... YOU ARE TRULY A MOST GENEROUS, THOUGHTFUL, KIND AND BEAUTIFUL HUMAN BEING.
leigh

Contrary to popular belief, Rudolph was actually a brown-nosed reindeer.

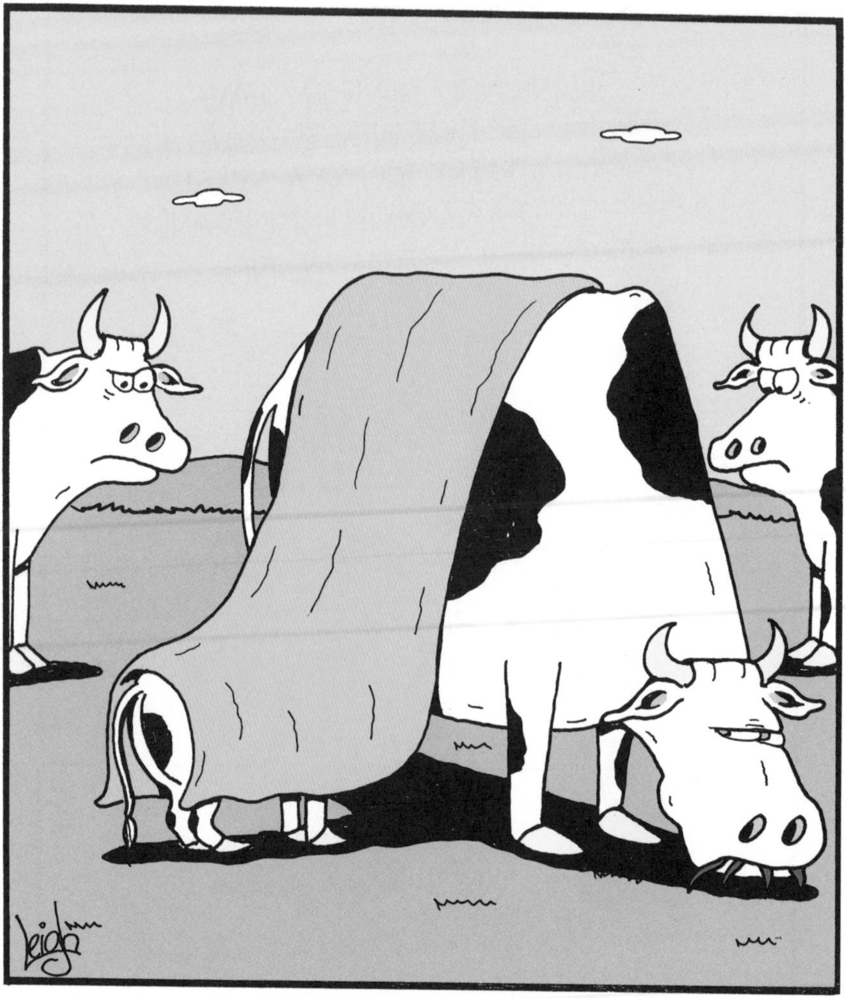

Even when practiced discreetly, raised eye-brows and disapproving glances still meet with those who dare to udder-feed in public.

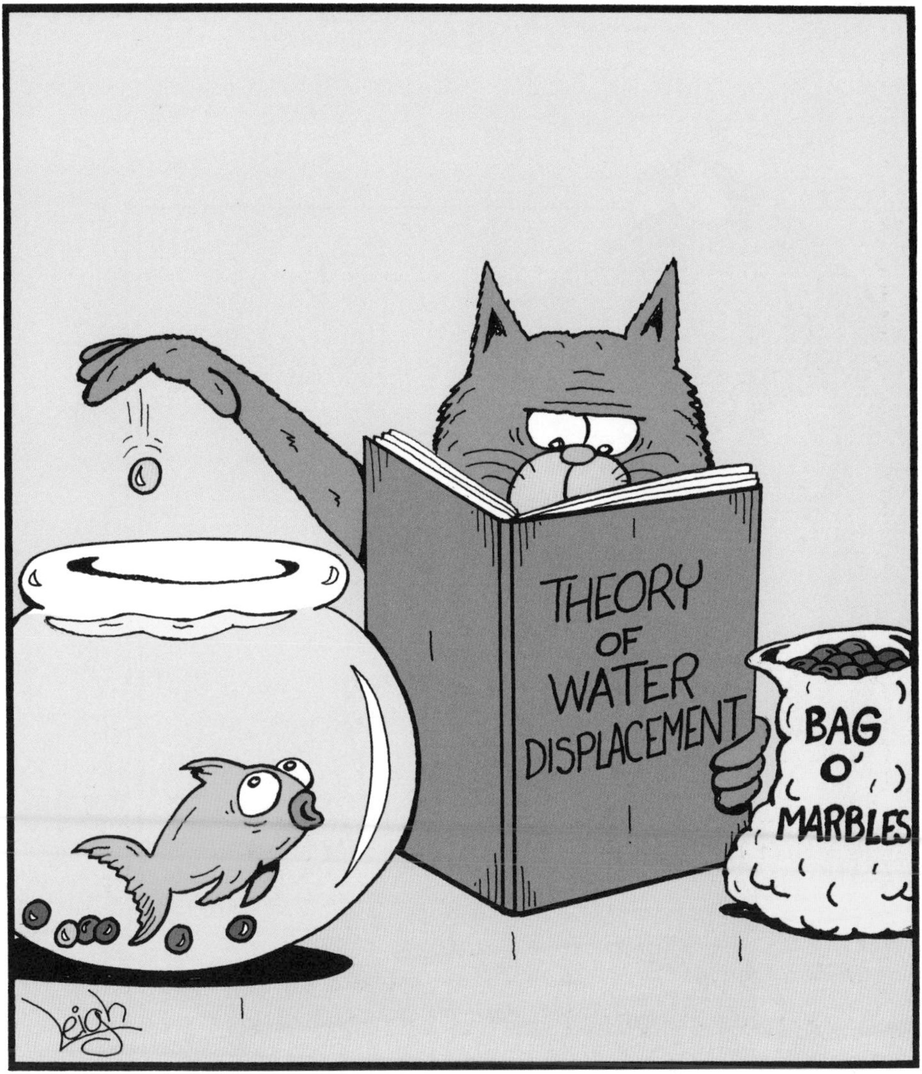
THEORY
OF
WATER
DISPLACEMENT
BAG
O'
MARBLES
Leigh

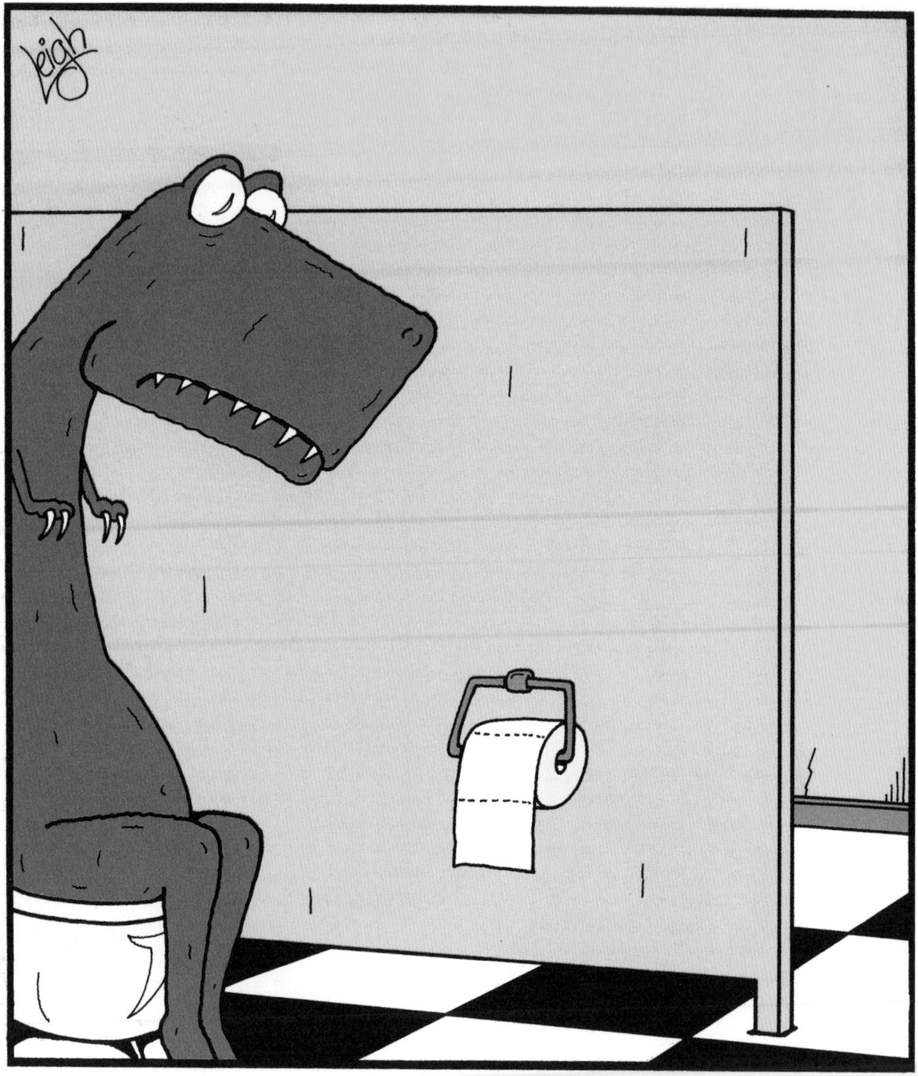
Leigh

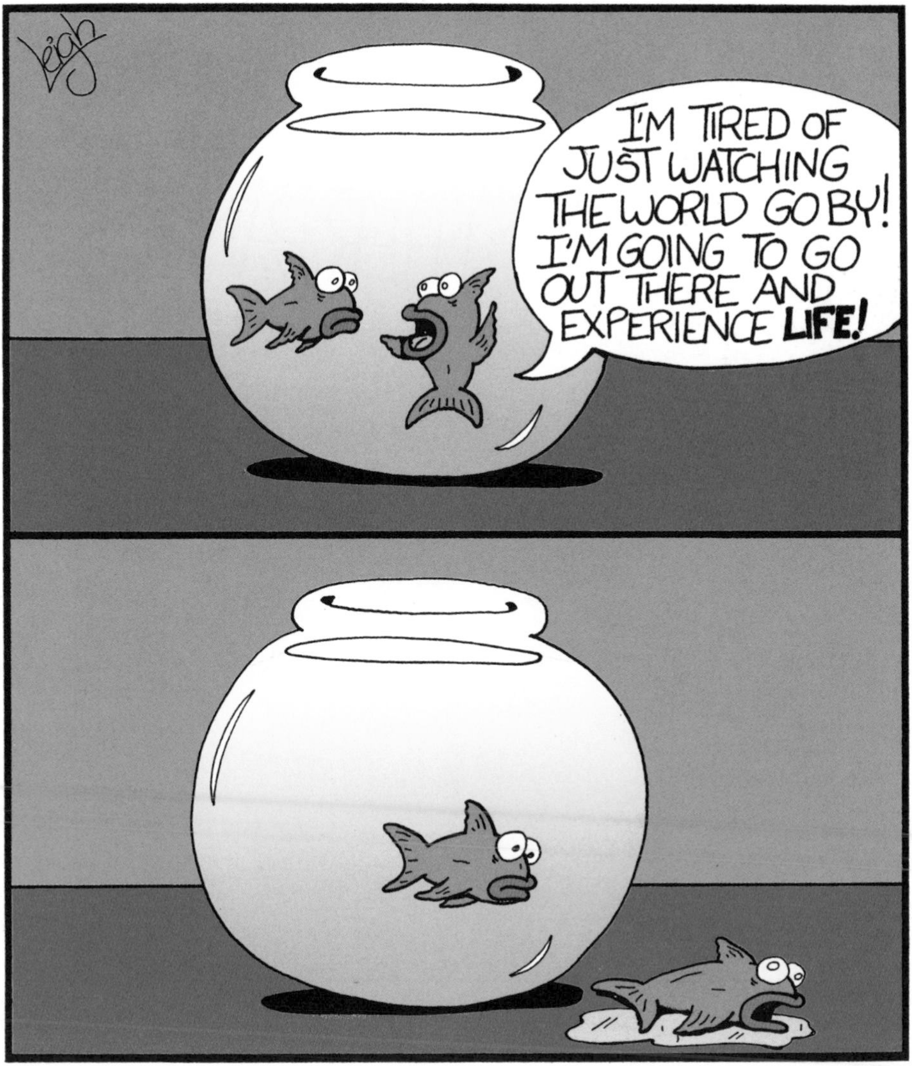
leigh
I'M TIRED OF JUST WATCHING THE WORLD GO BY! I'M GOING TO GO OUT THERE AND EXPERIENCE LIFE!

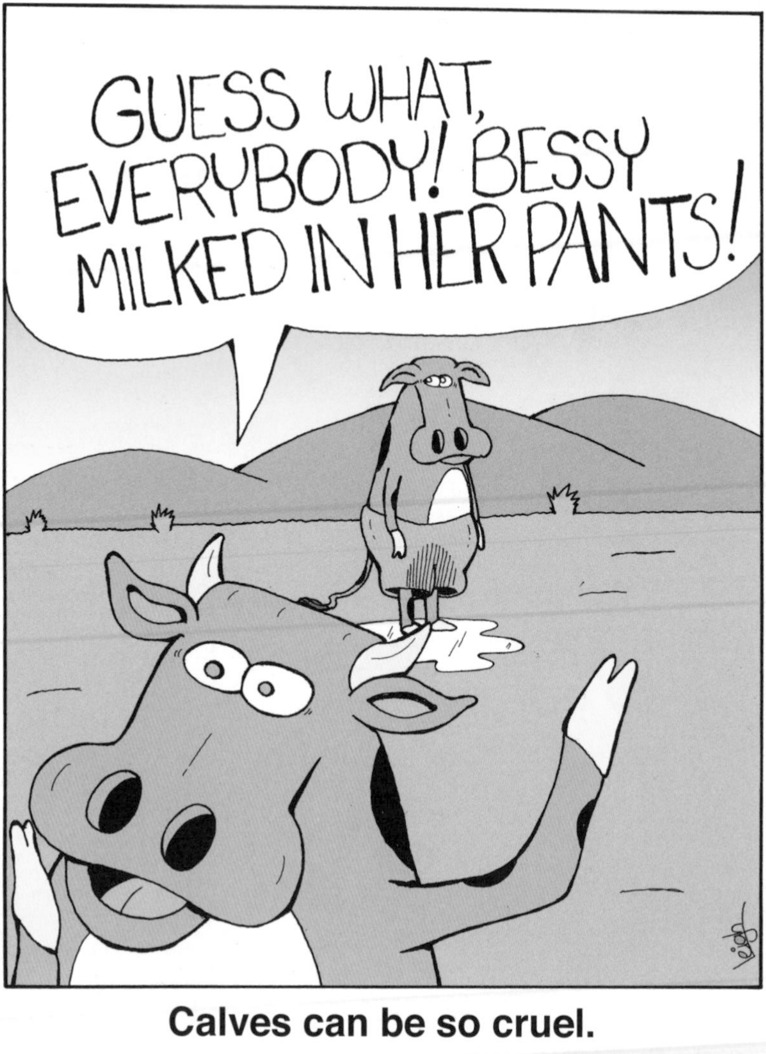
GUESS WHAT, EVERYBODY! BESSY MILKED IN HER PANTS!

Calves can be so cruel.

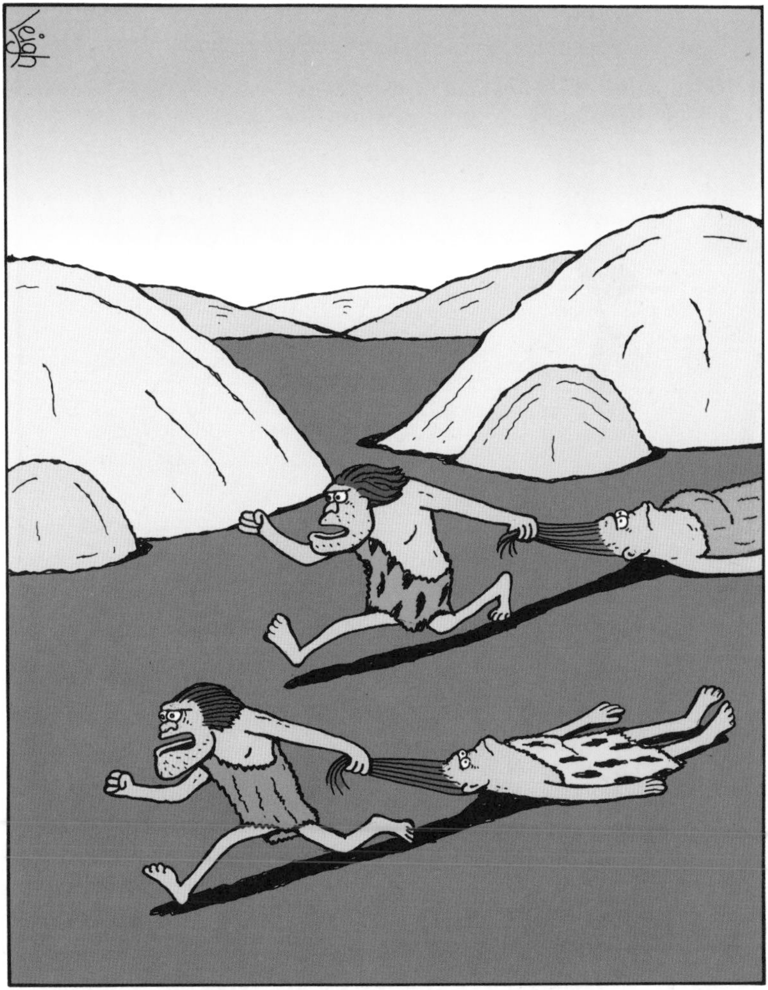
Leigh

Stone Age drag racing

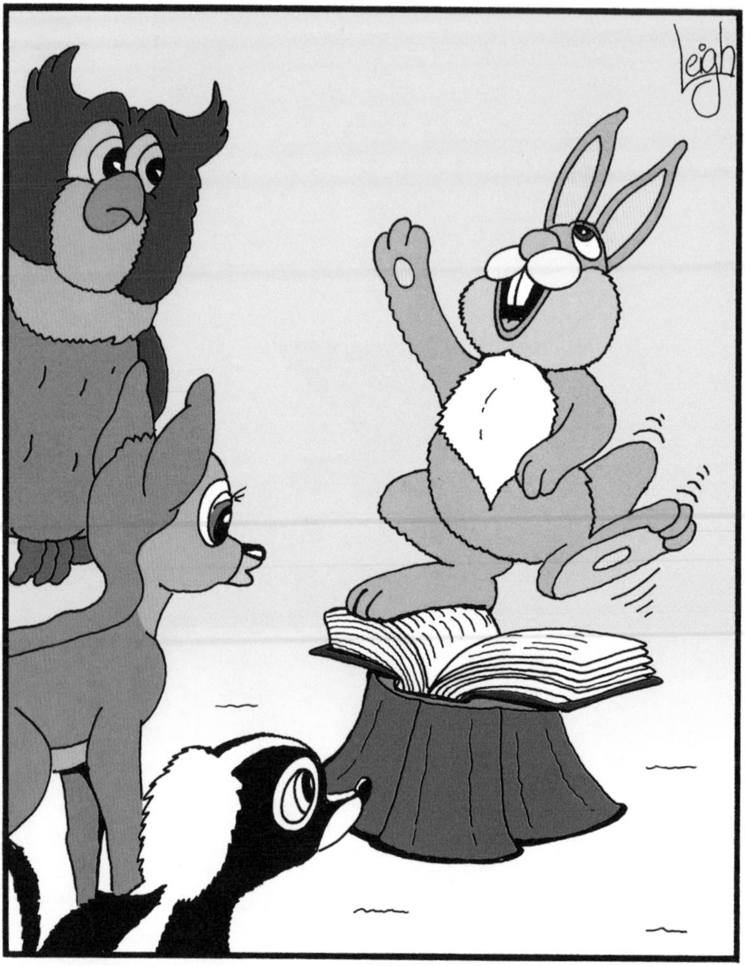
Leigh

Every Sunday morning, all the woodland creatures gathered around to hear an inspirational sermon delivered by the local Bible Thumper.

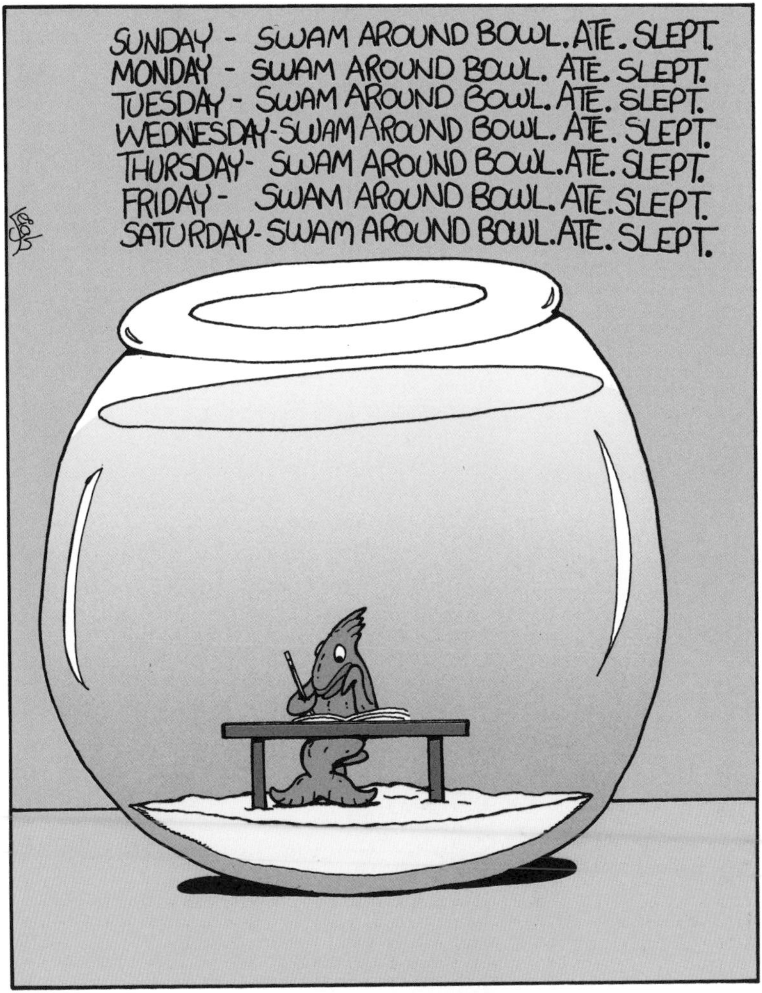
SUNDAY - SWAM AROUND BOWL. ATE. SLEPT.
MONDAY - SWAM AROUND BOWL. ATE. SLEPT.
TUESDAY - SWAM AROUND BOWL. ATE. SLEPT.
WEDNESDAY-SWAM AROUND BOWL. ATE. SLEPT.
THURSDAY- SWAM AROUND BOWL. ATE. SLEPT.
FRIDAY- SWAM AROUND BOWL. ATE. SLEPT.
SATURDAY-SWAM AROUND BOWL. ATE. SLEPT.

Diary of a fish

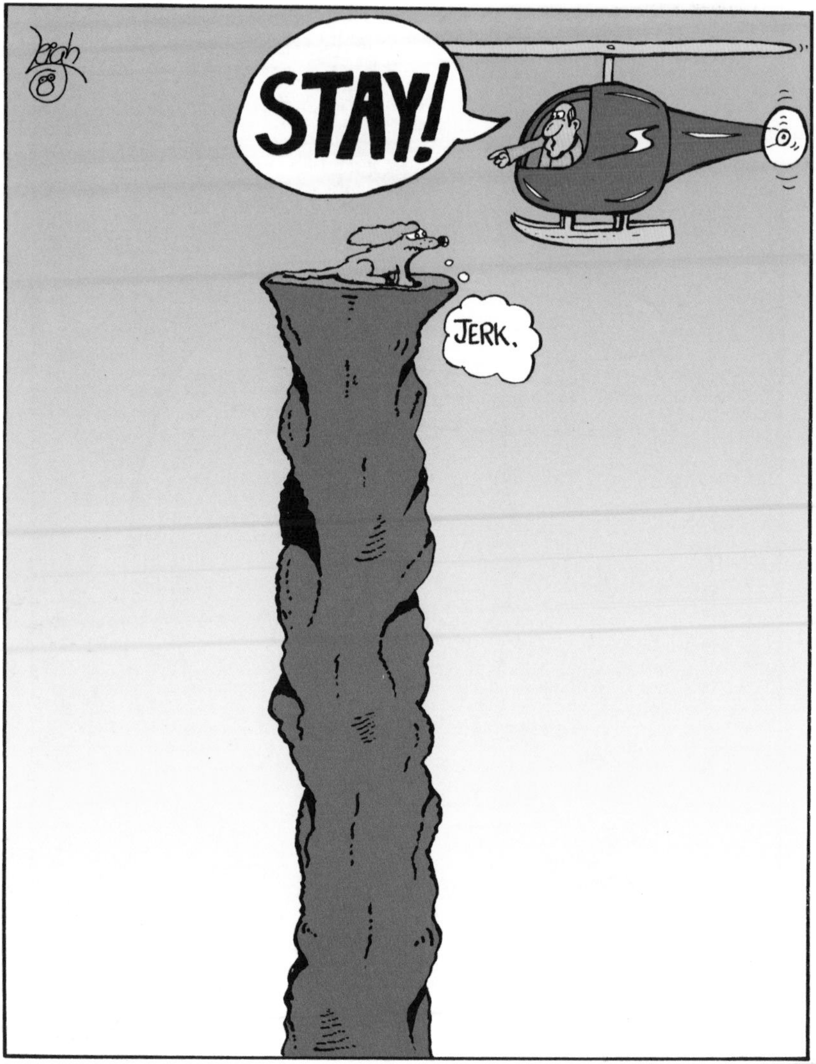
STAY!
JERK.

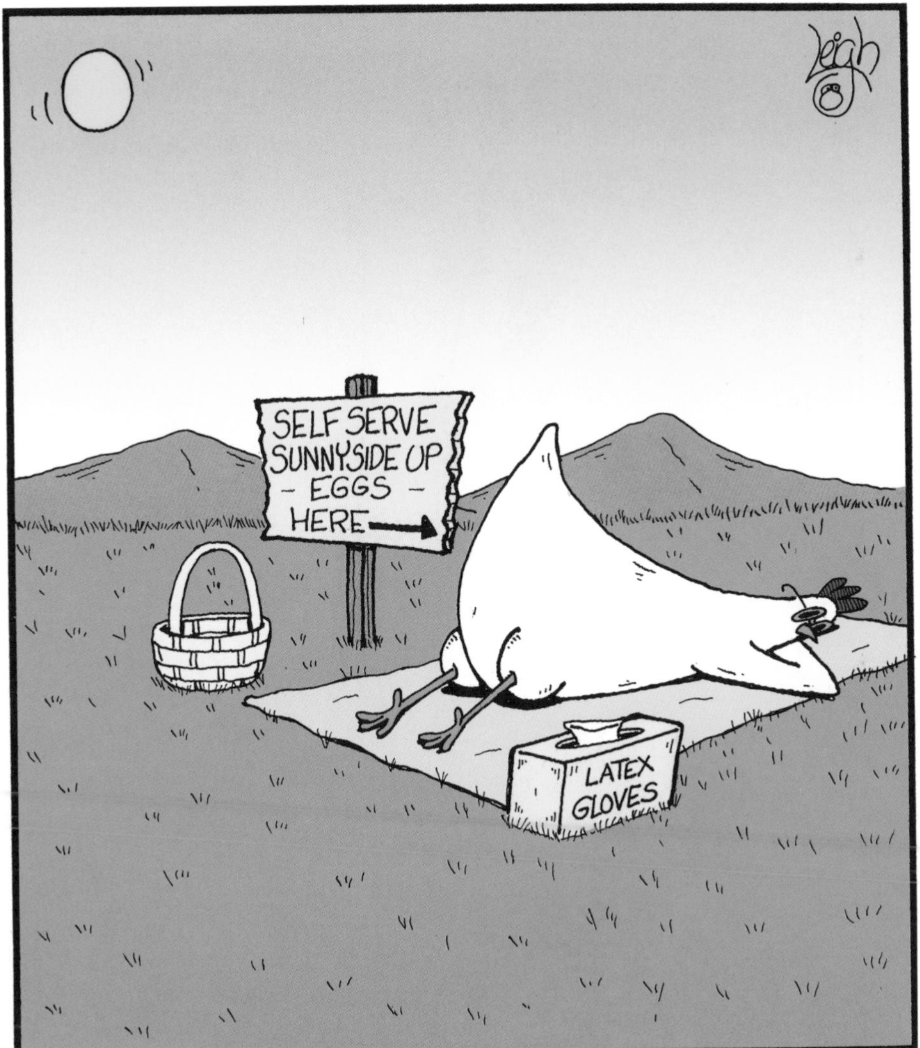
SELF SERVE
SUNNYSIDE UP
- EGGS -
HERE
LATEX
GLOVES
Leigh

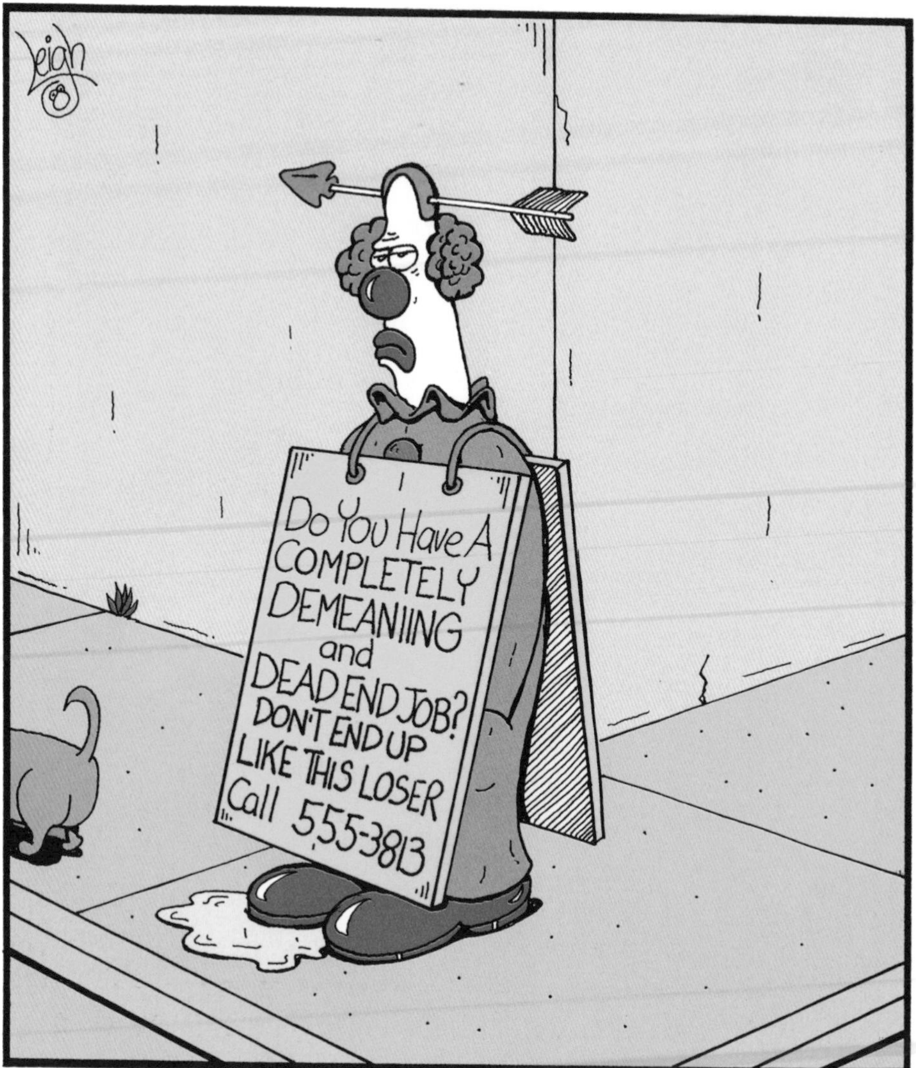
Do You Have A COMPLETELY DEMEANIING and DEAD END JOB? DON'T END UP LIKE THIS LOSER Call 555-3813

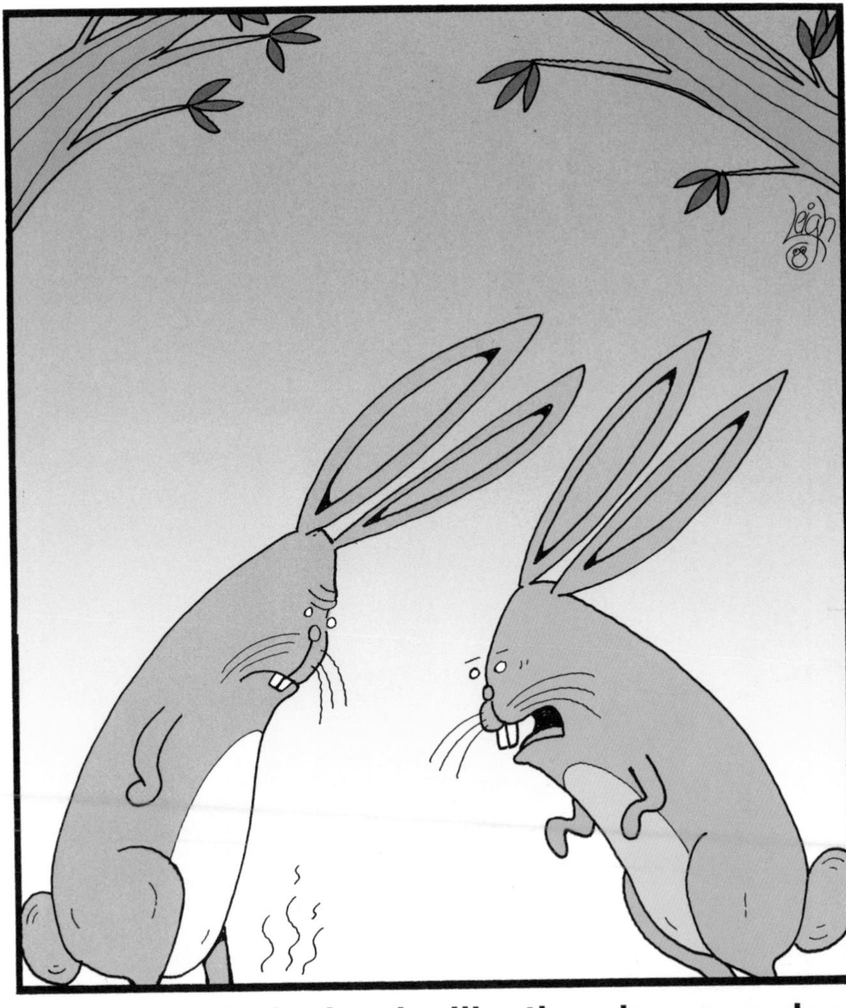

"Bummer, dude. Looks like there's a new dog in the neighborhood . . . I assume that's not your lucky rabbit's foot?"

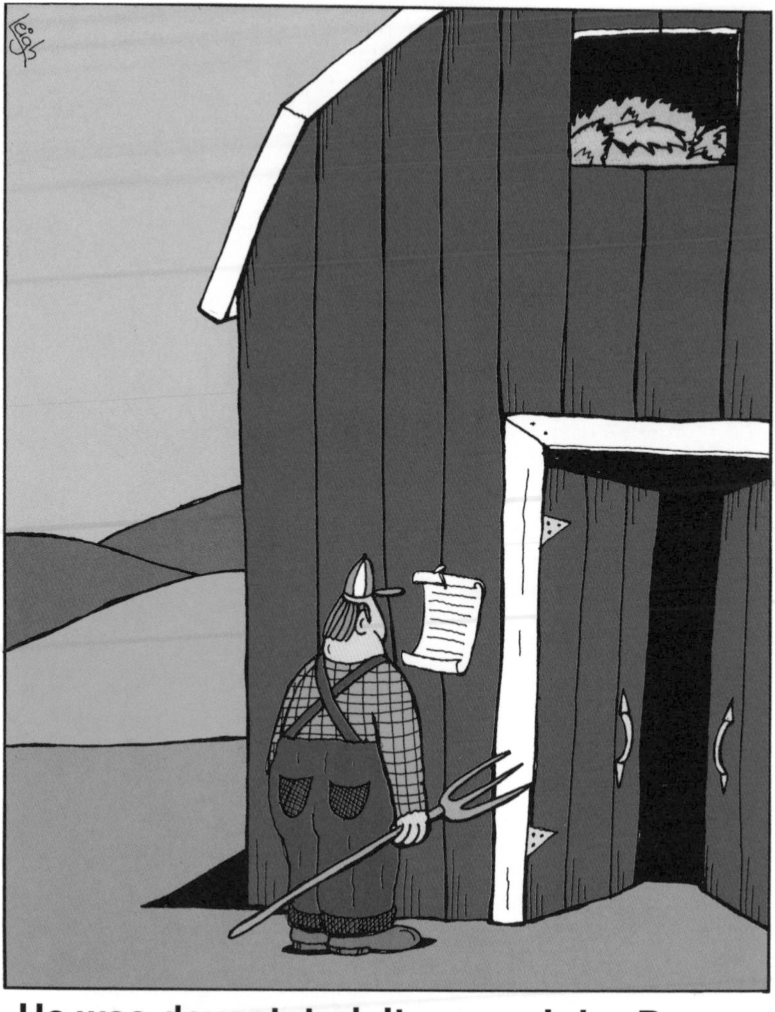

He was devastated. It was a John Deere letter. His tractor of twenty years had left him.

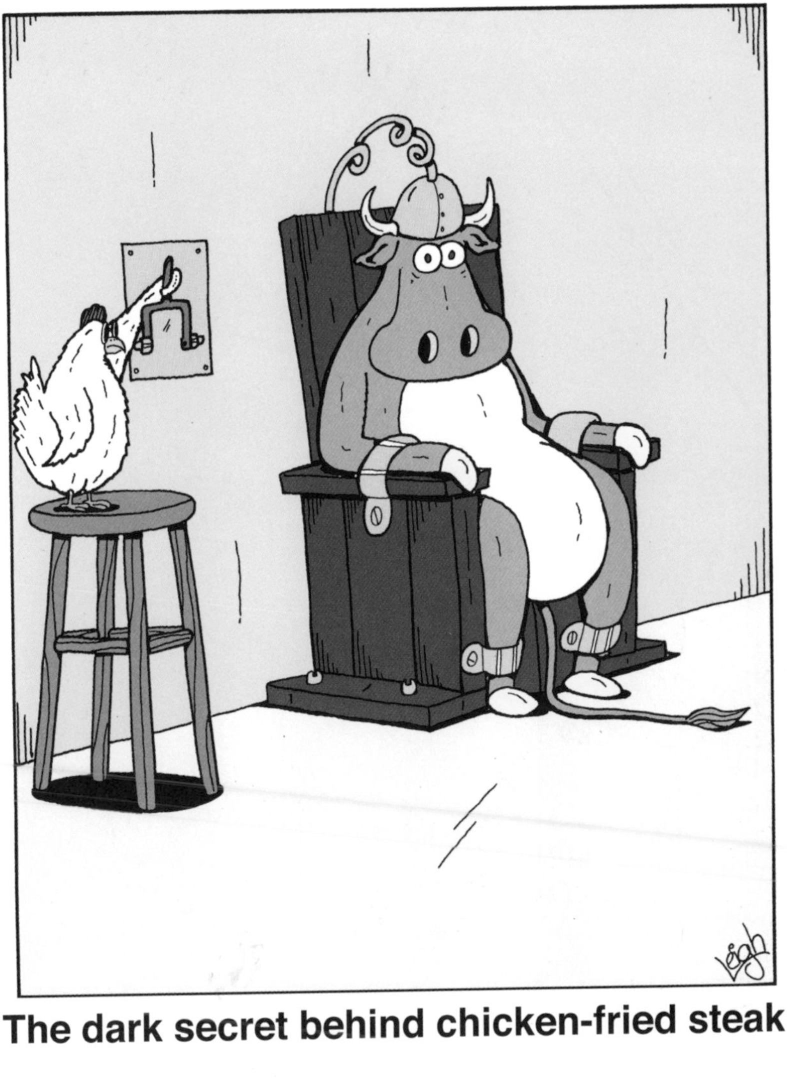

The dark secret behind chicken-fried steak

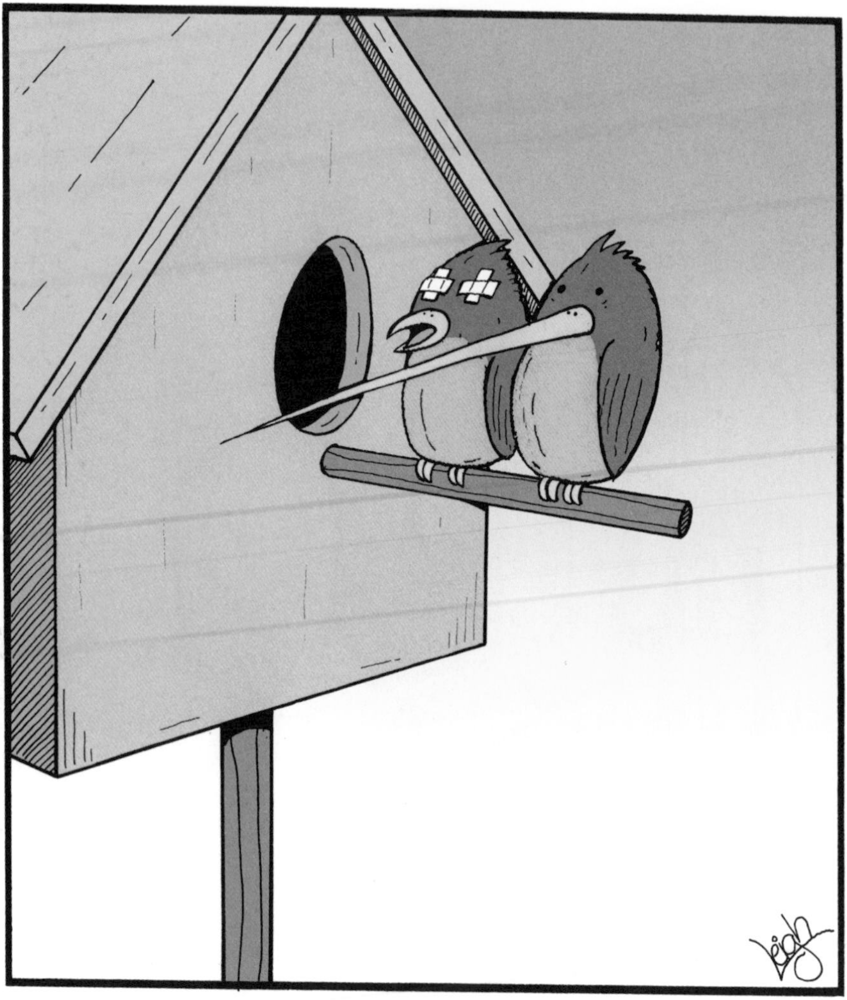

"It pains me to tell you this, Herb, but I'm afraid I can't see you anymore."

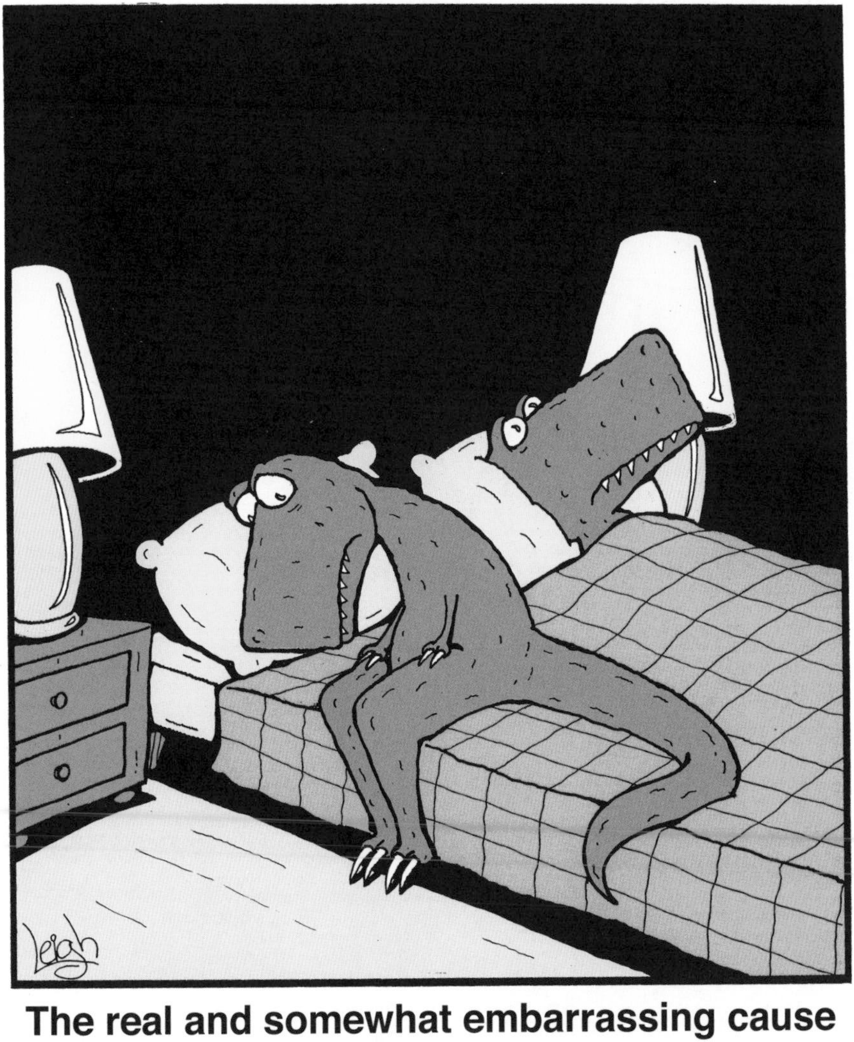
Leigh

The real and somewhat embarrassing cause of the mass extinction . . . reptile dysfunction

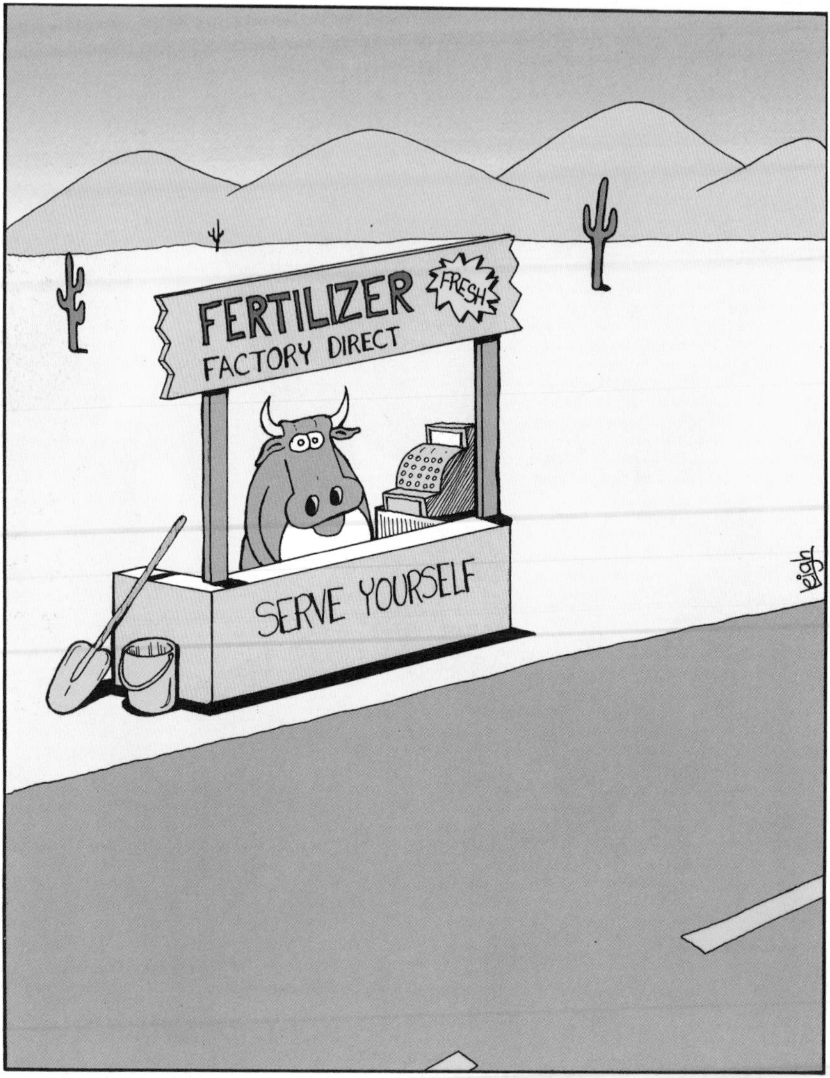
FERTILIZER
FRESH
FACTORY DIRECT
SERVE YOURSELF

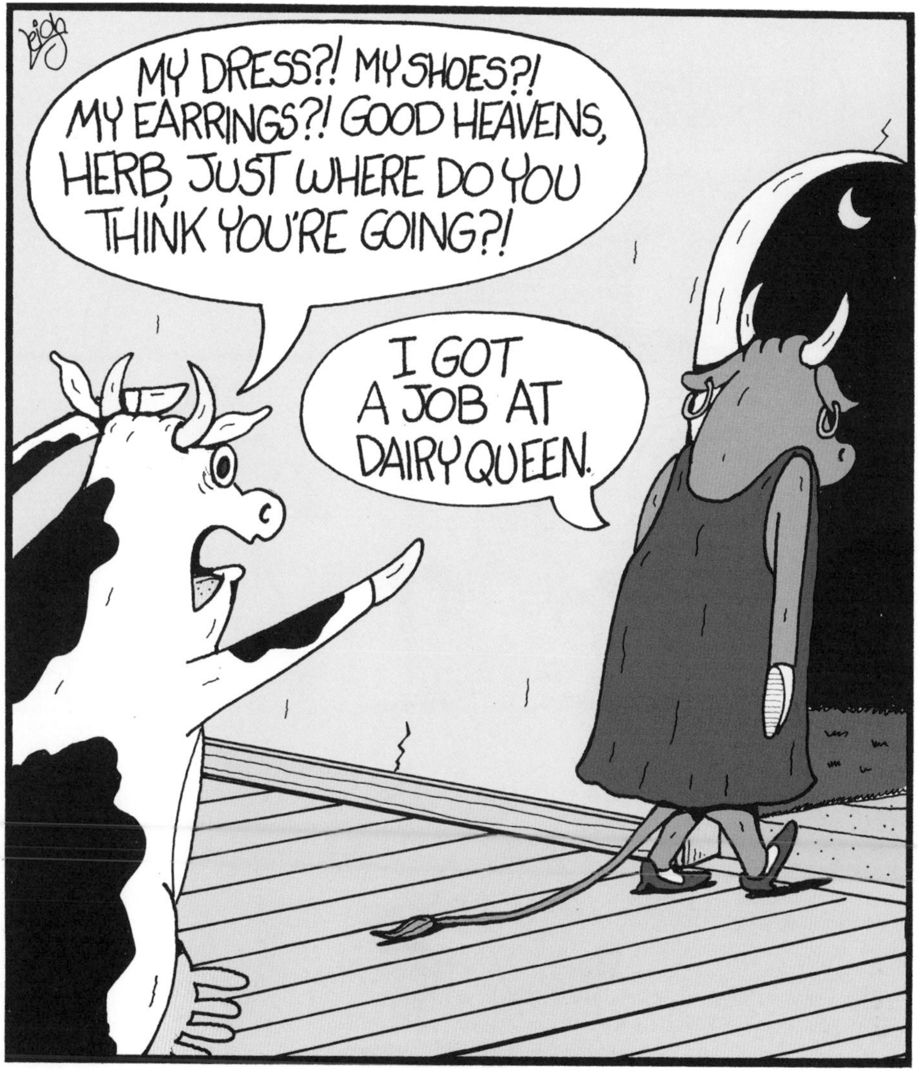
MY DRESS?! MY SHOES?! MY EARRINGS?! GOOD HEAVENS, HERB, JUST WHERE DO YOU THINK YOU'RE GOING?!
I GOT A JOB AT DAIRY QUEEN.

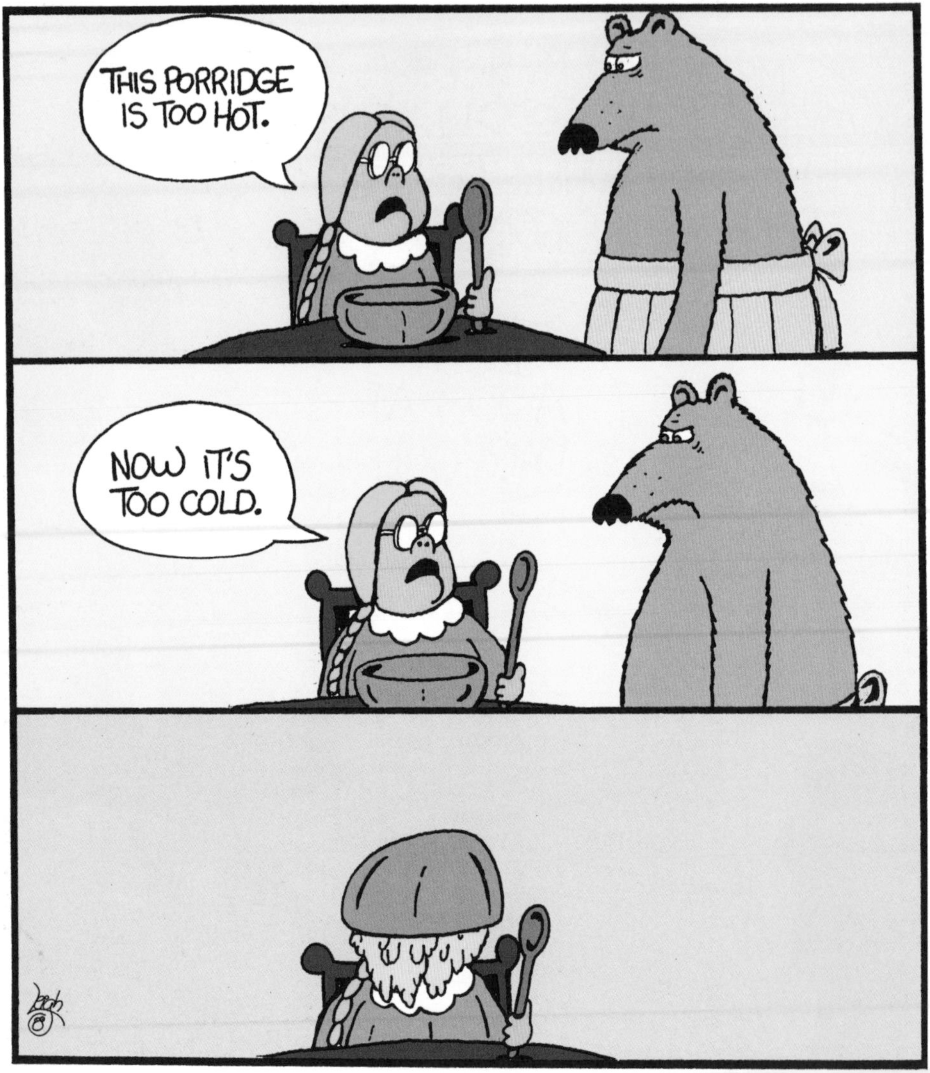
THIS PORRIDGE IS TOO HOT.
NOW IT'S TOO COLD.

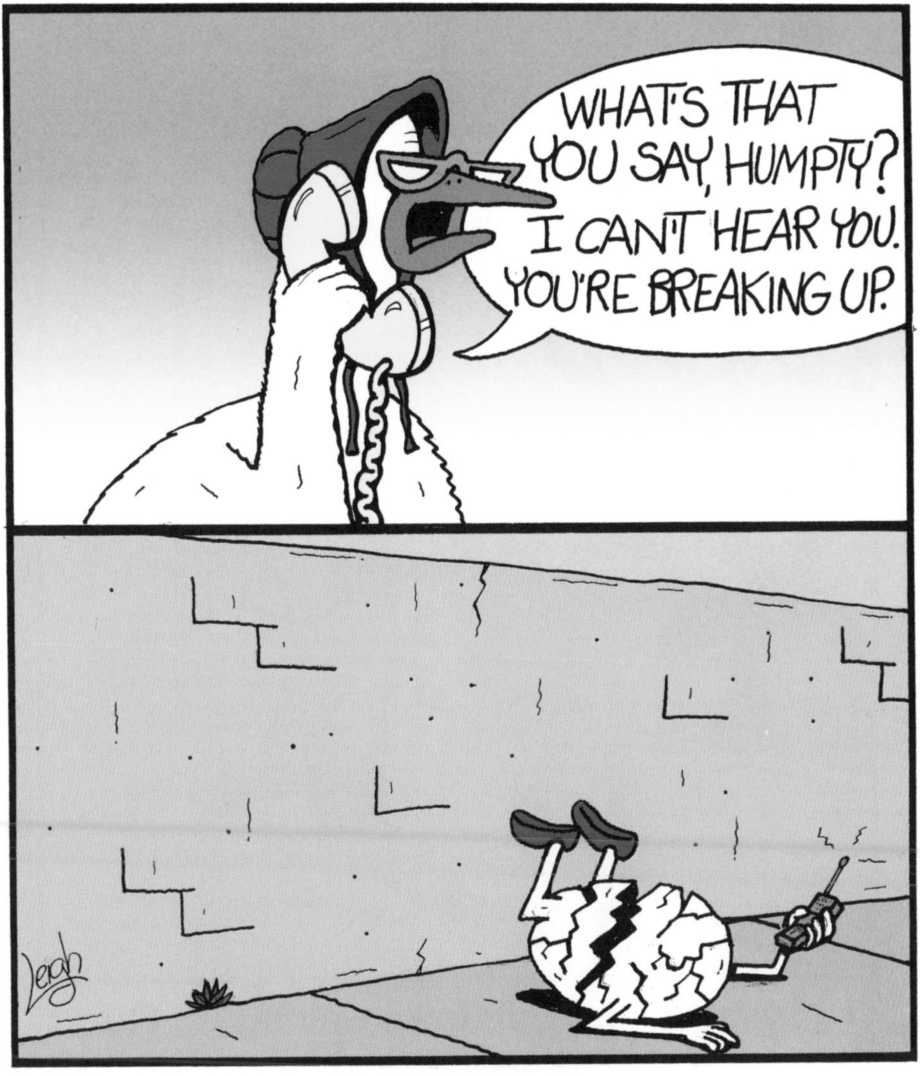
WHAT'S THAT YOU SAY, HUMPTY? I CAN'T HEAR YOU. YOU'RE BREAKING UP.
Leigh

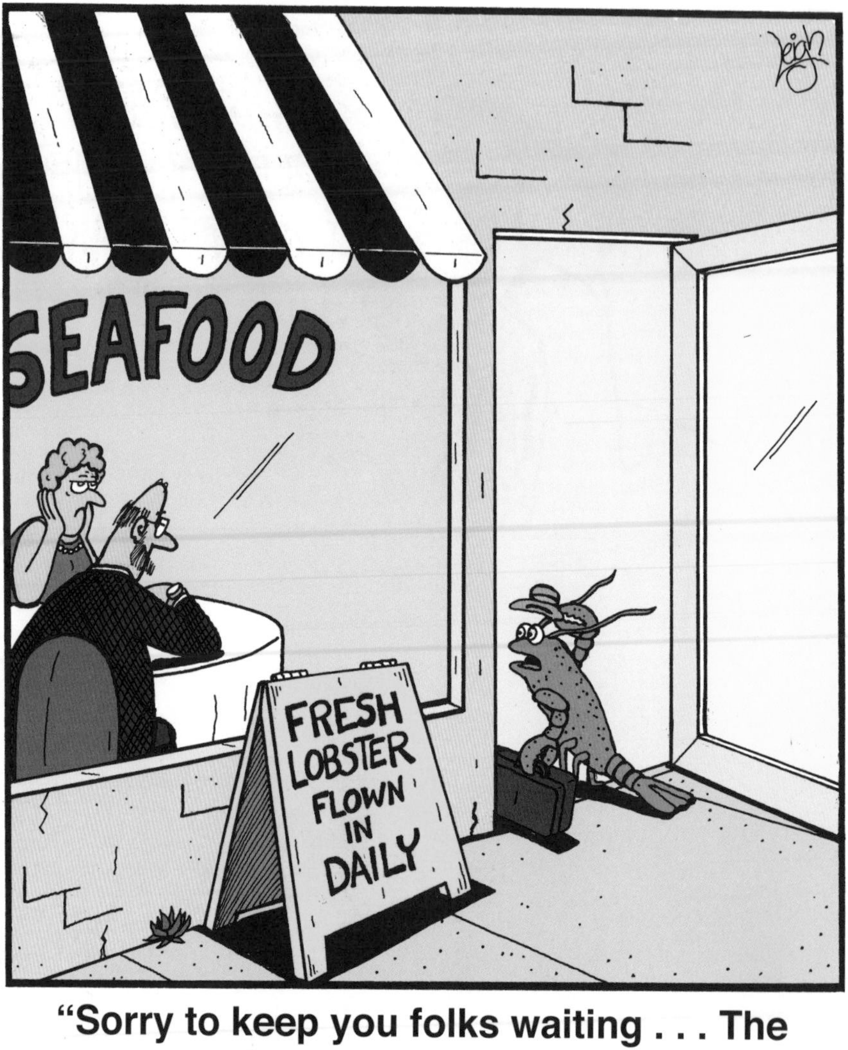
SEAFOOD
FRESH
LOBSTER
FLOWN
IN
DAILY
Leigh

"Sorry to keep you folks waiting . . . The flight was delayed."

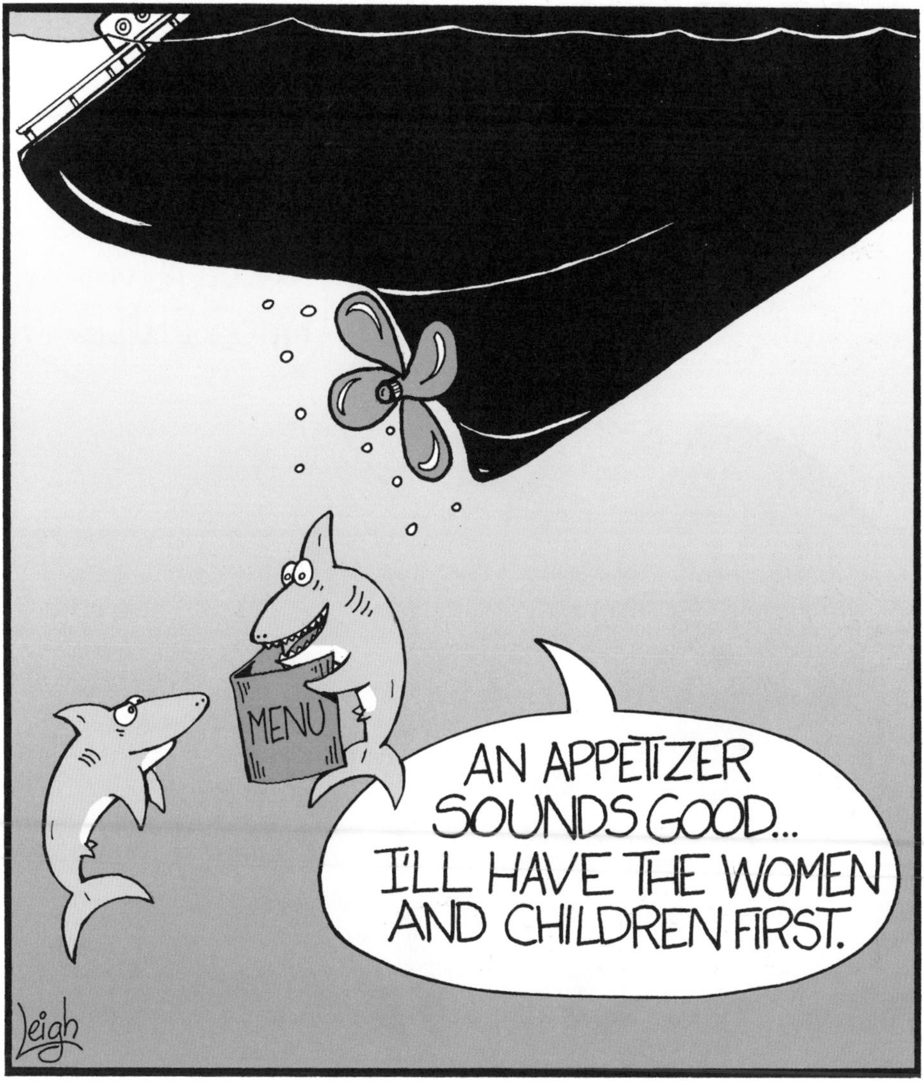
MENU
AN APPETIZER SOUNDS GOOD... I'LL HAVE THE WOMEN AND CHILDREN FIRST.
Leigh

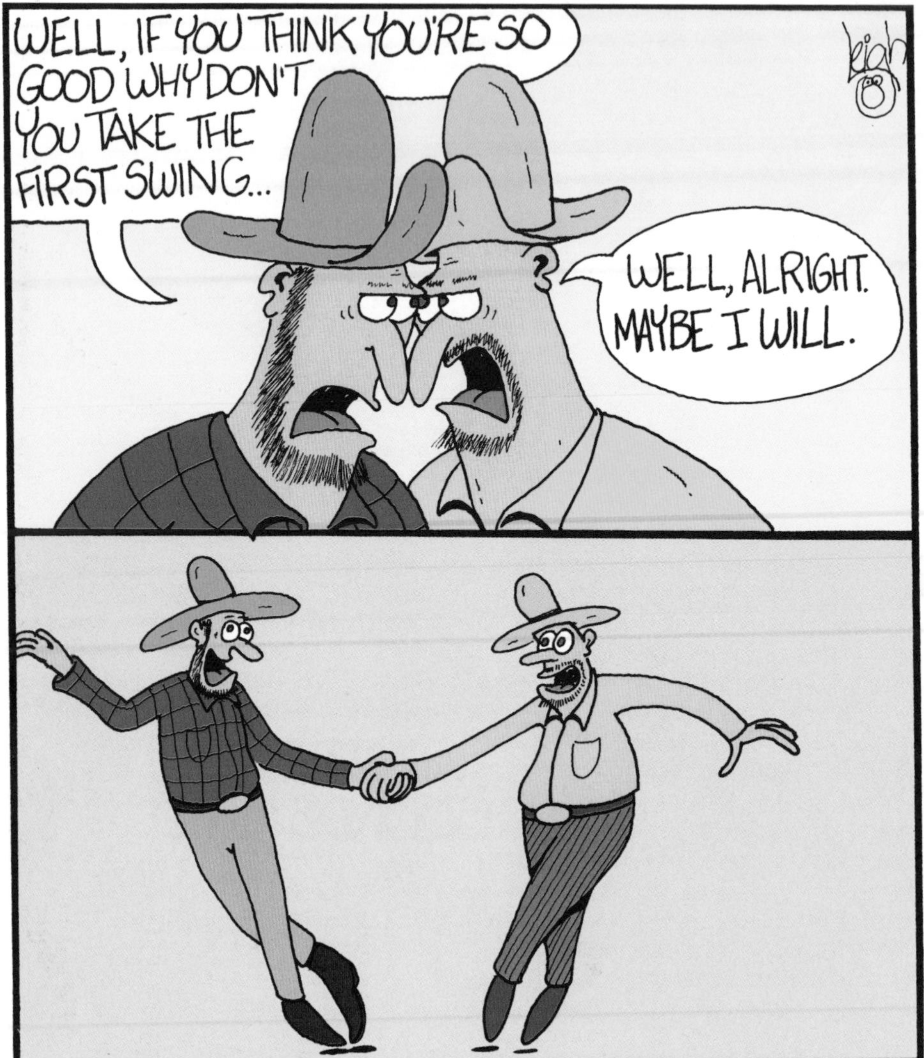
WELL, IF YOU THINK YOU'RE SO GOOD WHY DON'T YOU TAKE THE FIRST SWING...
WELL, ALRIGHT. MAYBE I WILL.

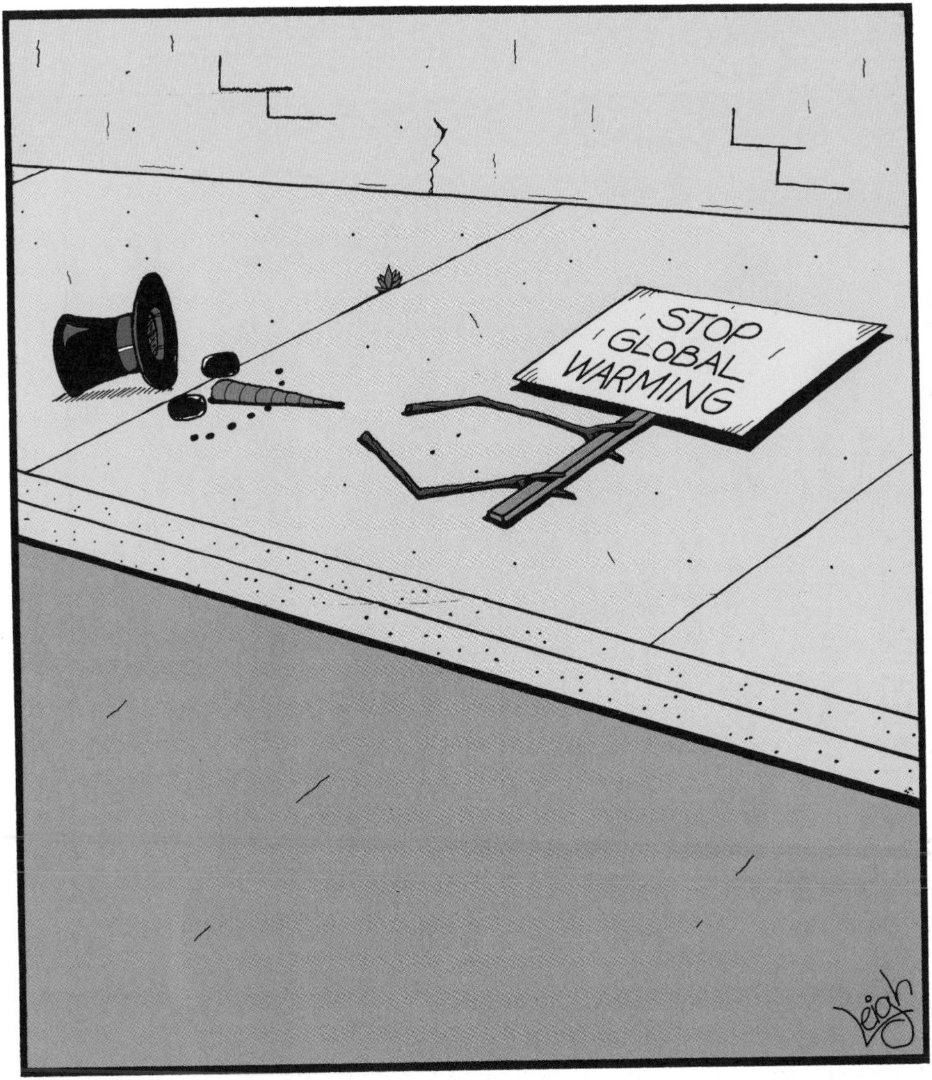
STOP GLOBAL WARMING
Leigh

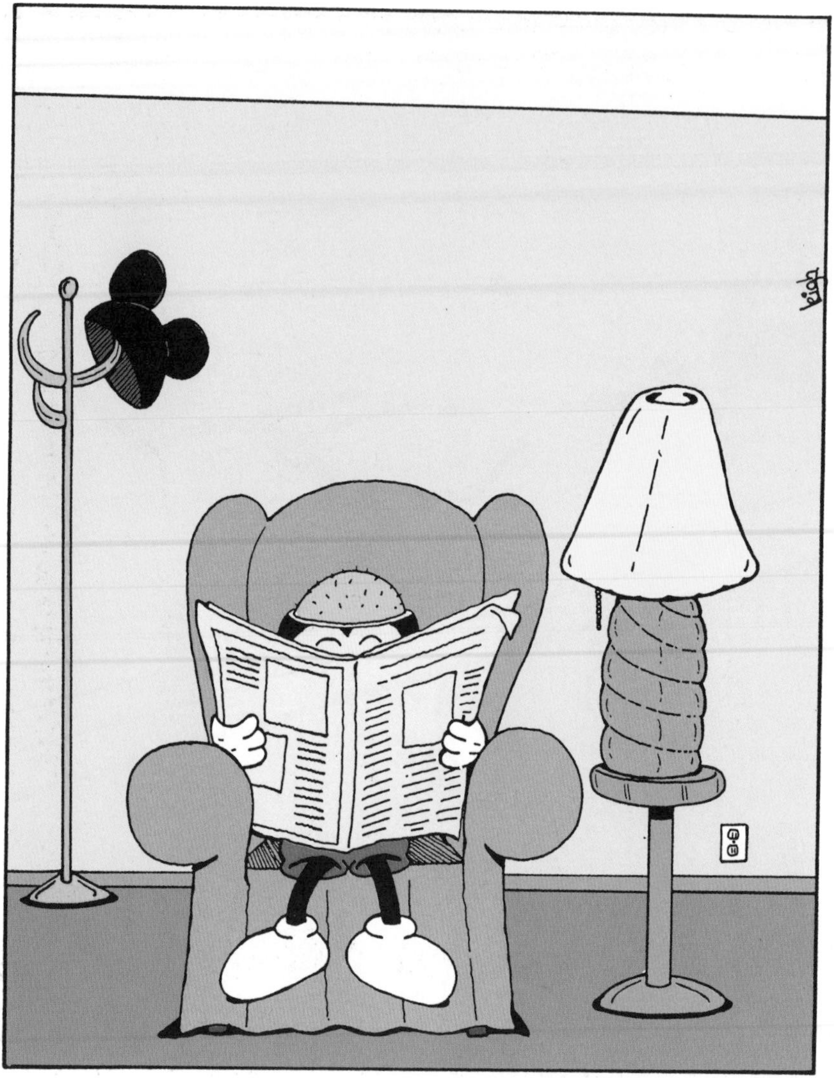

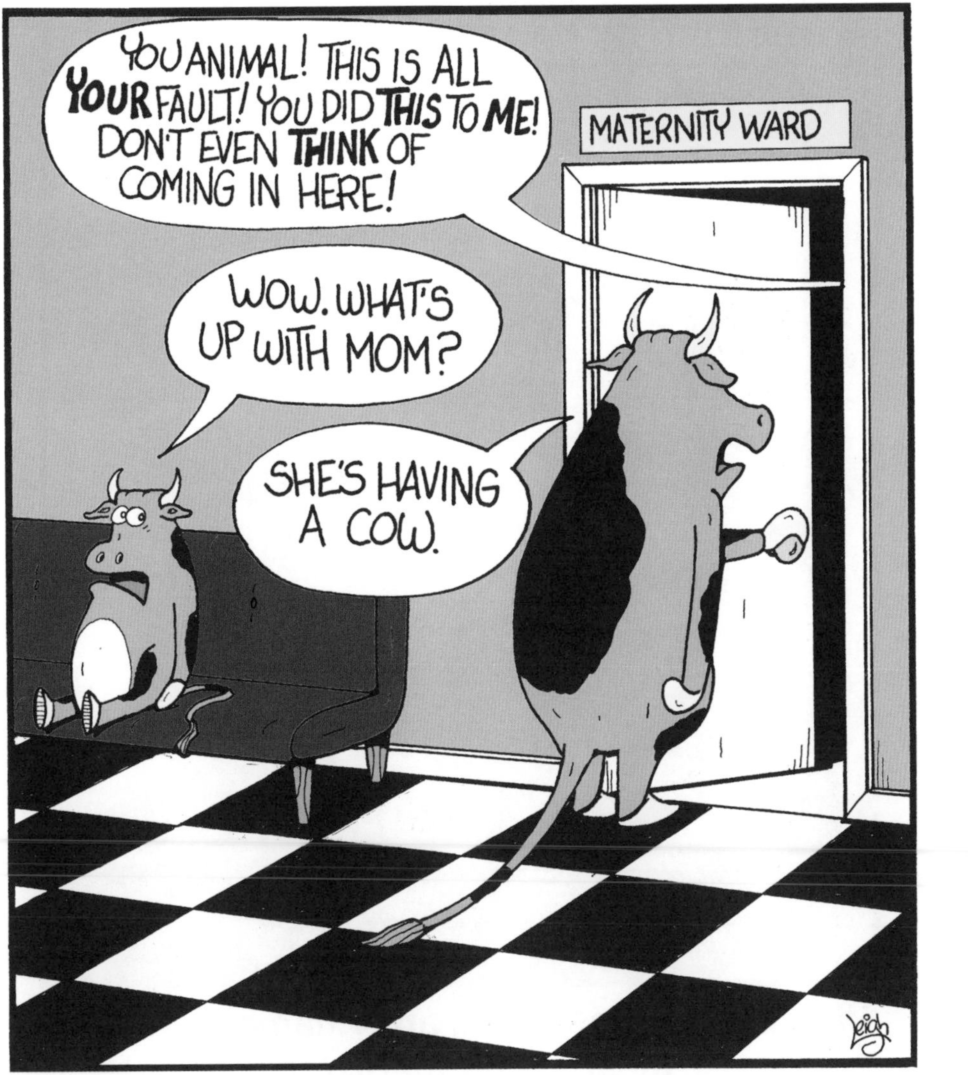
YOU ANIMAL! THIS IS ALL YOUR FAULT! YOU DID THIS TO ME! DON'T EVEN THINK OF COMING IN HERE!
MATERNITY WARD
WOW. WHAT'S UP WITH MOM?
SHE'S HAVING A COW.
Leigh

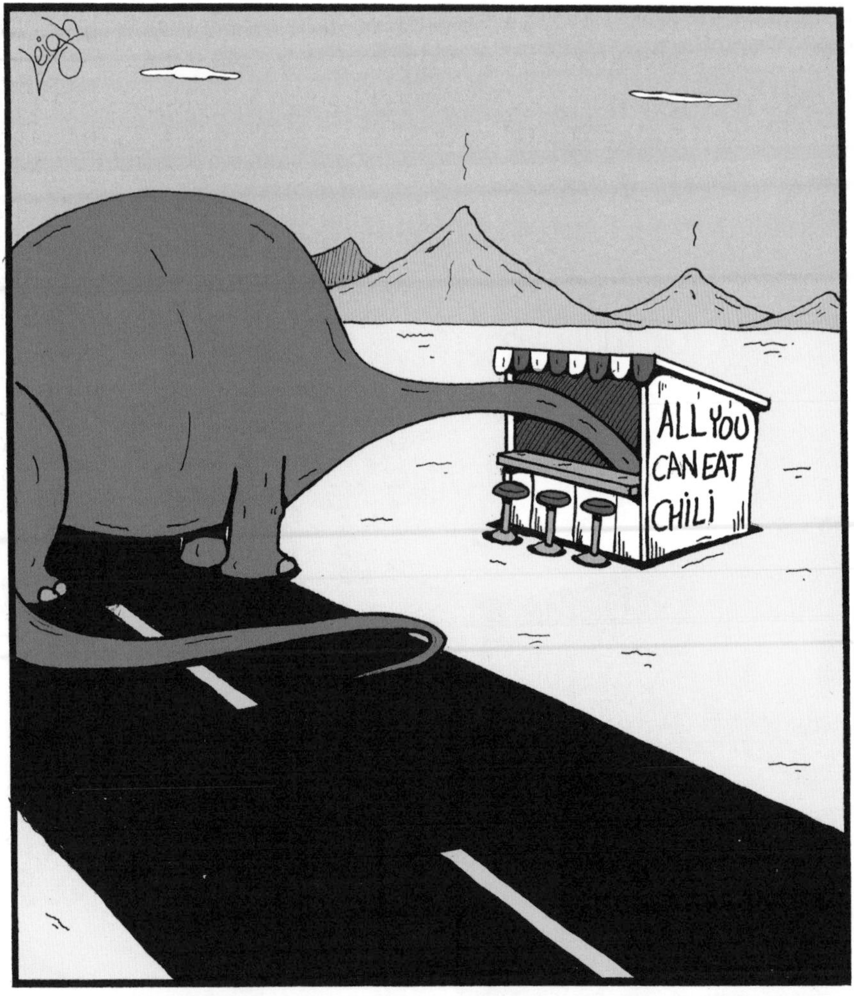
ALL YOU CAN EAT CHILI

Why the brontosaurus, aptly named, literally means "thunderlizard"

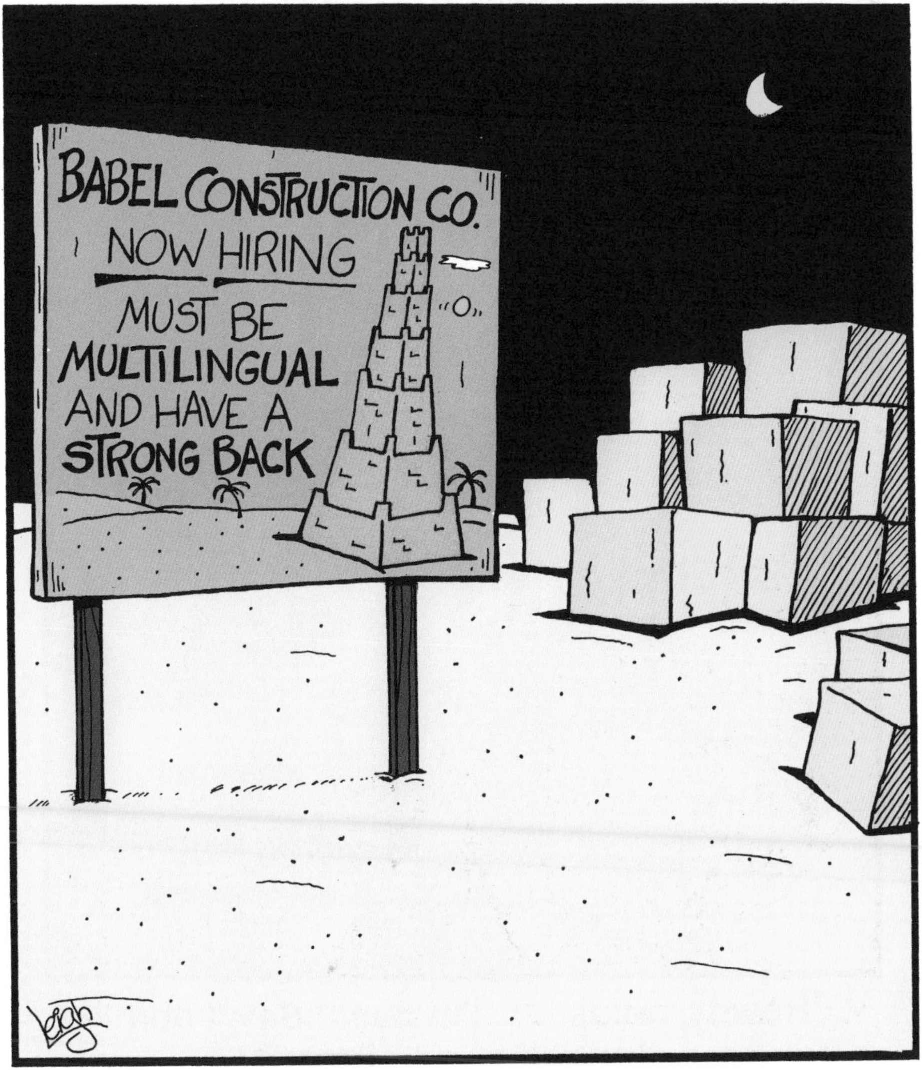
BABEL CONSTRUCTION CO.
NOW HIRING
MUST BE MULTILINGUAL AND HAVE A STRONG BACK

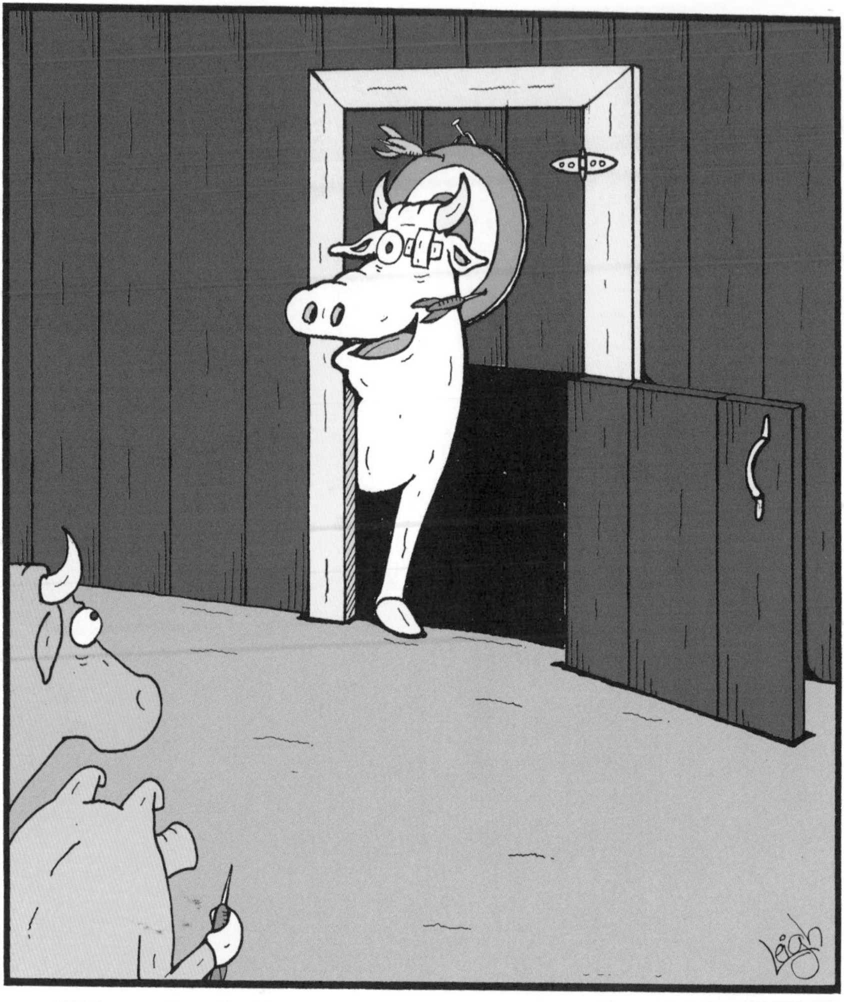
Leigh

"Howdy, fellas . . . I'm back! Say, I don't suppose either of you noticed a touch of irony in my tragic little mishap?"

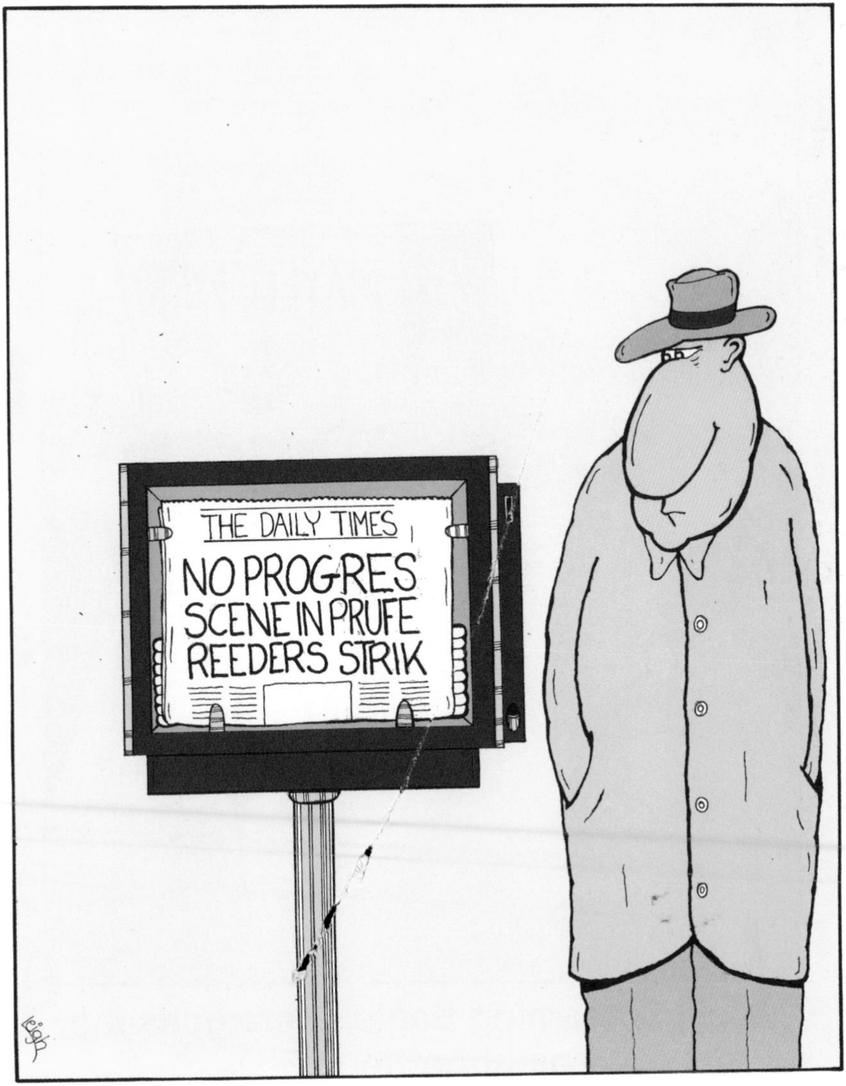
THE DAILY TIMES
NO PROGRES
SCENE IN PRUFE
REEDERS STRIK
Leigh

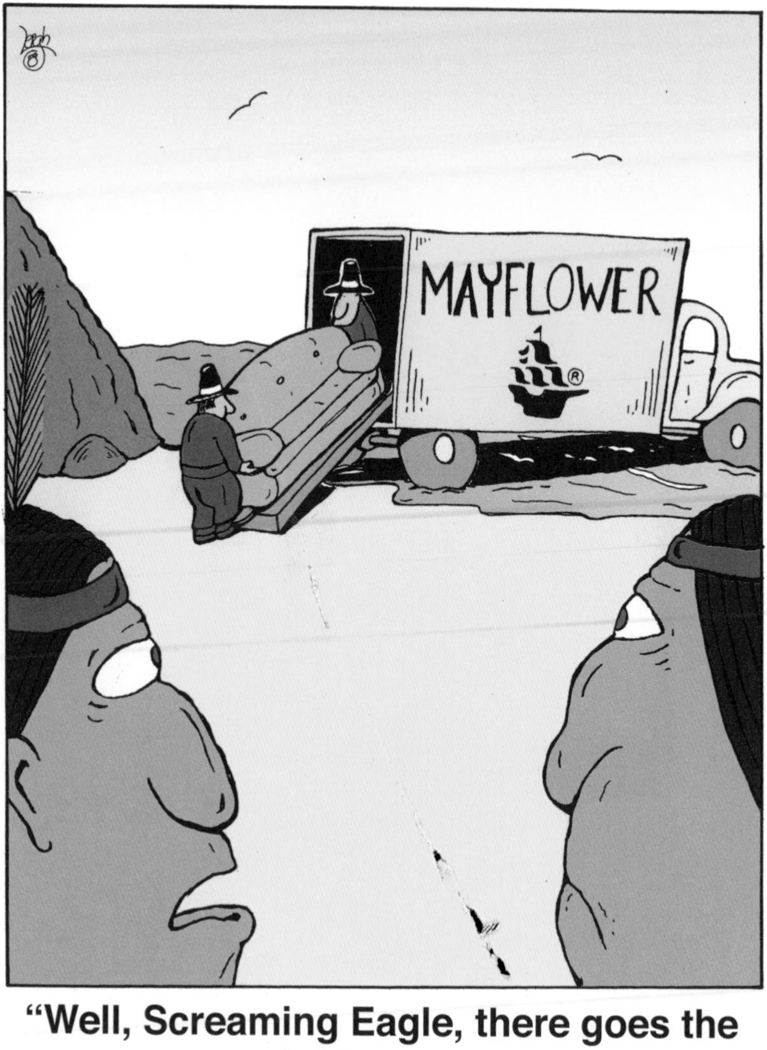
MAYFLOWER

"Well, Screaming Eagle, there goes the neighborhood."

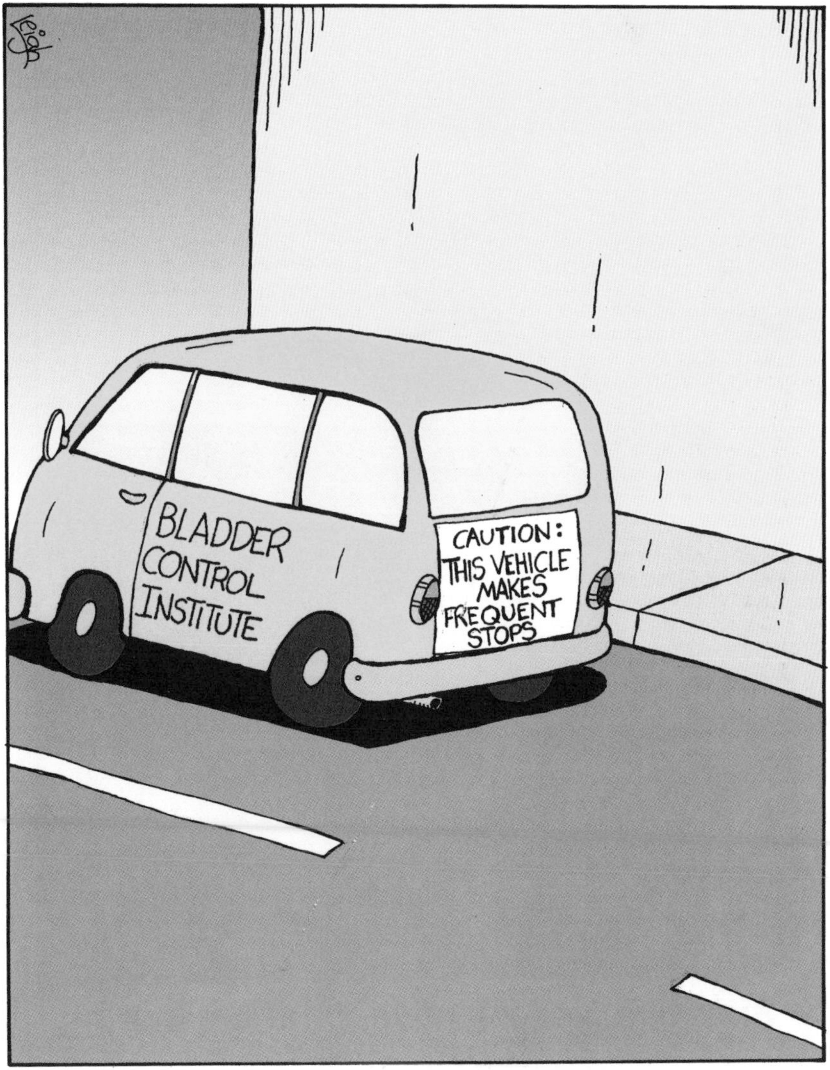
BLADDER
CONTROL
INSTITUTE
CAUTION:
THIS VEHICLE
MAKES
FREQUENT
STOPS

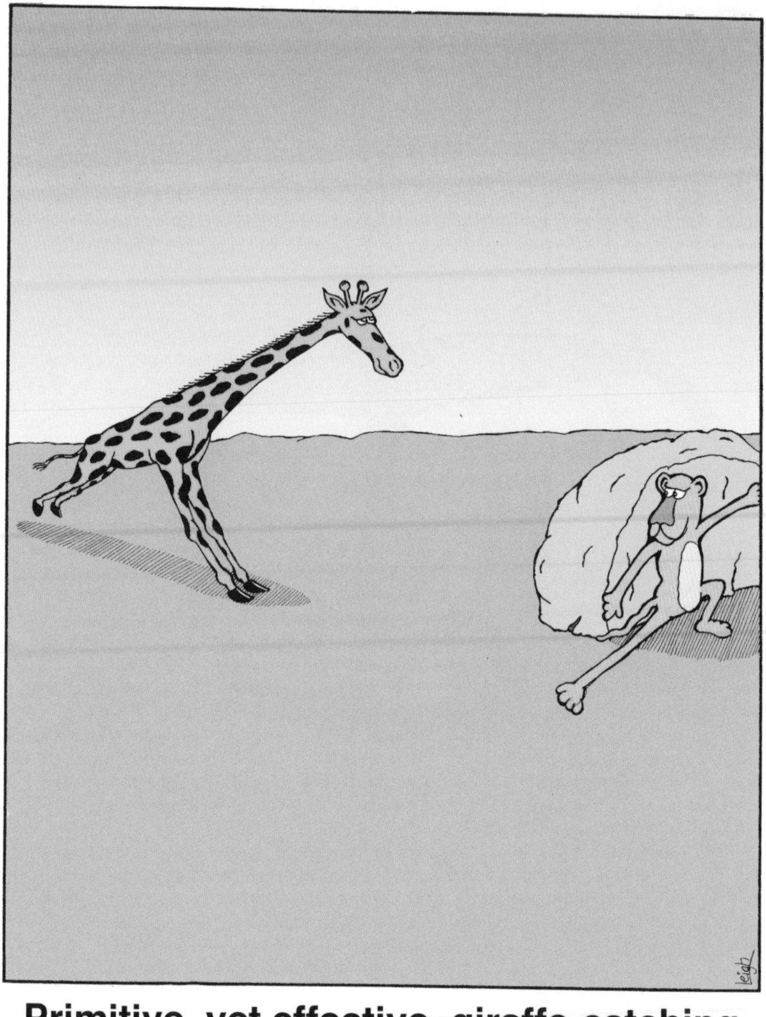
leigh

Primitive, yet effective, giraffe-catching techniques

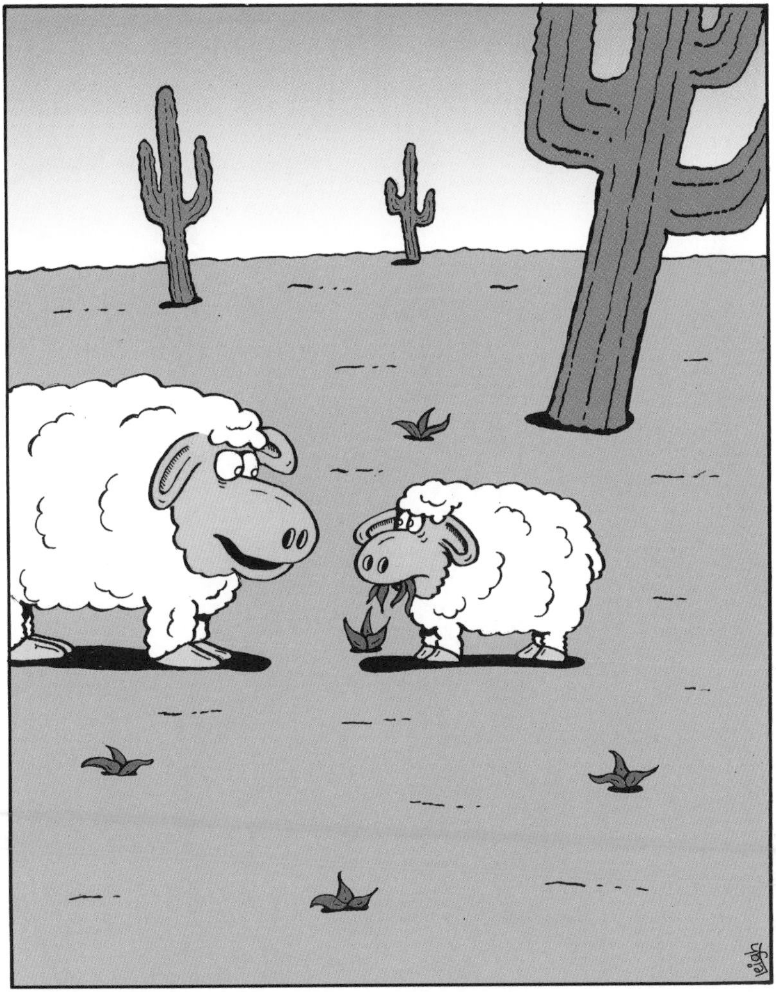
leigh

"Be a good little lamb and eat all of your grass so you'll grow up big and strong and become a seat cover like your father."

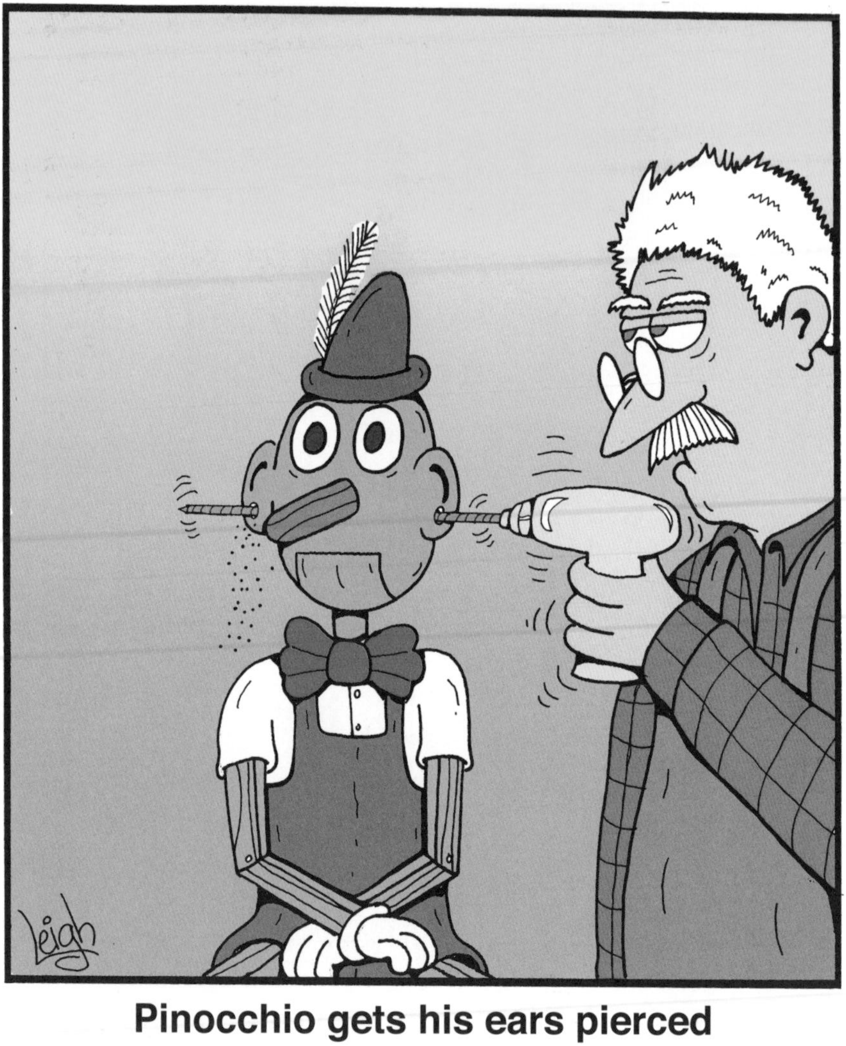
Leigh

Pinocchio gets his ears pierced

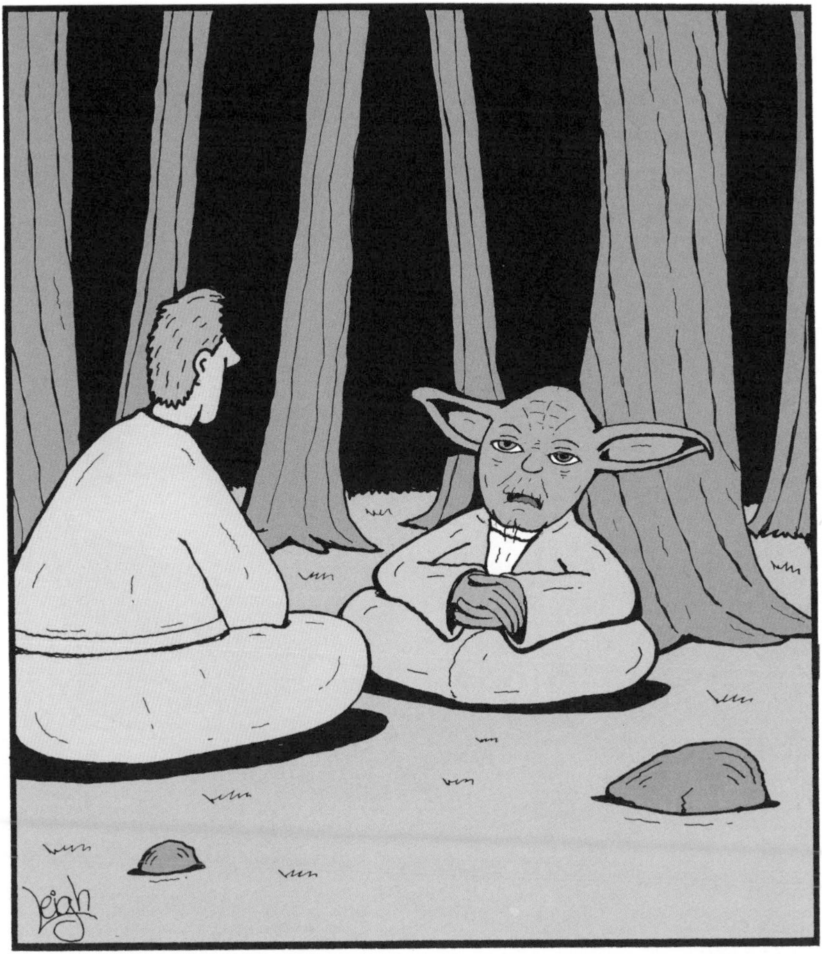
Leigh

"Yes, young Jedi, I too sense a great disturbance in the Force. May I suggest that in the future you go a bit easier on those burritos from the Dark Side."

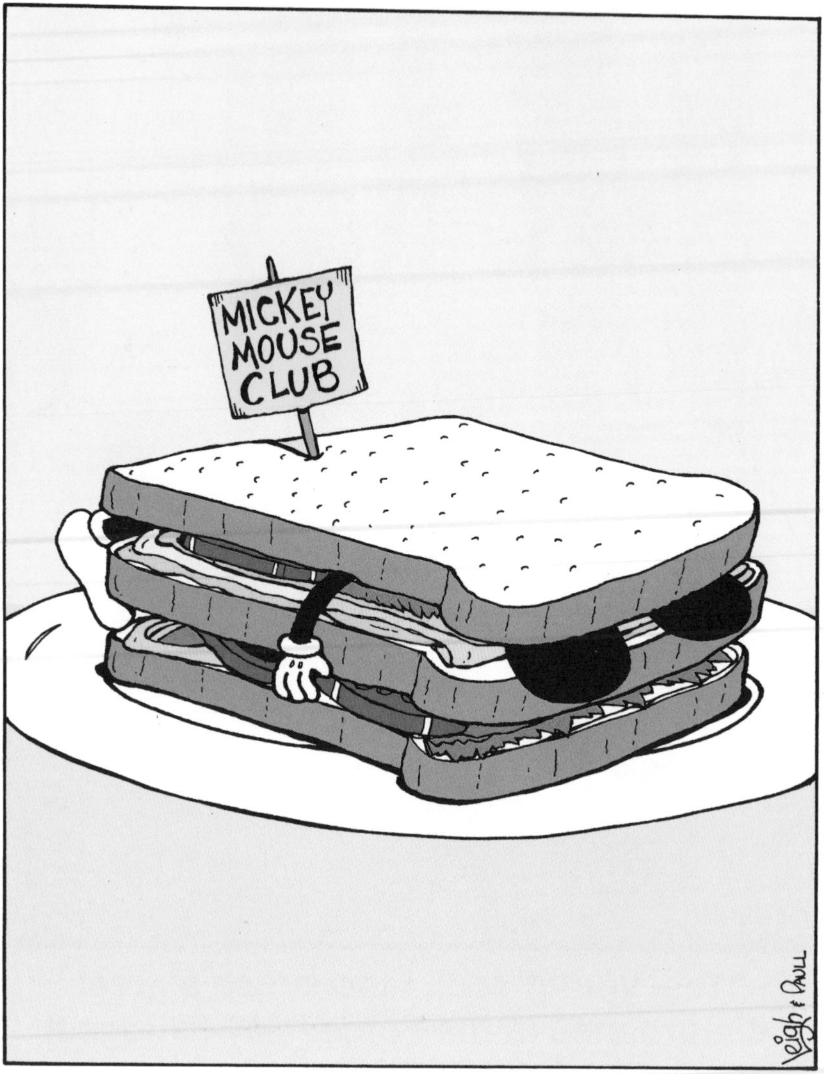
MICKEY MOUSE CLUB
Leigh & Paull

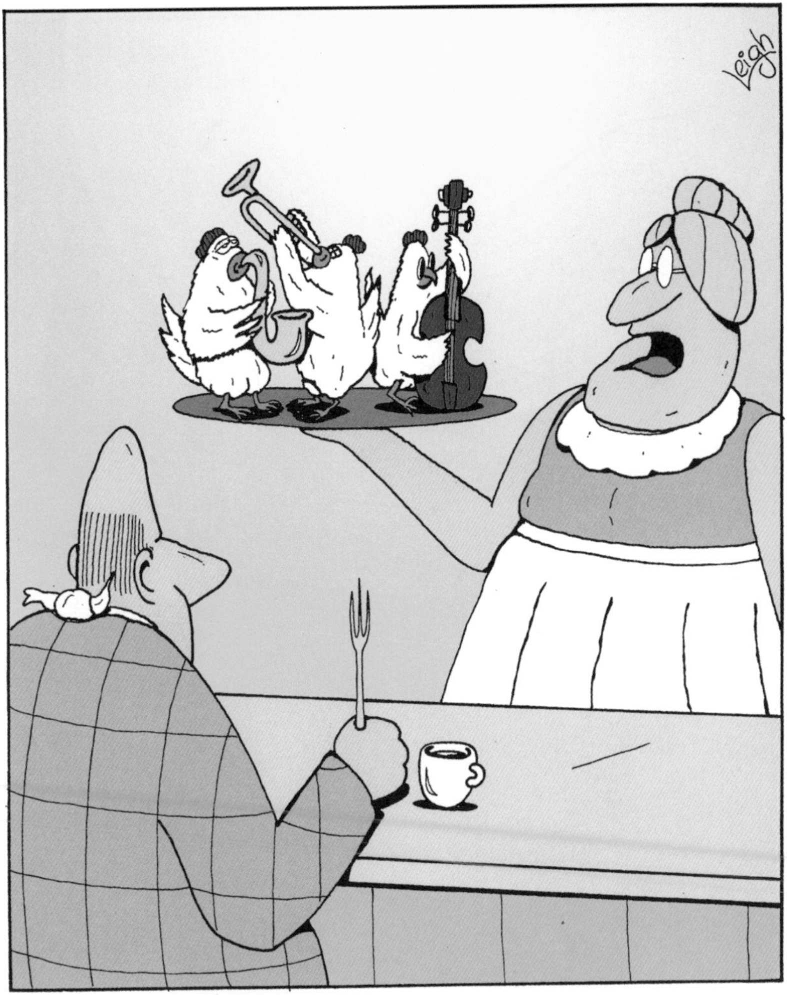
Leigh

"Here's your three-piece
chicken combo, sir."

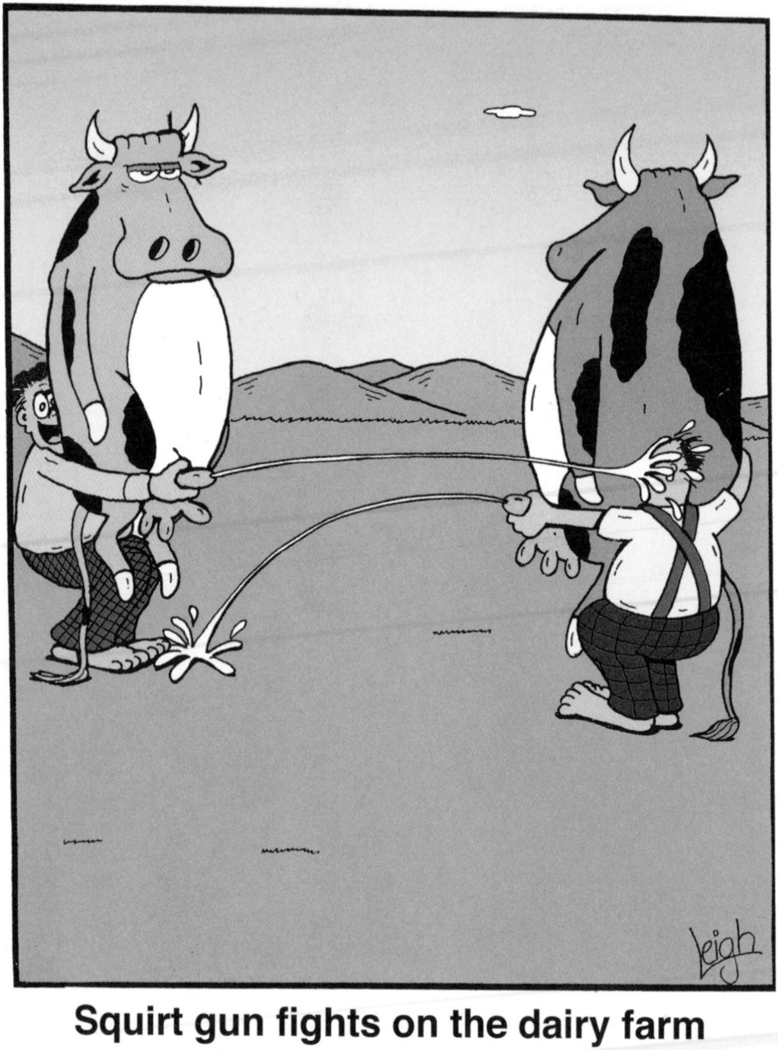
Leigh

Squirt gun fights on the dairy farm

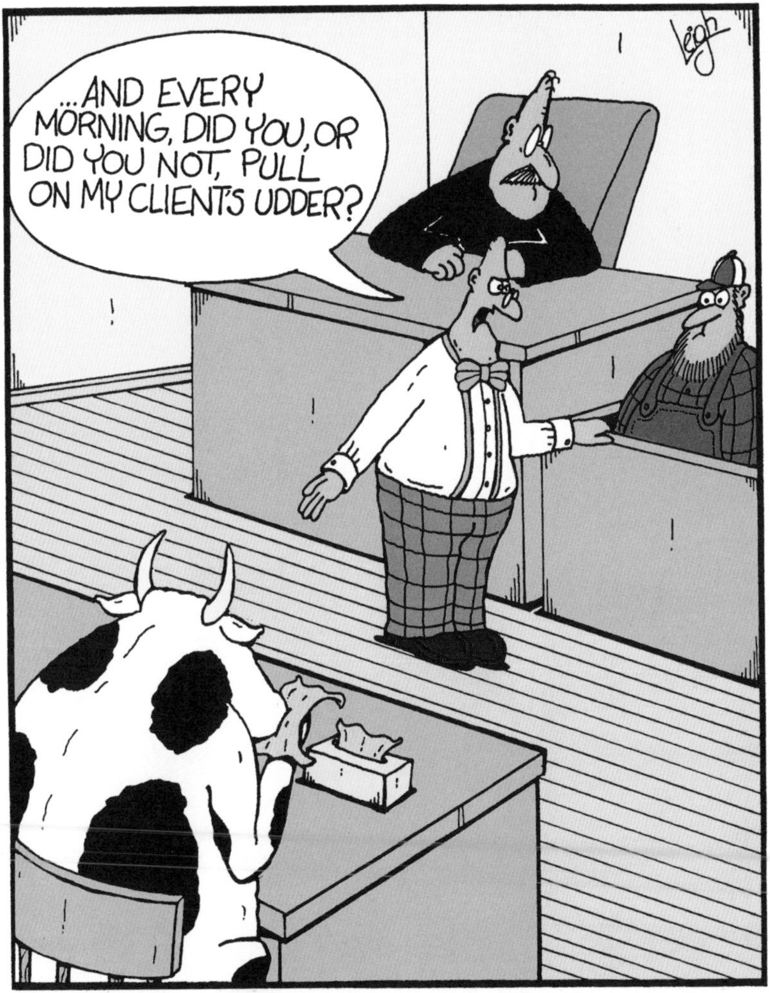
...AND EVERY MORNING, DID YOU, OR DID YOU NOT, PULL ON MY CLIENT'S UDDER?
Leigh

The sexual harassment suit that sent shock waves through the dairy industry

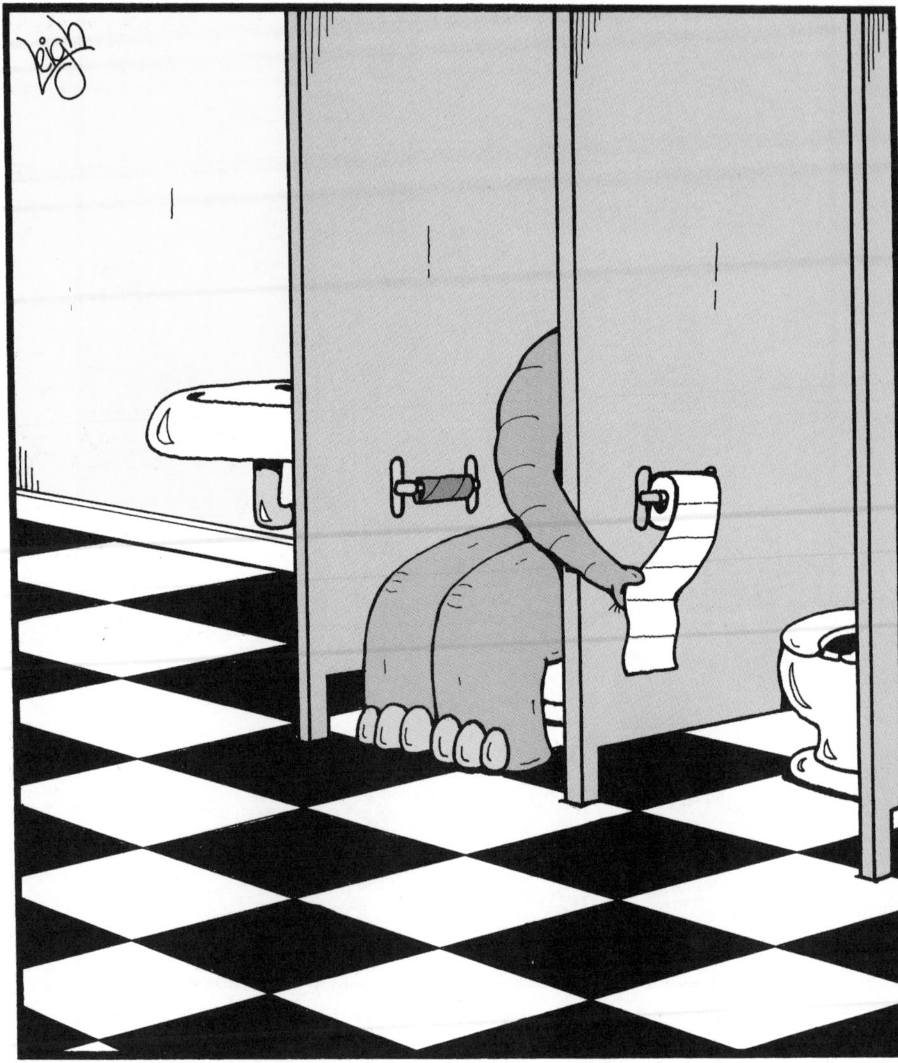

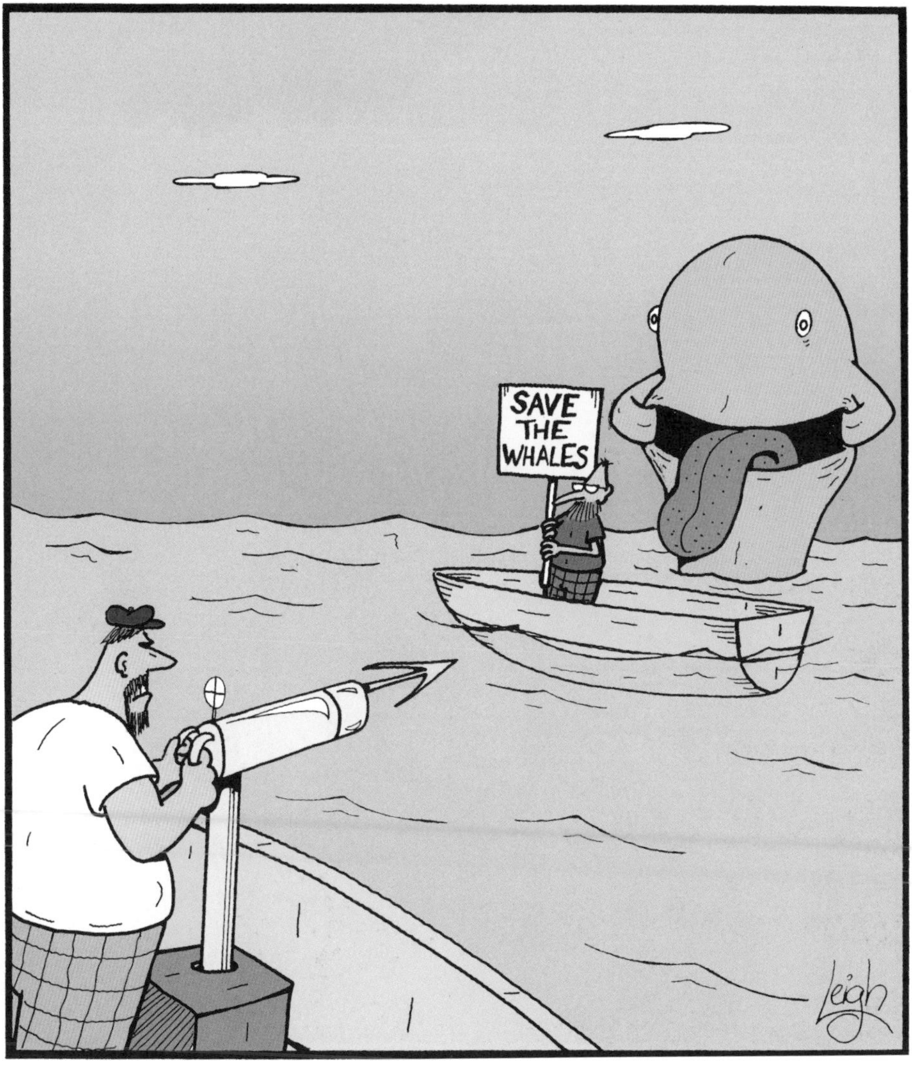
SAVE
THE
WHALES
Leigh

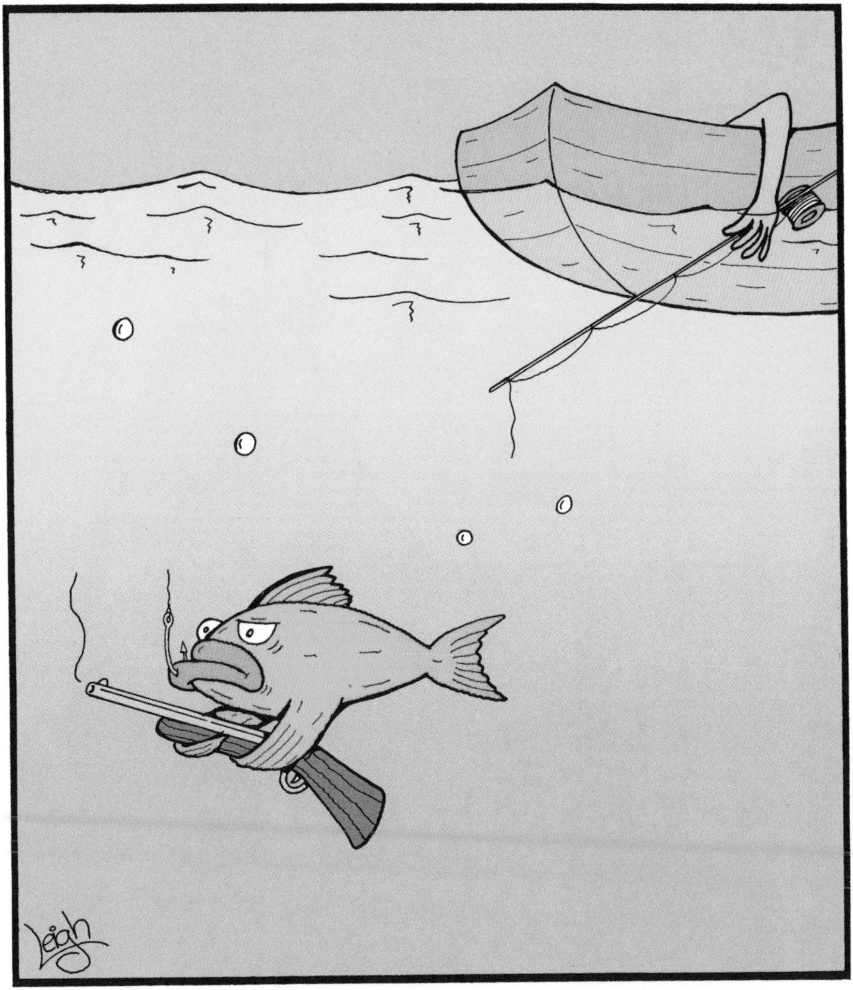
Leigh

The one that got away . . . with murder

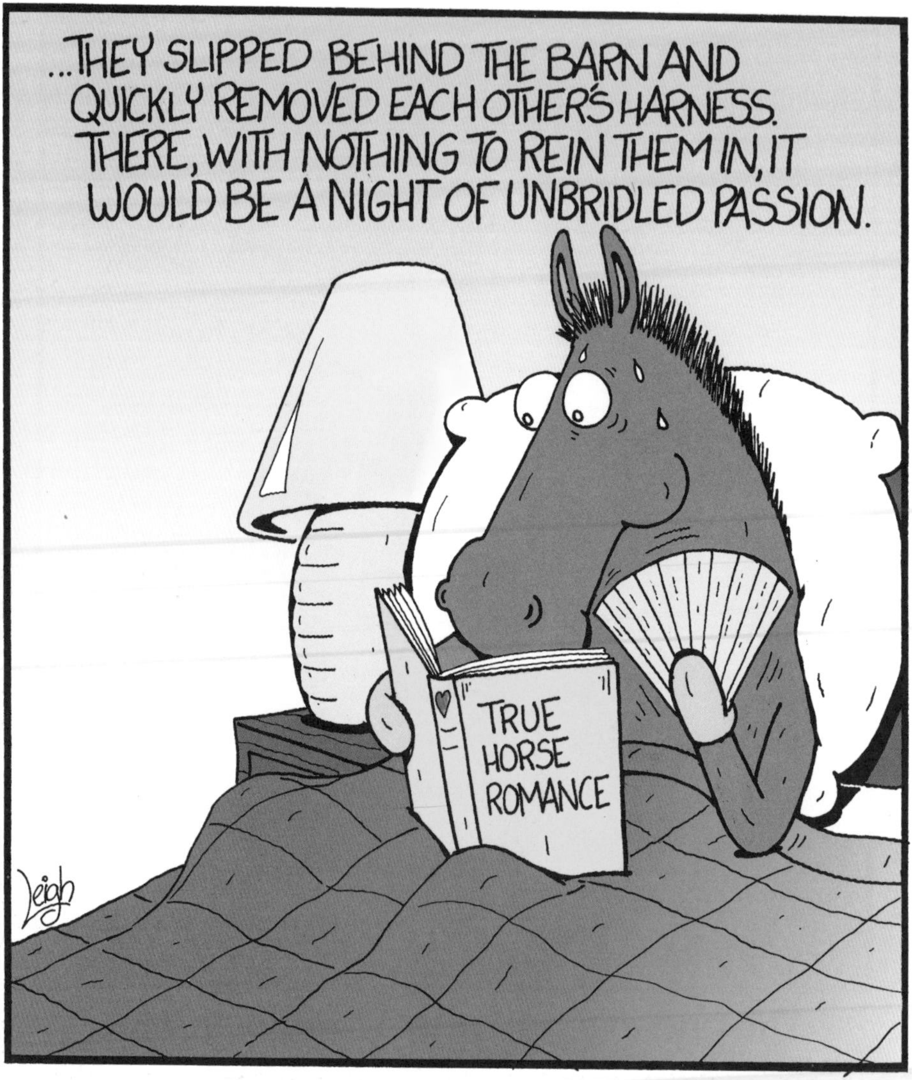
...THEY SLIPPED BEHIND THE BARN AND QUICKLY REMOVED EACH OTHER'S HARNESS. THERE, WITH NOTHING TO REIN THEM IN, IT WOULD BE A NIGHT OF UNBRIDLED PASSION.
TRUE HORSE ROMANCE
Leigh

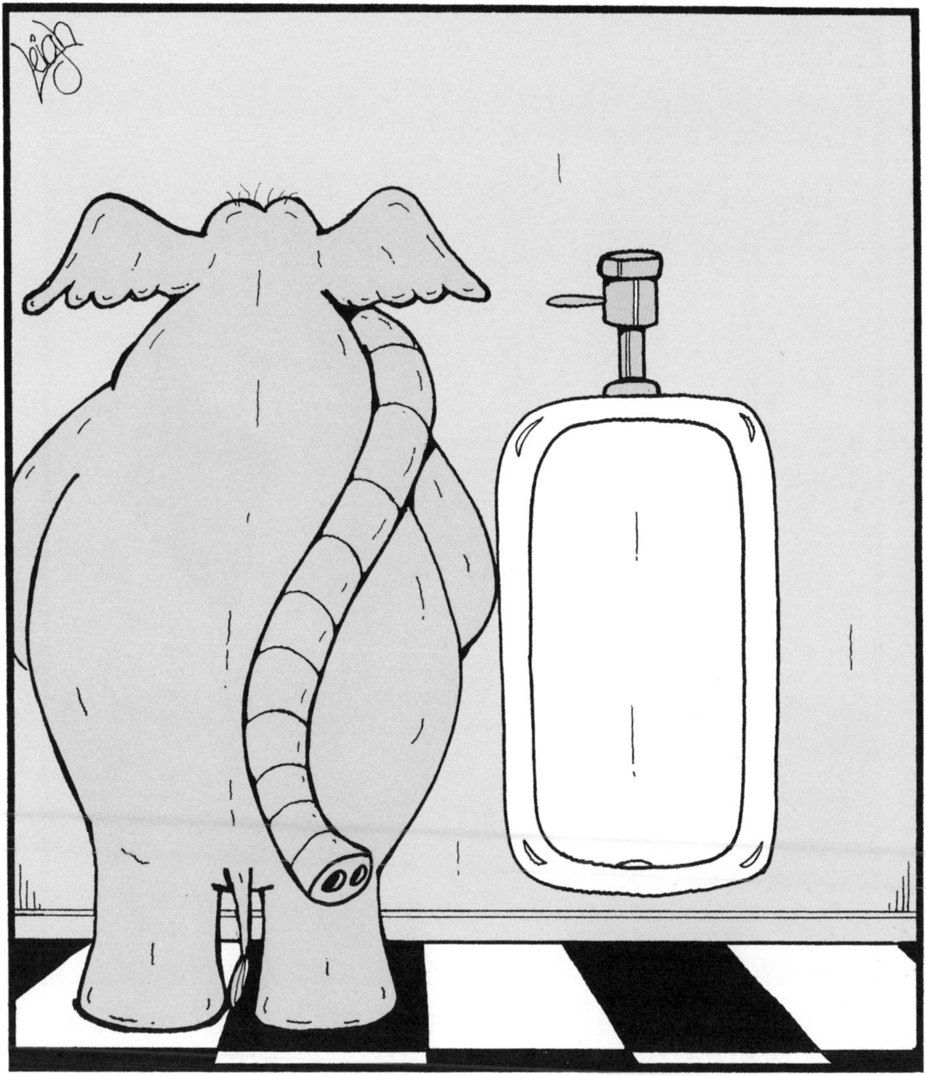

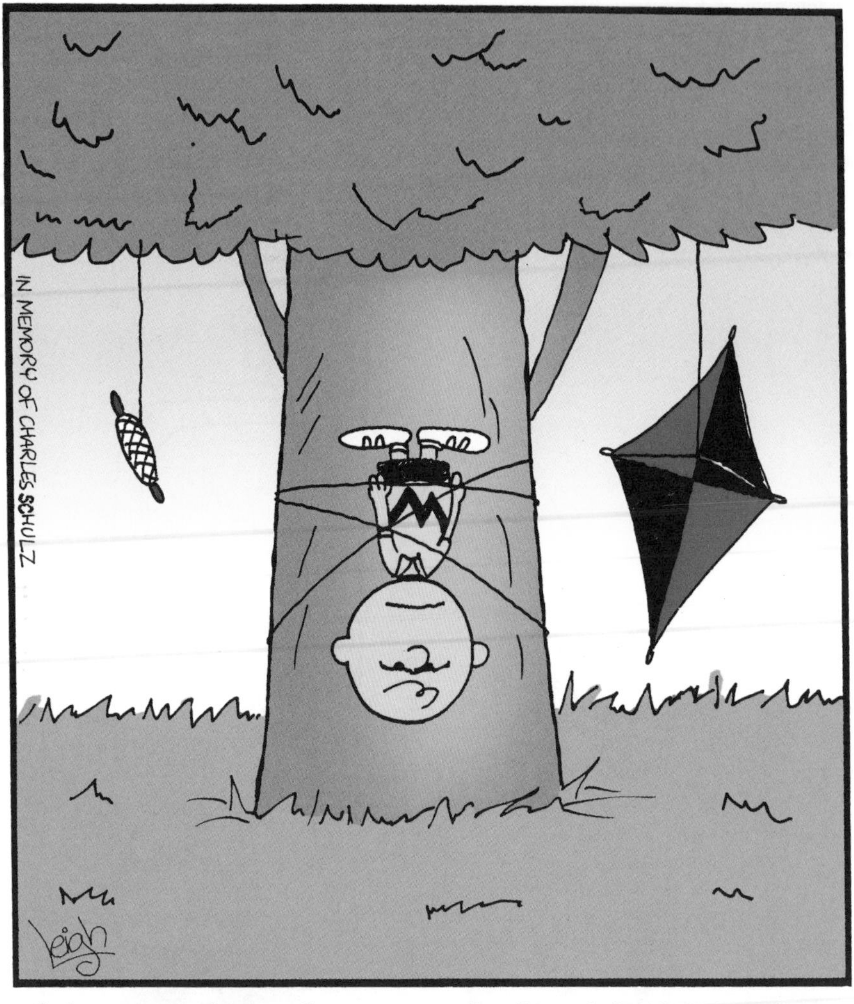
IN MEMORY OF CHARLES SCHULZ
Leigh

A long string of events during his formative years would ultimately help determine Charlie's extremely strong pro-logging position.

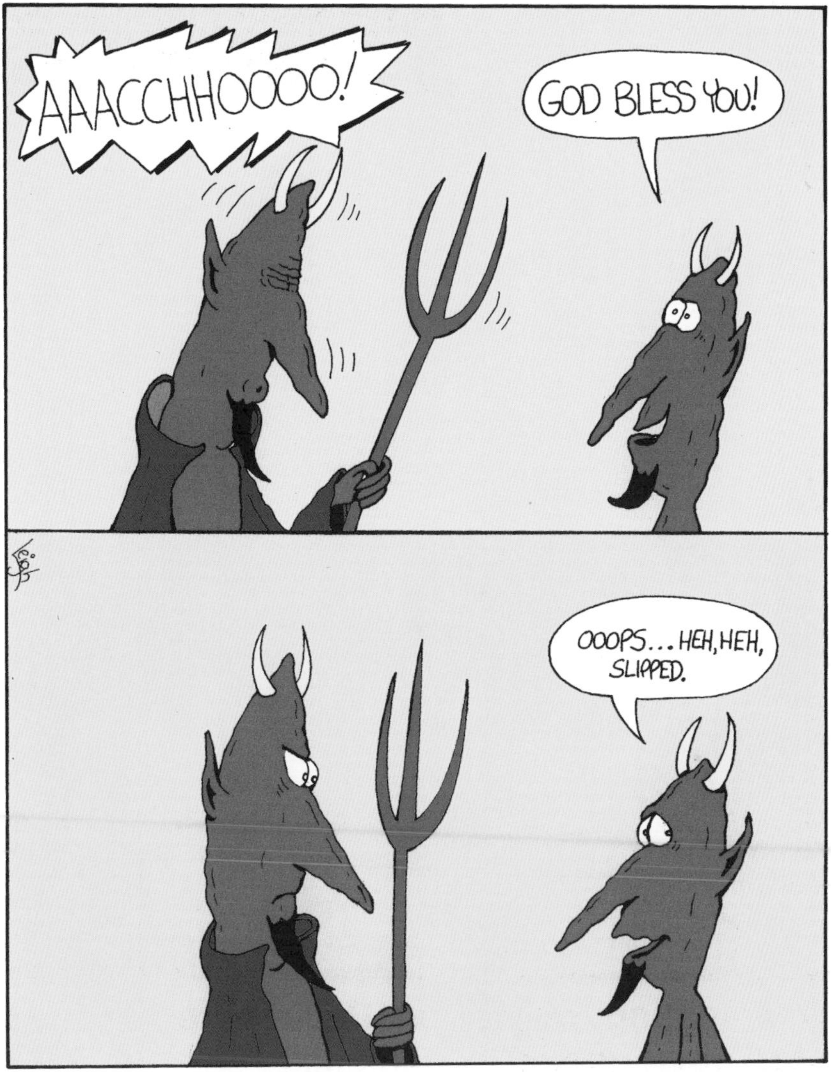
AAACCHHOOOO!
GOD BLESS YOU!
OOOPS... HEH, HEH, SLIPPED.

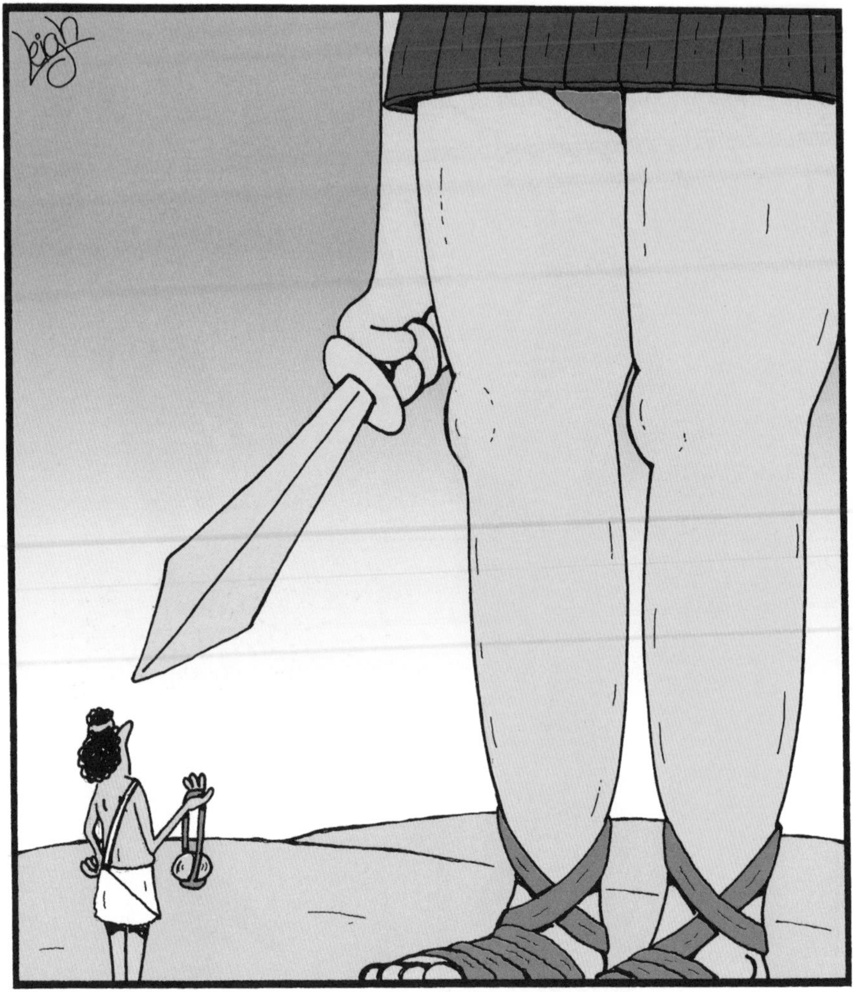

Overcoming temptation, David opted against the obvious, unsportsmanlike cheap shot.

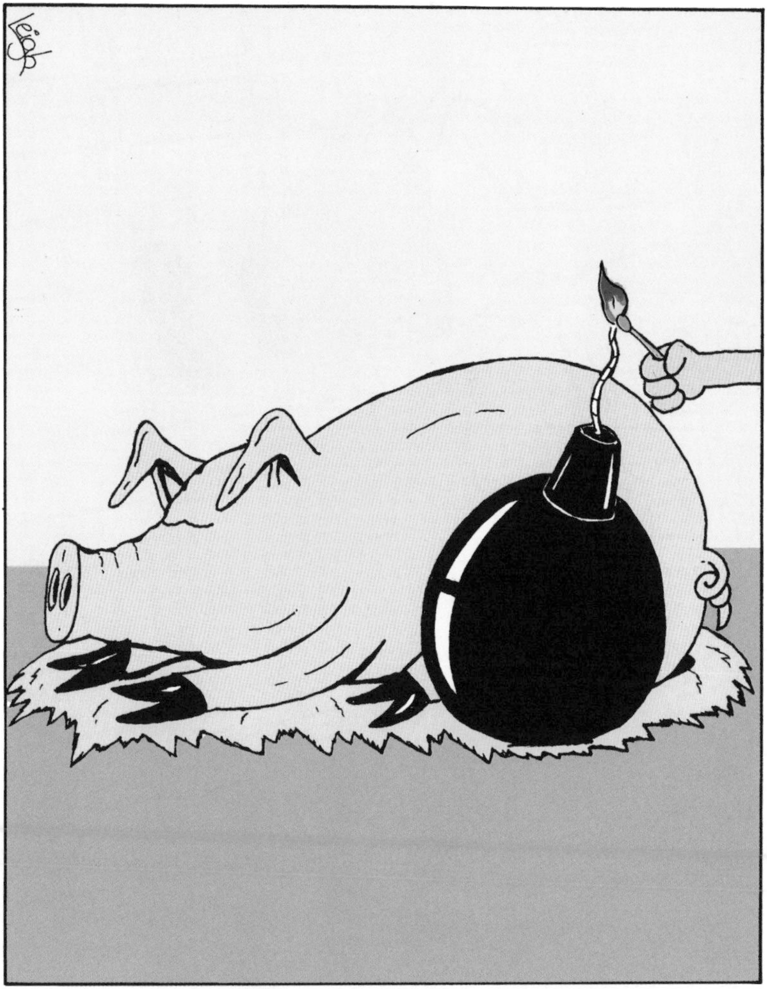
Leigh

How they make bacon bits

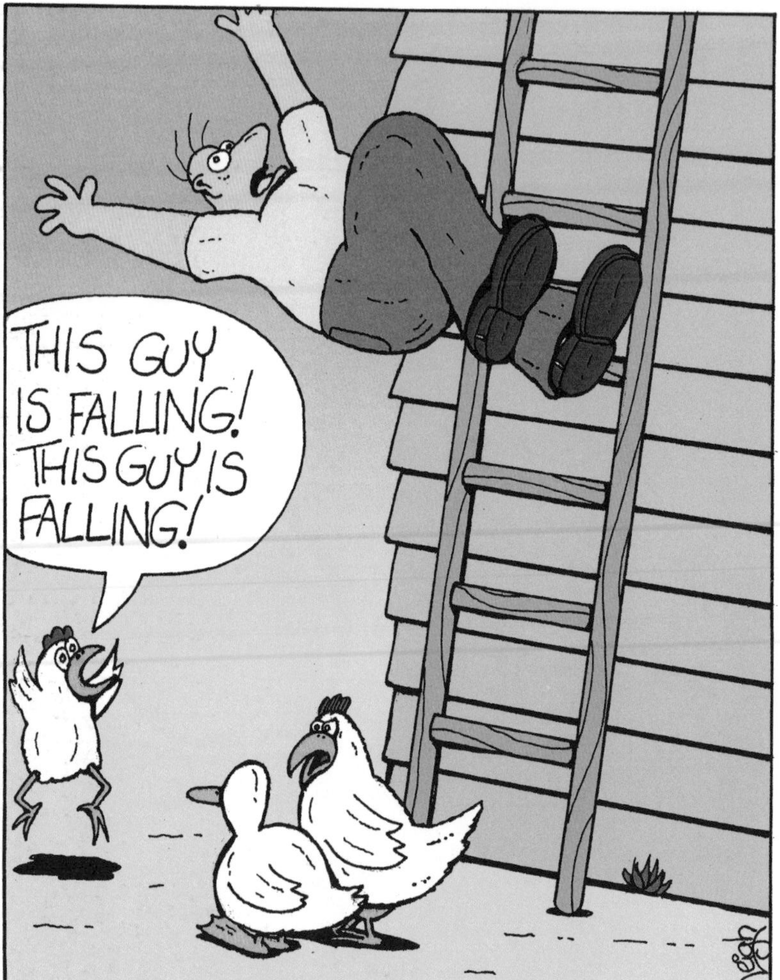
THIS GUY IS FALLING! THIS GUY IS FALLING!

"Boy, he must think we're pretty stupid to fall for that again."

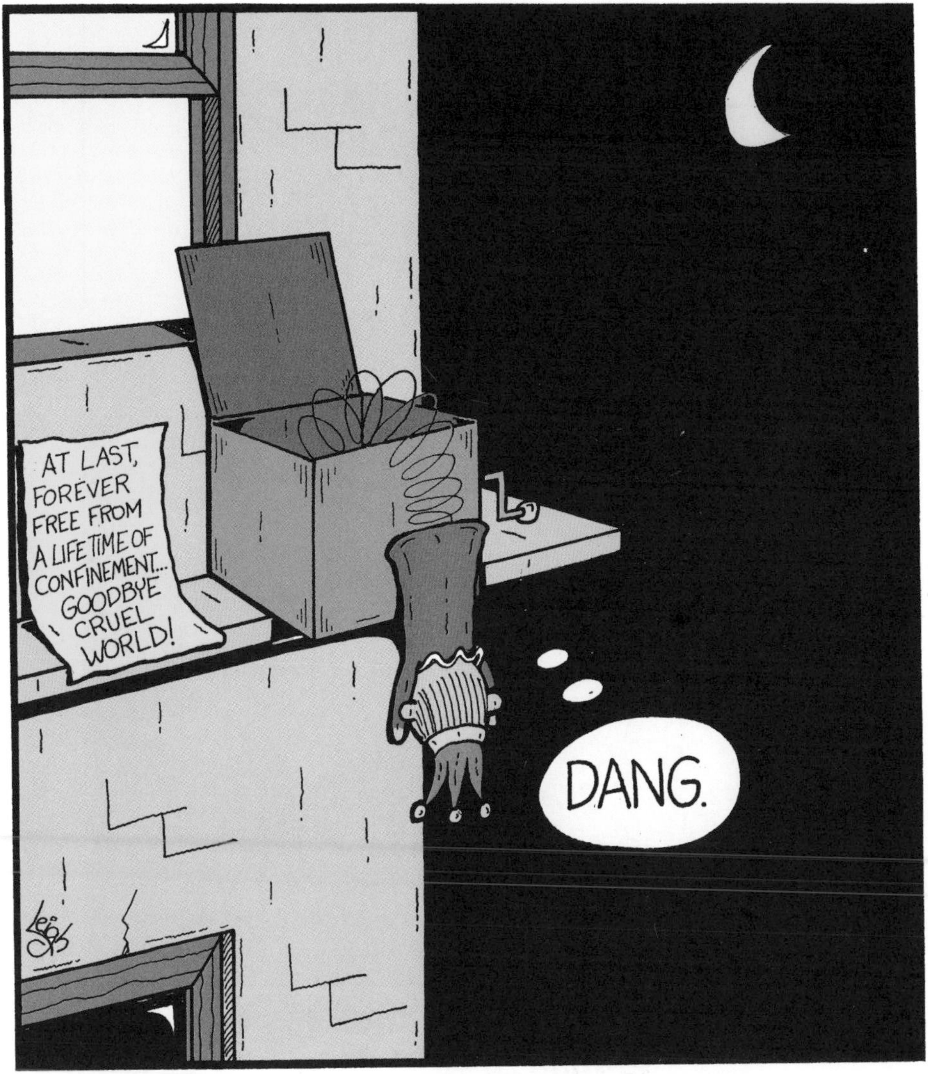
AT LAST, FOREVER FREE FROM A LIFE TIME OF CONFINEMENT... GOODBYE CRUEL WORLD!
DANG.

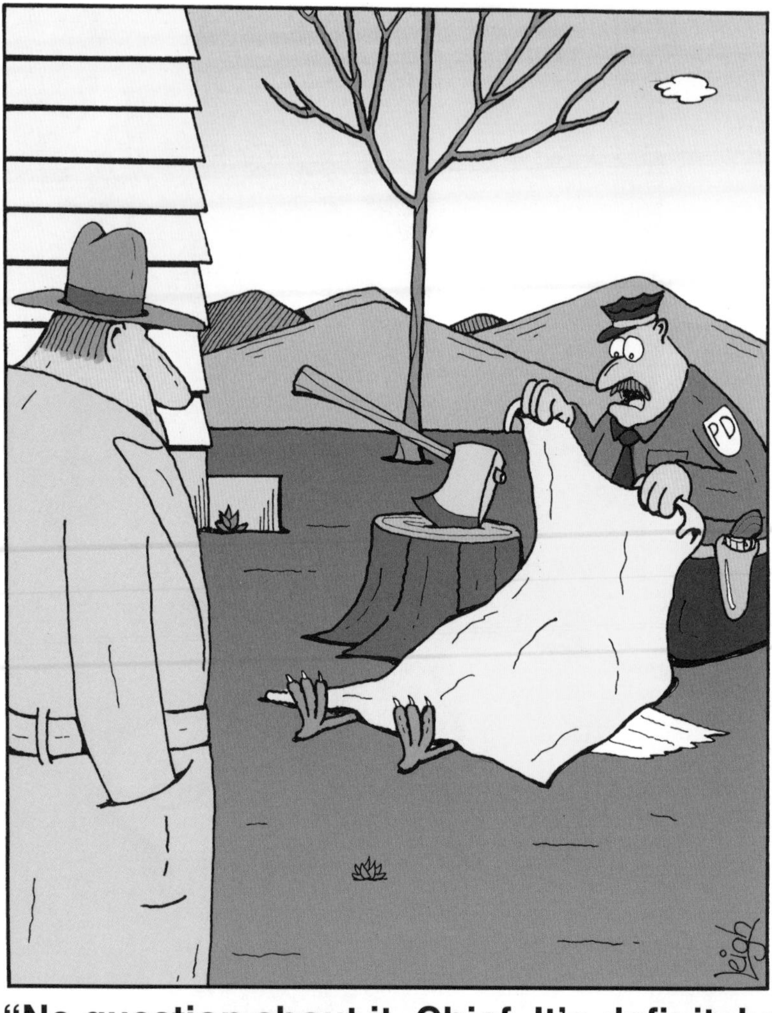
PD

"No question about it, Chief. It's definitely a case of fowl play."

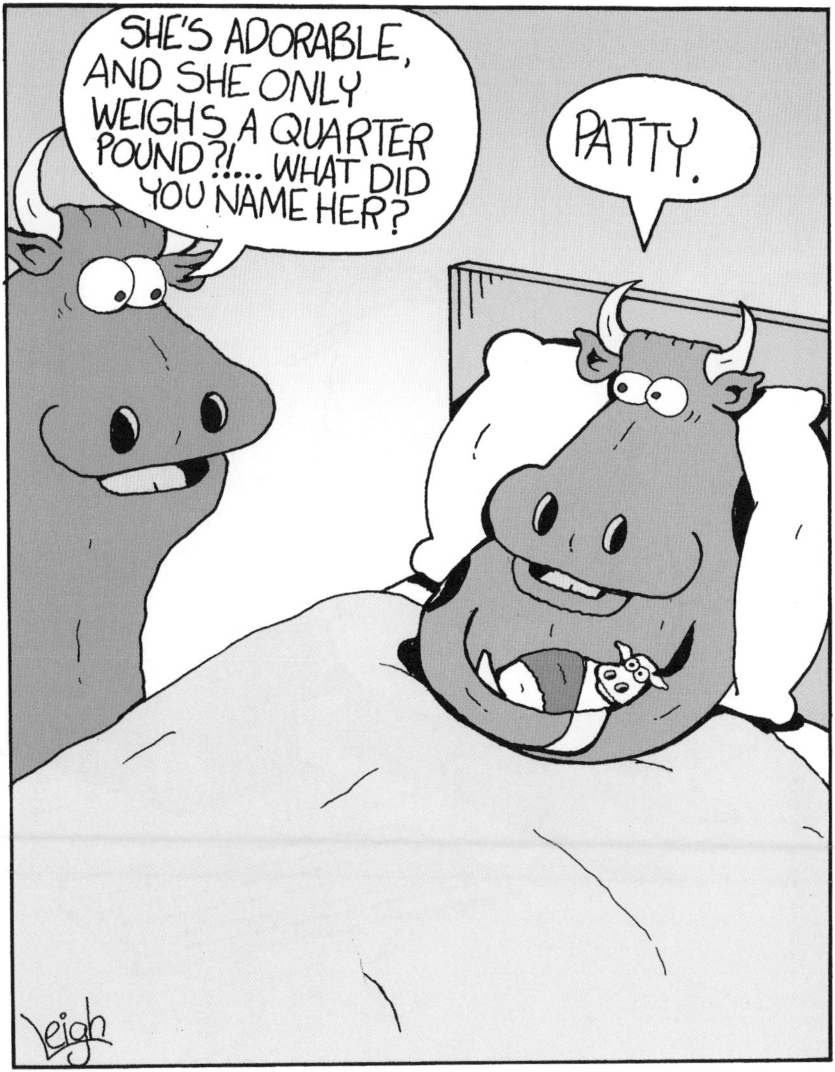
SHE'S ADORABLE, AND SHE ONLY WEIGHS A QUARTER POUND?!.... WHAT DID YOU NAME HER?
PATTY.
Leigh

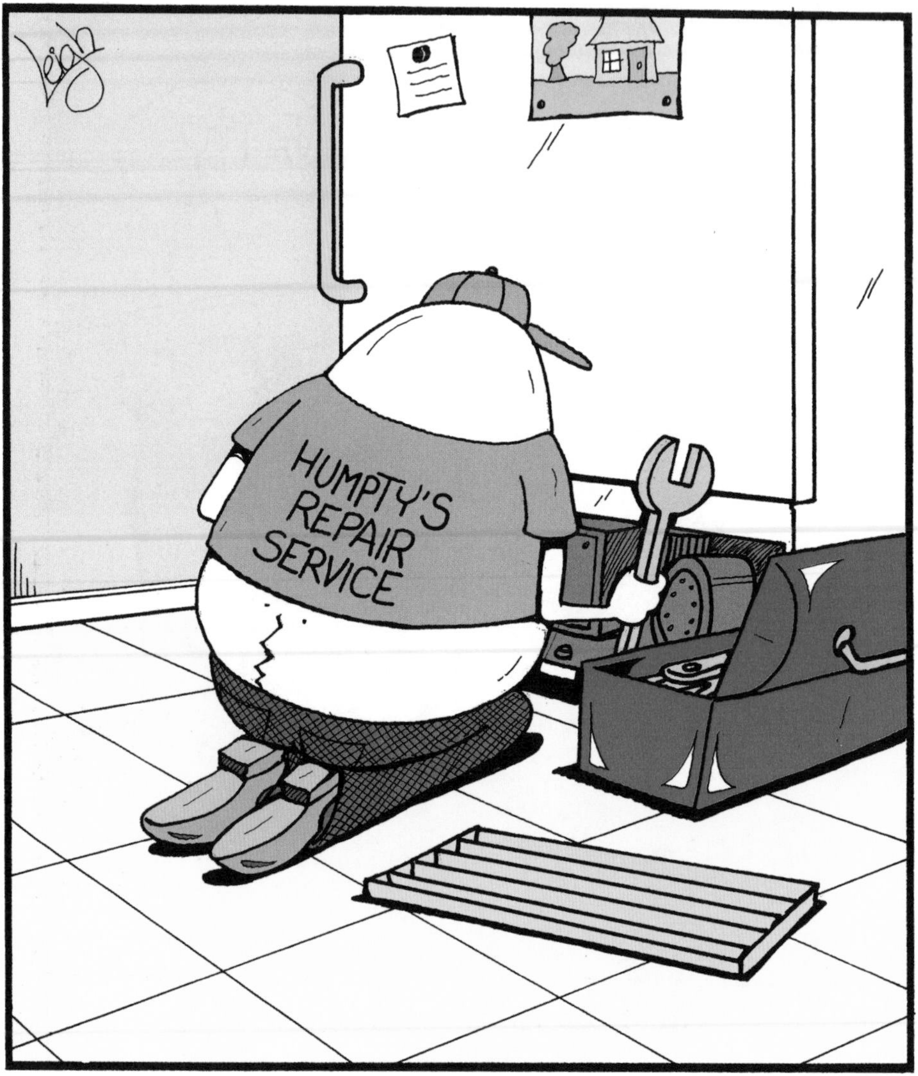
HUMPTY'S
REPAIR
SERVICE

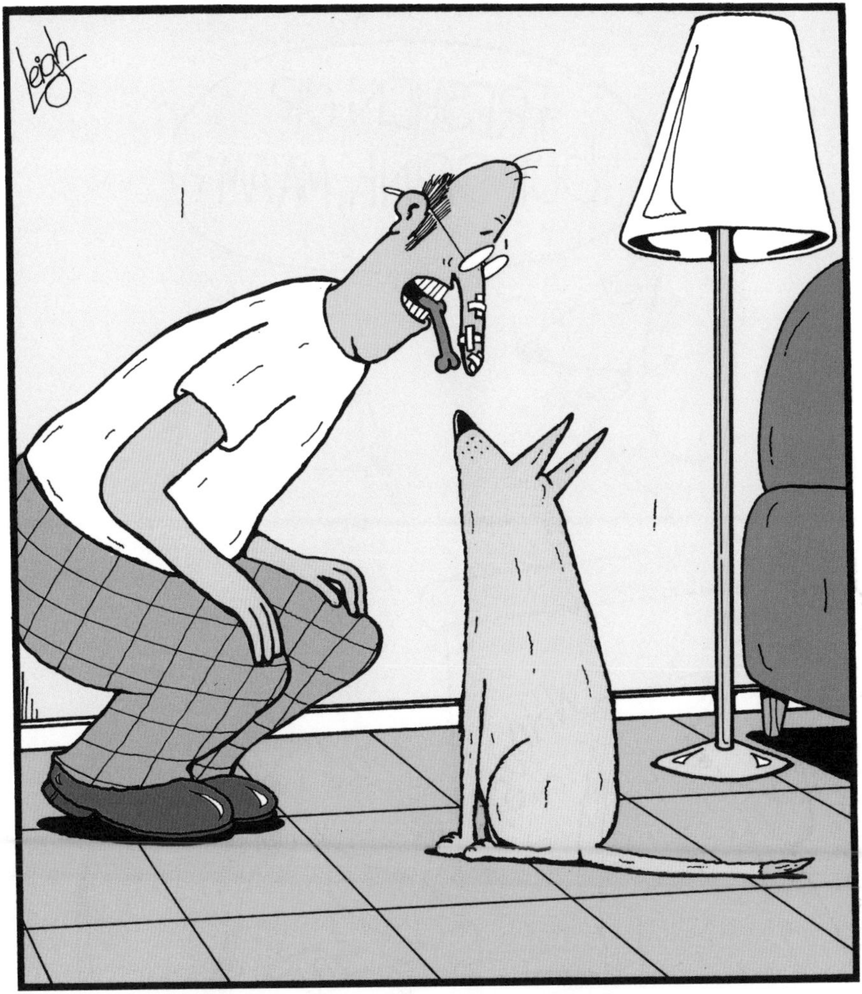
leigh

"OK, boy, let's try it again . . ."

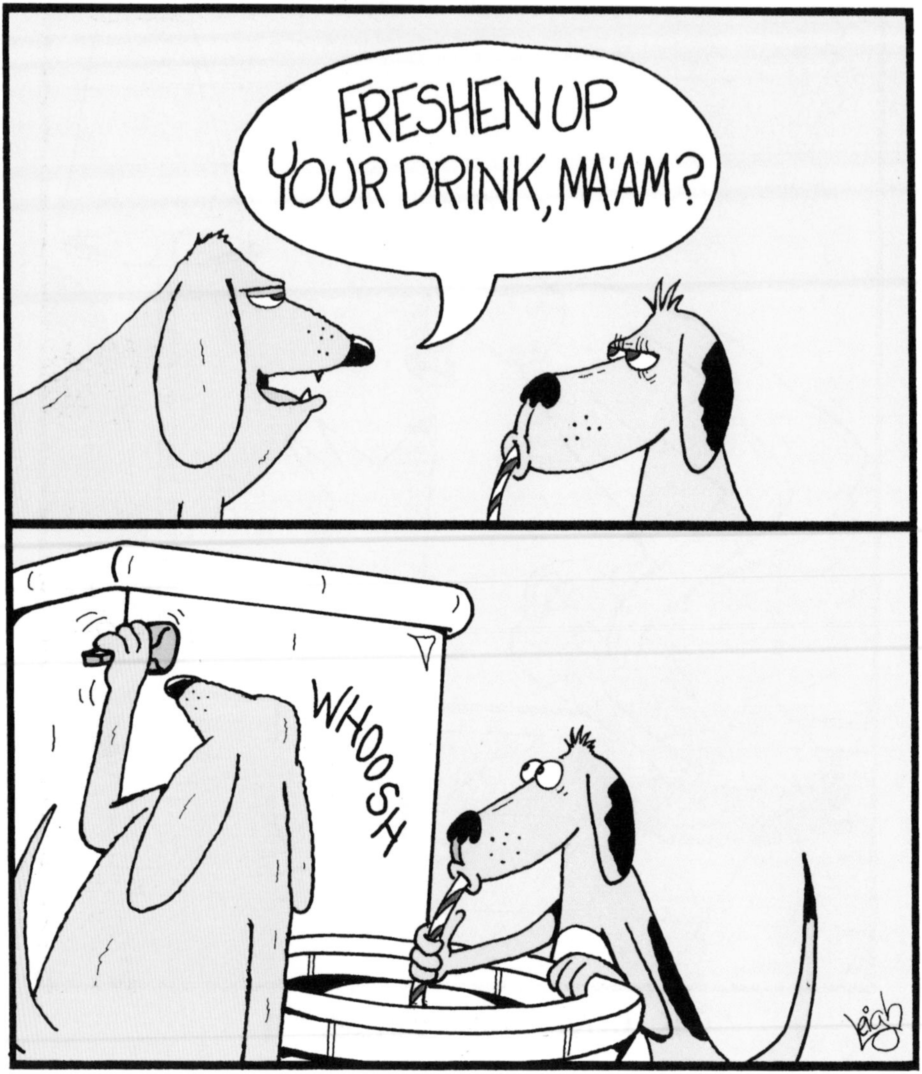
FRESHEN UP YOUR DRINK, MA'AM?
WHOOOSH
Leigh

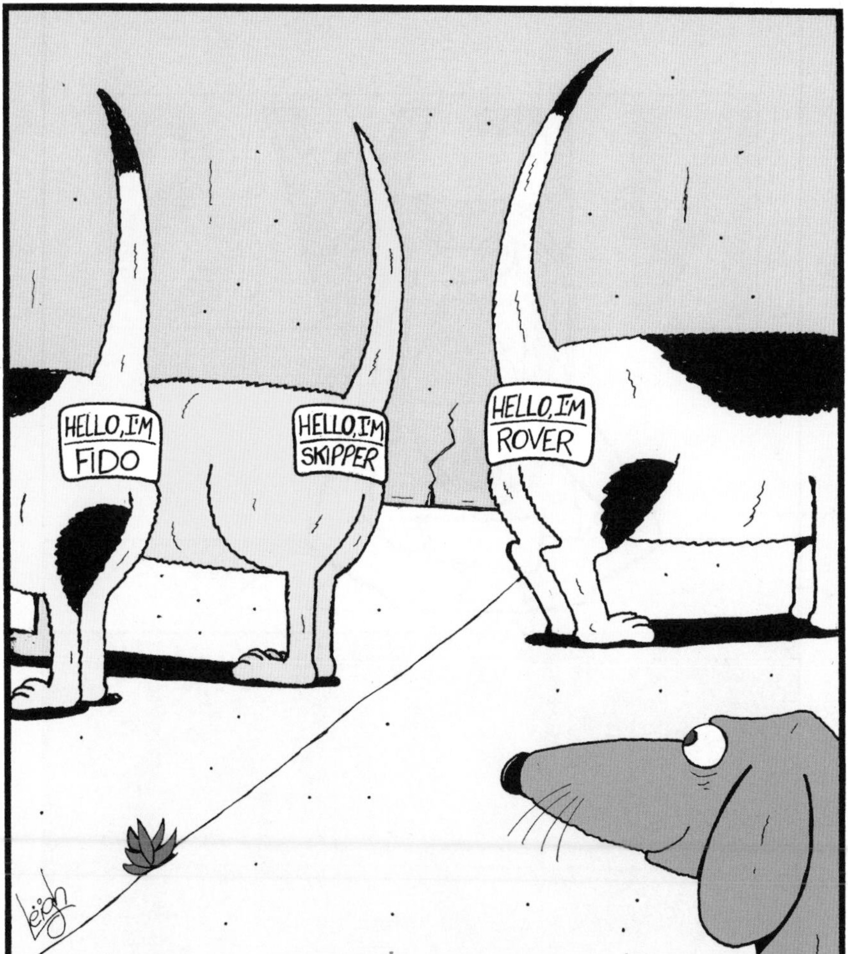
HELLO, I'M FIDO
HELLO, I'M SKIPPER
HELLO, I'M ROVER

Canine mixers

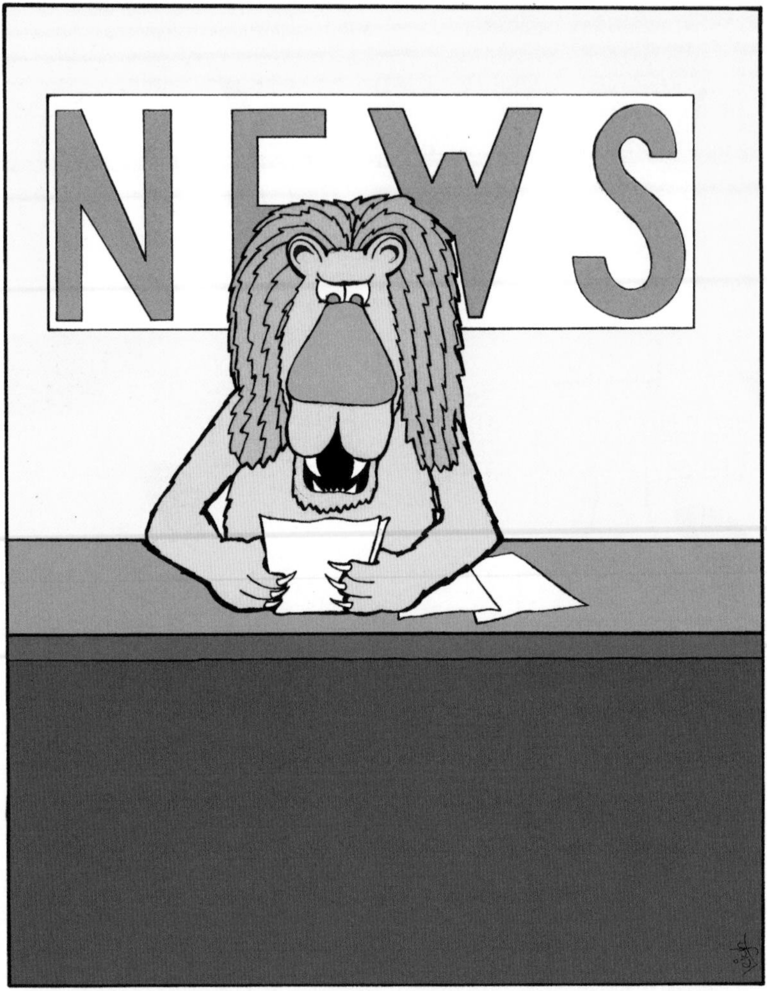
NEWS

"This just in . . . ferocious escaped lion devours anchorman . . . details at 11:00."

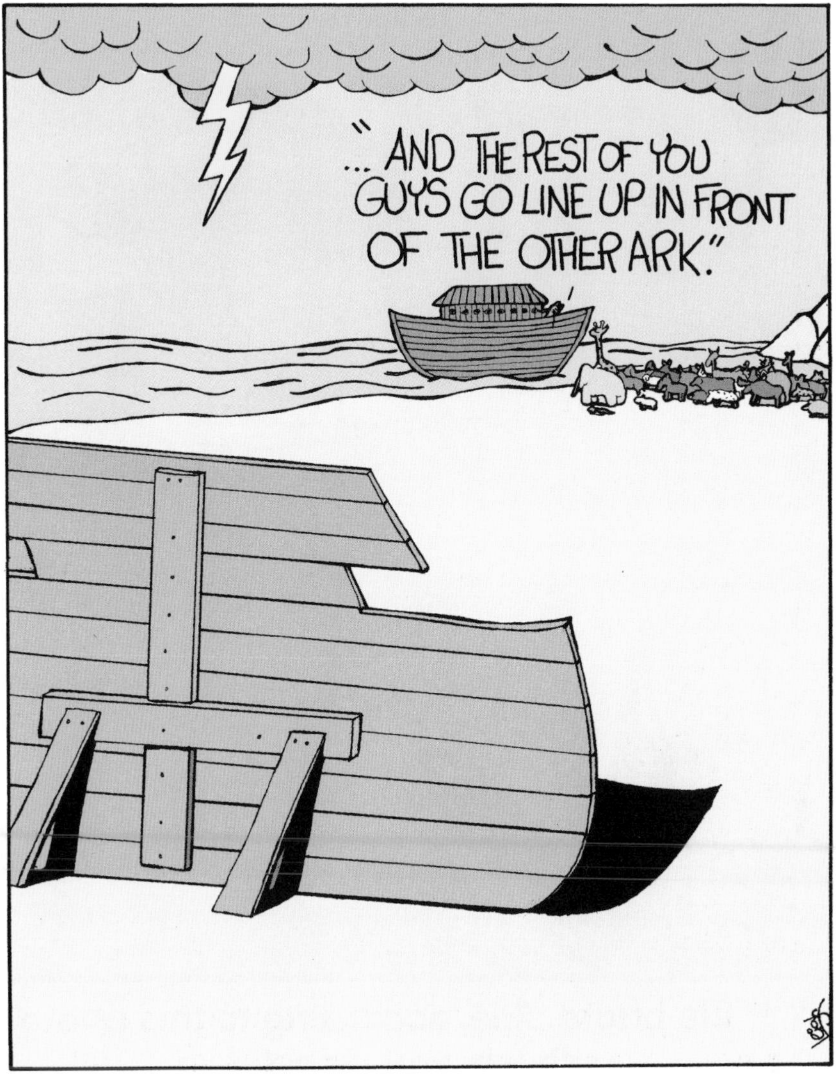
"... AND THE REST OF YOU GUYS GO LINE UP IN FRONT OF THE OTHER ARK."

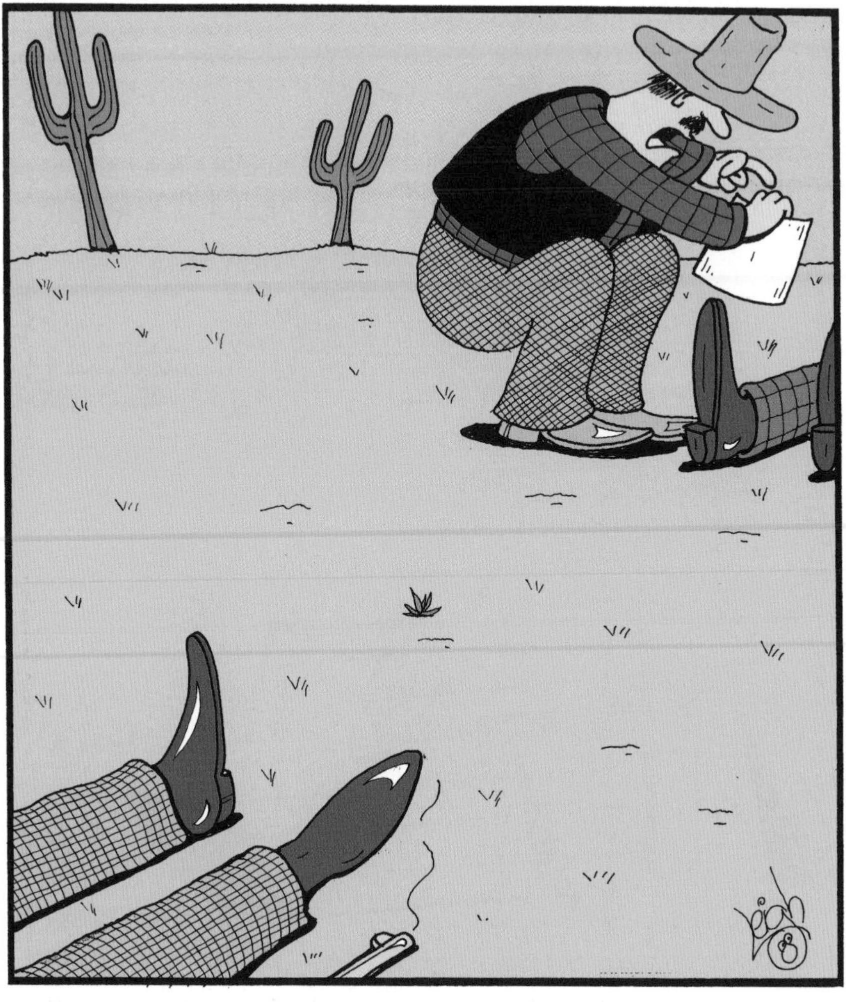

“On the bright side, according to this photo finish, you won.”

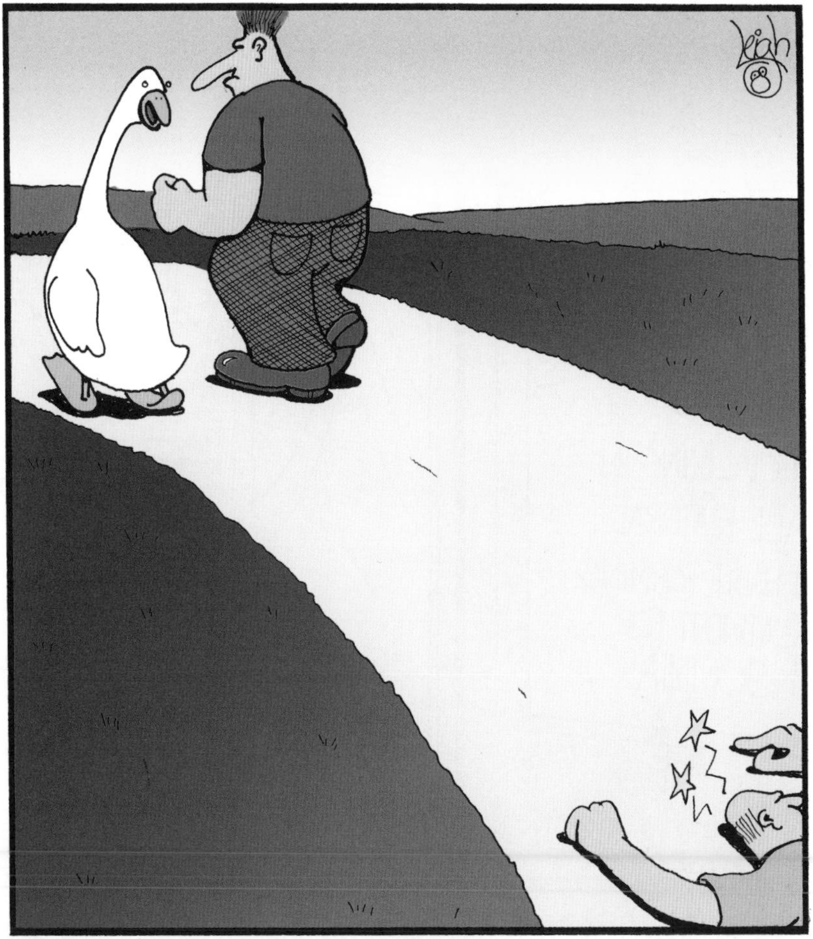

"Seriously, Murray, if we're going to keep hanging out together, you're going to have to be a little less sensitive whenever someone points and says, 'Hey, look at that guy with the huge honker!'"

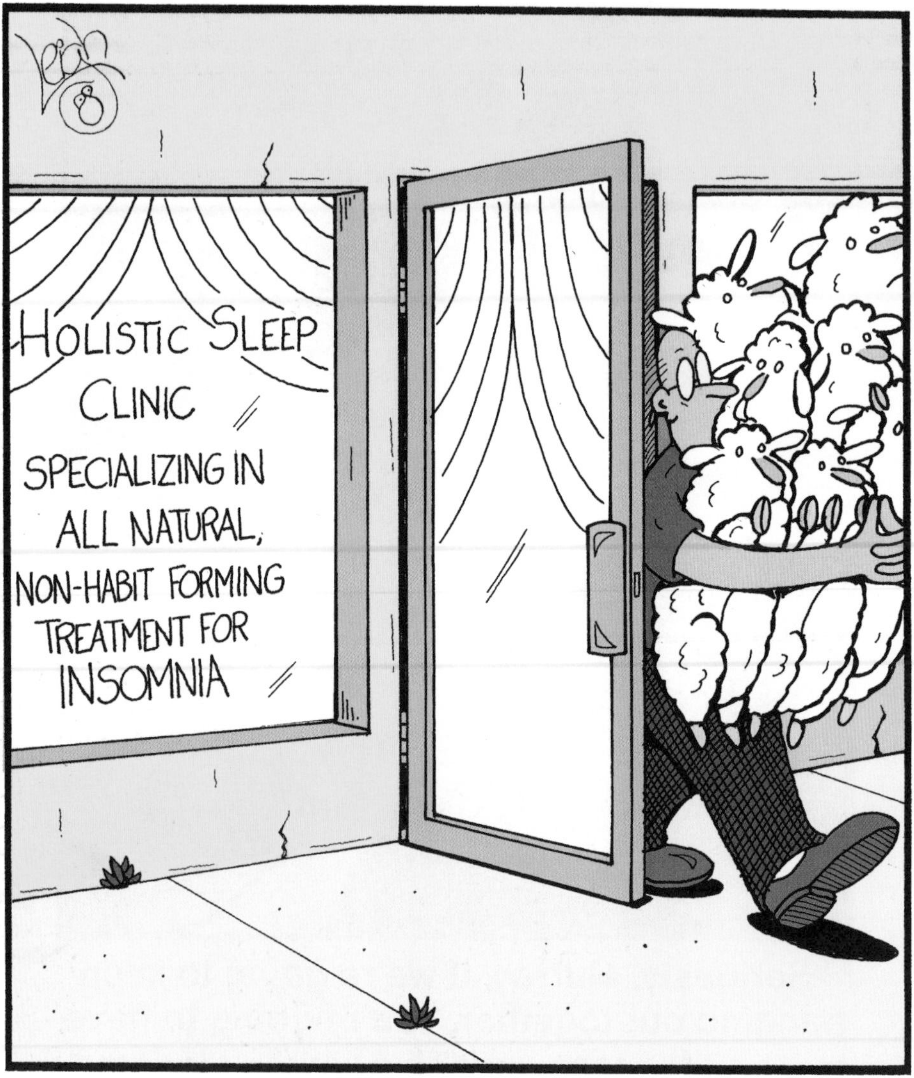
HOLISTIC SLEEP CLINIC
SPECIALIZING IN ALL NATURAL, NON-HABIT FORMING TREATMENT FOR INSOMNIA

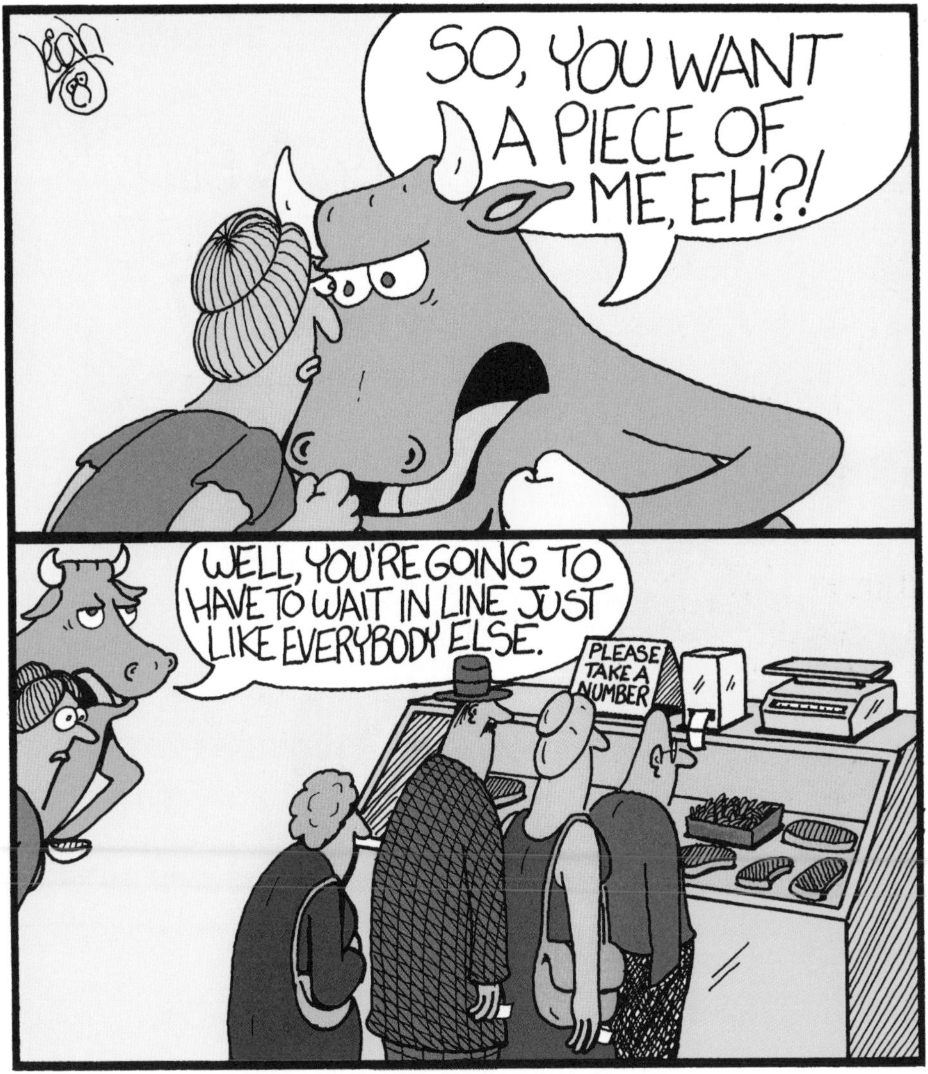
SO, YOU WANT A PIECE OF ME, EH?!
WELL, YOU'RE GOING TO HAVE TO WAIT IN LINE JUST LIKE EVERYBODY ELSE.
PLEASE TAKE A NUMBER

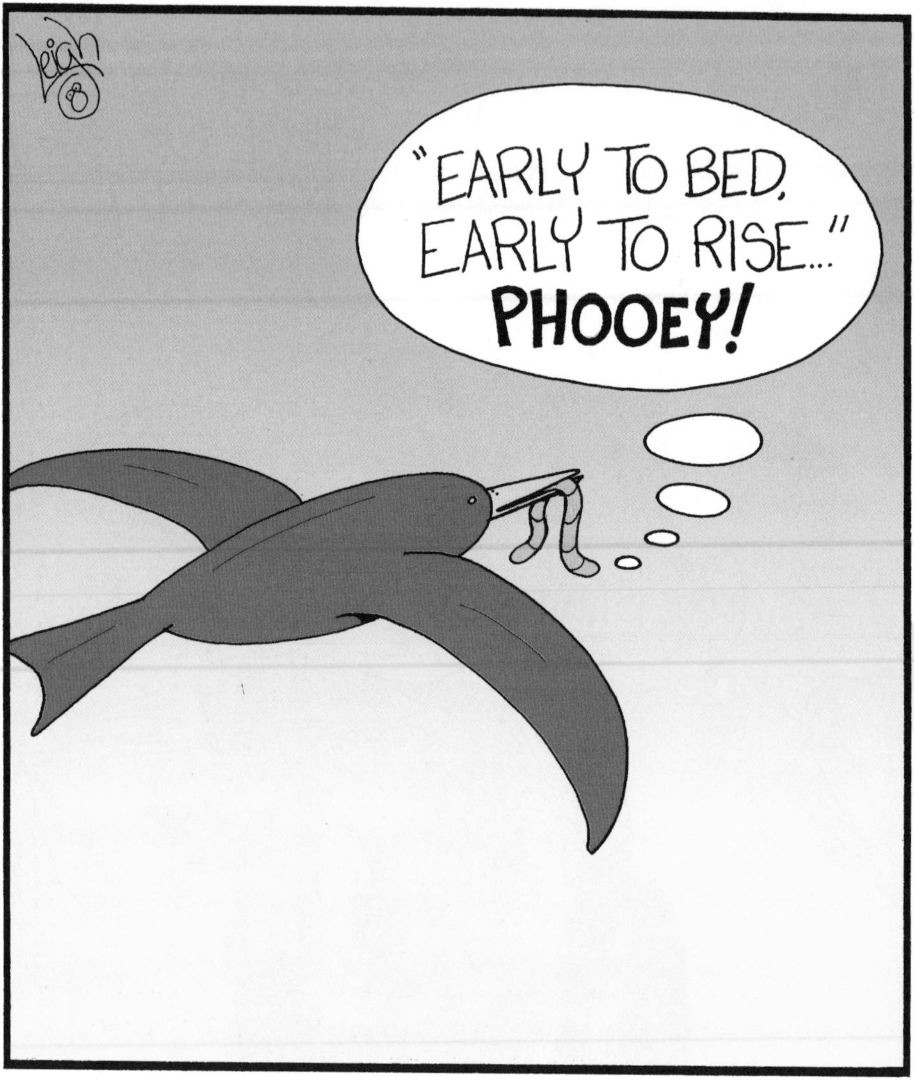
"EARLY TO BED, EARLY TO RISE..." PHOOEY!

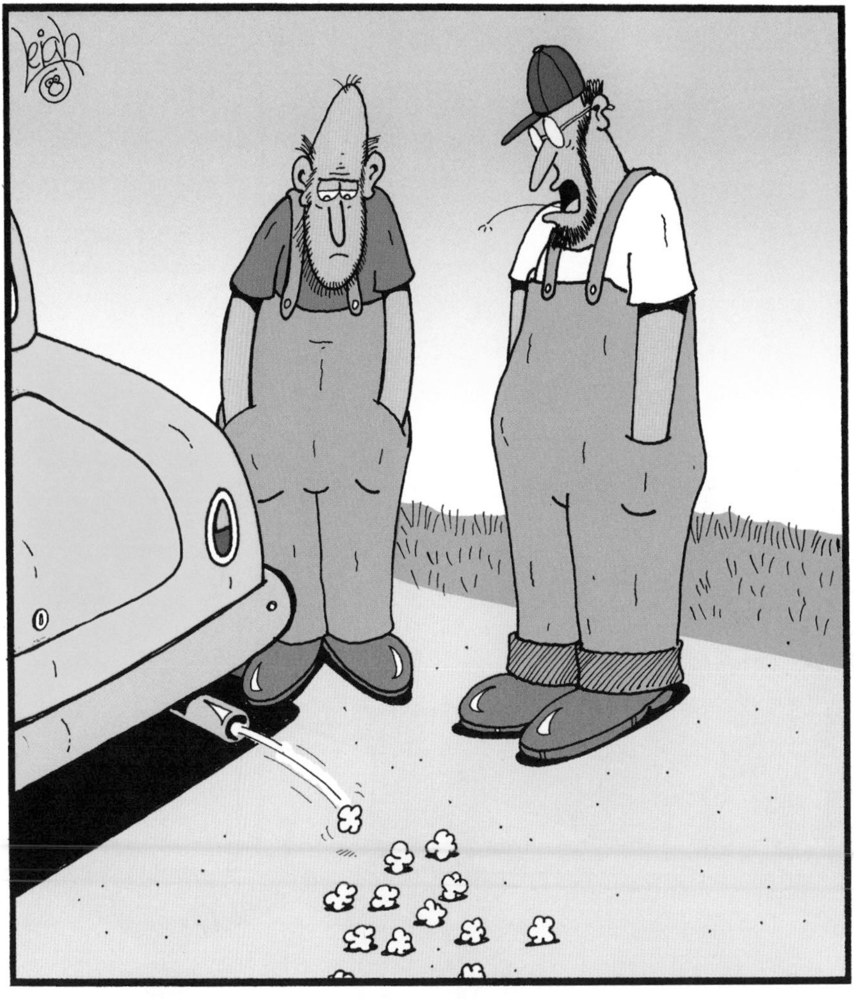

"Better call the fellas down at the ethanol plant. Seems they may want to consider using another variety of corn."

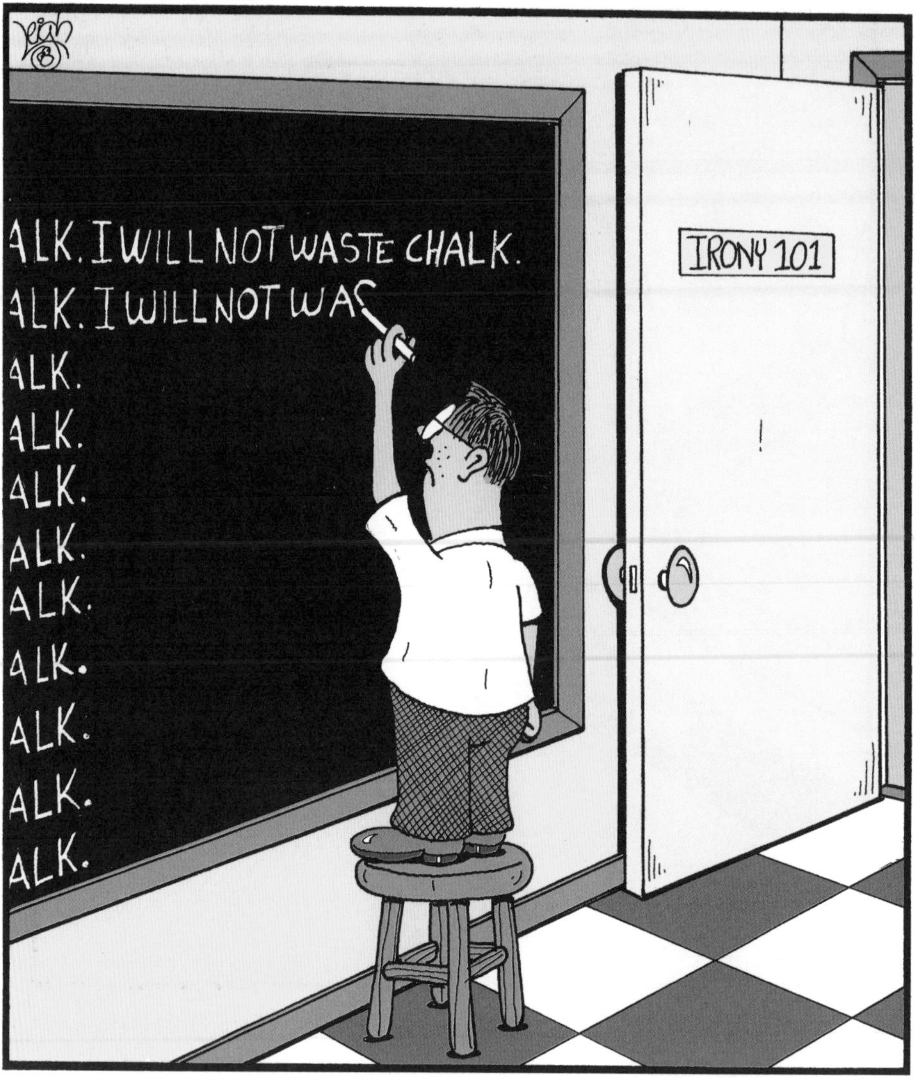

ALK. I WILL NOT WASTE CHALK.
ALK. I WILL NOT WAS
ALK.
ALK.
ALK.
ALK.
ALK.
ALK.
ALK.
ALK.
ALK.
IRONY 101

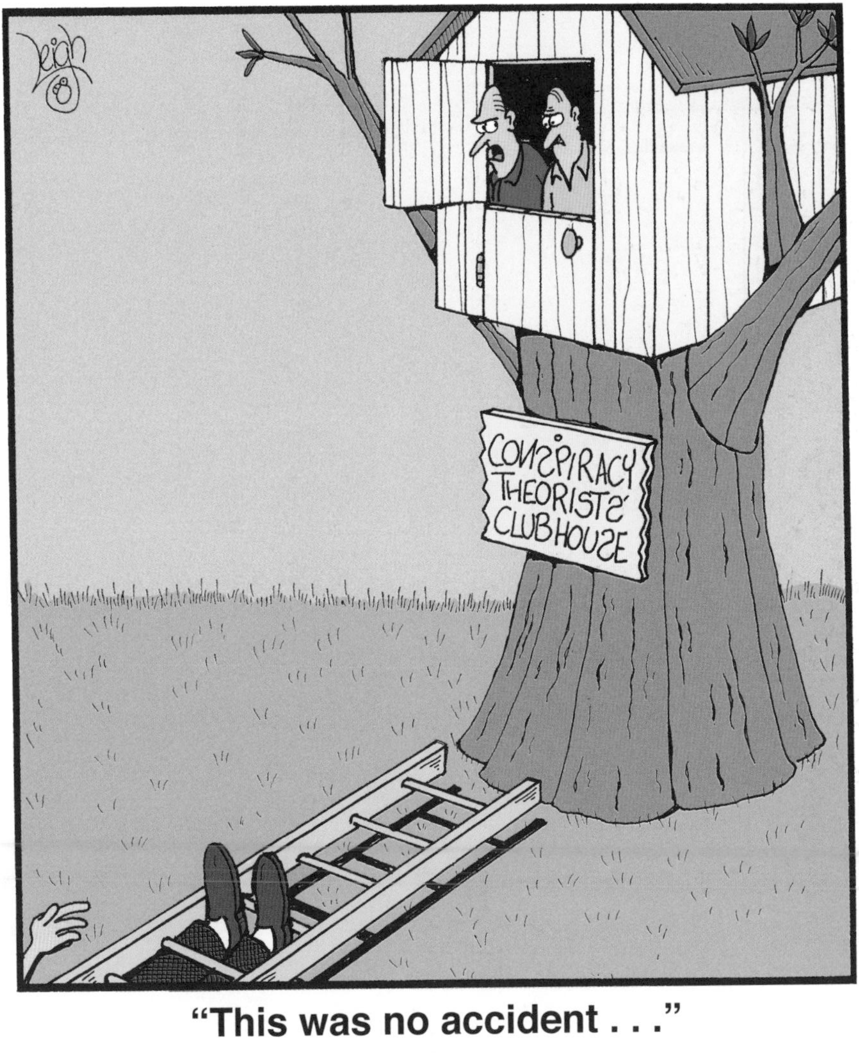
CONSPIRACY
THEORISTS'
CLUBHOUSE

"This was no accident . . ."

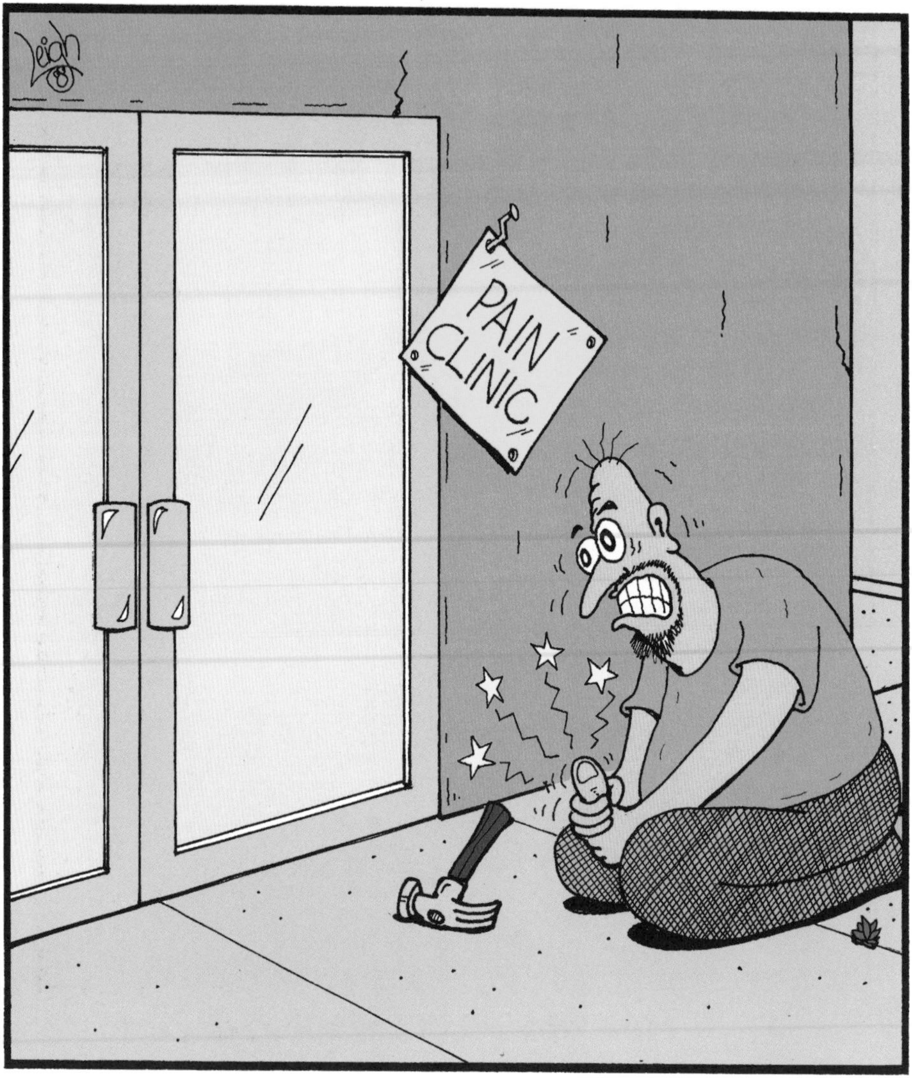
Leigh 08
PAIN CLINIC

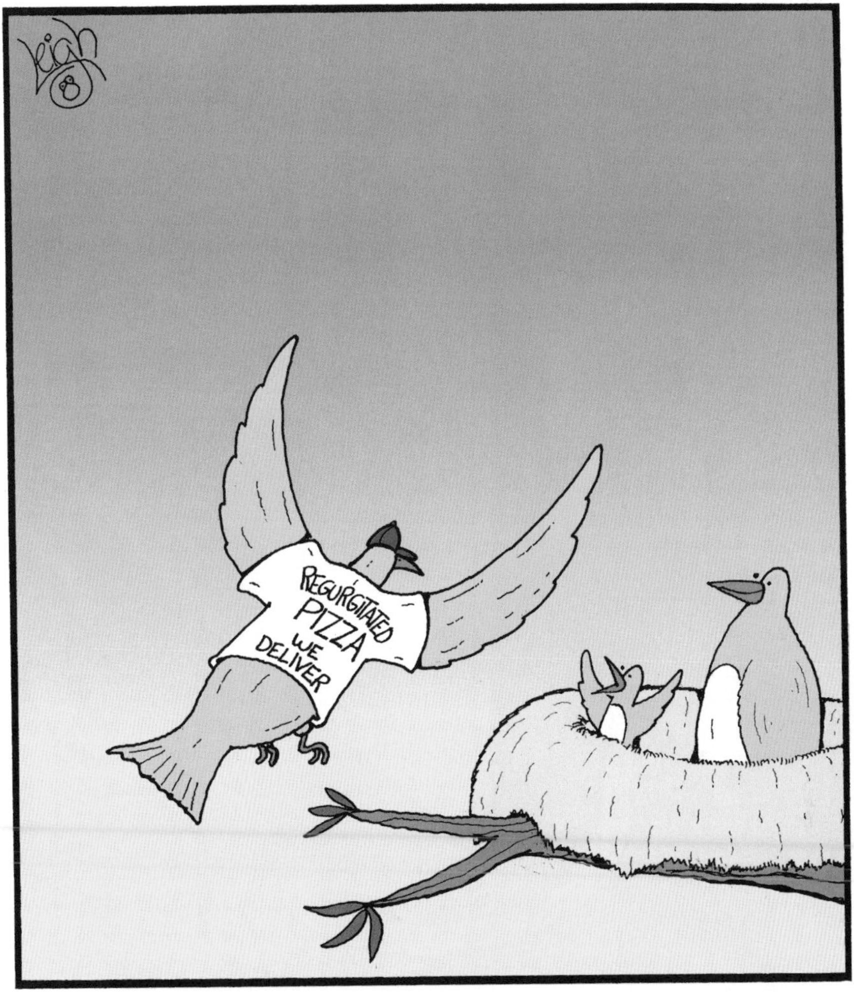
REGURGITATED
PIZZA
WE
DELIVER

When mother birds take the night off

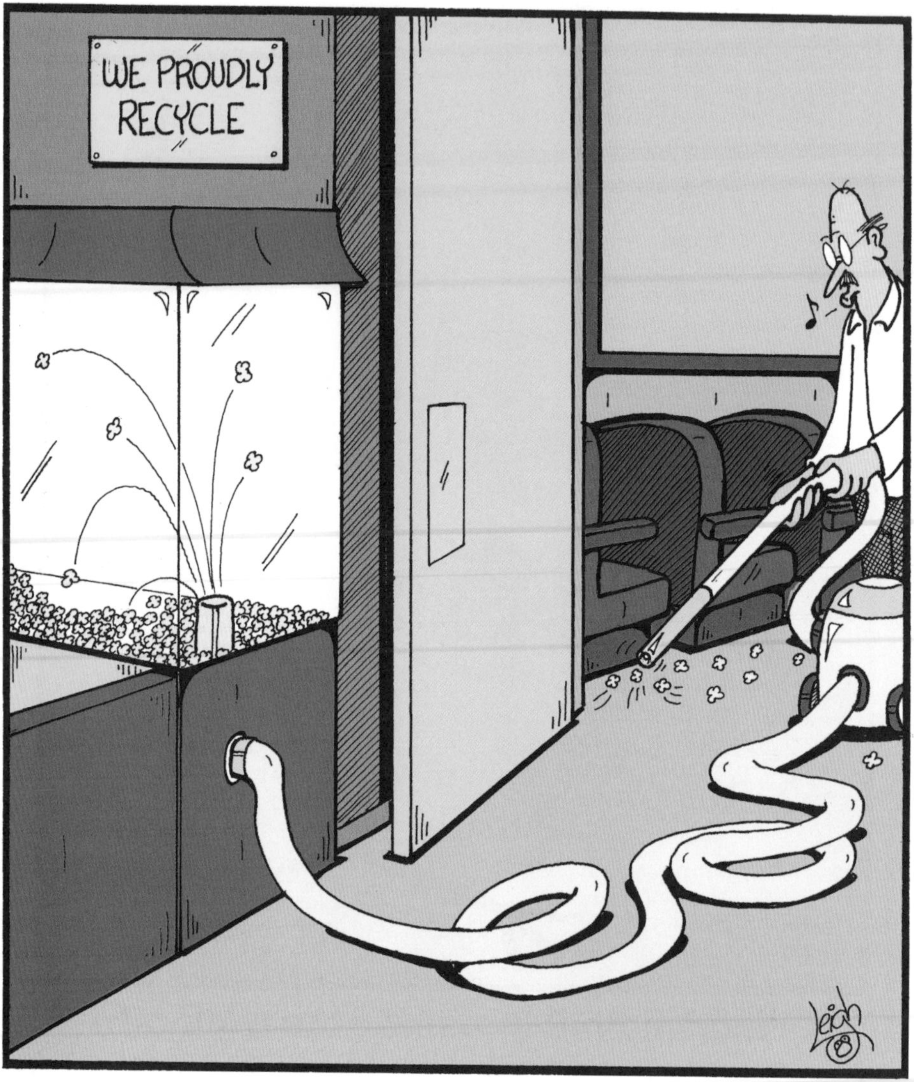
WE PROUDLY RECYCLE

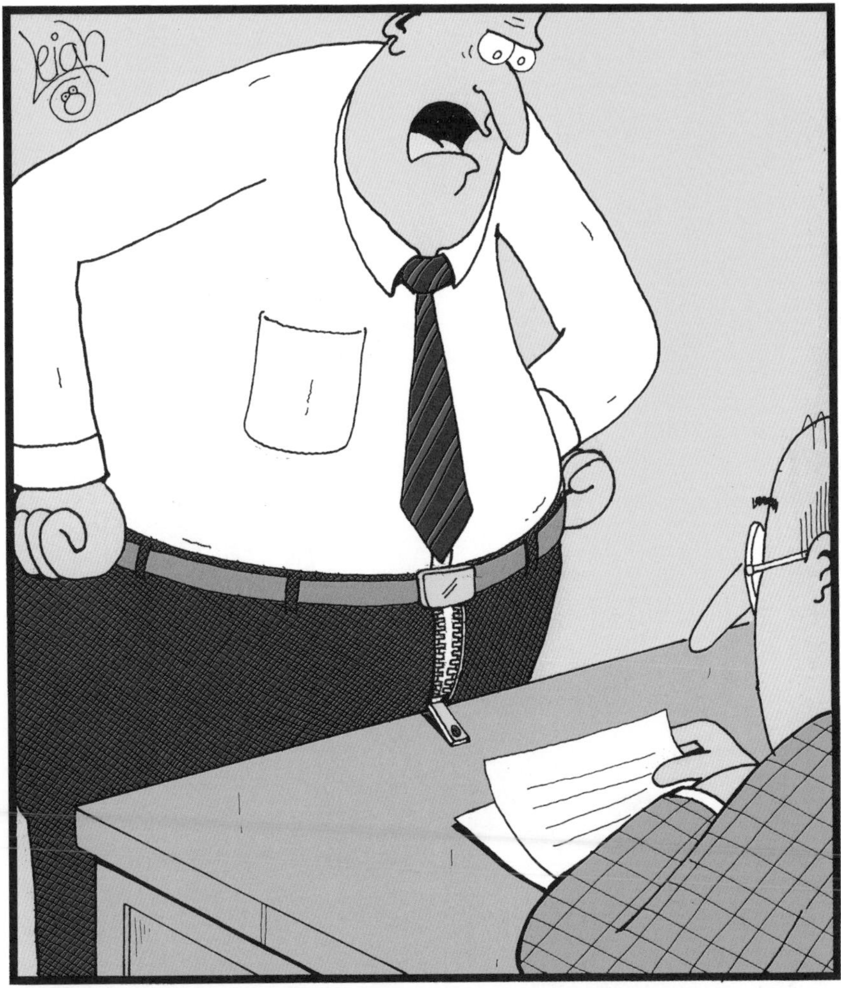

“Oh yeah?! Well, give me one good reason why I’m not cut out for a job in quality control!”

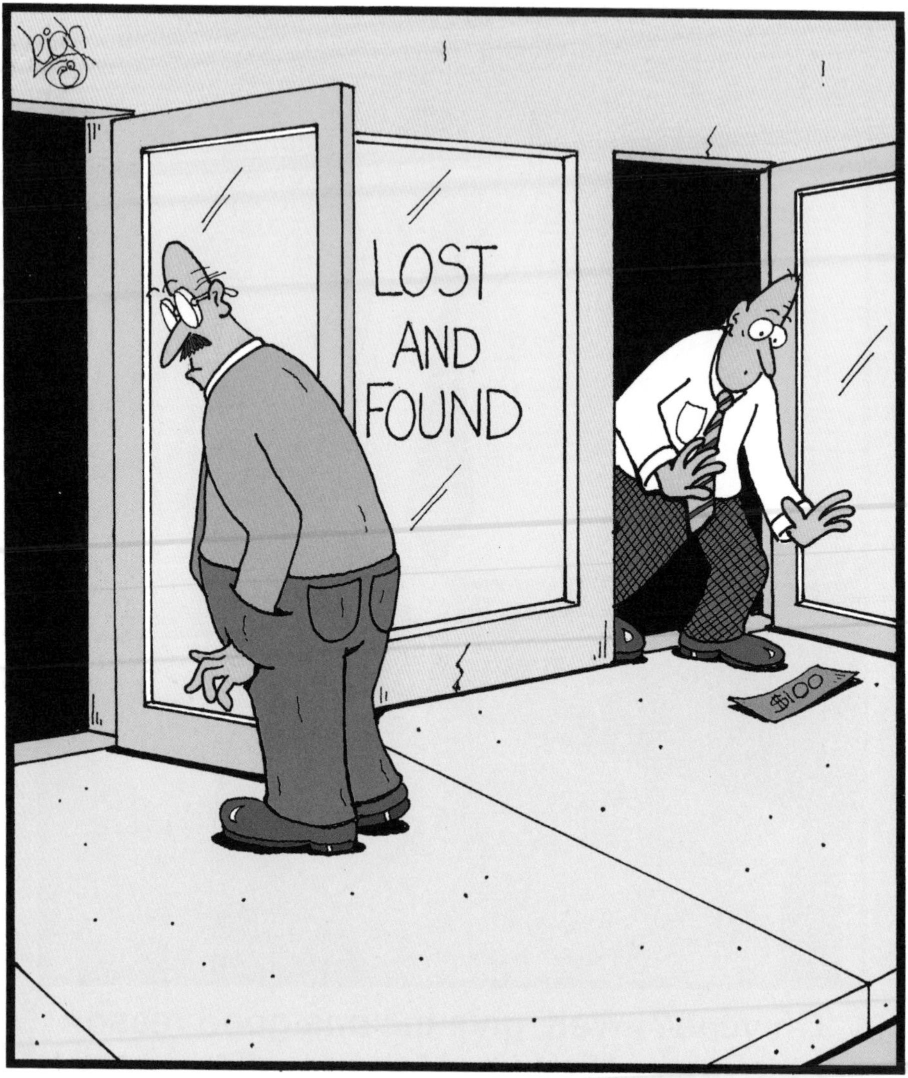
LOST
AND
FOUND
$100

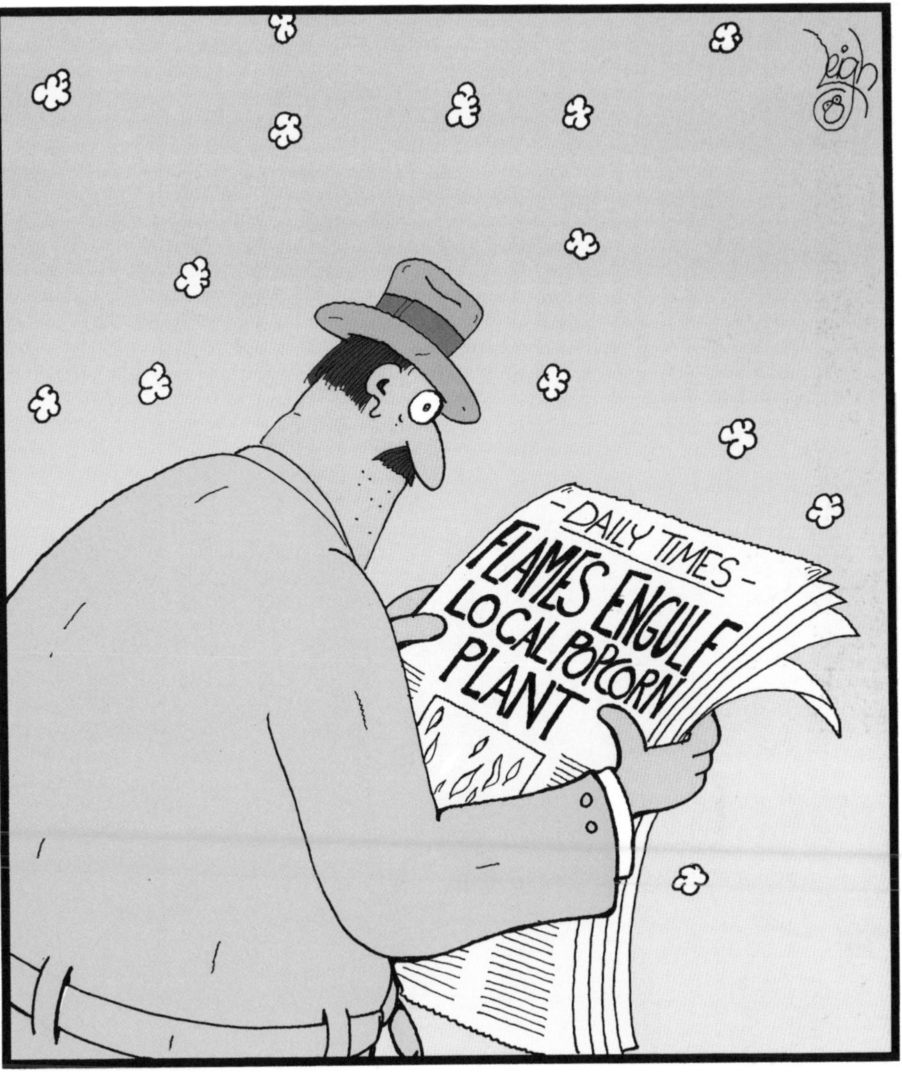
DAILY TIMES
FLAMES ENGULF LOCAL POPCORN PLANT

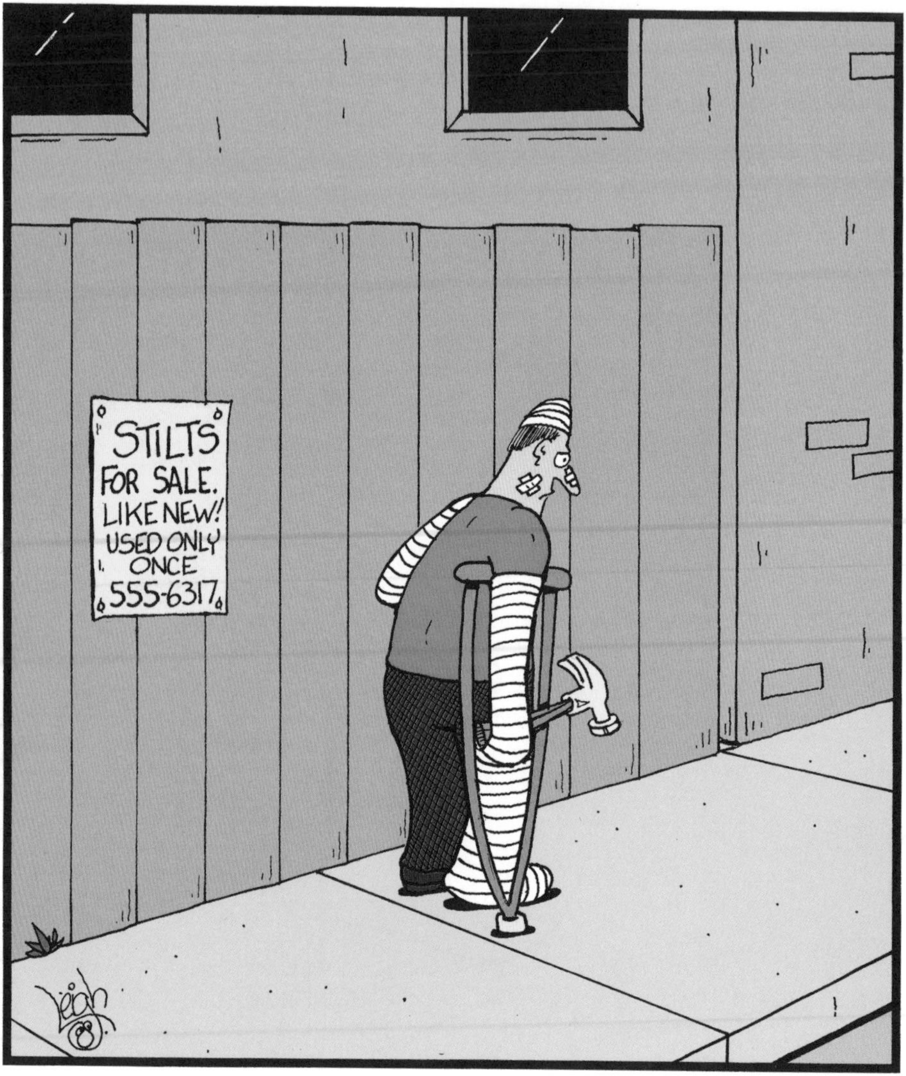
STILTS
FOR SALE.
LIKE NEW!
USED ONLY
ONCE
555-6317

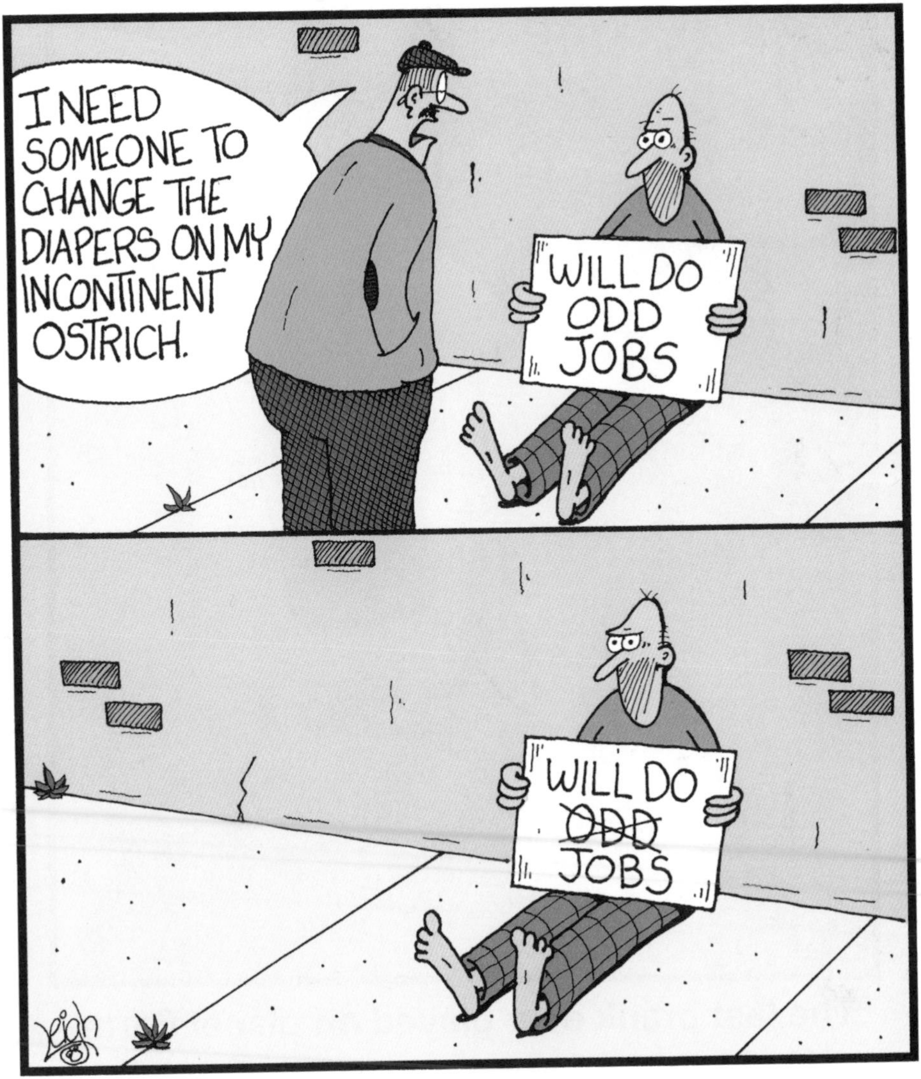
I NEED SOMEONE TO CHANGE THE DIAPERS ON MY INCONTINENT OSTRICH.
WILL DO ODD JOBS
WILL DO ODD JOBS

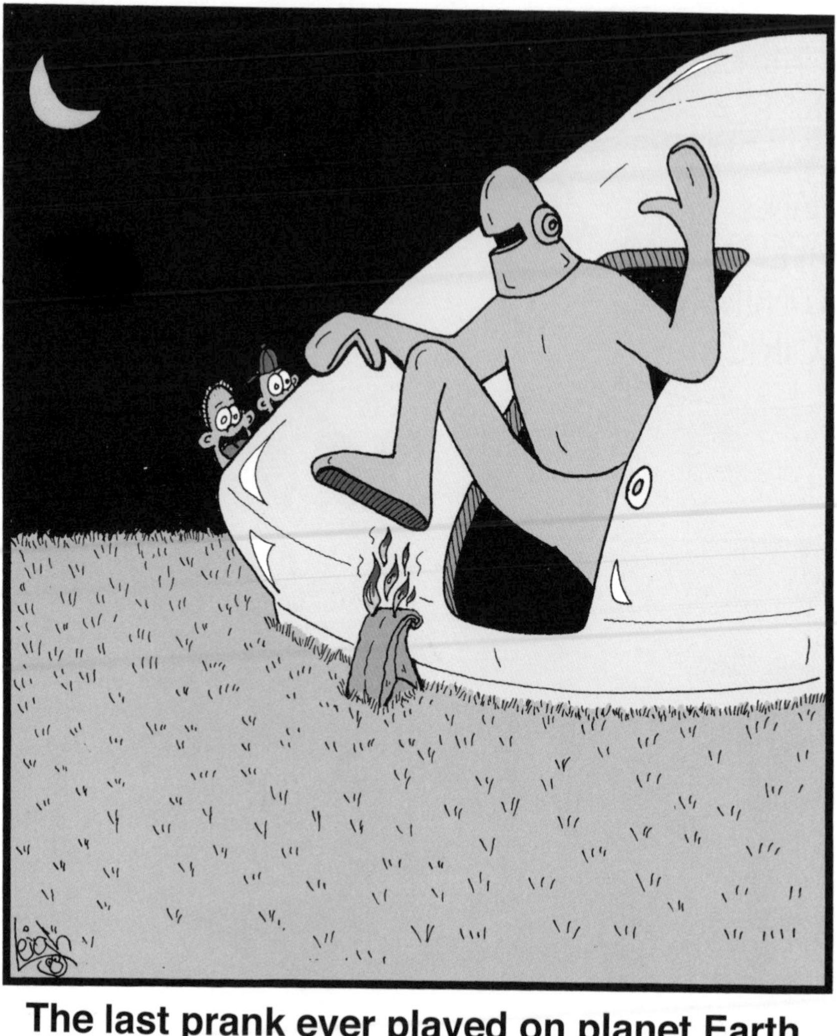

The last prank ever played on planet Earth

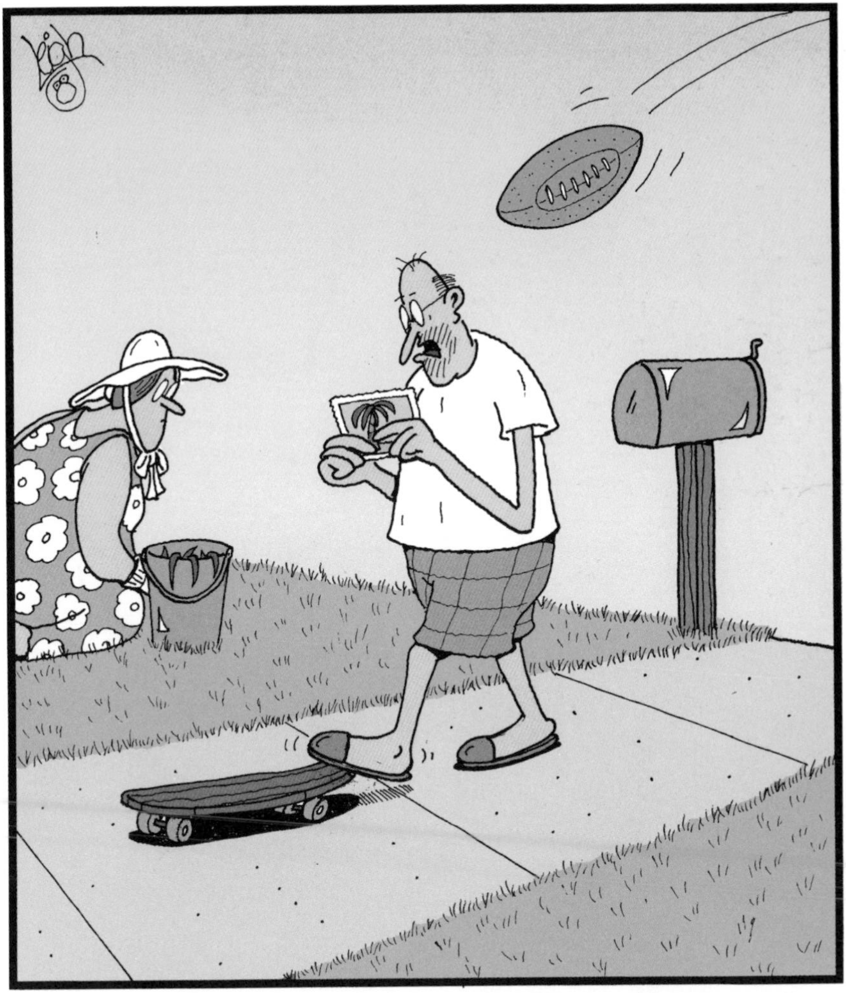

"Oh, nothing much, just a postcard from my guardian angel. He's on vacation."

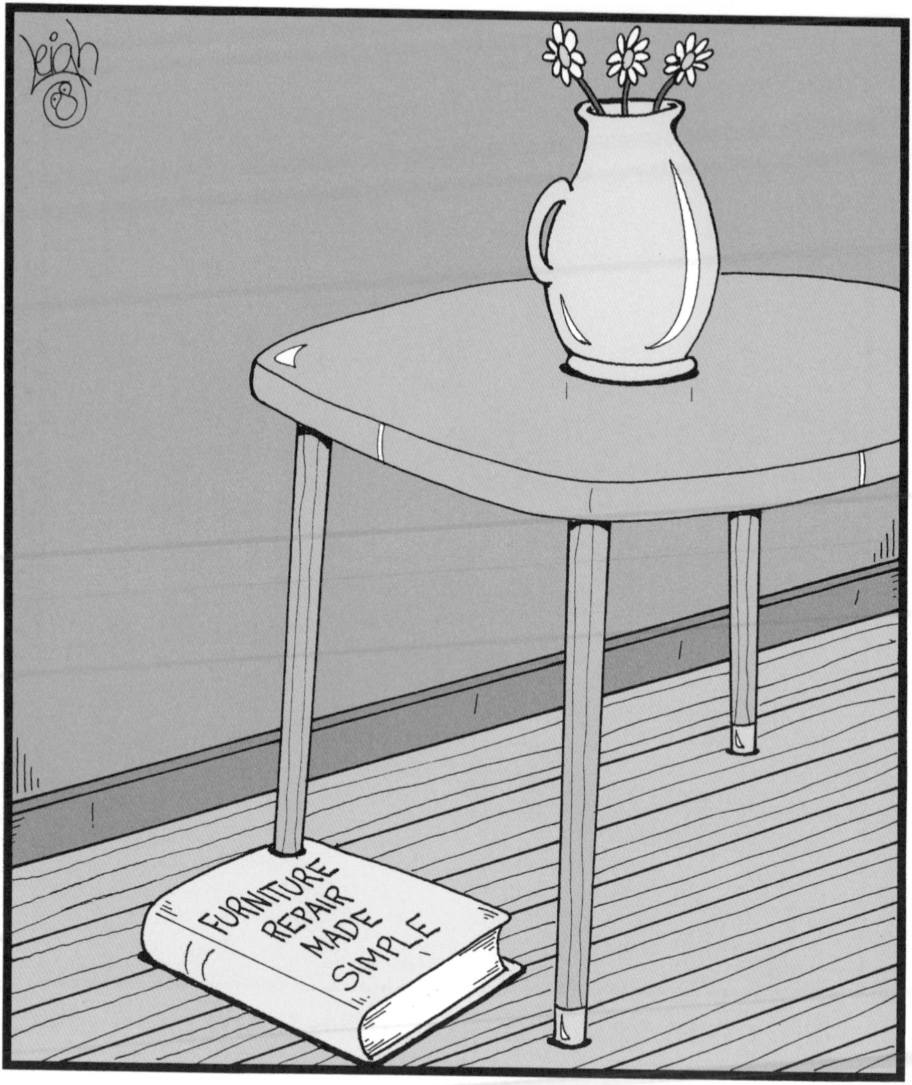
FURNITURE
REPAIR
MADE
SIMPLE

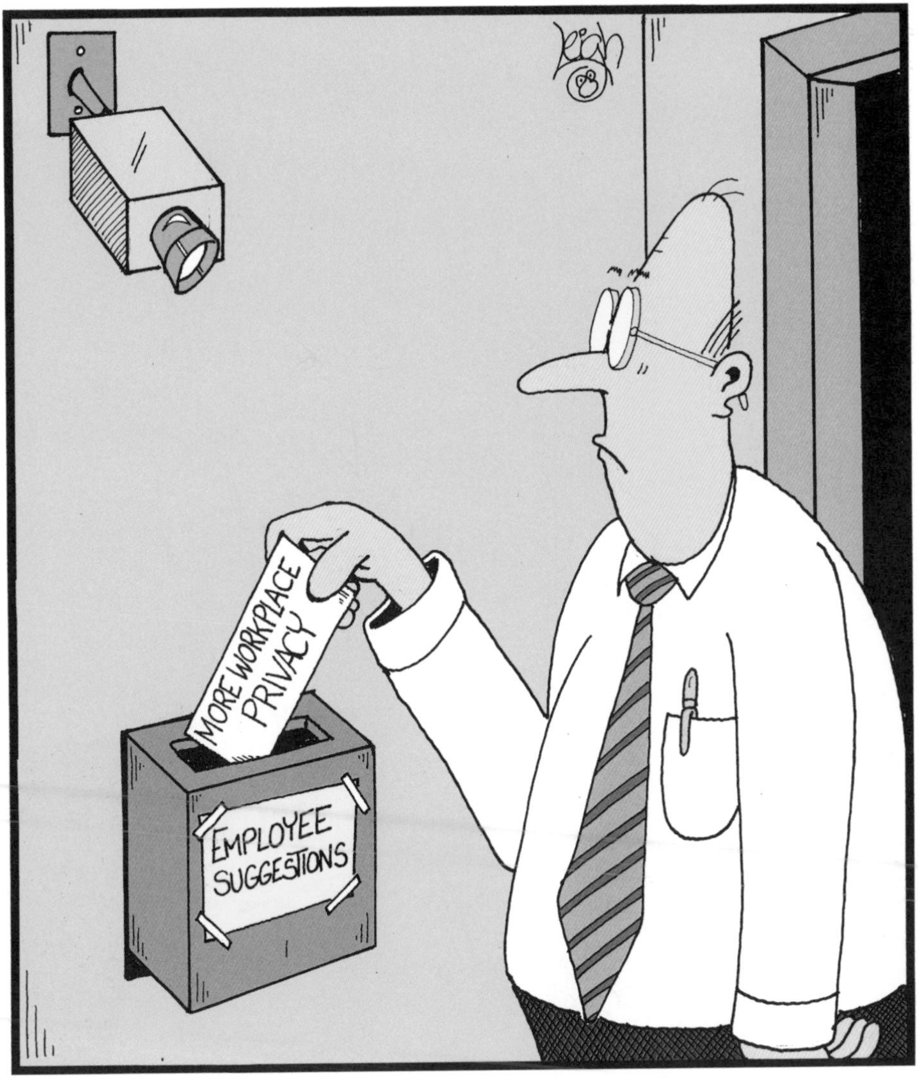
MORE WORKPLACE PRIVACY
EMPLOYEE SUGGESTIONS

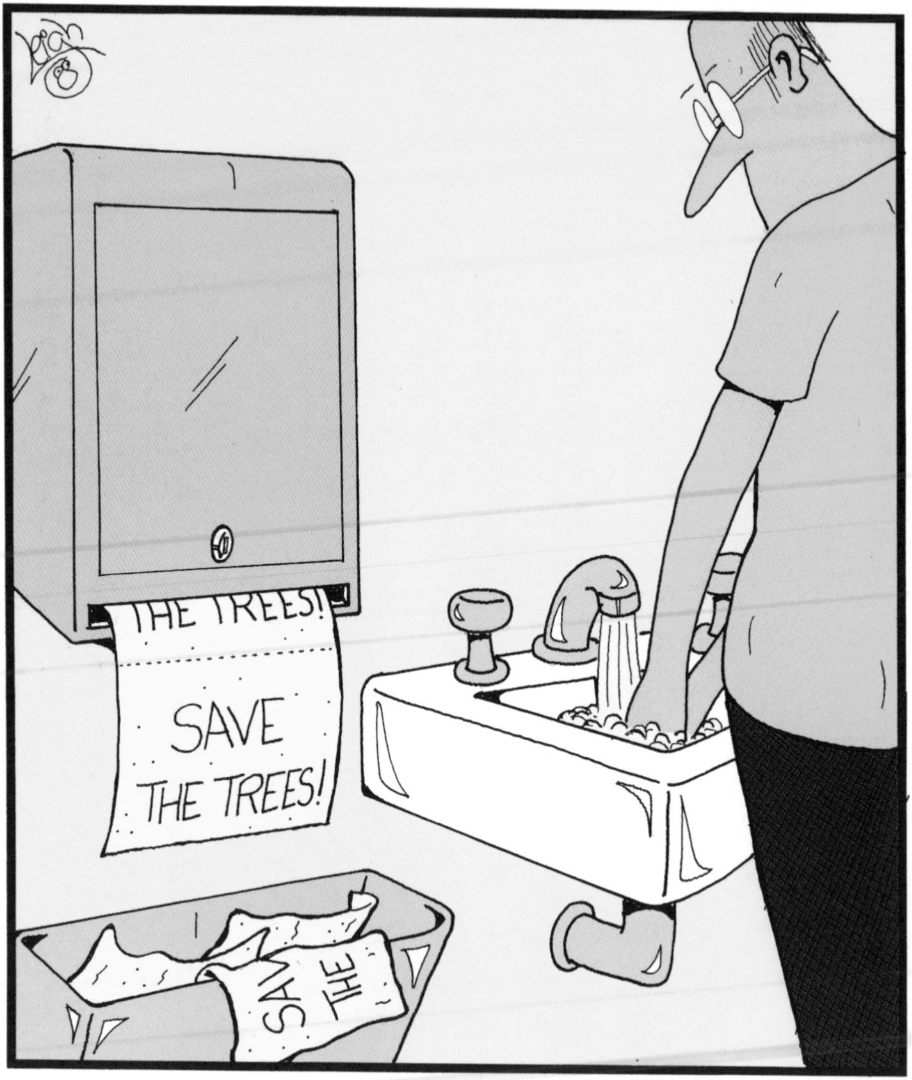
THE TREES!
SAVE
THE TREES!
SA
THE

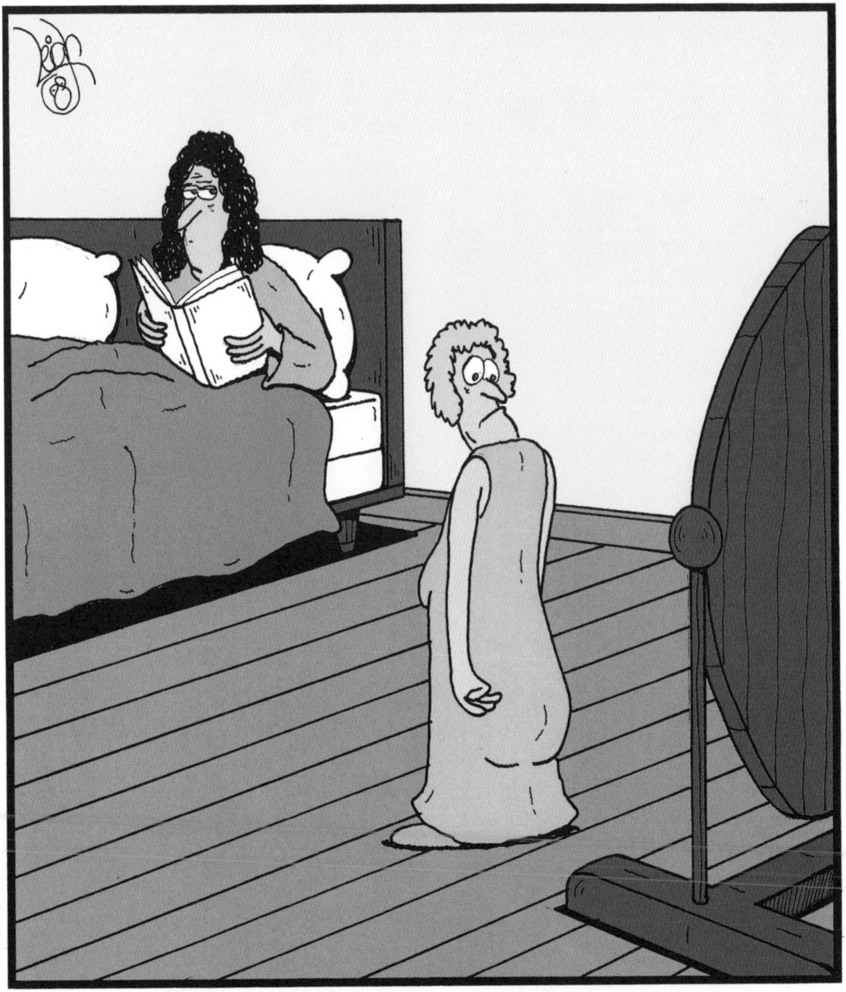

Apparently, Mrs. Isaac Newton also discovered gravity.

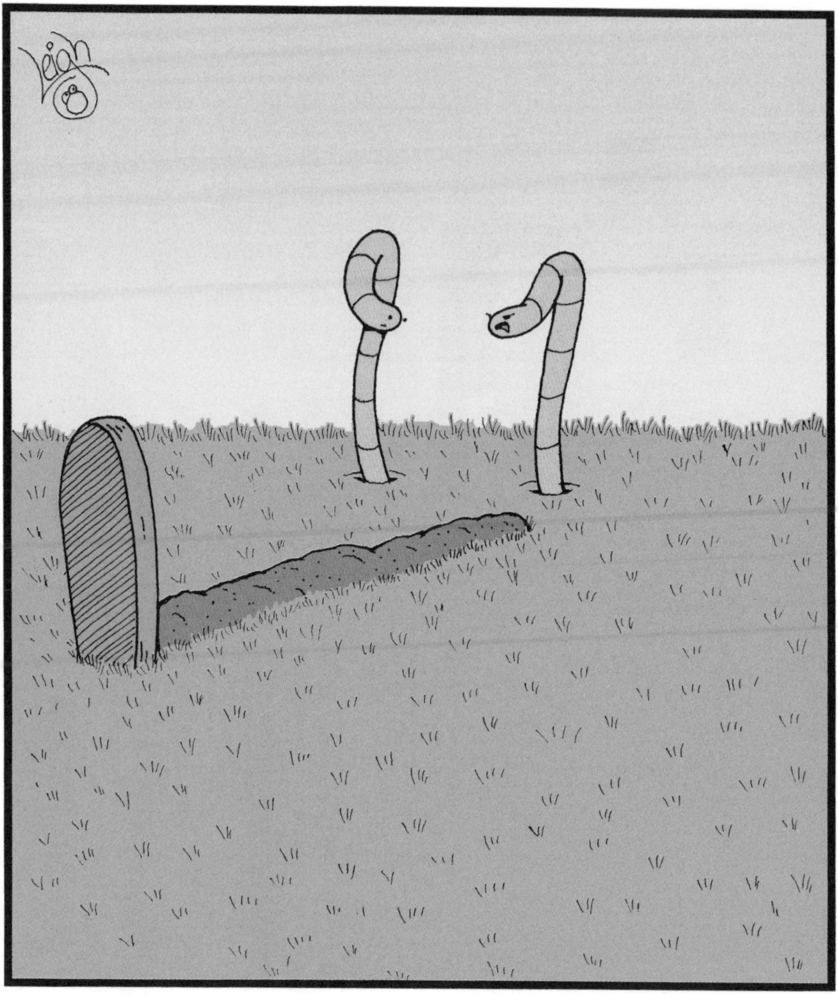

“What do you mean, ‘He’s gone to better place?’ . . . He’s in the same place he’s always been.”

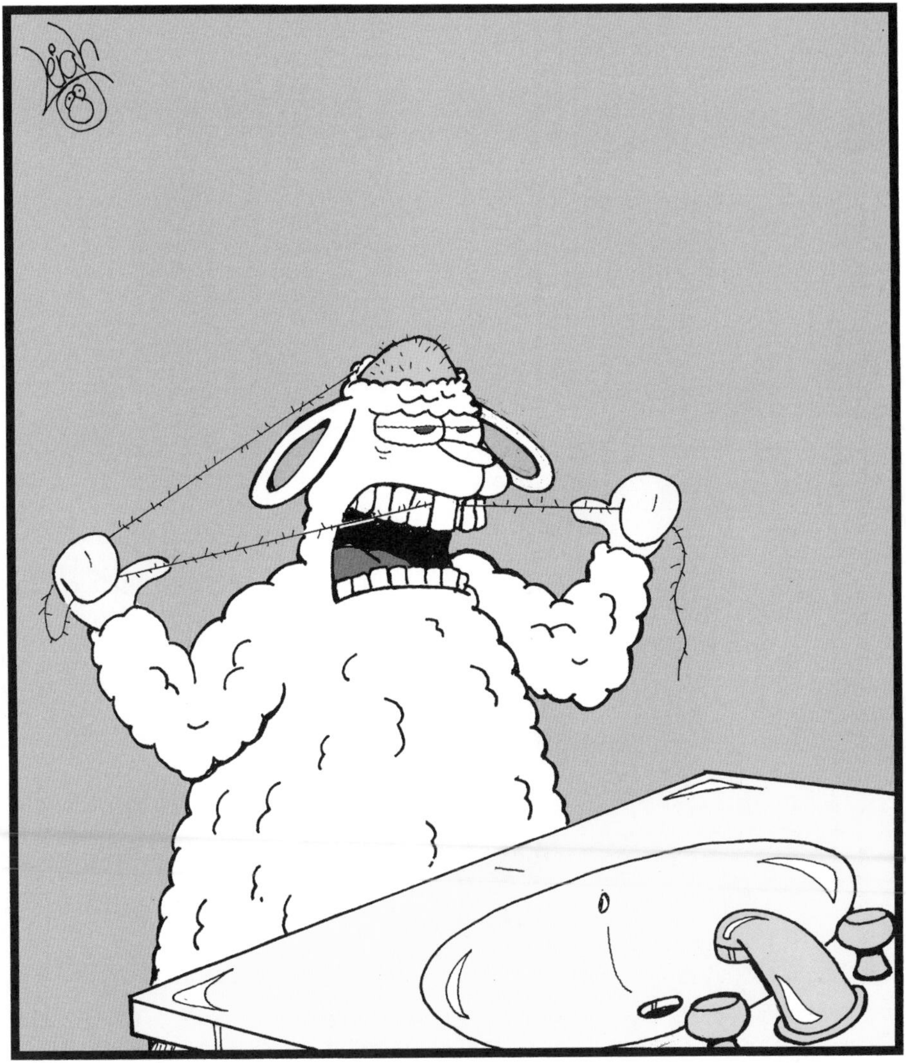

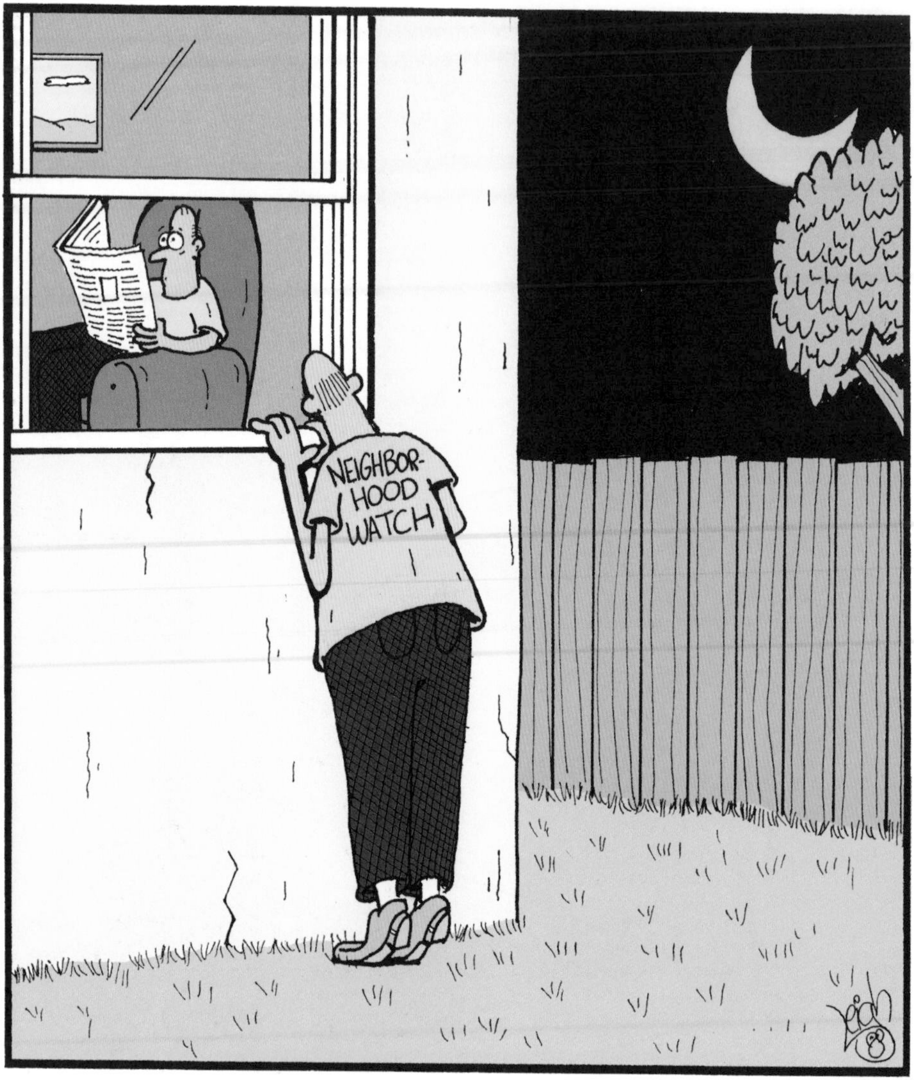
NEIGHBOR-
HOOD
WATCH

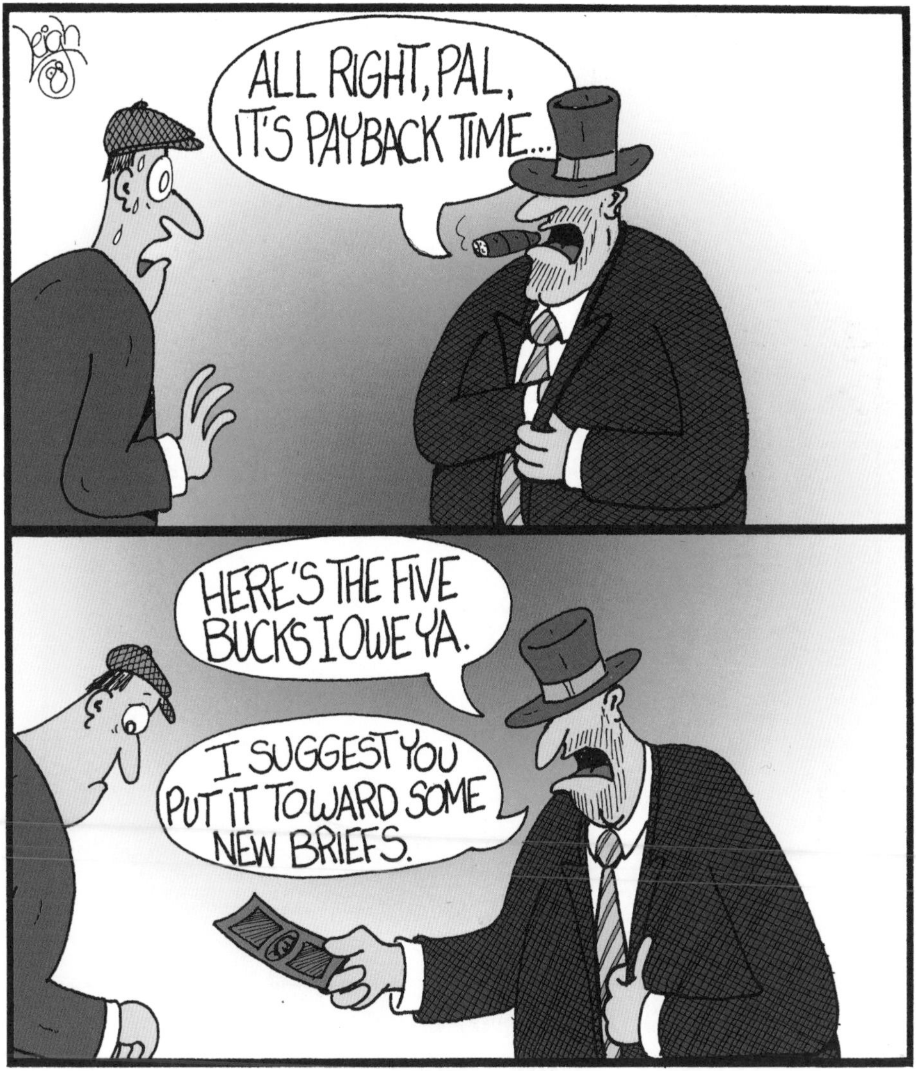
ALL RIGHT, PAL, IT'S PAYBACK TIME...
HERE'S THE FIVE BUCKS I OWE YA.
I SUGGEST YOU PUT IT TOWARD SOME NEW BRIEFS.

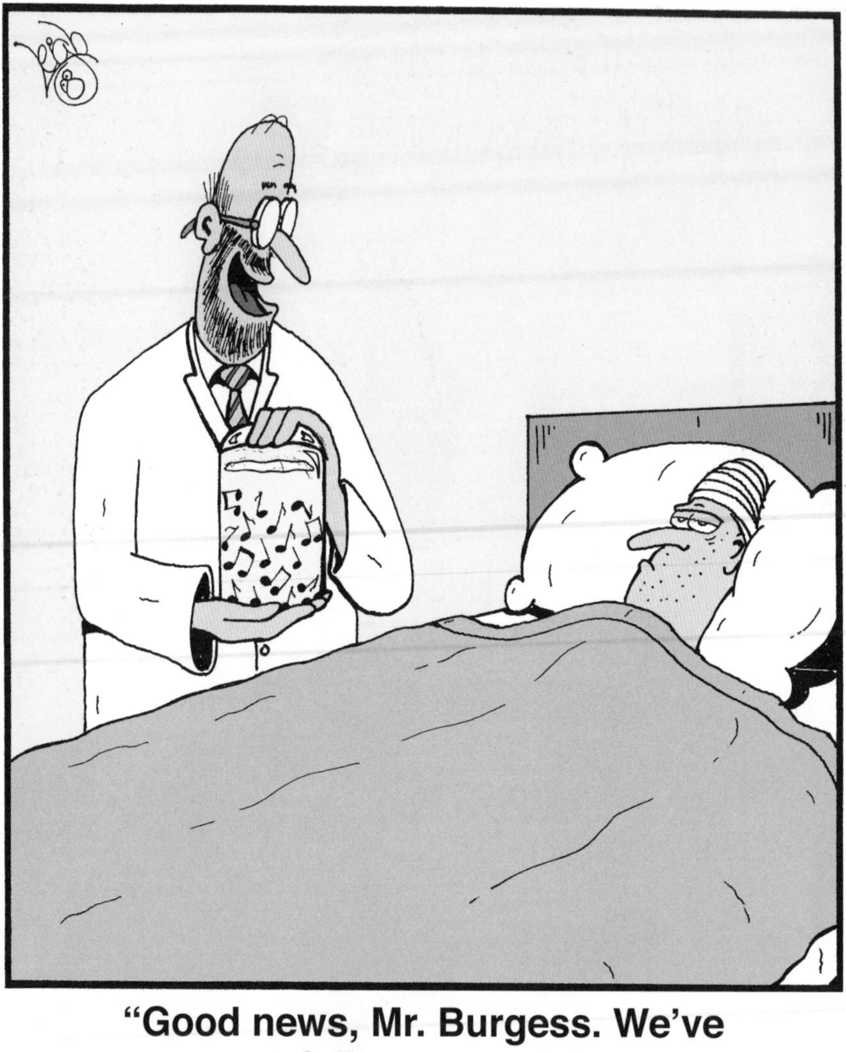

"Good news, Mr. Burgess. We've successfully removed the tune that was stuck in your head."

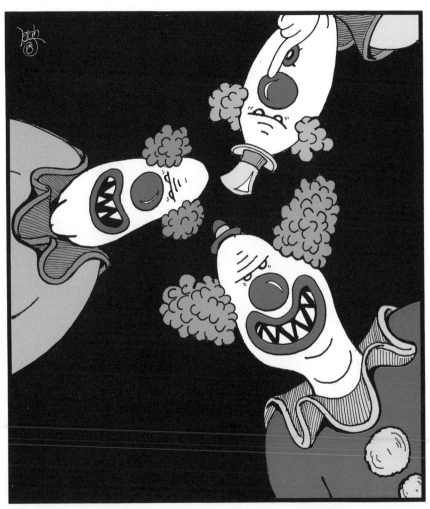

It had been the worst nightmare Danny had ever had, until he woke up.

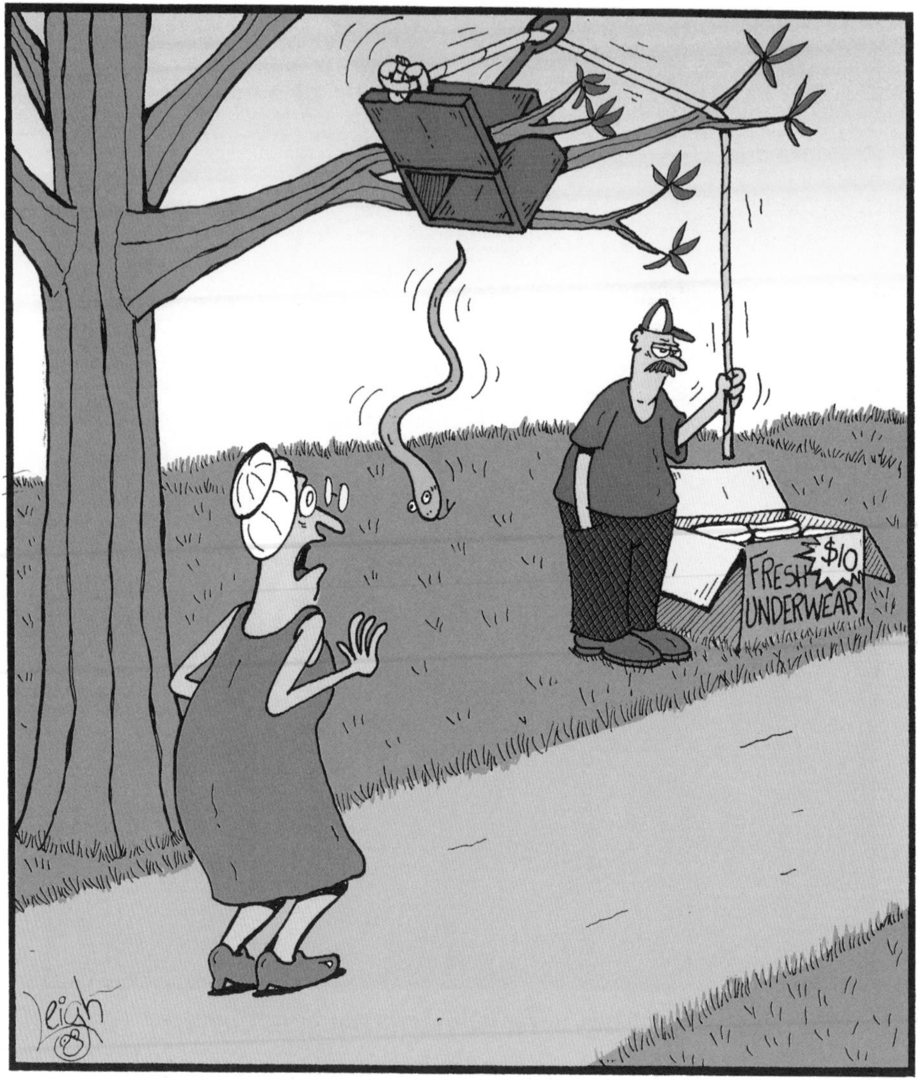
FRESH
$10
UNDERWEAR
Leigh

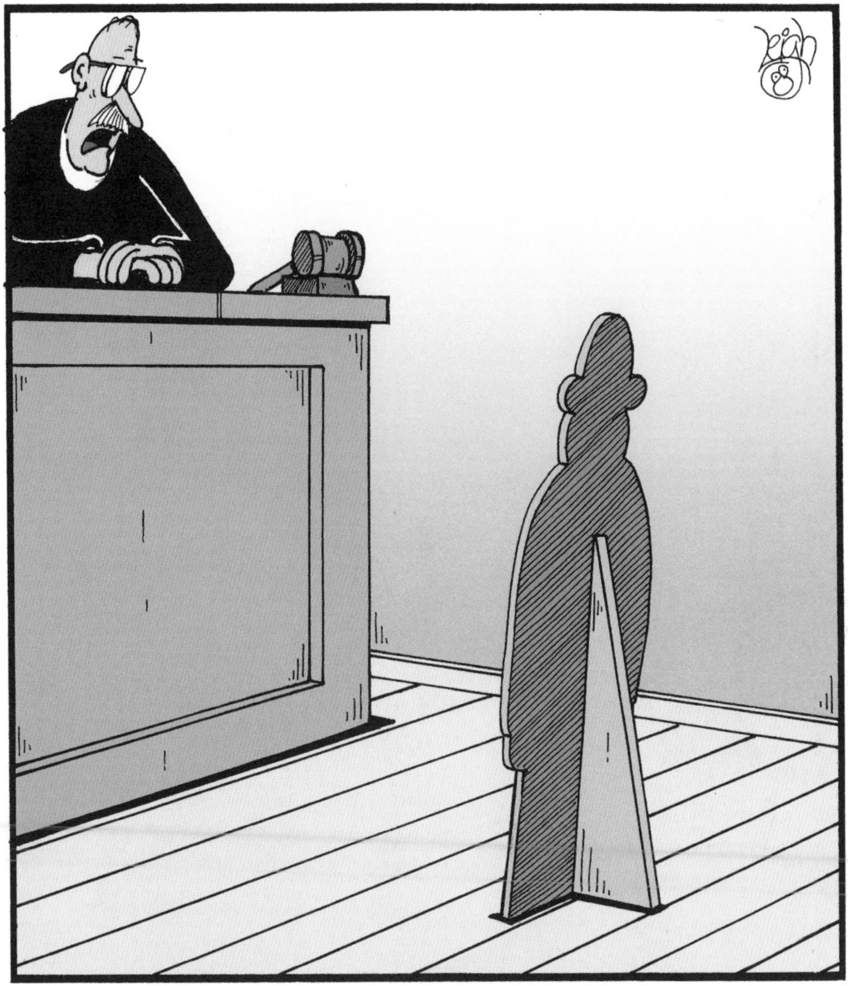

“In case you didn’t hear me the first time, you have been charged with fraud; how do you plead?”

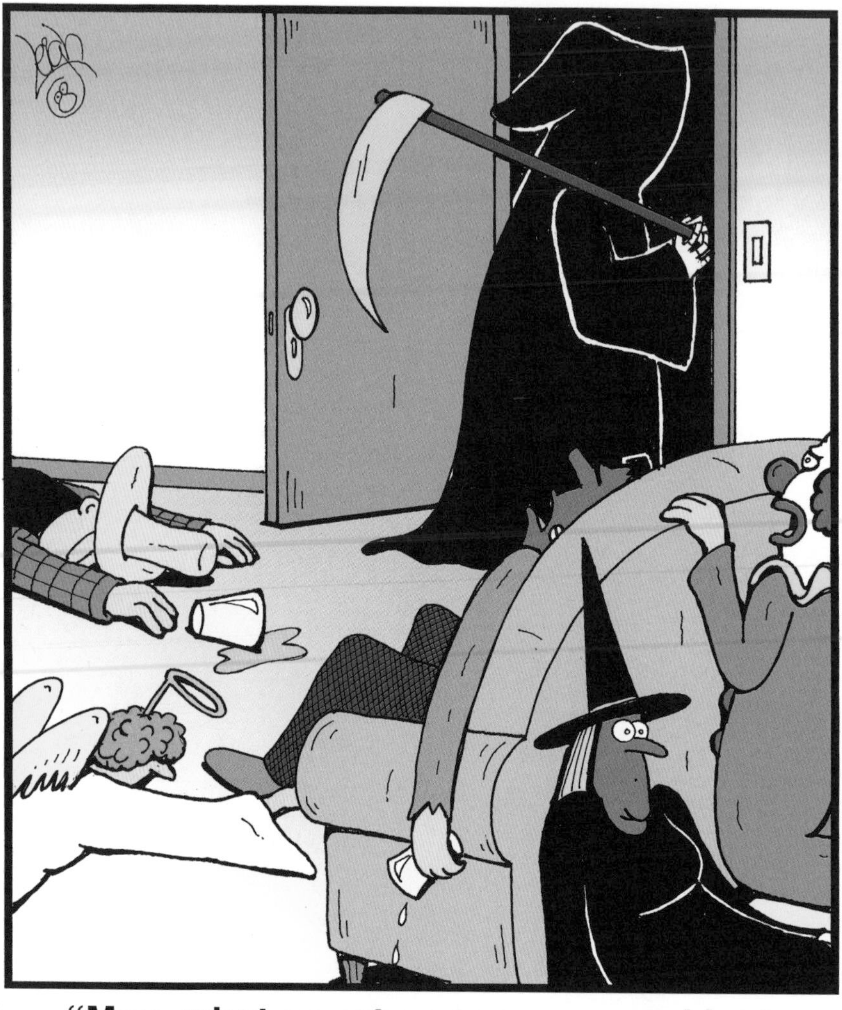

"Man, what a party pooper . . . and just because he didn't win the costume contest."

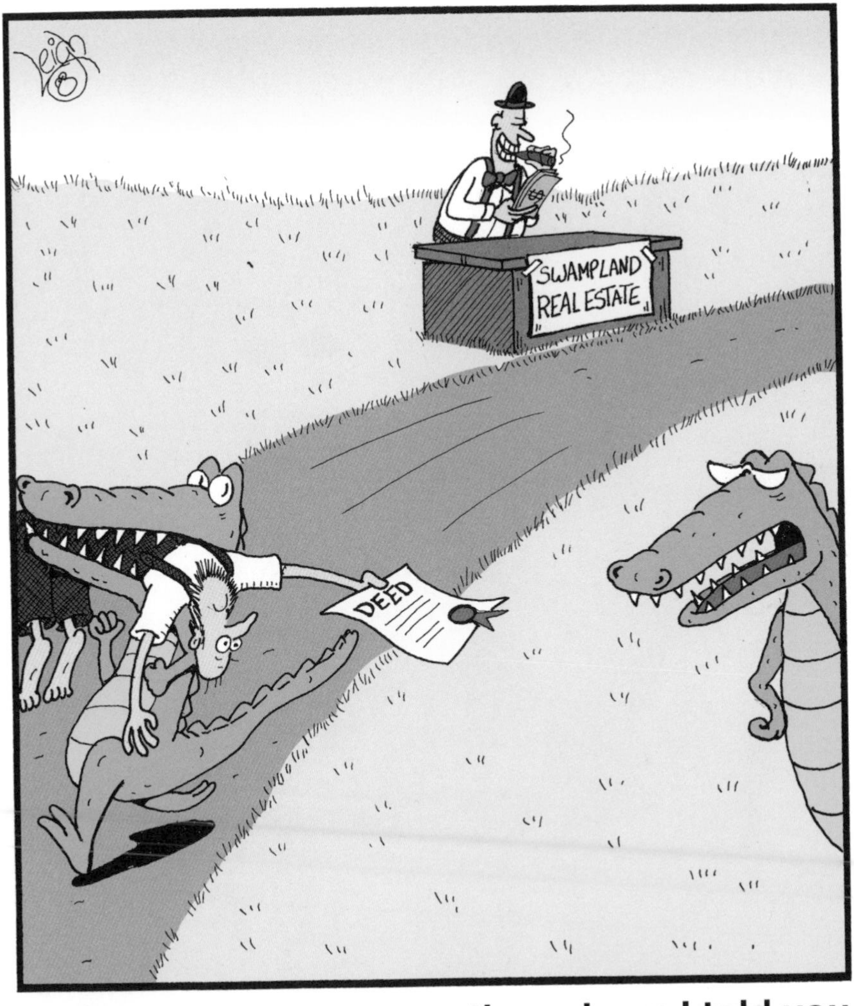
SWAMPLAND
REAL ESTATE
DEED

"Young man, how many times have I told you never to run with a sucker in your mouth?!"

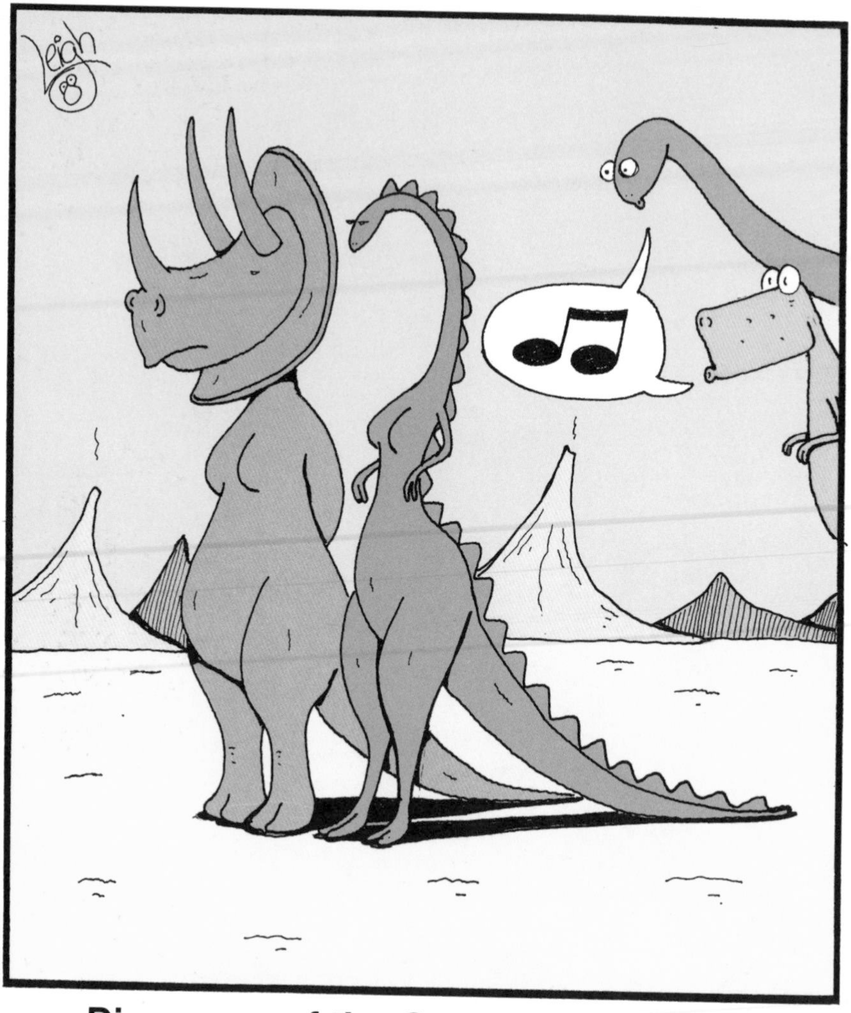

Dinosaurs of the Curvaceous Period

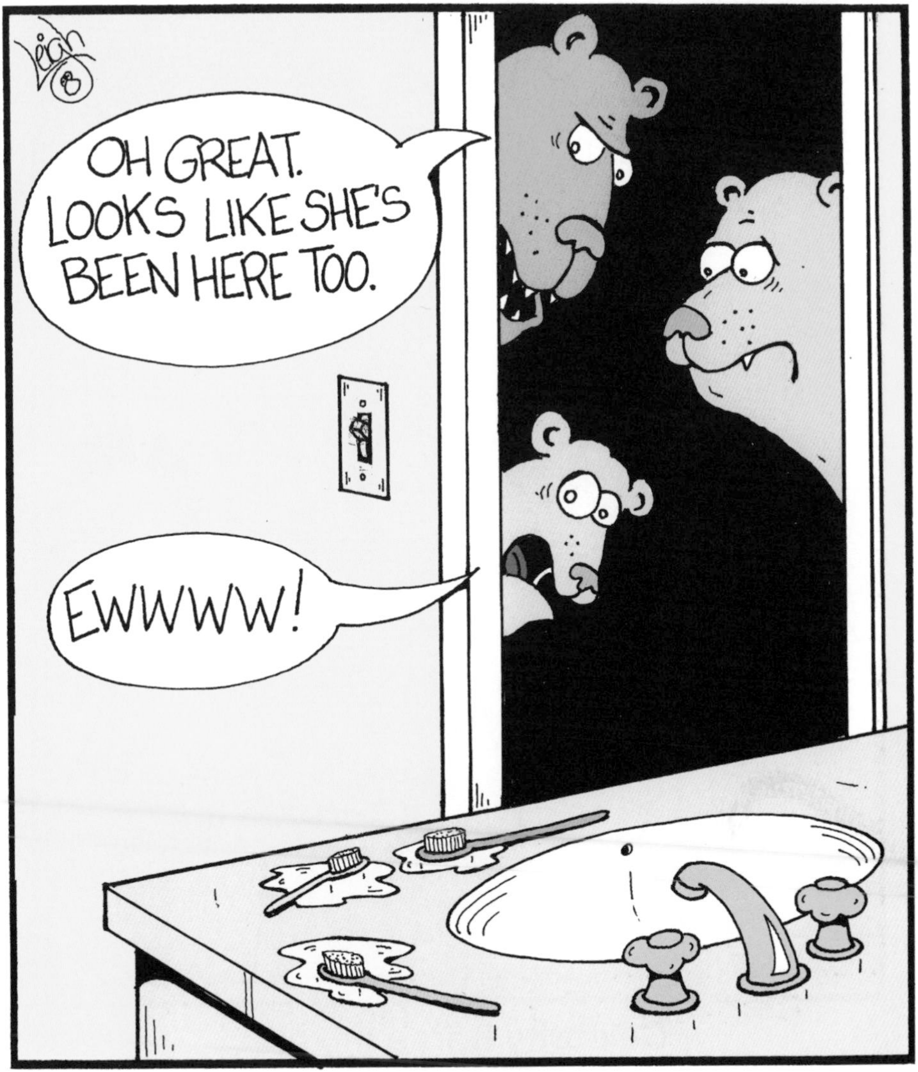
OH GREAT. LOOKS LIKE SHE'S BEEN HERE TOO.
EWWWW!

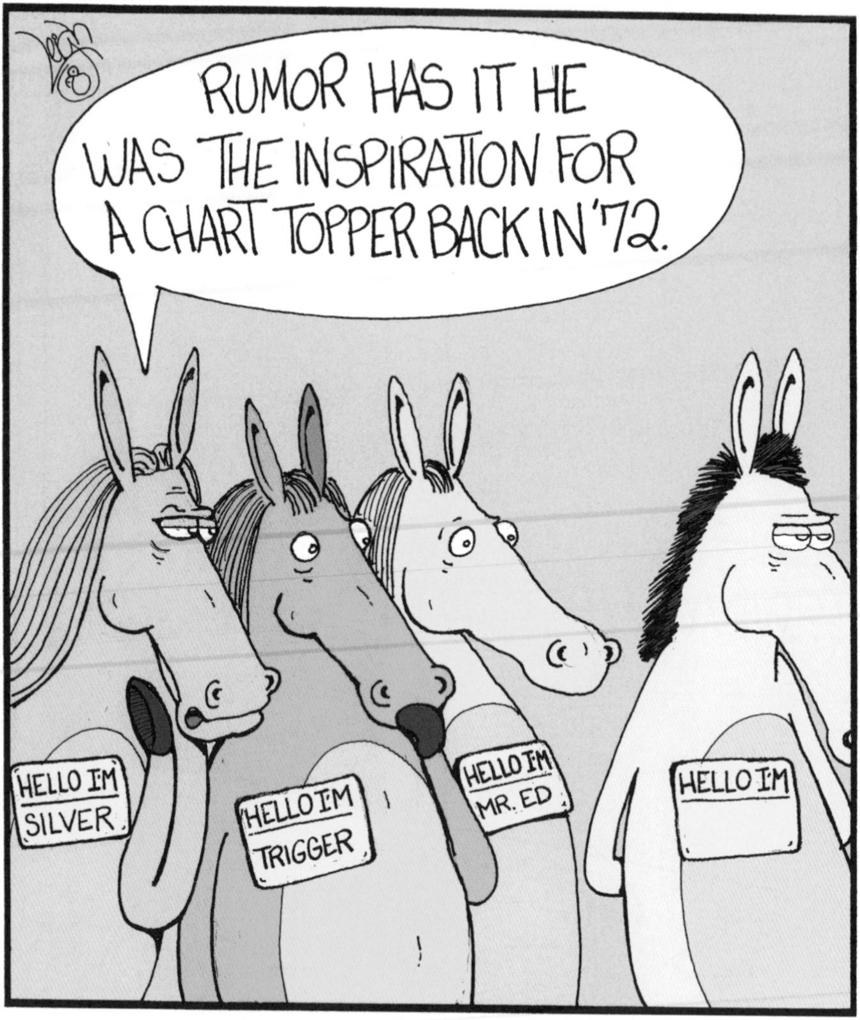
RUMOR HAS IT HE WAS THE INSPIRATION FOR A CHART TOPPER BACK IN '72.
HELLO I'M SILVER
HELLO I'M TRIGGER
HELLO I'M MR. ED
HELLO I'M

Celebrity horse mixers

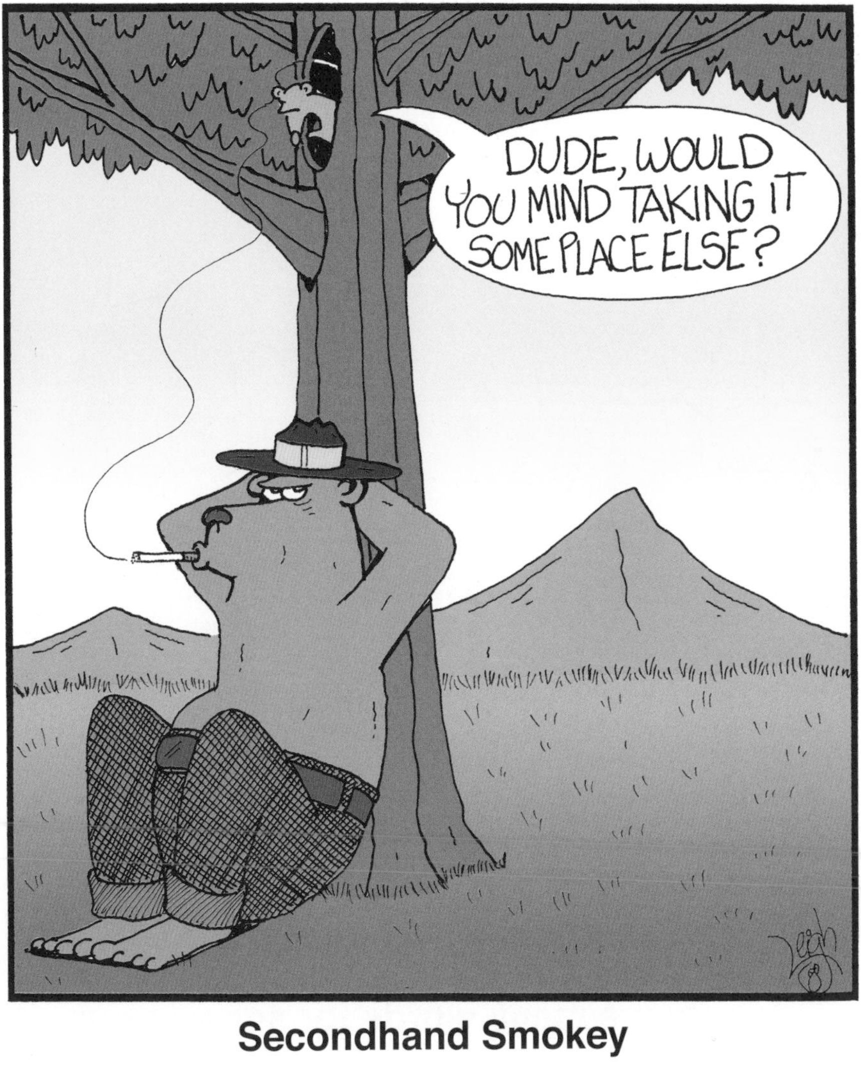
DUDE, WOULD YOU MIND TAKING IT SOME PLACE ELSE?

Secondhand Smokey

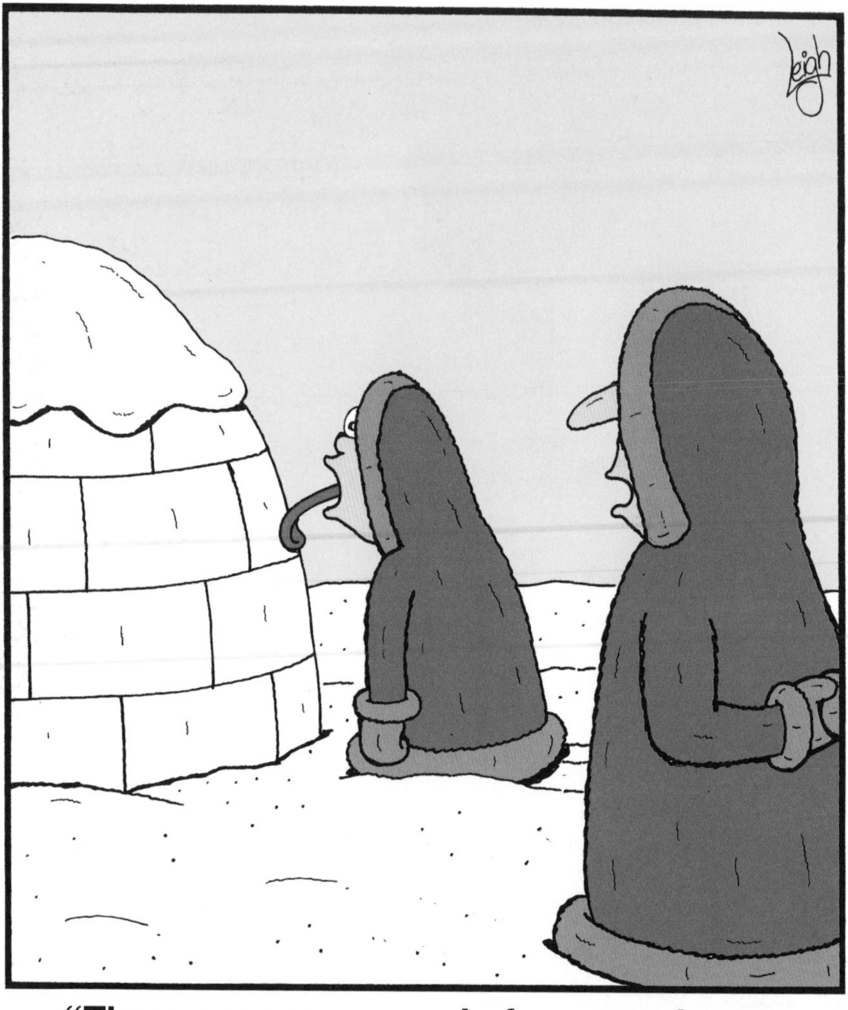
Leigh

"There are many words for snow in our language, Son . . . but only one for moron."

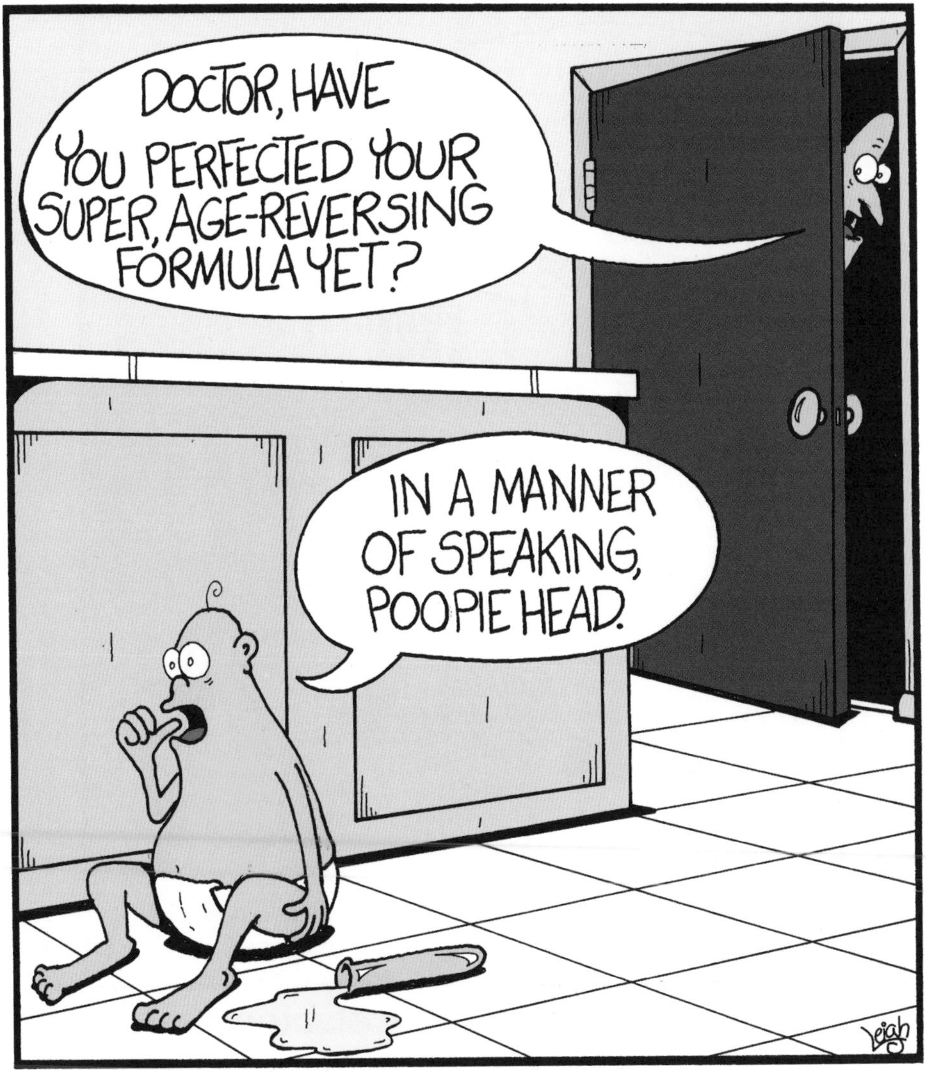
DOCTOR, HAVE YOU PERFECTED YOUR SUPER, AGE-REVERSING FORMULA YET?
IN A MANNER OF SPEAKING, POOPIE HEAD.
Leigh

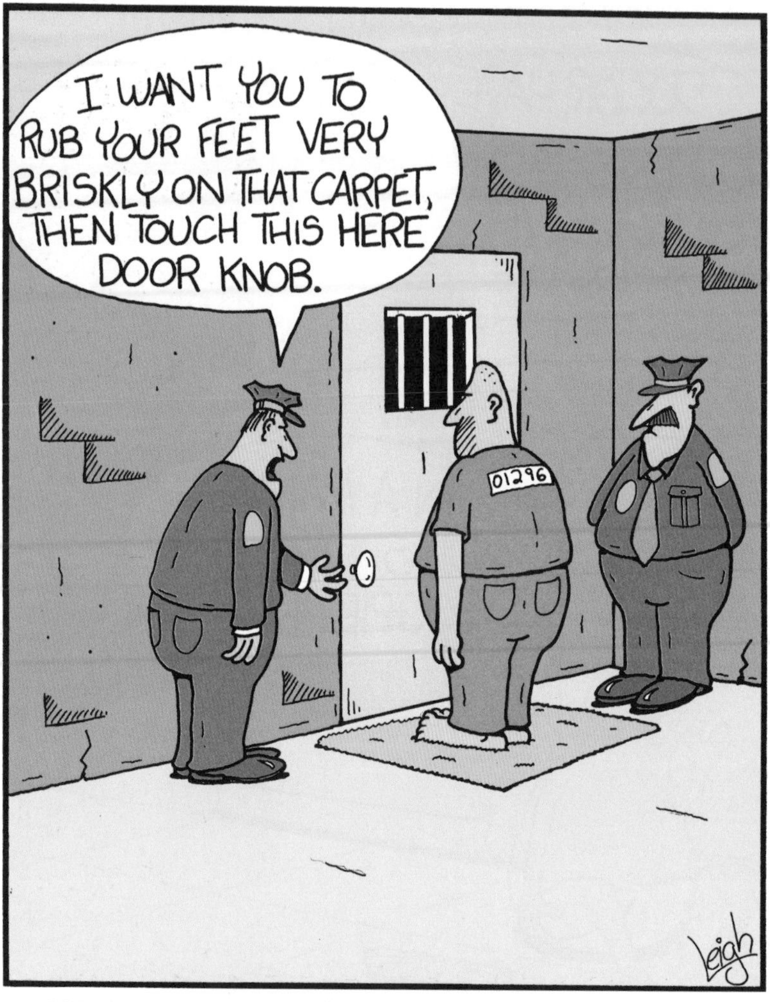
I WANT YOU TO RUB YOUR FEET VERY BRISKLY ON THAT CARPET, THEN TOUCH THIS HERE DOOR KNOB.
01296
Leigh

What they do when the electric chair goes on the blink

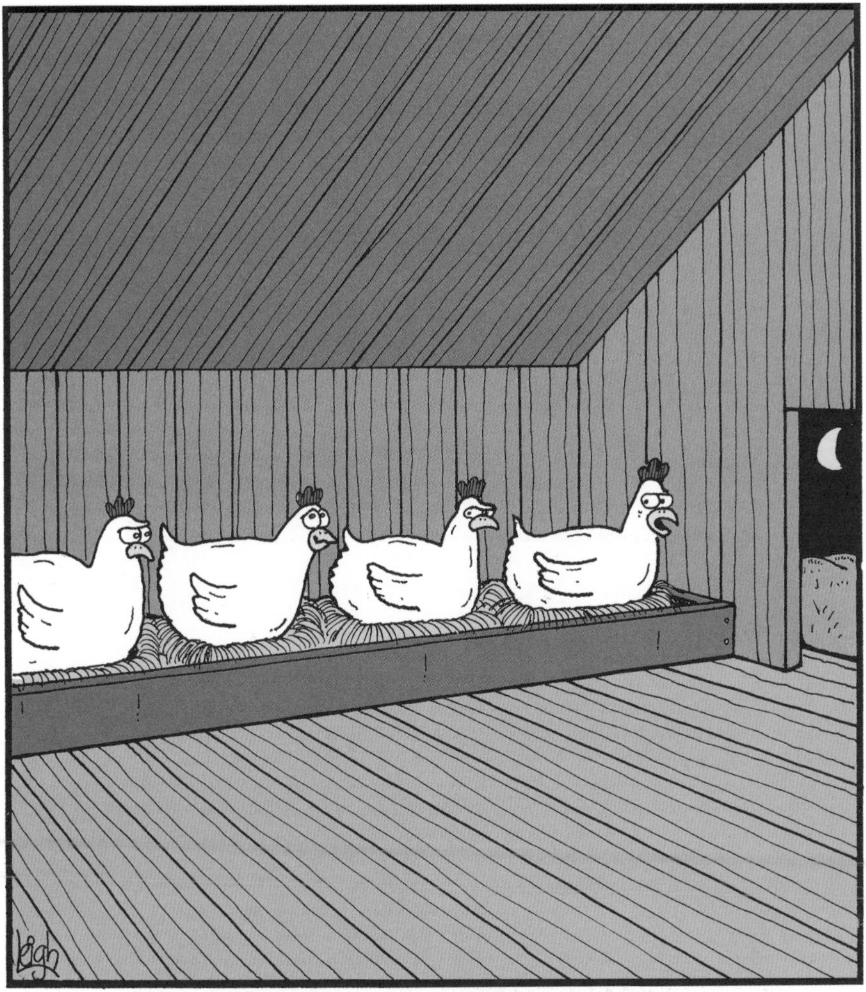
Leigh

"I'm not one to point the finger, but someone around here just laid a particularly rotten egg."

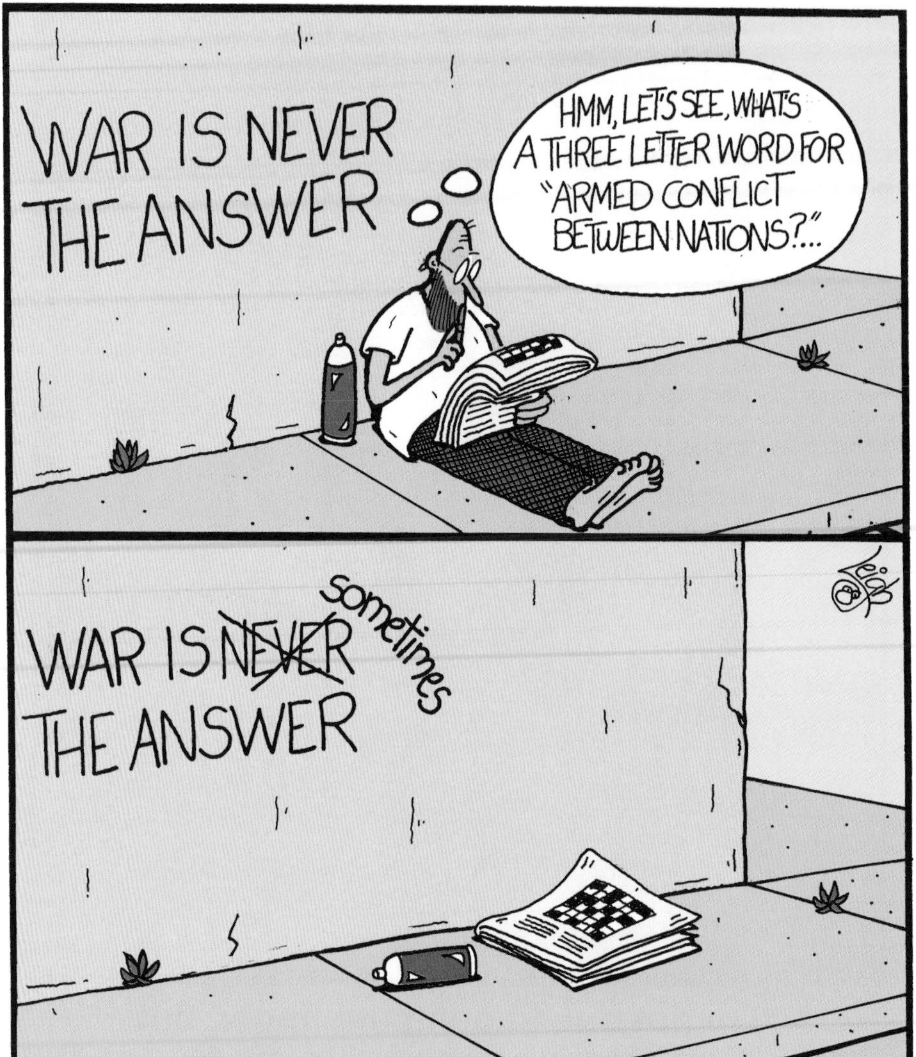
WAR IS NEVER THE ANSWER
HMM, LET'S SEE, WHAT'S A THREE LETTER WORD FOR "ARMED CONFLICT BETWEEN NATIONS?"...
WAR IS NEVER sometimes THE ANSWER

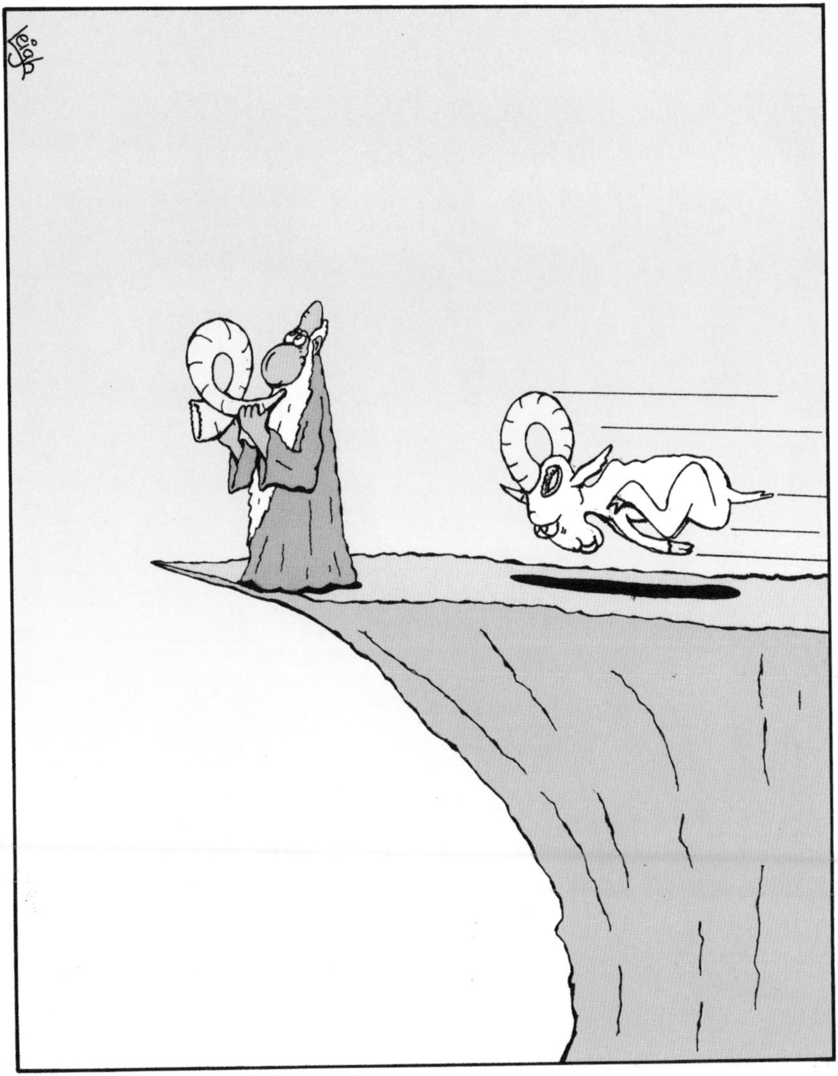
Leigh

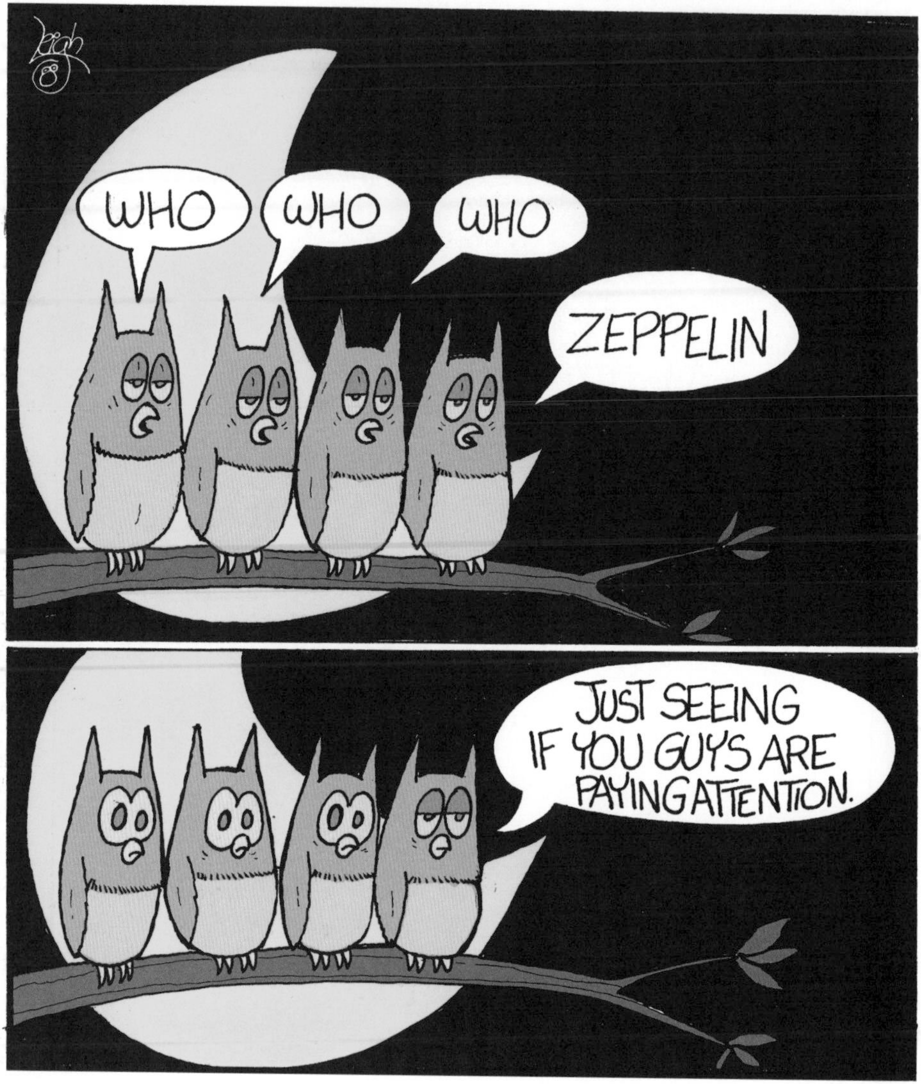
WHO
WHO
WHO
ZEPPELIN
JUST SEEING IF YOU GUYS ARE PAYING ATTENTION.

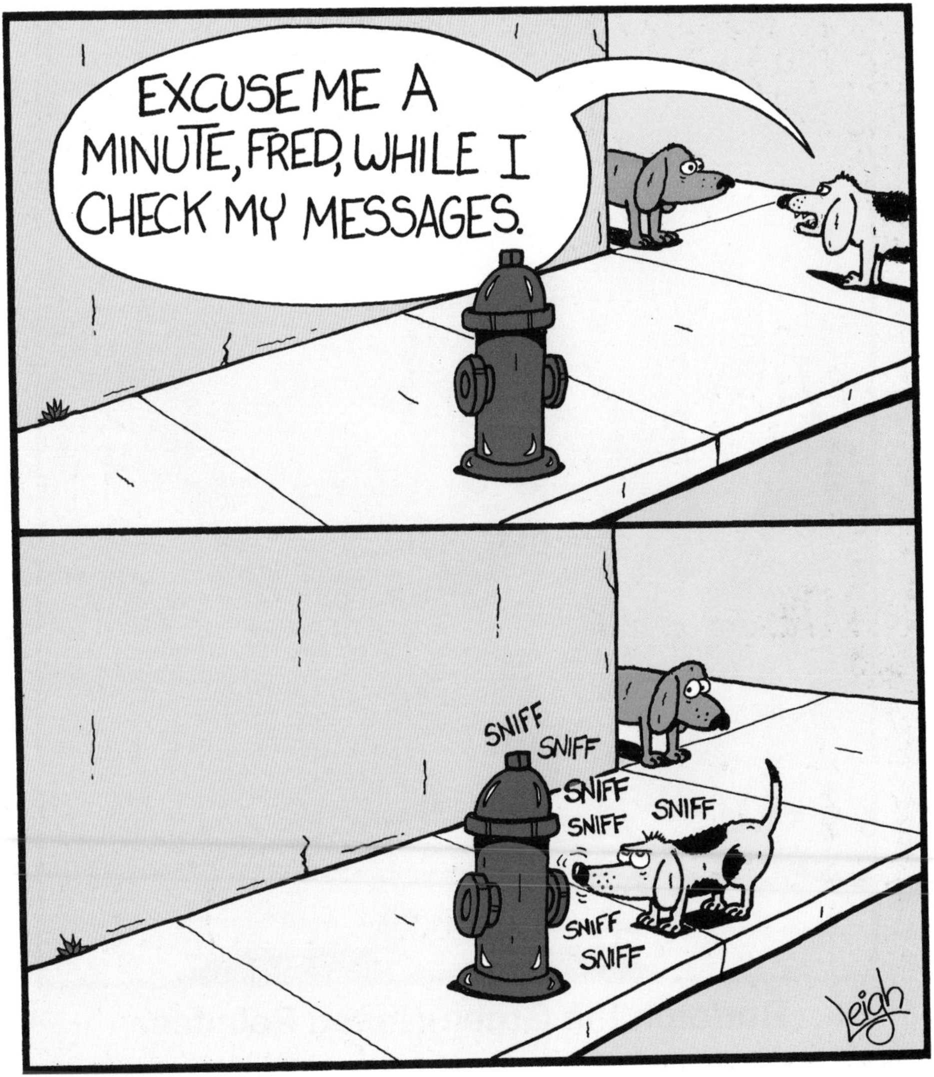
EXCUSE ME A MINUTE, FRED, WHILE I CHECK MY MESSAGES.
SNIFF SNIFF SNIFF SNIFF SNIFF SNIFF SNIFF
Leigh

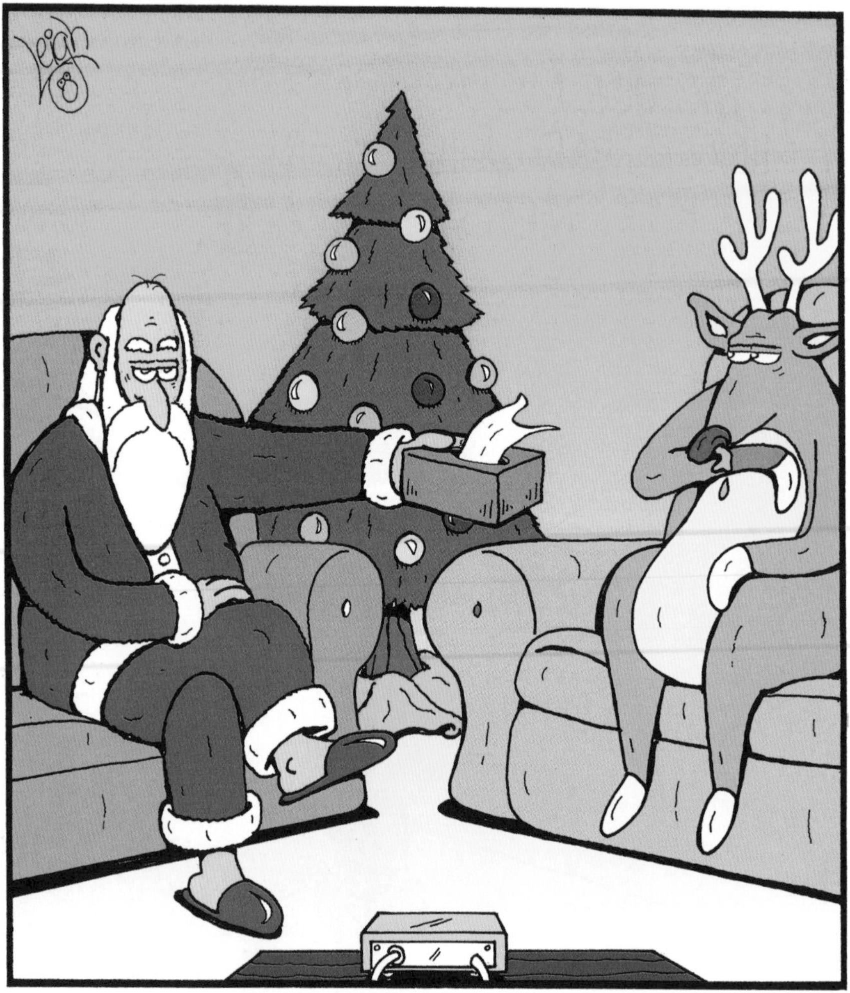
Leigh

Rudolph the Green-Nosed Reindeer

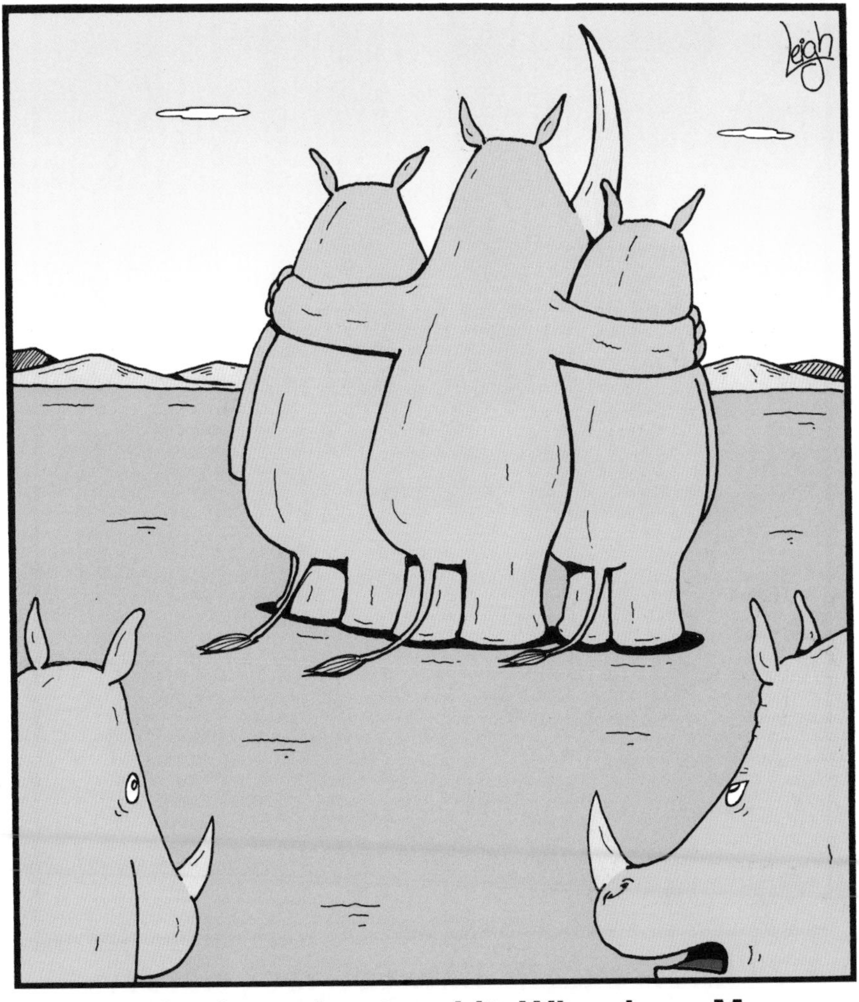
Leigh

"I just don't understand it. Why does Murray always get all the girls? What does he have that we don't?!"

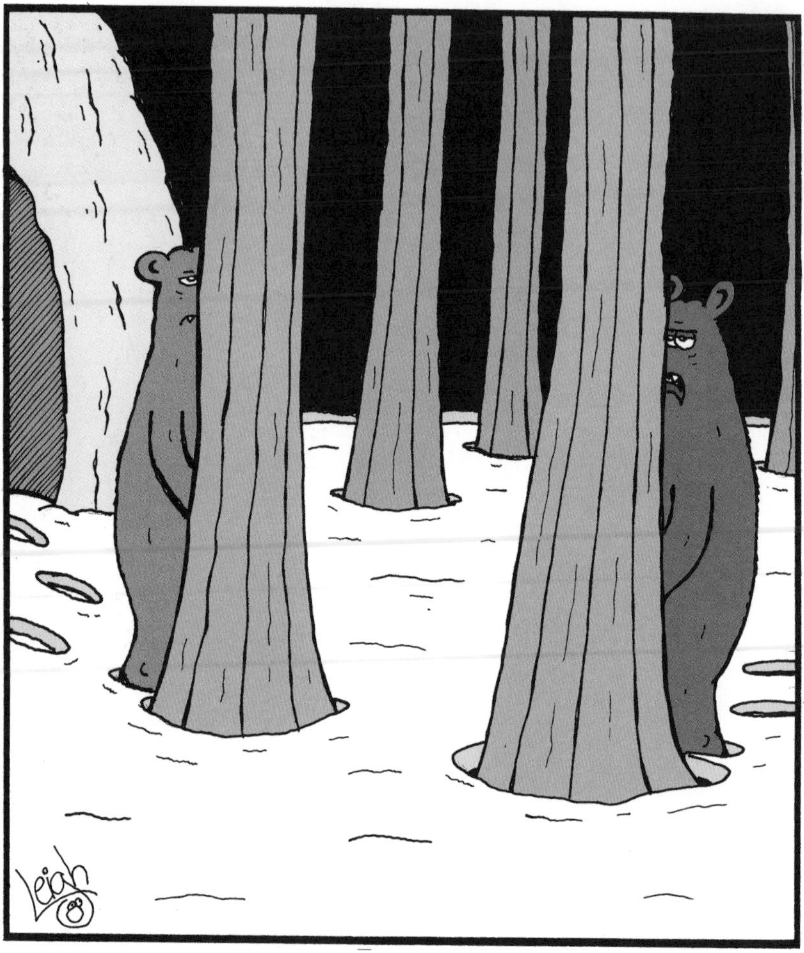
Leigh
88

"I know exactly how you feel, Harvey. Middle age definitely has its drawbacks. I used to be able to sleep through the entire winter. Now I'm lucky to last a week."

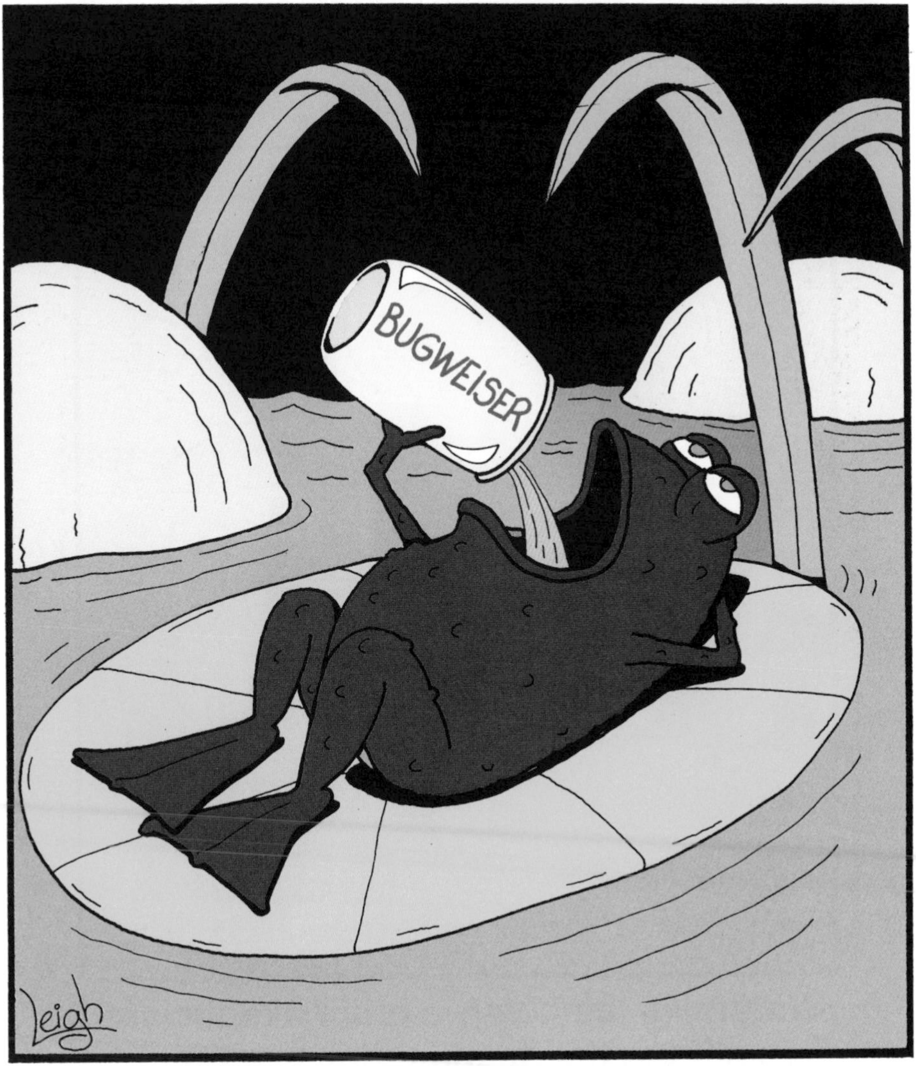
BUGWEISER
Leigh

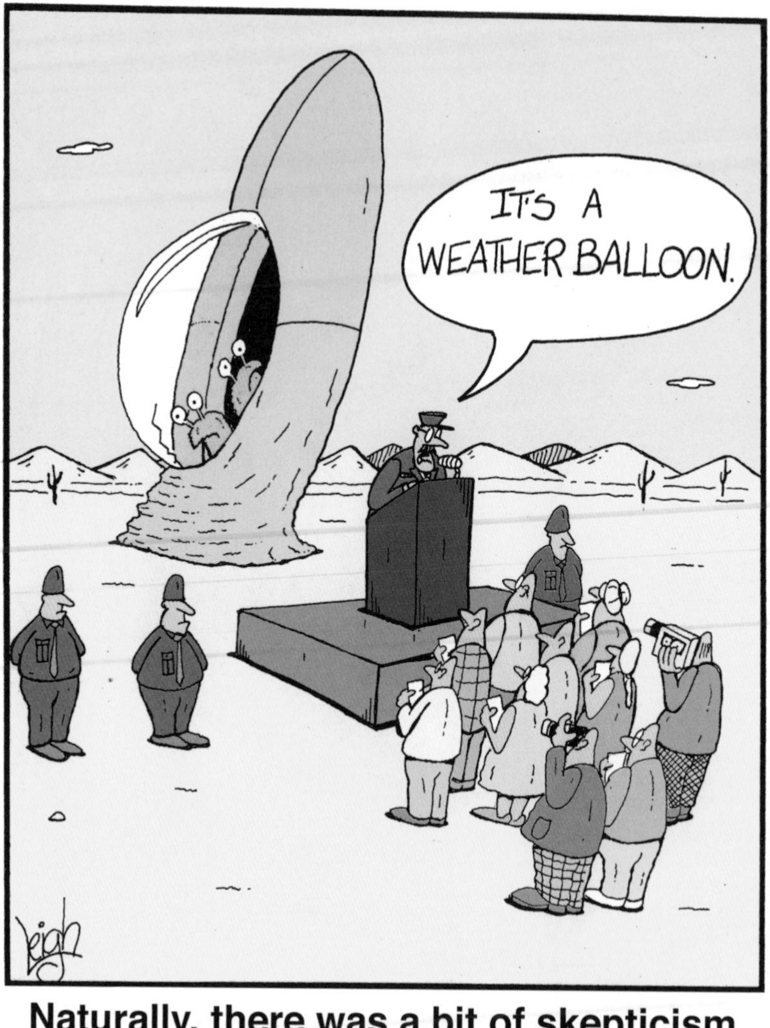
IT'S A WEATHER BALLOON.
Leigh

Naturally, there was a bit of skepticism among the media regarding the official Air Force explanation.

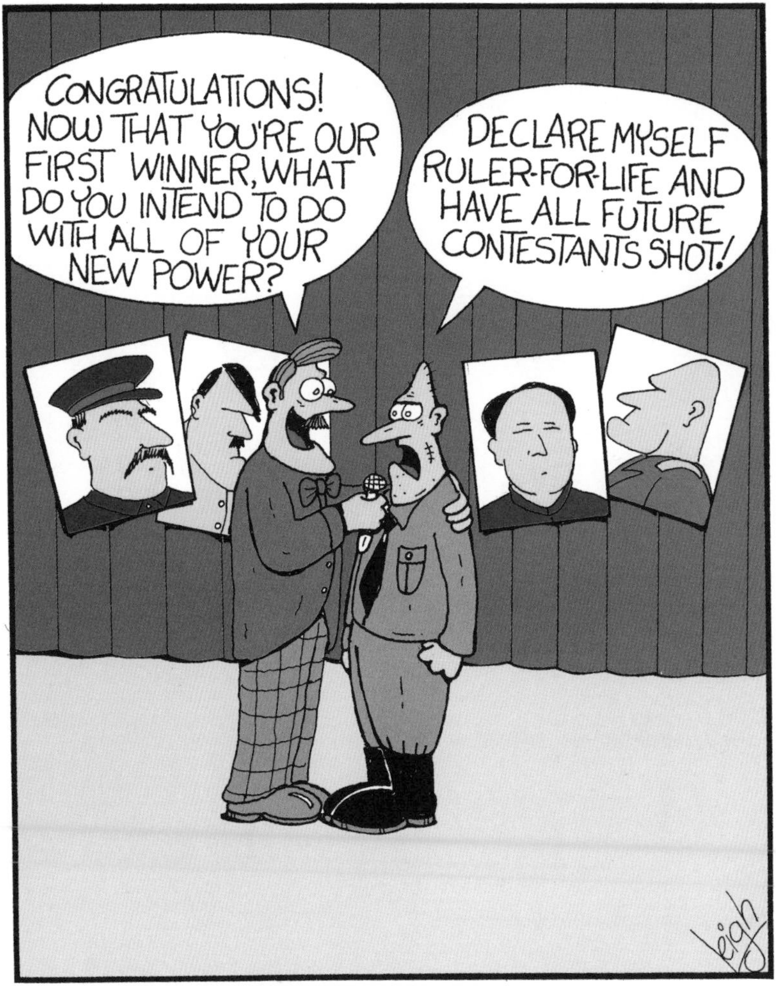
CONGRATULATIONS! NOW THAT YOU'RE OUR FIRST WINNER, WHAT DO YOU INTEND TO DO WITH ALL OF YOUR NEW POWER?
DECLARE MYSELF RULER-FOR-LIFE AND HAVE ALL FUTURE CONTESTANTS SHOT!
leigh

Why the *Dictator for a Day* show only lasted one episode

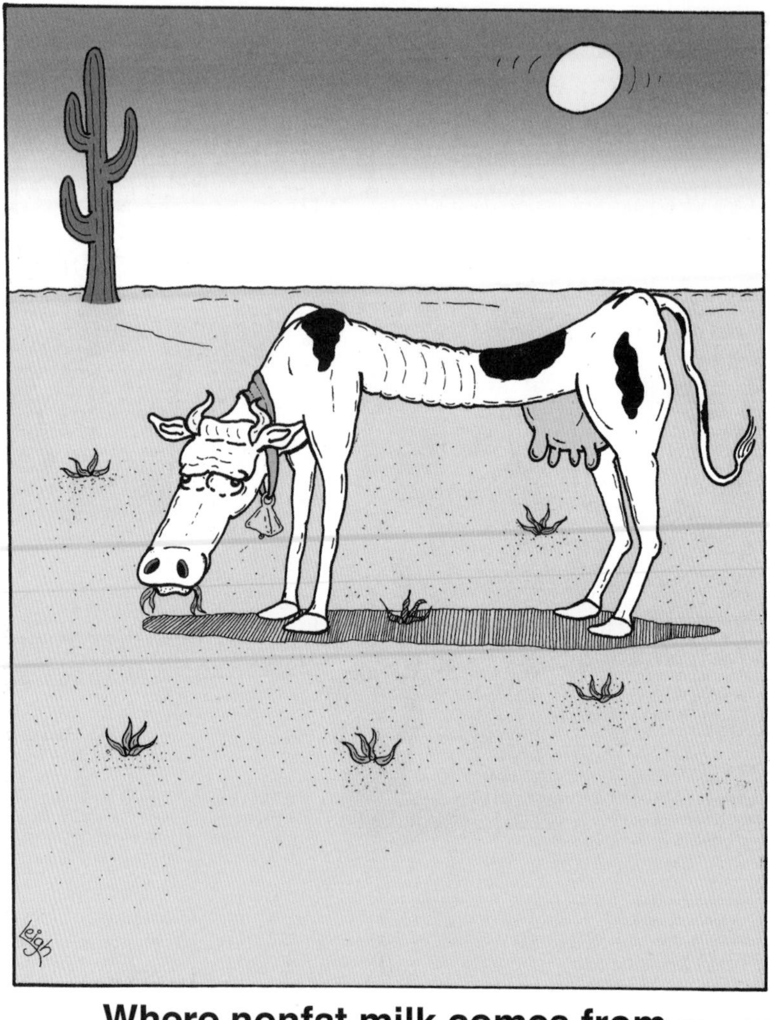
Leigh

Where nonfat milk comes from

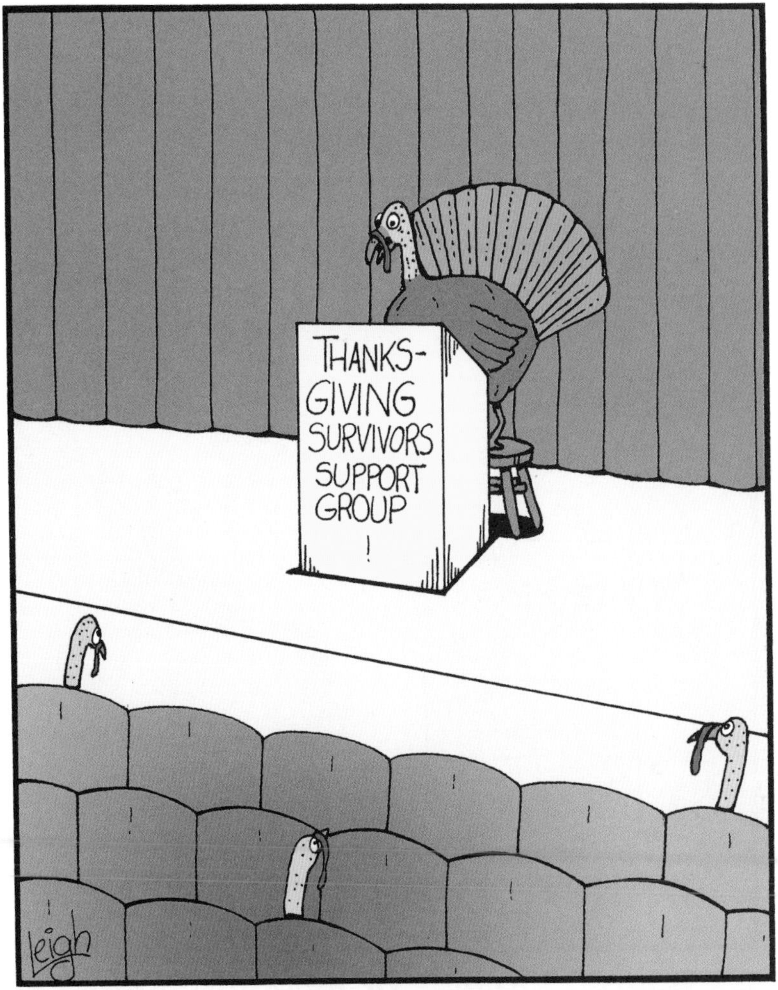
THANKS-
GIVING
SURVIVORS
SUPPORT
GROUP
Leigh

"I'm sure you've all noticed by now that after the holiday there aren't many of us, pardon the expression, 'leftover.'"

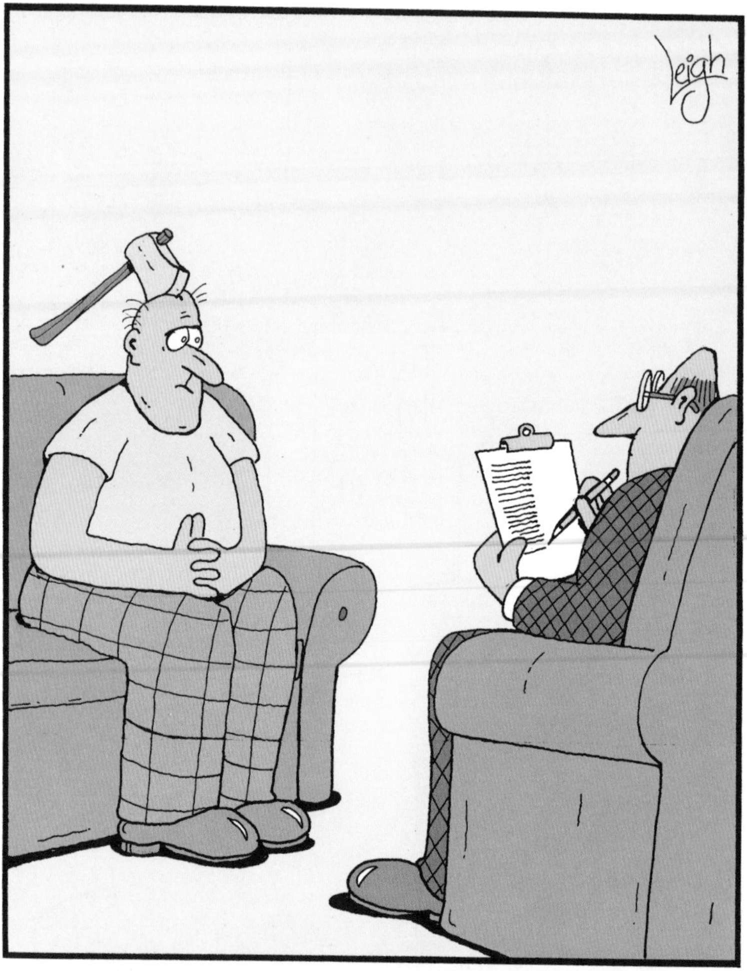
Leigh

Everything was proceeding quite smoothly on Edgar's health insurance application, until the nagging question about preexisting conditions came up.

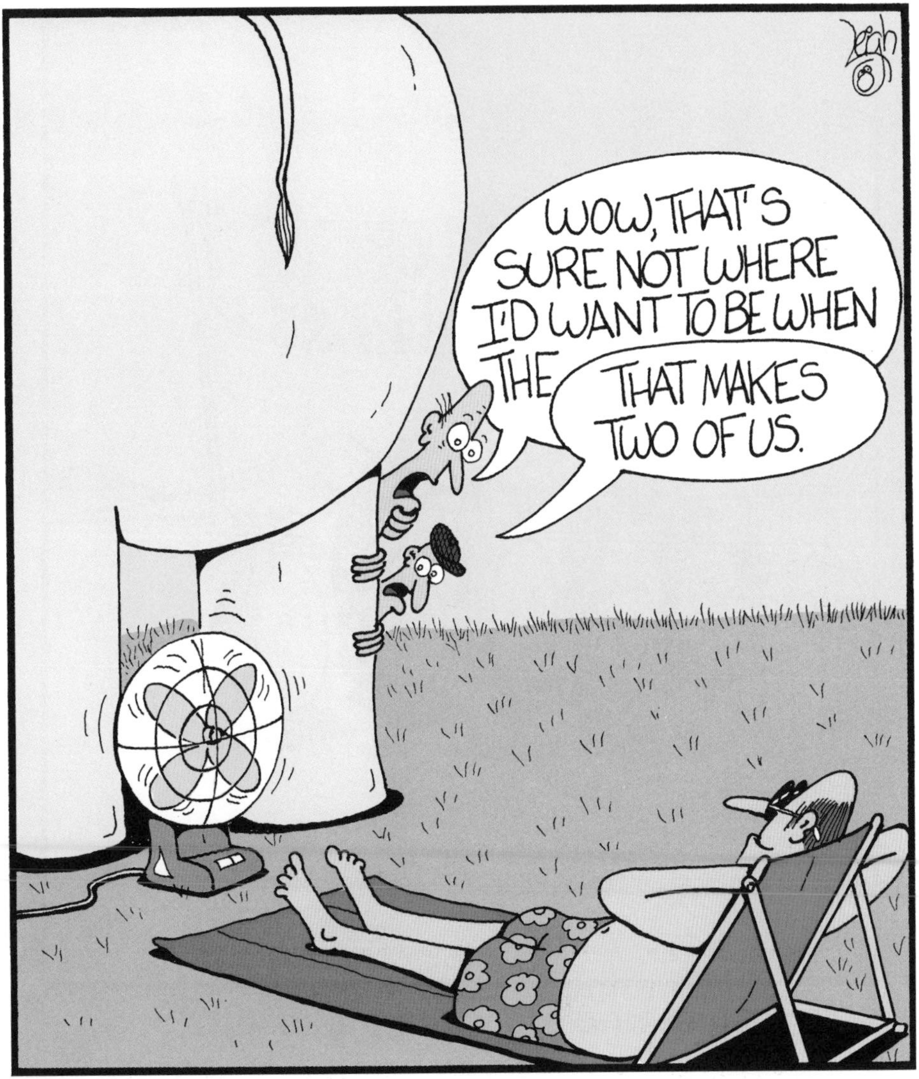
WOW, THAT'S SURE NOT WHERE I'D WANT TO BE WHEN THE
THAT MAKES TWO OF US.

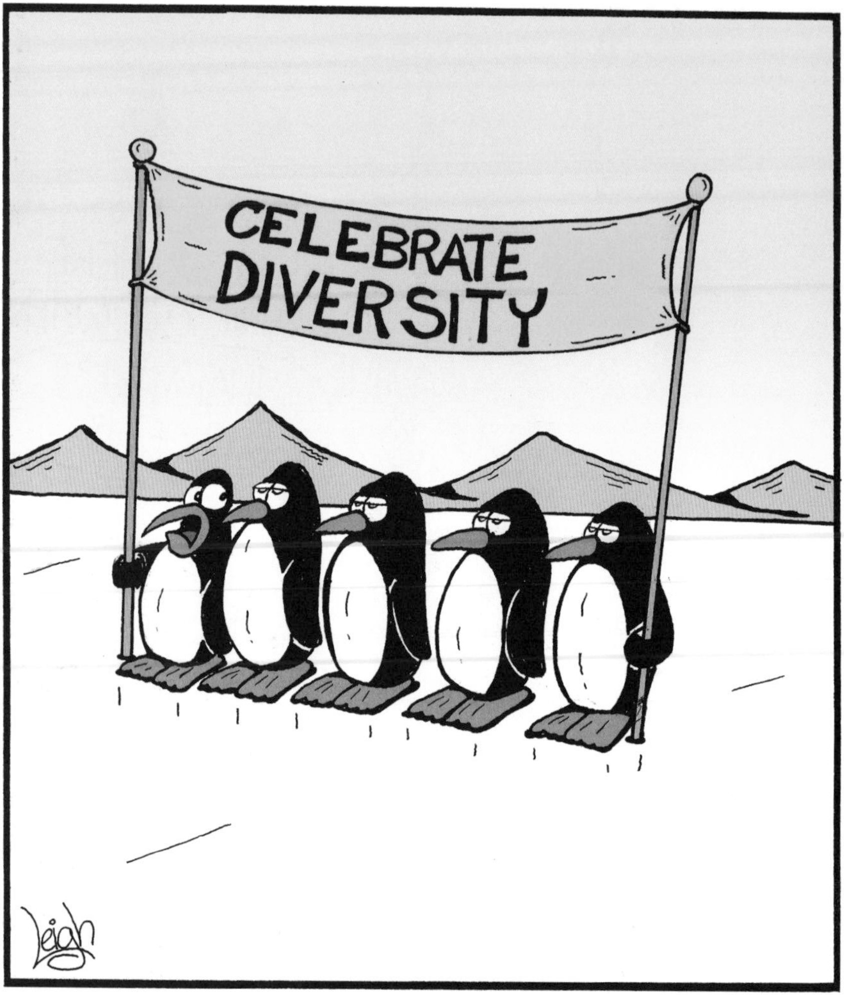
CELEBRATE
DIVERSITY
Leigh

"Just who are we trying to kid?"

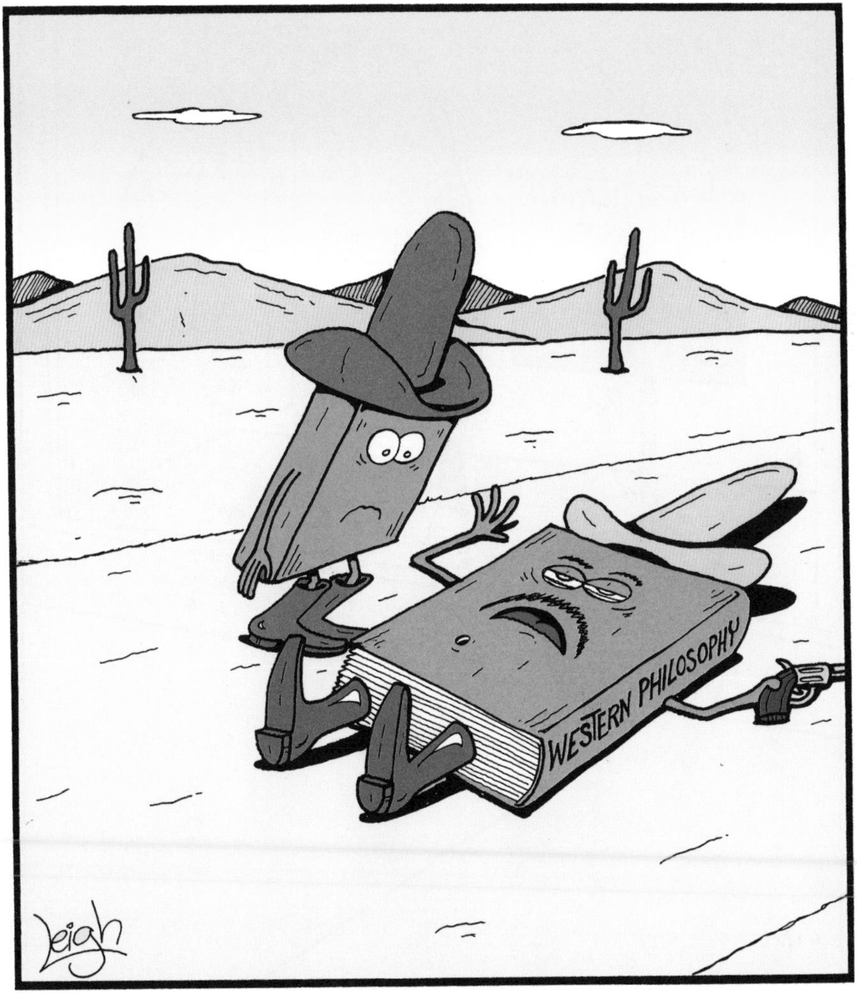
WESTERN PHILOSOPHY
Leigh

"It looks as though this is my final chapter, Son. But don't worry about me . . . sooner or later we all have to check out."

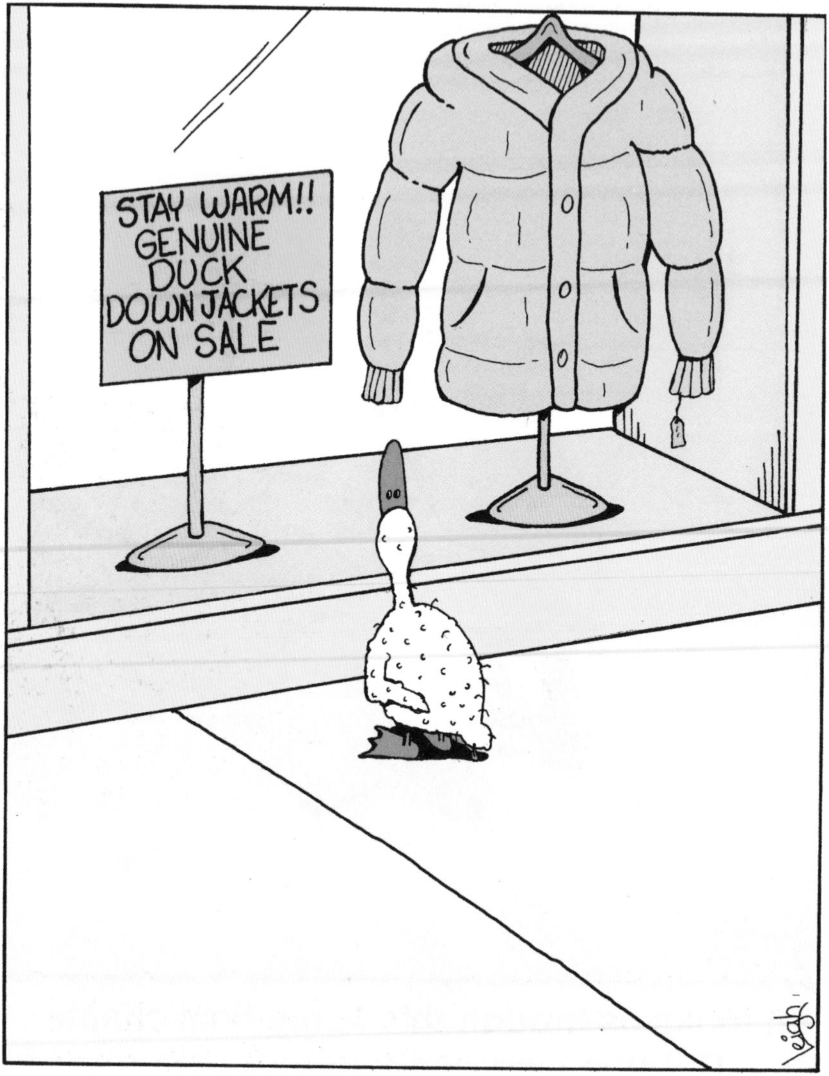
STAY WARM!!
GENUINE
DUCK
DOWN JACKETS
ON SALE

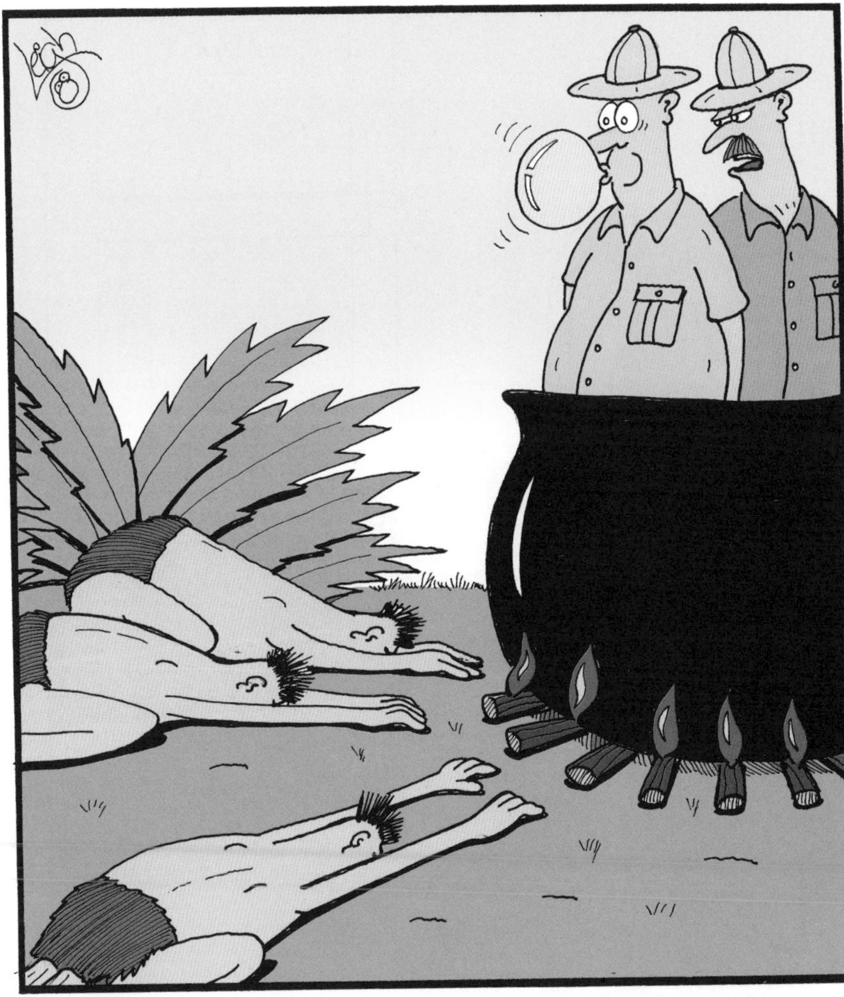

“Well, Winthrop, it seems as though that annoying little habit of yours may prove somewhat useful after all.”

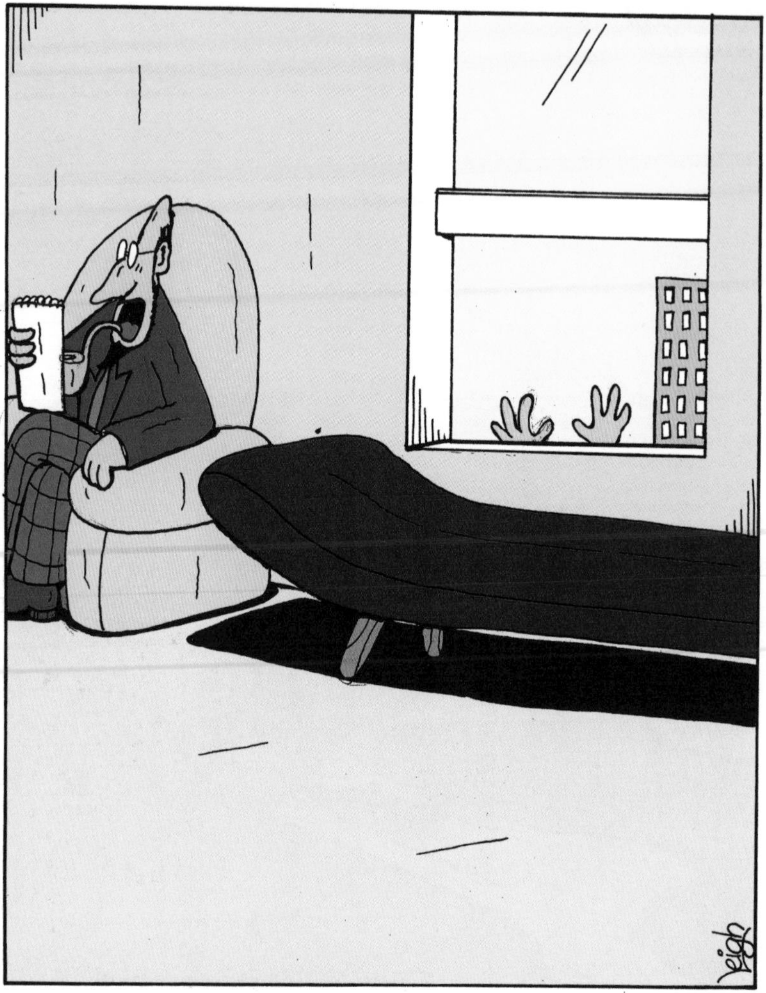
Leigh

"Well, Mr. Johnson, now that your fear of heights is cured, perhaps we can get to work on those suicidal tendencies of yours."

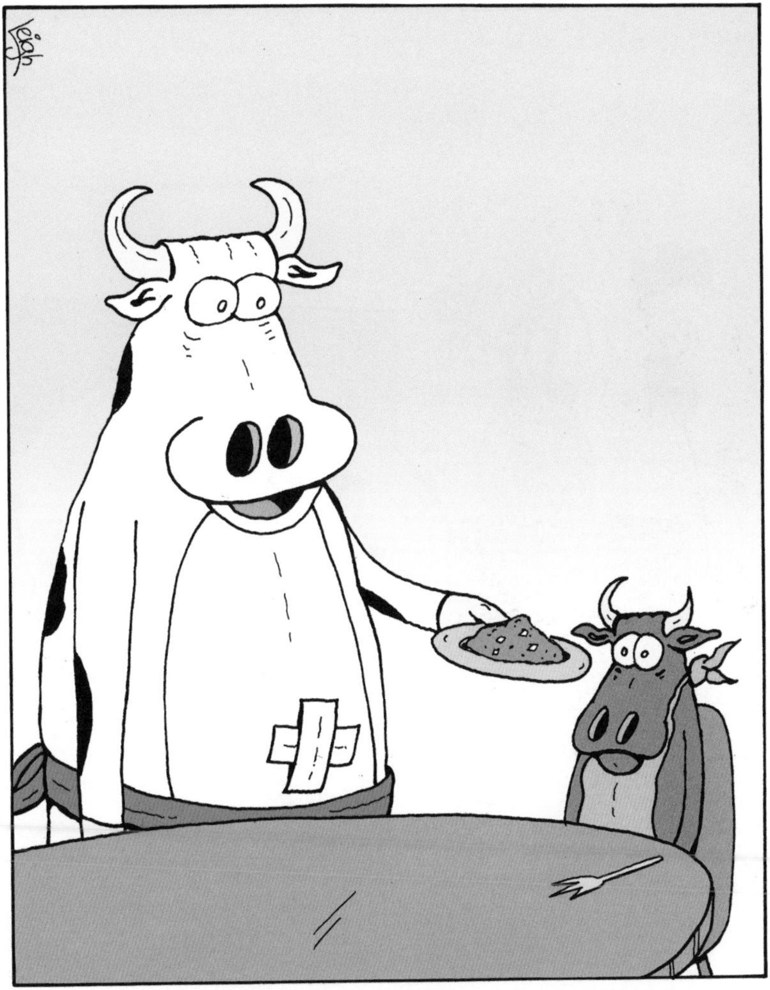
Leigh

"Here you go . . . It's my famous liver and onions."

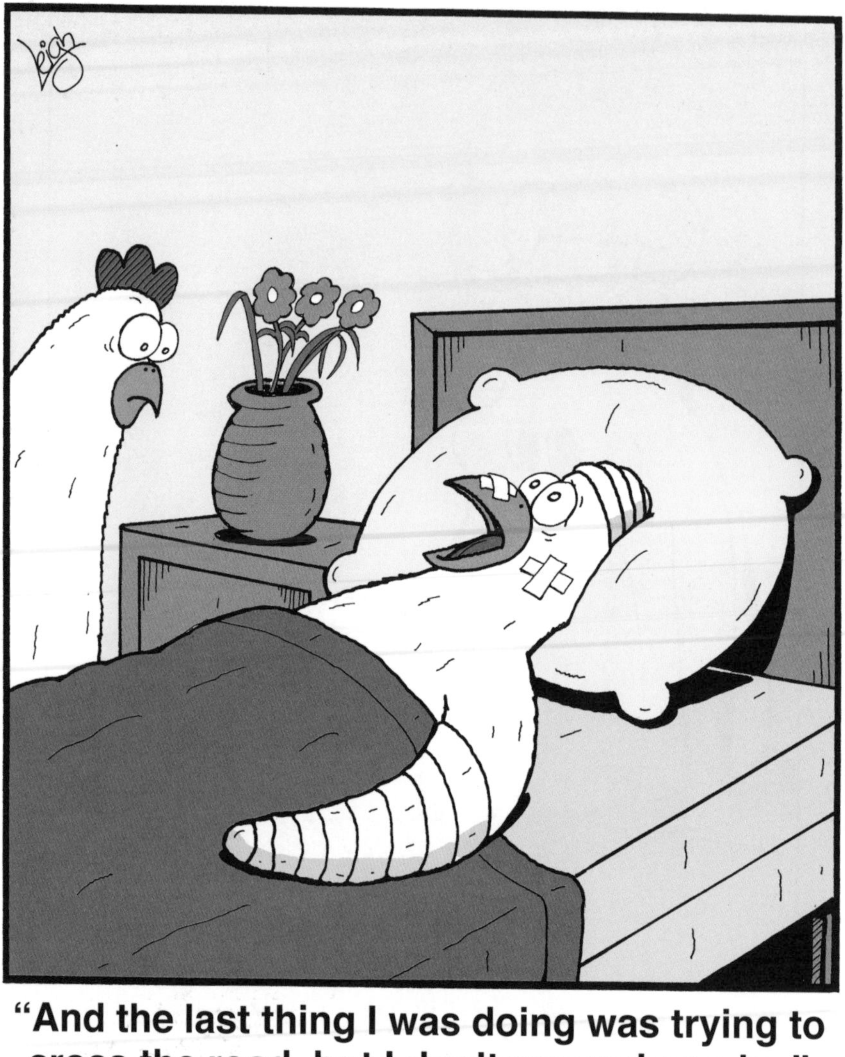
Leigh

"And the last thing I was doing was trying to cross the road, but I don't remember why."

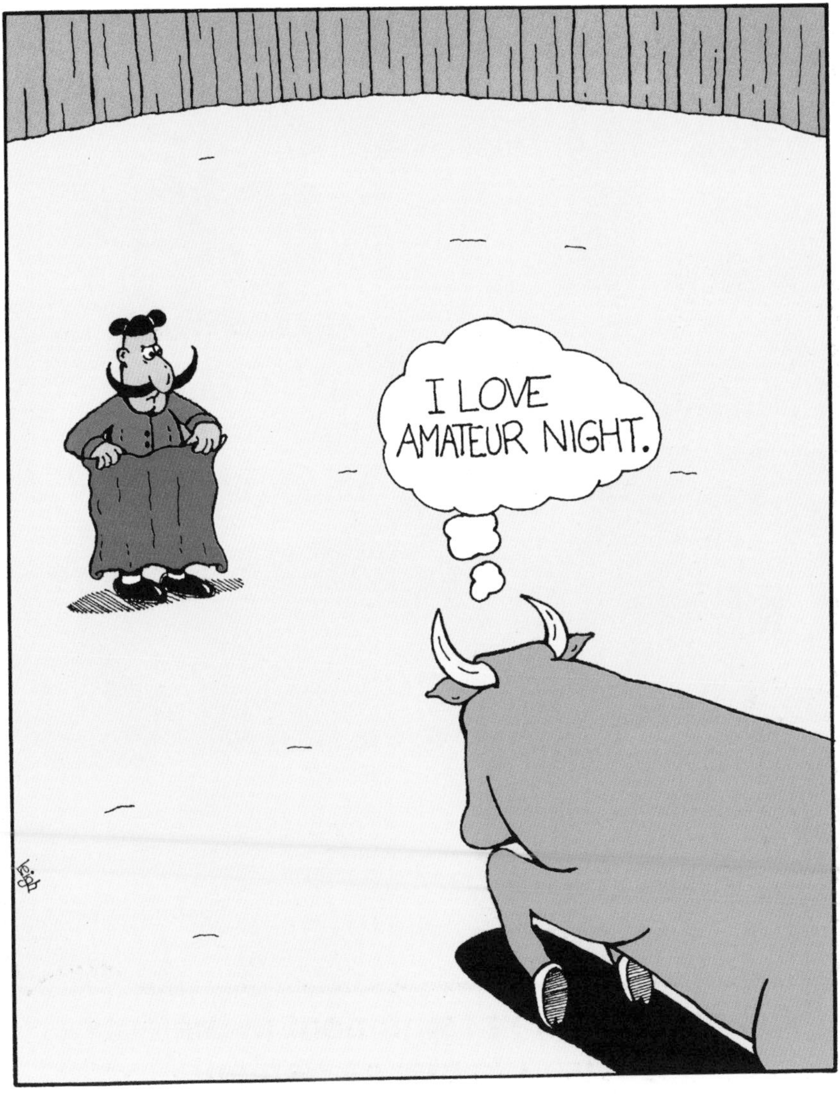
I LOVE AMATEUR NIGHT.

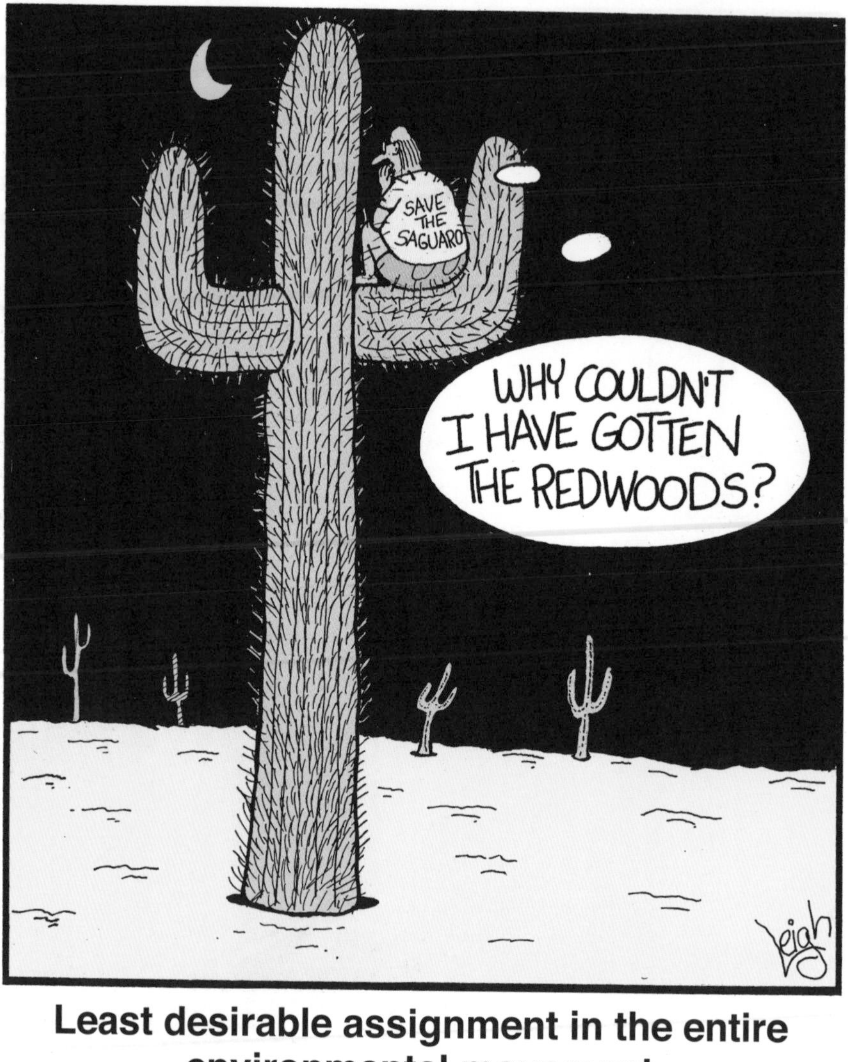
SAVE THE SAGUARO
WHY COULDN'T I HAVE GOTTEN THE REDWOODS?
leigh

Least desirable assignment in the entire environmental movement

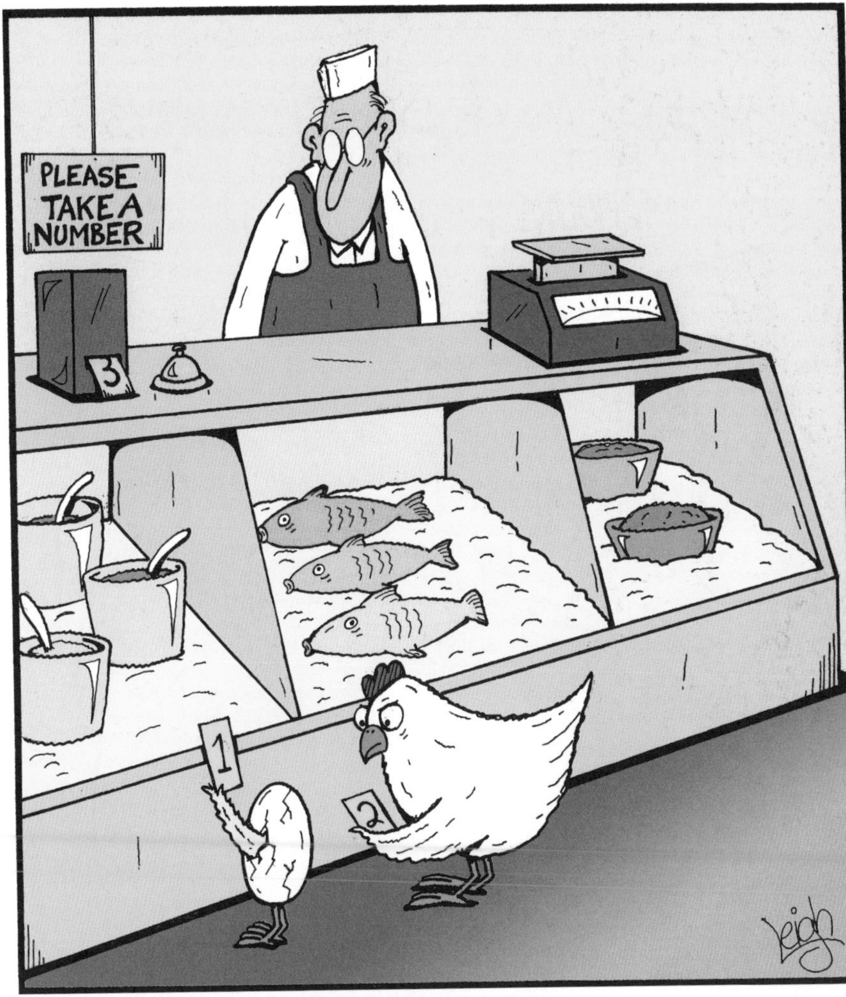
PLEASE
TAKE A
NUMBER
3
1
2
Leigh

The age-old question at long last put to rest

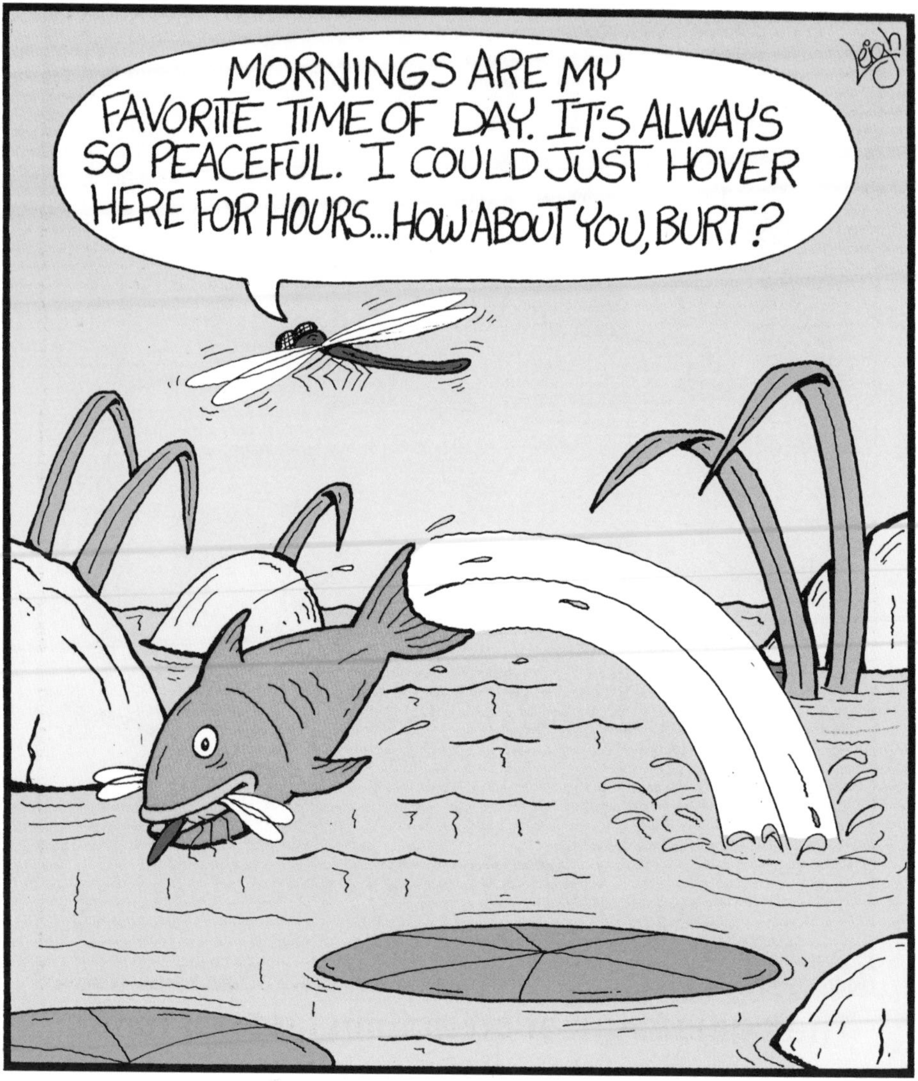
MORNINGS ARE MY FAVORITE TIME OF DAY. IT'S ALWAYS SO PEACEFUL. I COULD JUST HOVER HERE FOR HOURS...HOW ABOUT YOU, BURT?
Leigh

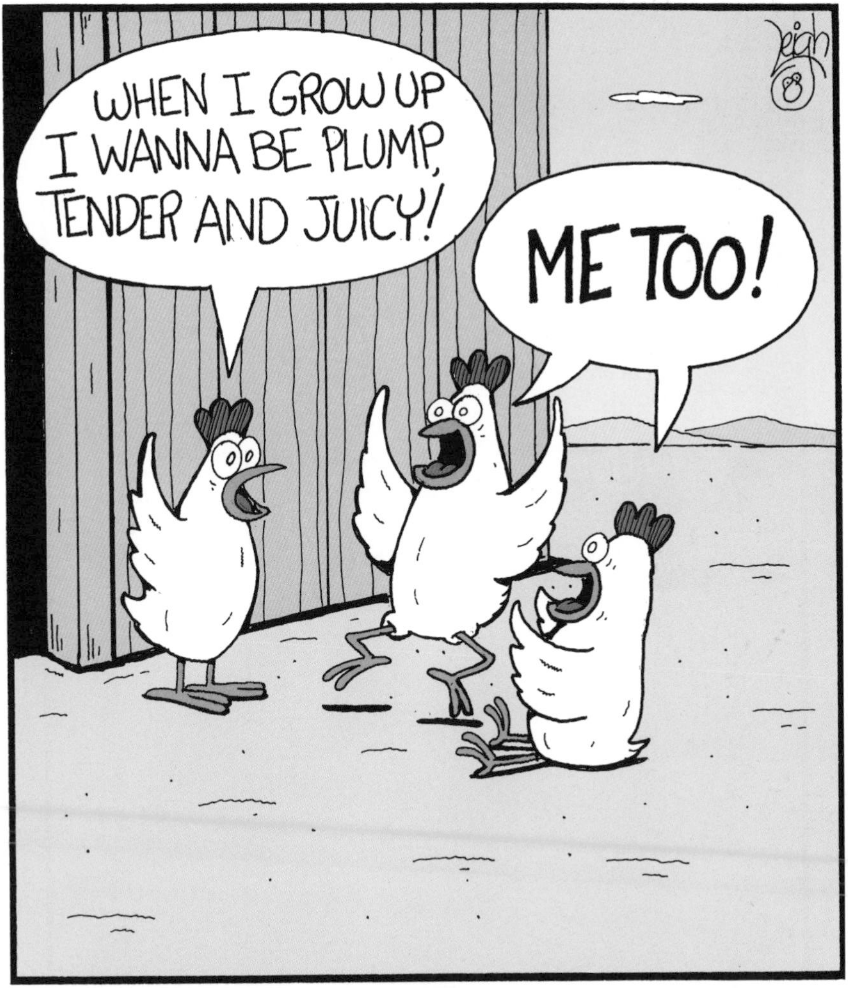
WHEN I GROW UP I WANNA BE PLUMP, TENDER AND JUICY!
ME TOO!

The hazards of advertising on young, impressionable minds

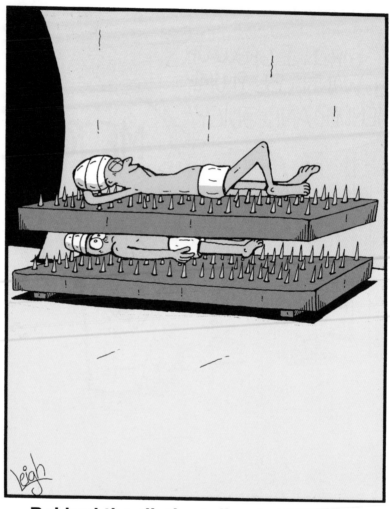

**Raj had the distinct disadvantage of
always getting the bottom bunk.**

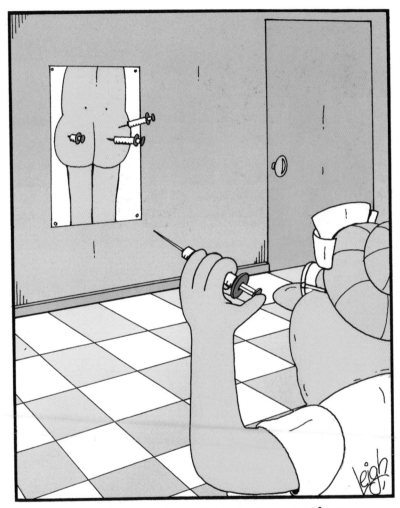

Nursing school target practice

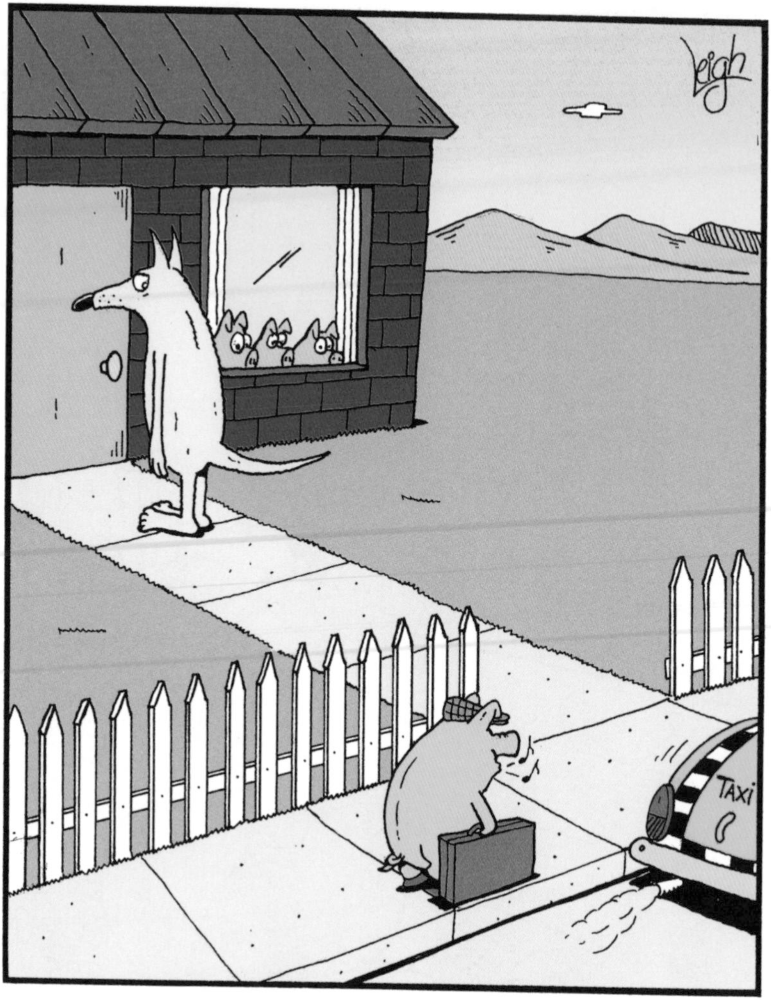
Leigh
TAXI

The timing could not have been worse for an impromptu visit from the fourth little pig.

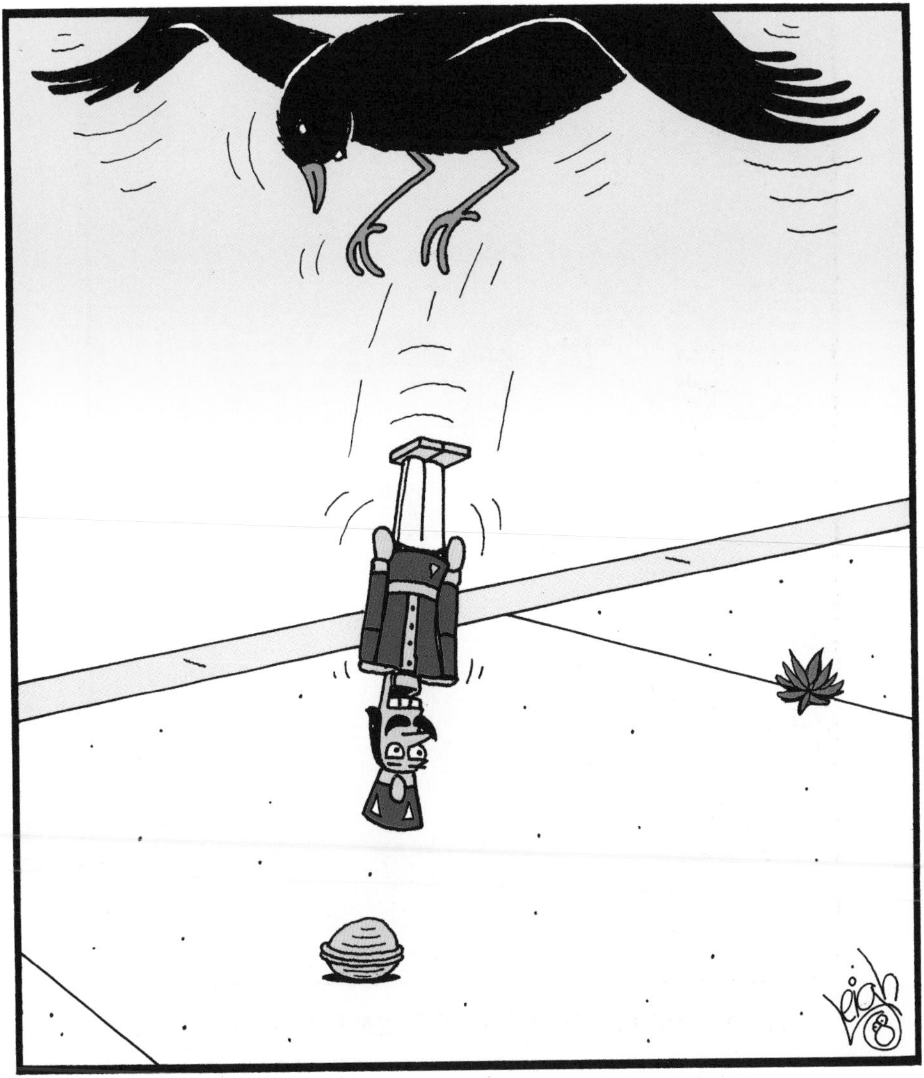

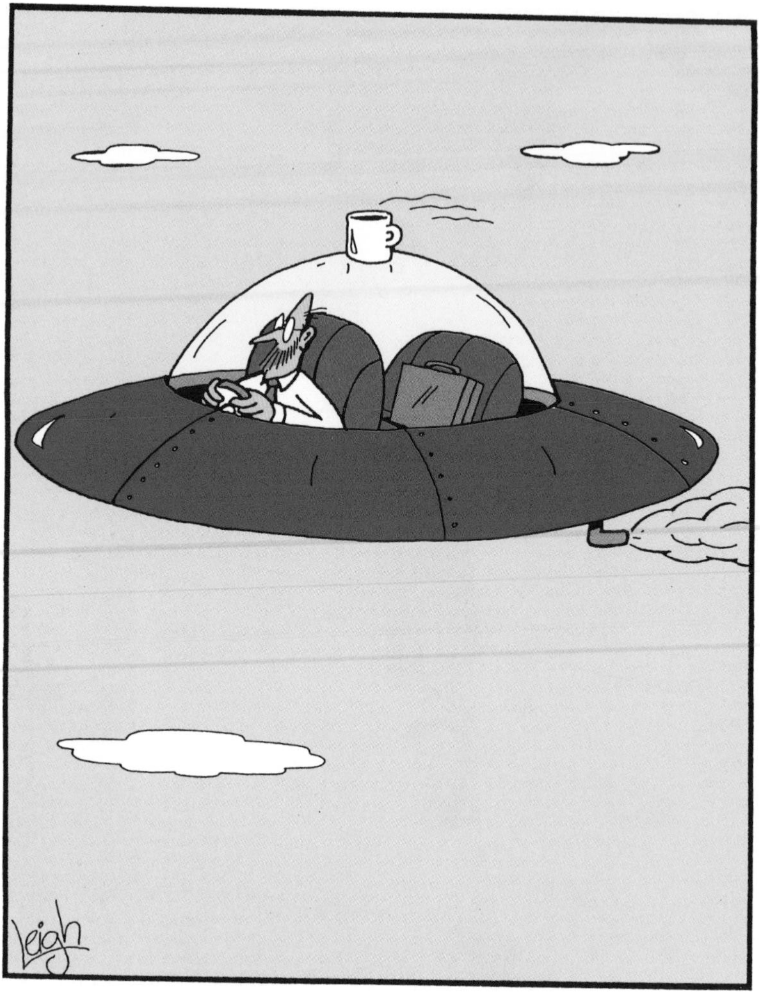
Leigh

**Technology advances;
people stay the same.**

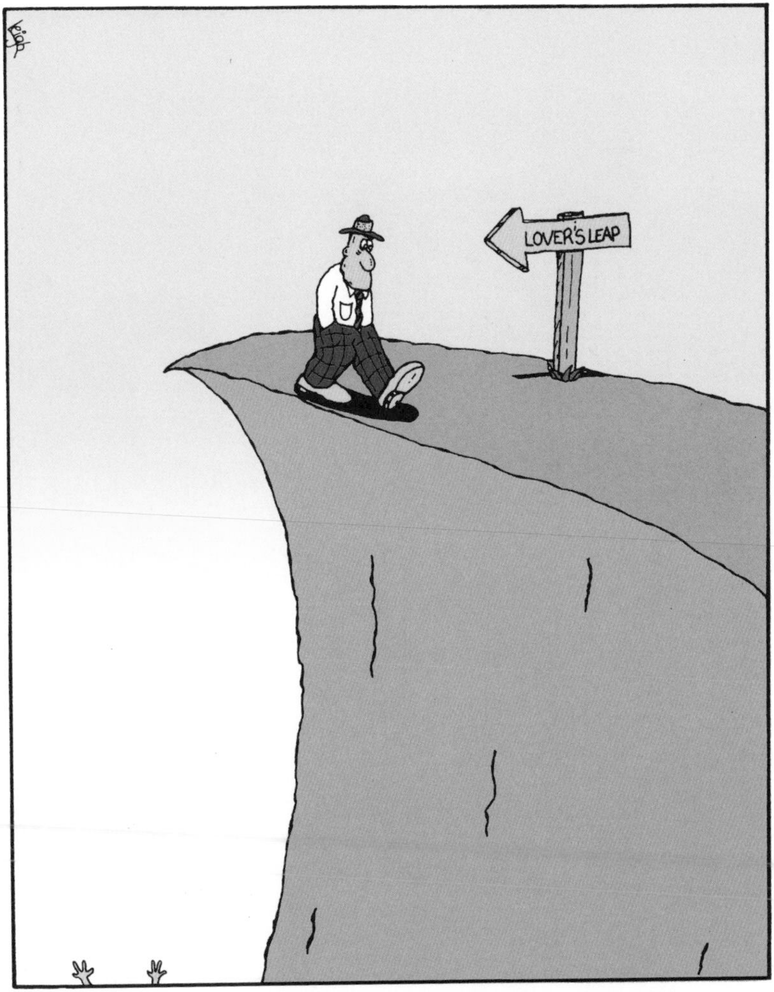
LOVER'S LEAP

After Marcie leapt, Herb realized it was just infatuation.

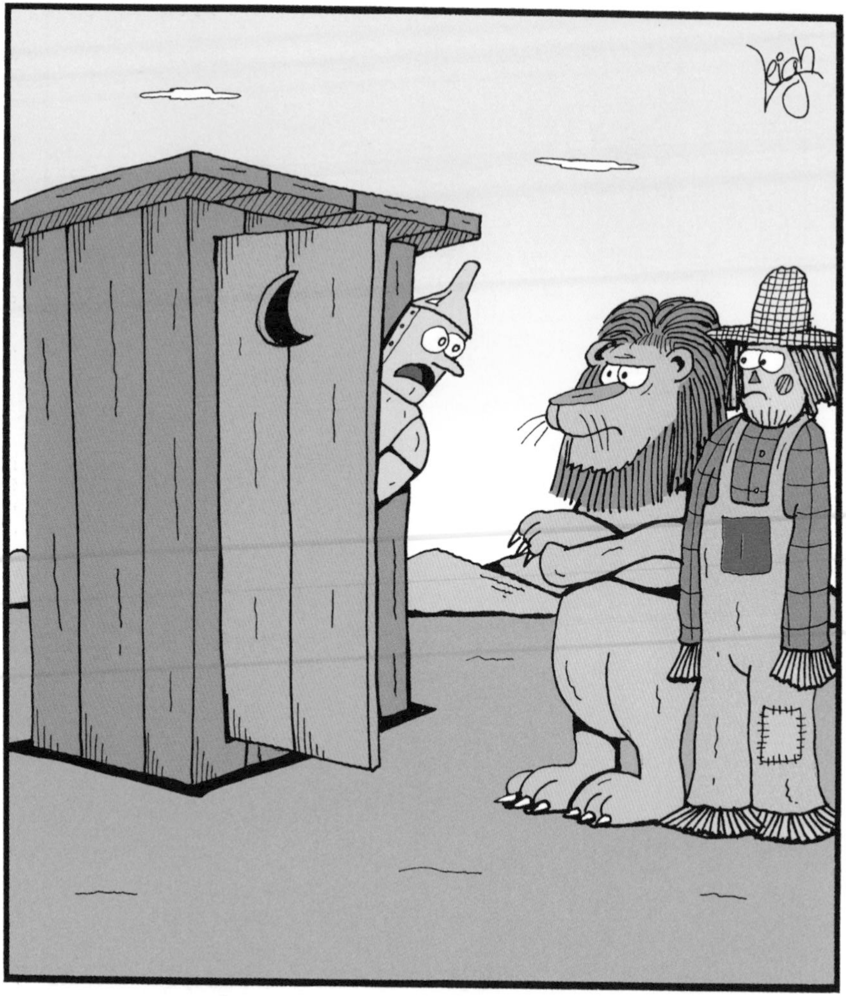

“Sorry to keep you waiting, fellas. I guess I should have asked the Wizard for a zipper.”

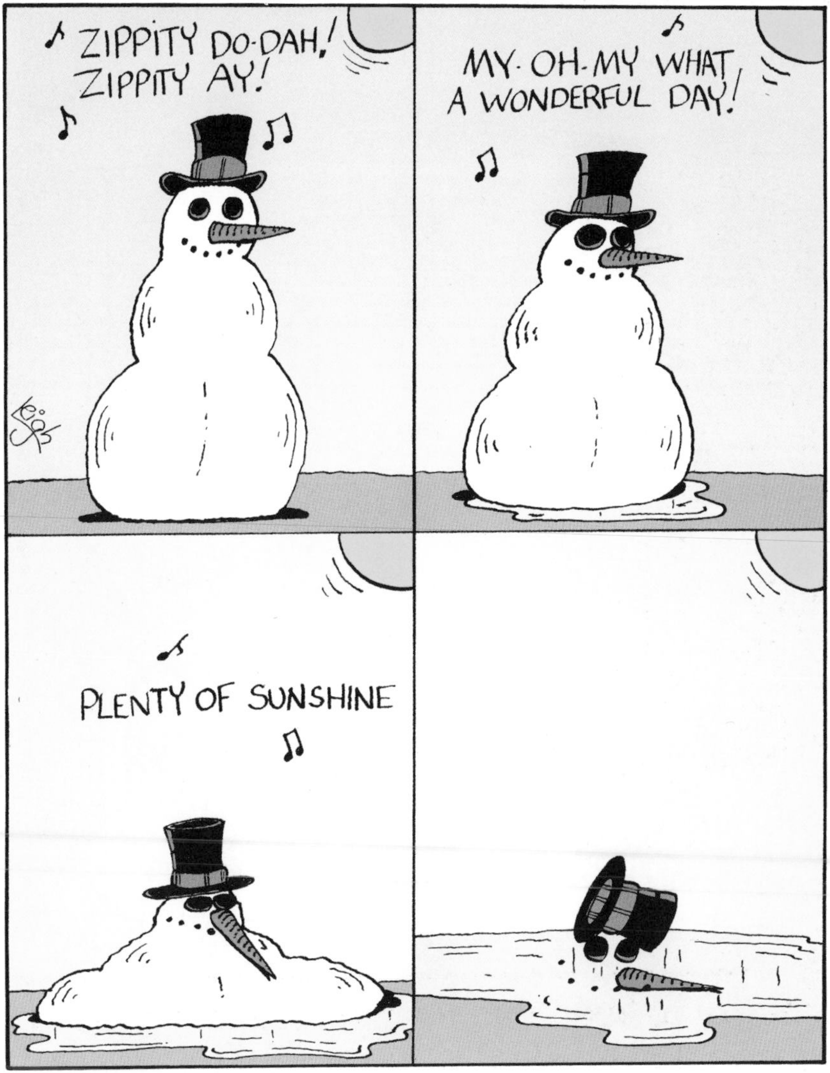
ZIPPITY DO-DAH!
ZIPPITY AY!
MY-OH-MY WHAT A WONDERFUL DAY!
PLENTY OF SUNSHINE

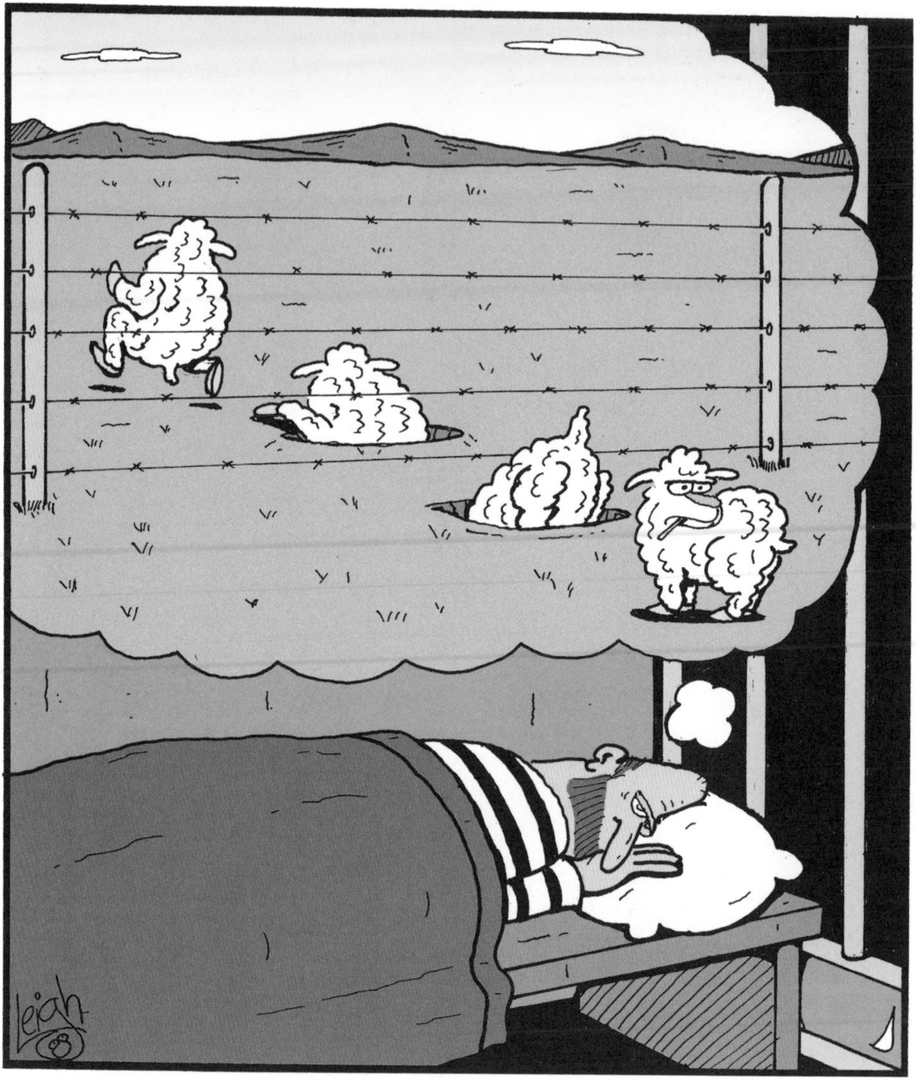

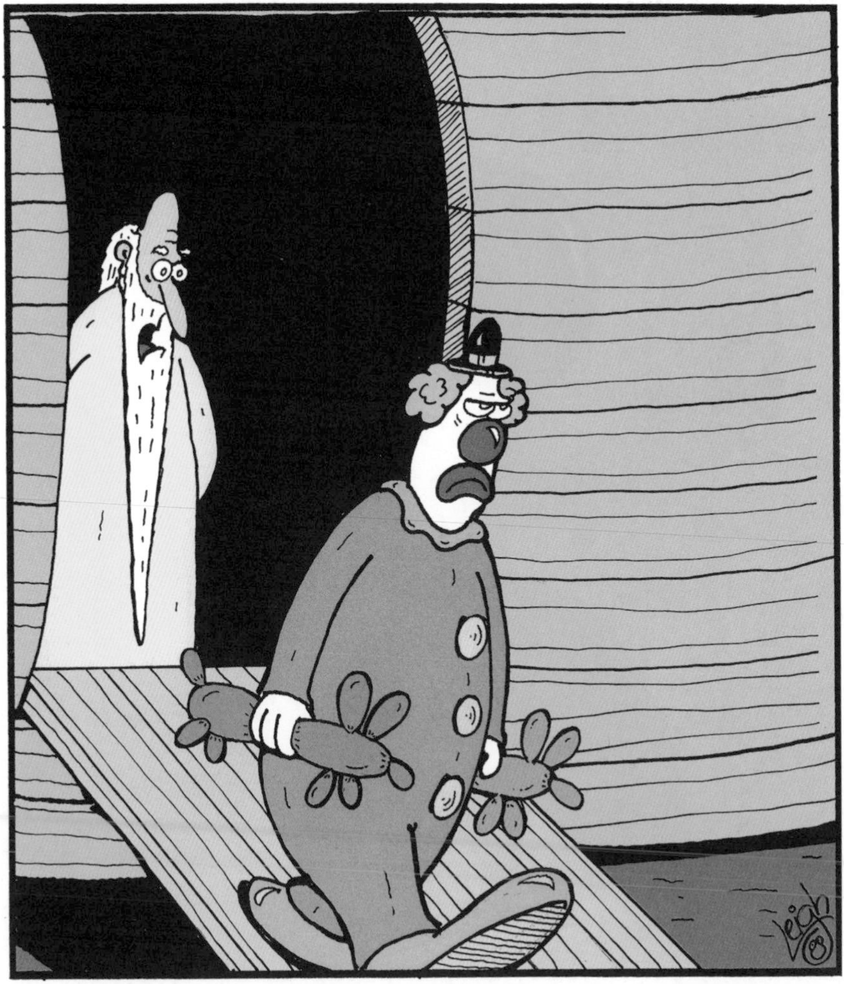

"If it's any consolation, I really admire your creativity."

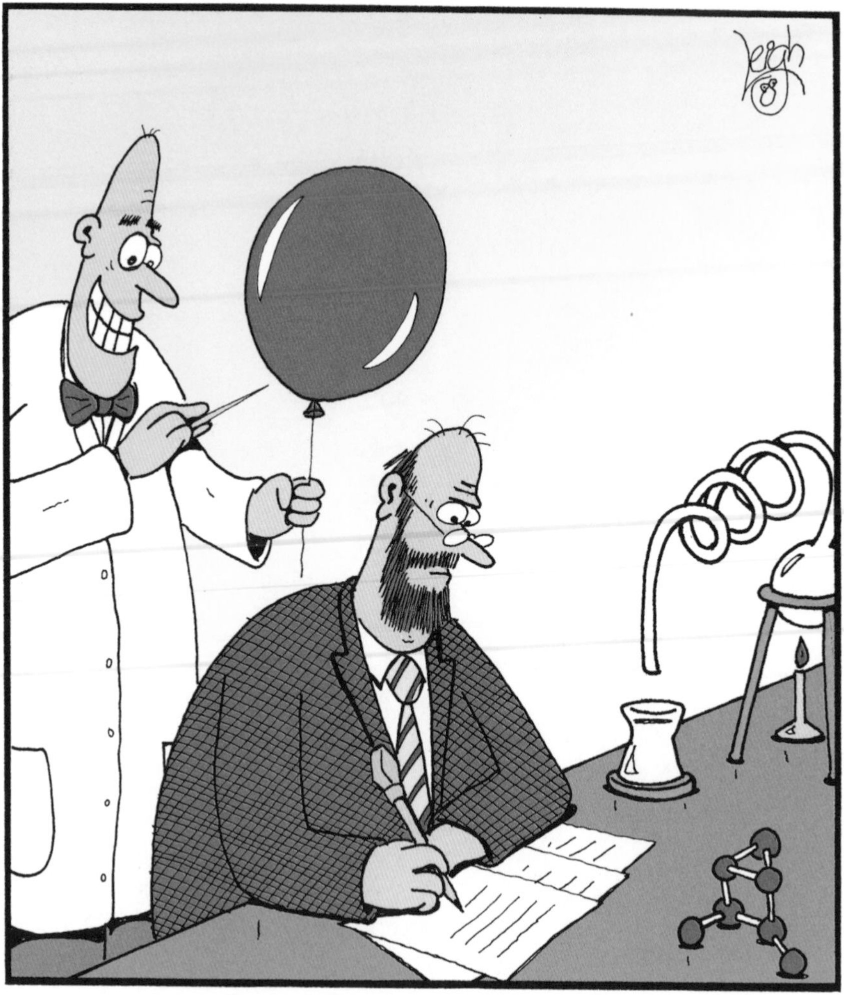

Late one evening in the physics lab, with a little help from a colleague, Professor Rittenberg discovers the element of surprise.

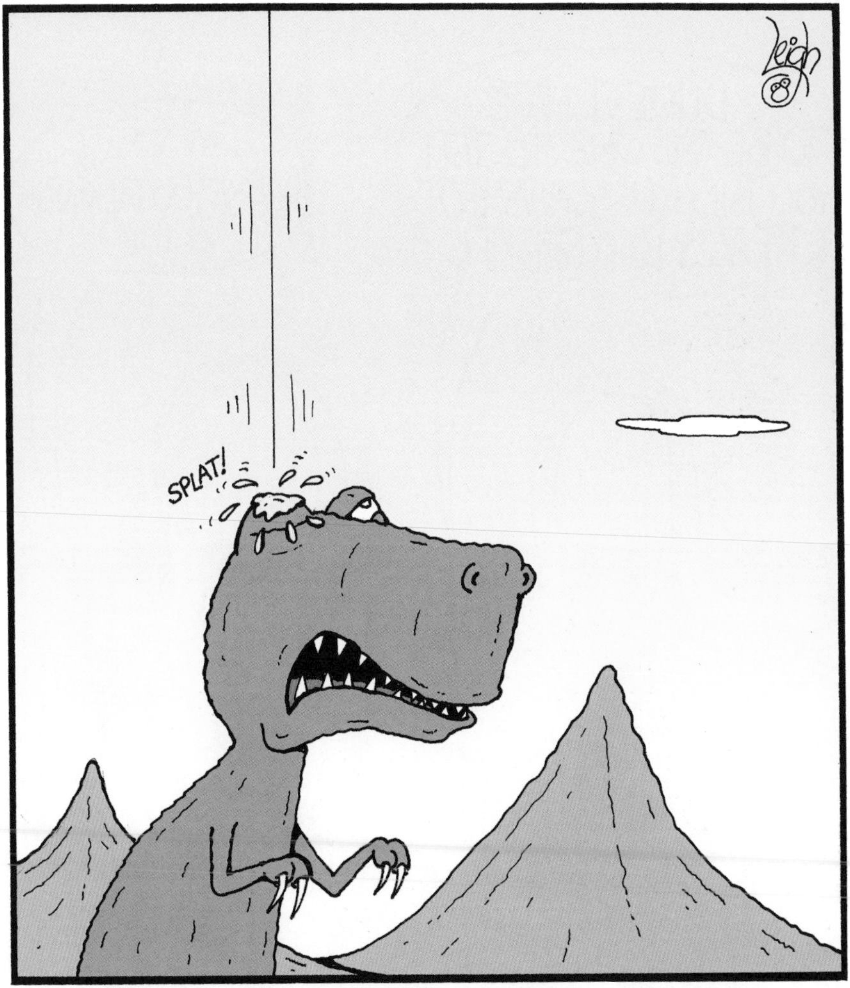
SPLAT!

The Jurassic period—when the first birds appeared

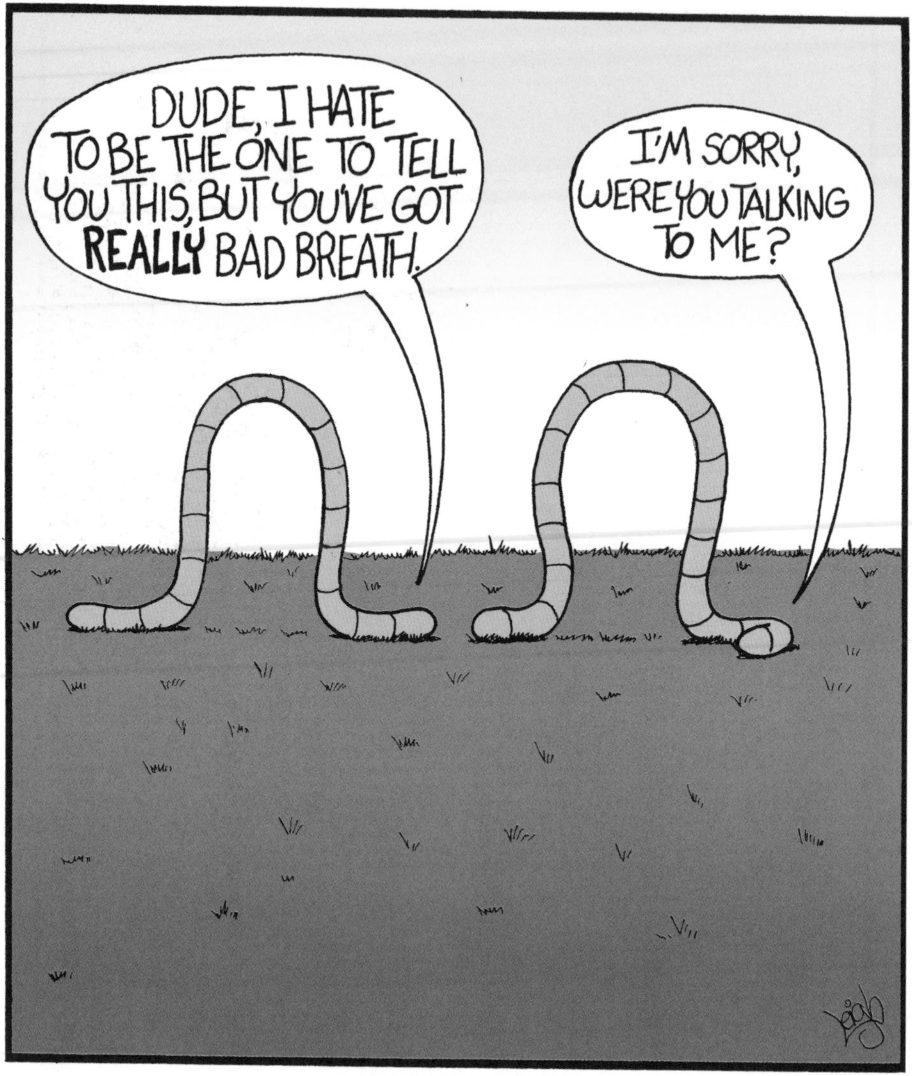
DUDE, I HATE TO BE THE ONE TO TELL YOU THIS, BUT YOU'VE GOT **REALLY** BAD BREATH.
I'M SORRY, WERE YOU TALKING TO ME?

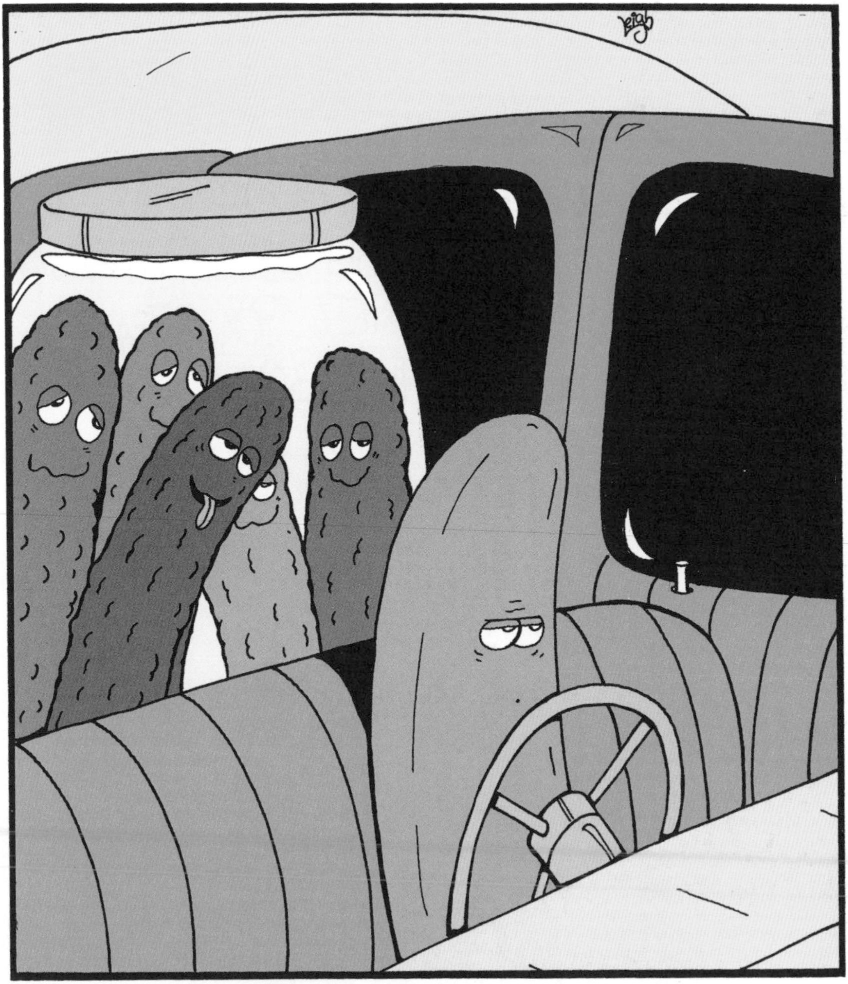
Leigh

Cucumber designated drivers

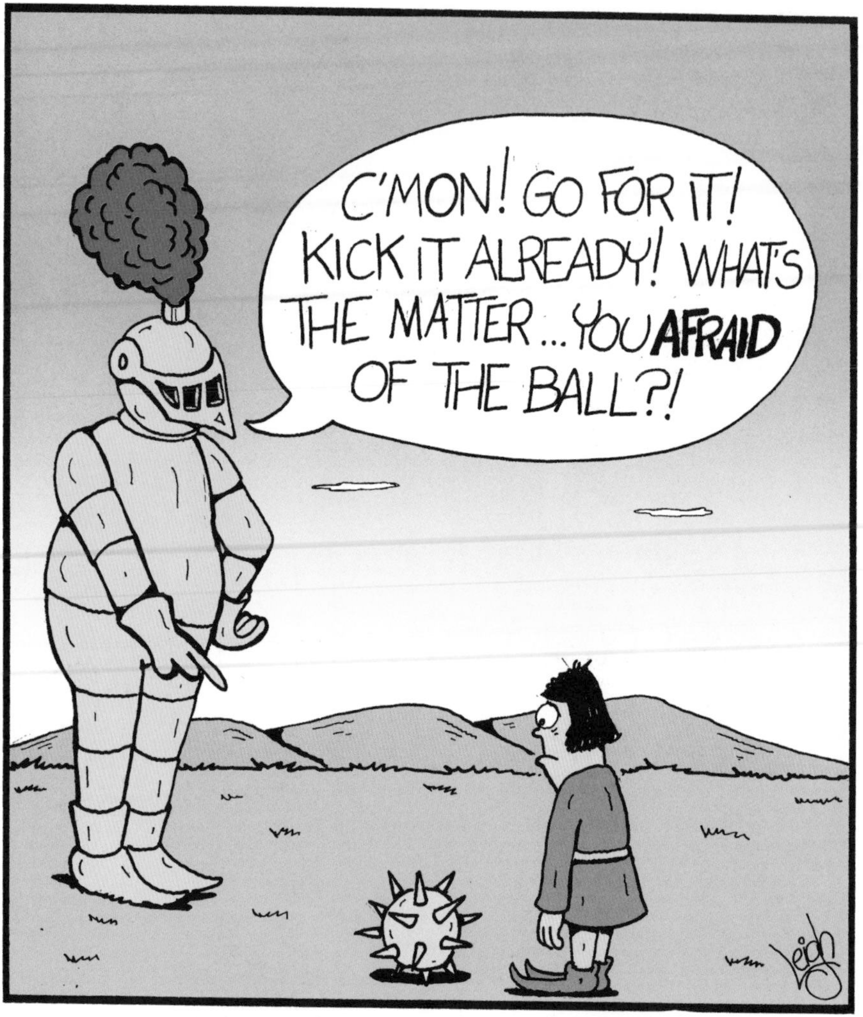
C'MON! GO FOR IT! KICK IT ALREADY! WHAT'S THE MATTER... YOU AFRAID OF THE BALL?!

Medieval soccer coaches

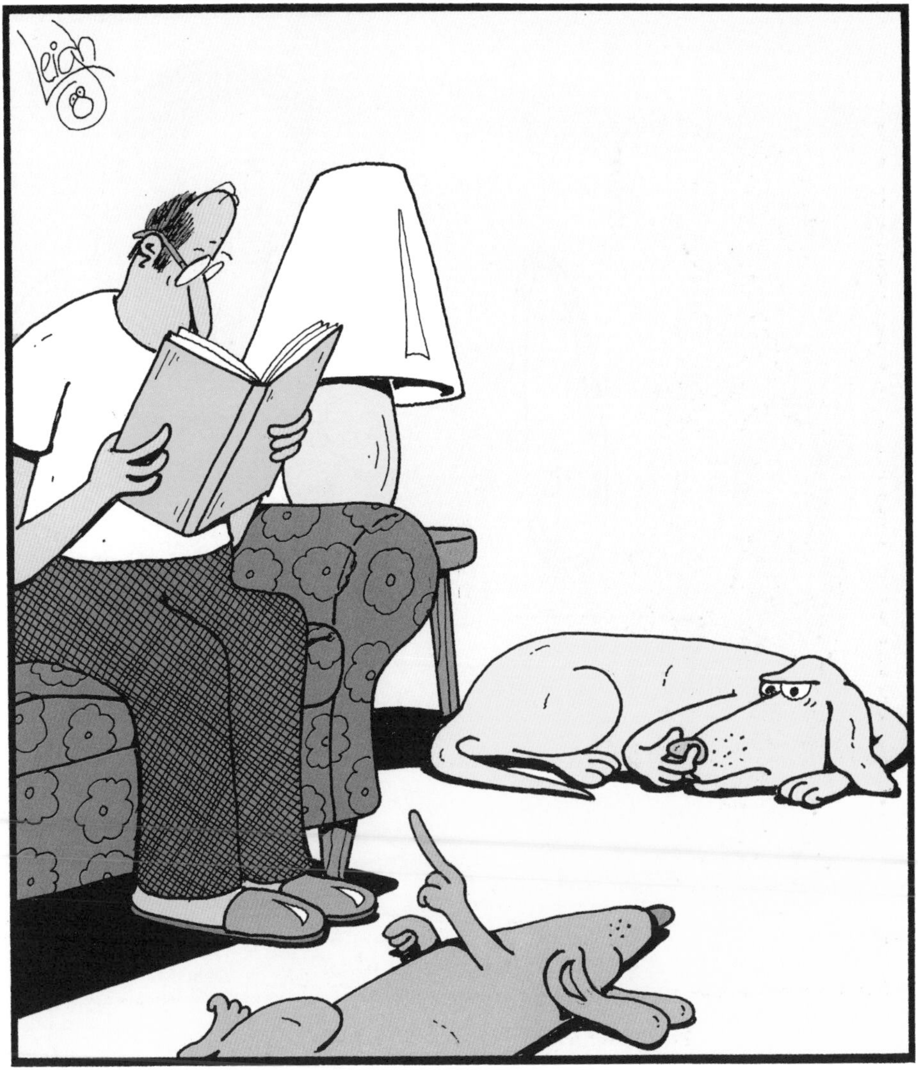

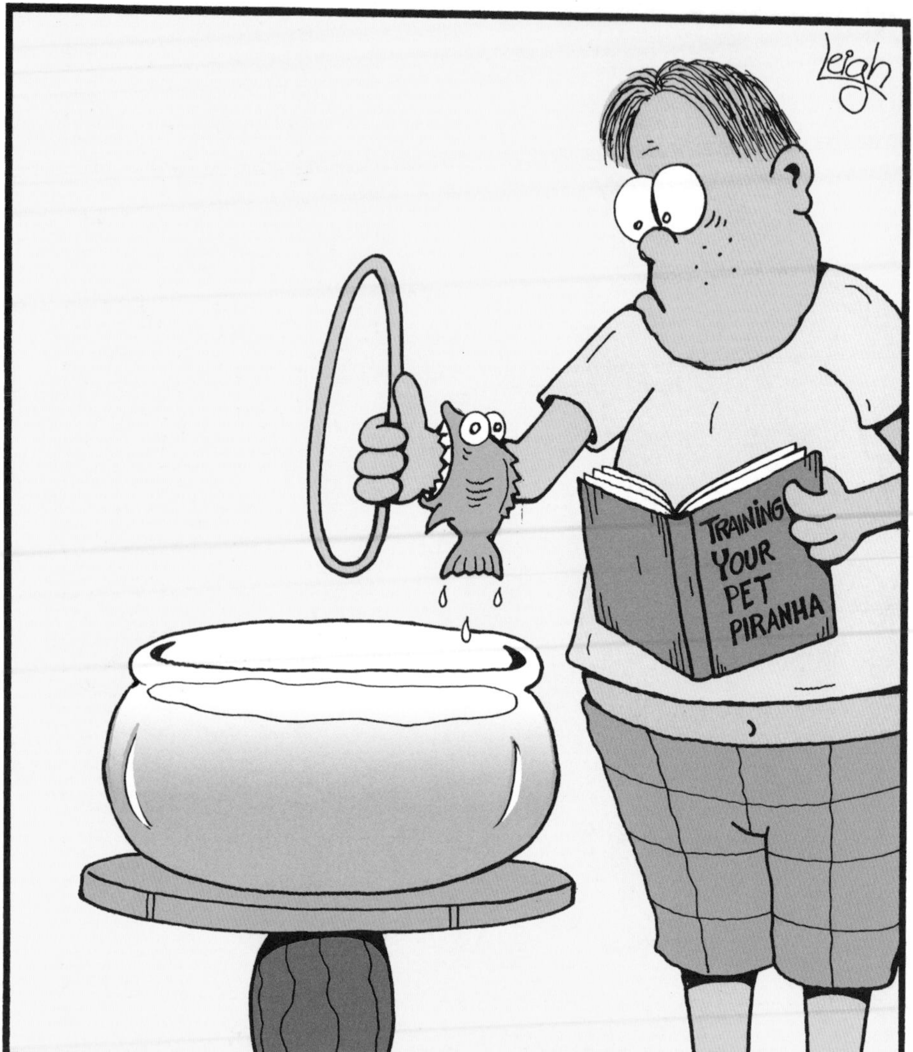
Leigh
TRAINING YOUR PET PIRANHA

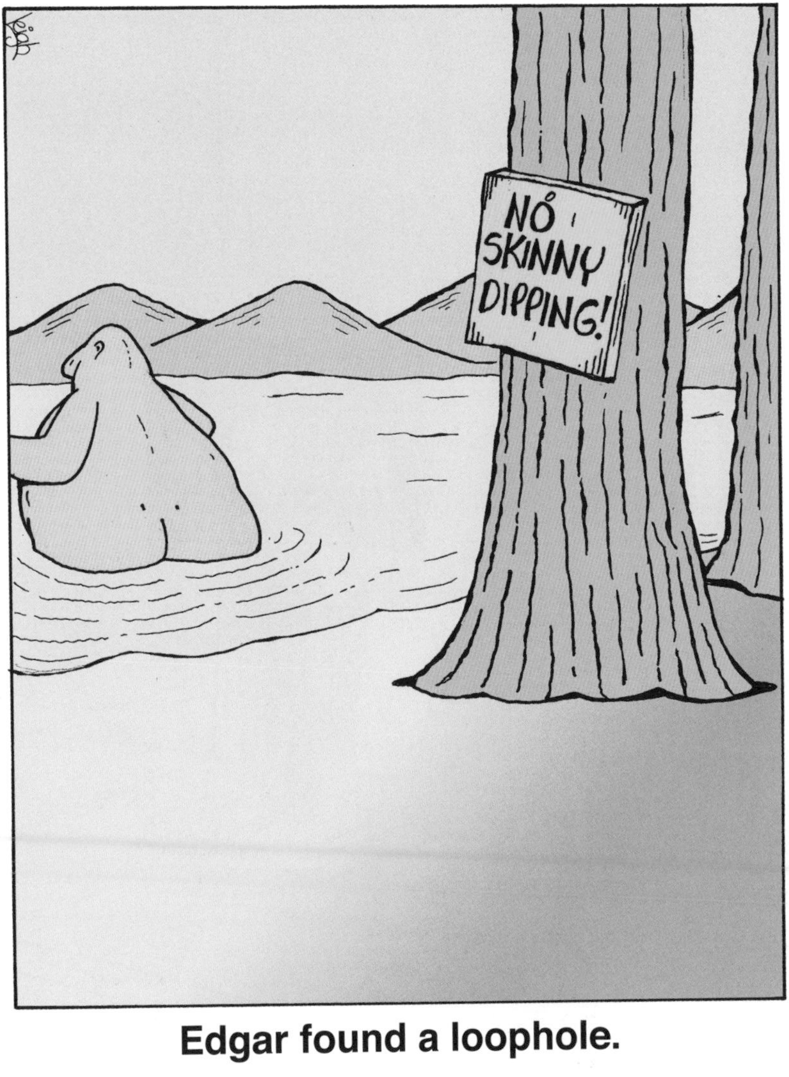
NO SKINNY DIPPING!

Edgar found a loophole.

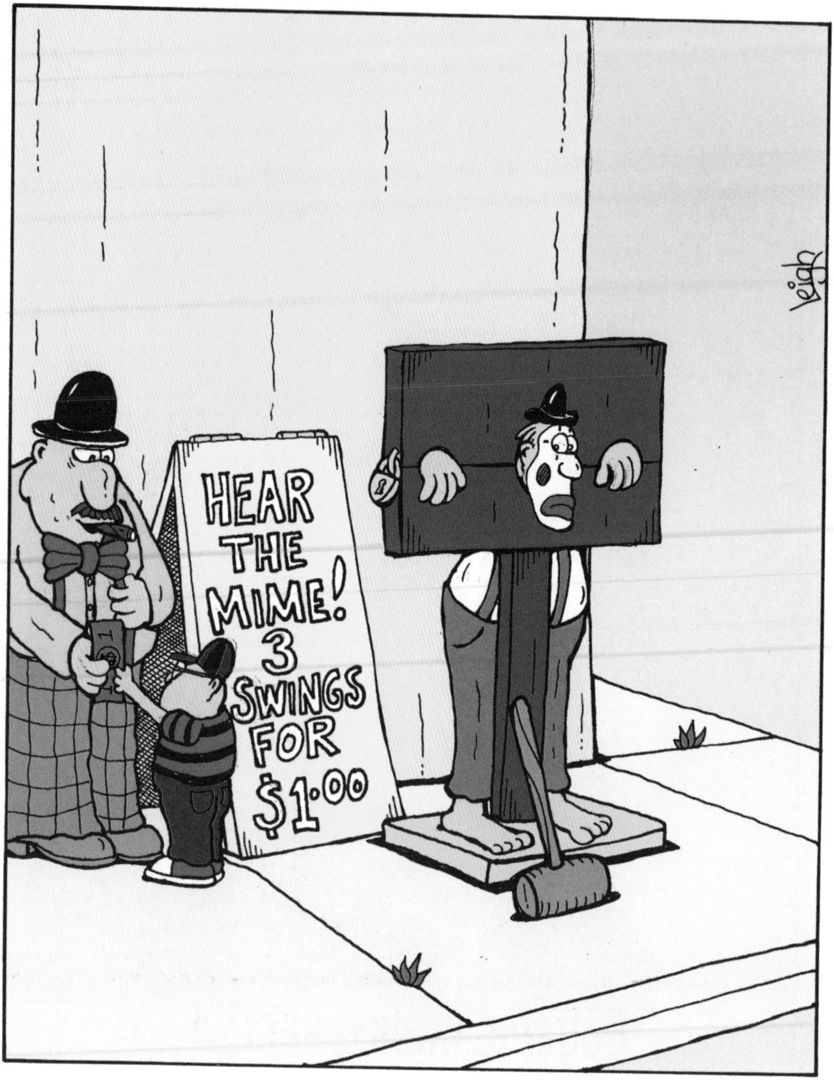
HEAR
THE
MIME!
3
SWINGS
FOR
$1.00
leigh

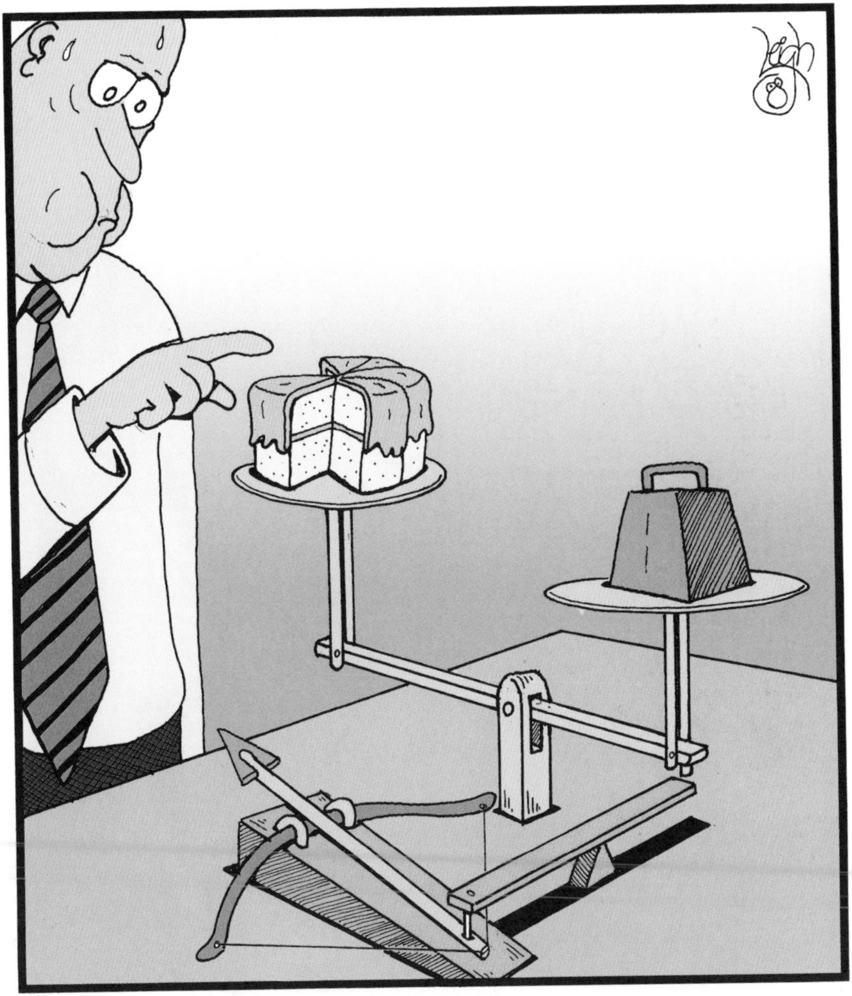

Extreme portion control

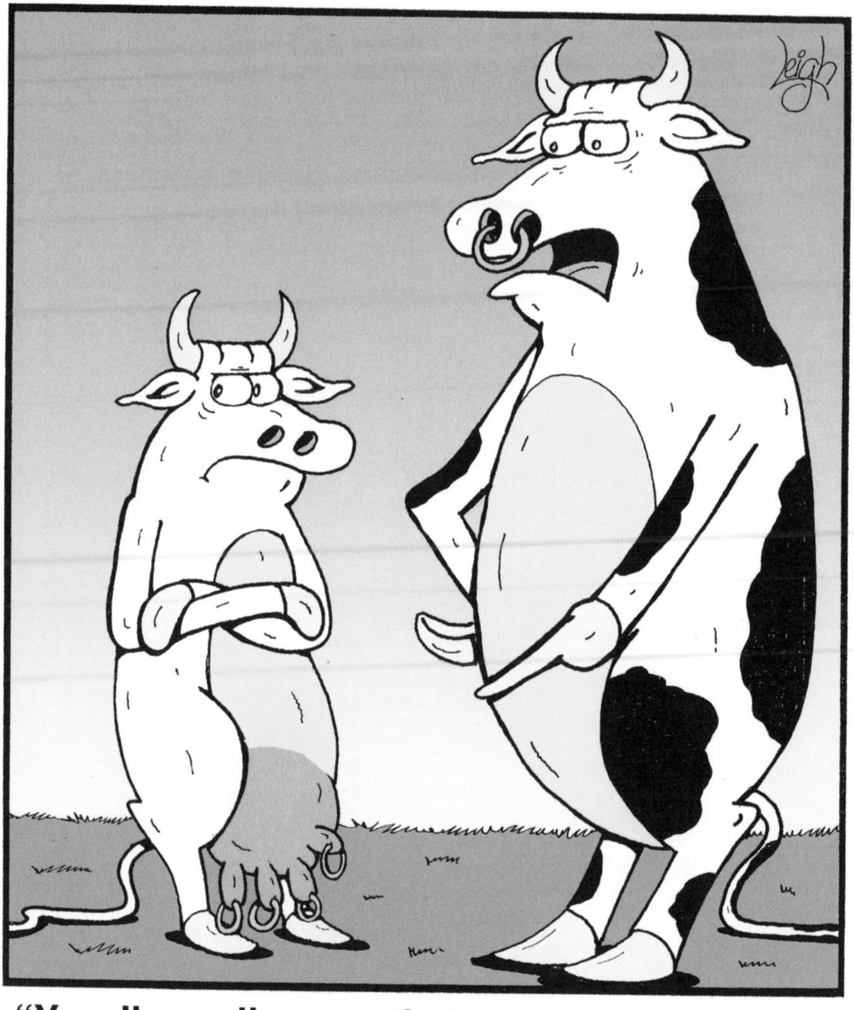
Leigh

"Yes, I'm well aware that my nose is pierced, but *those* are different!"

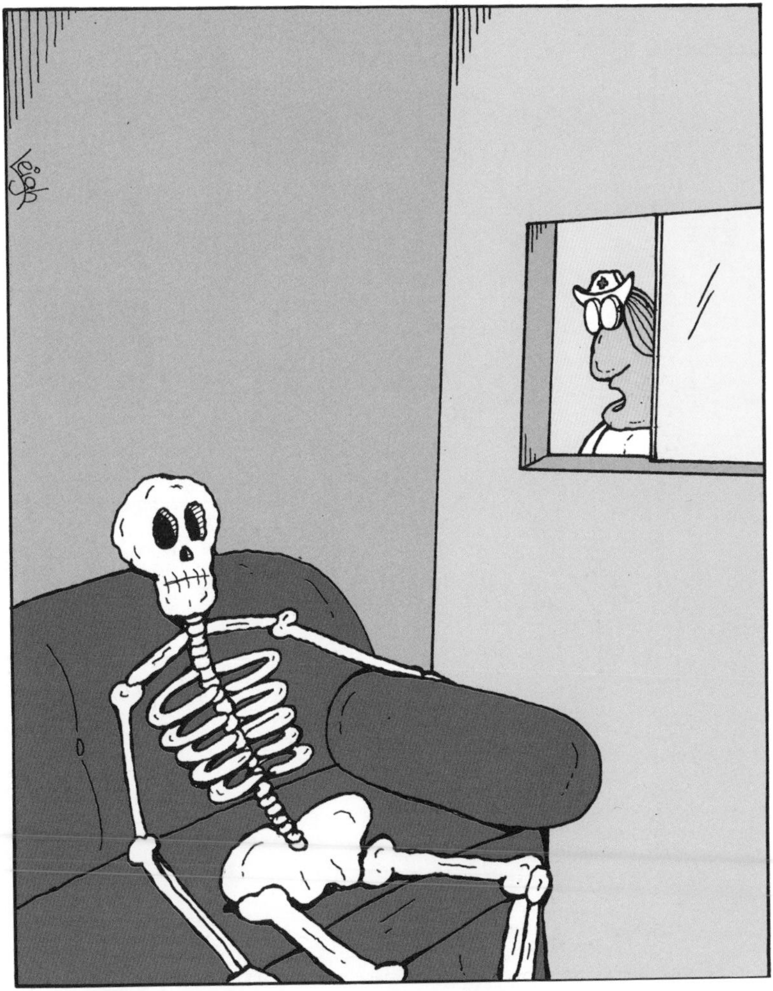
Leigh

"The doctor will be with you in just five more minutes."

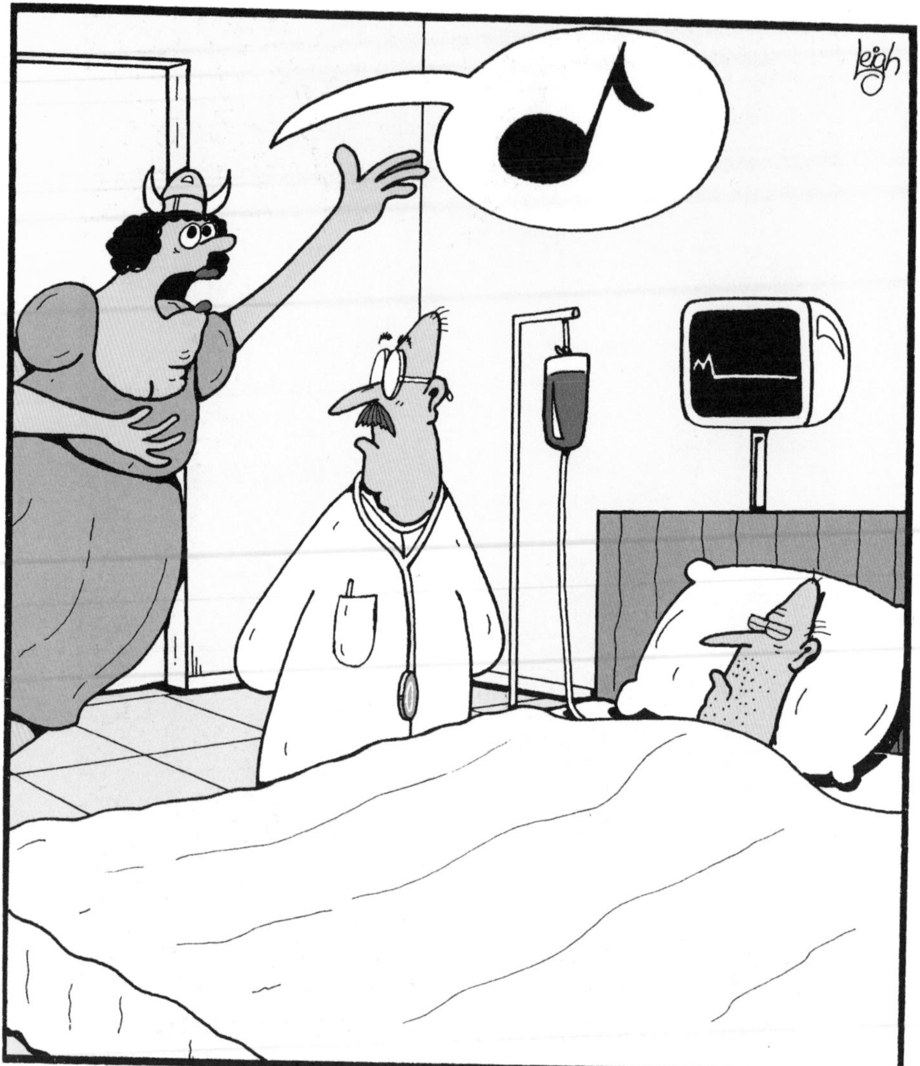

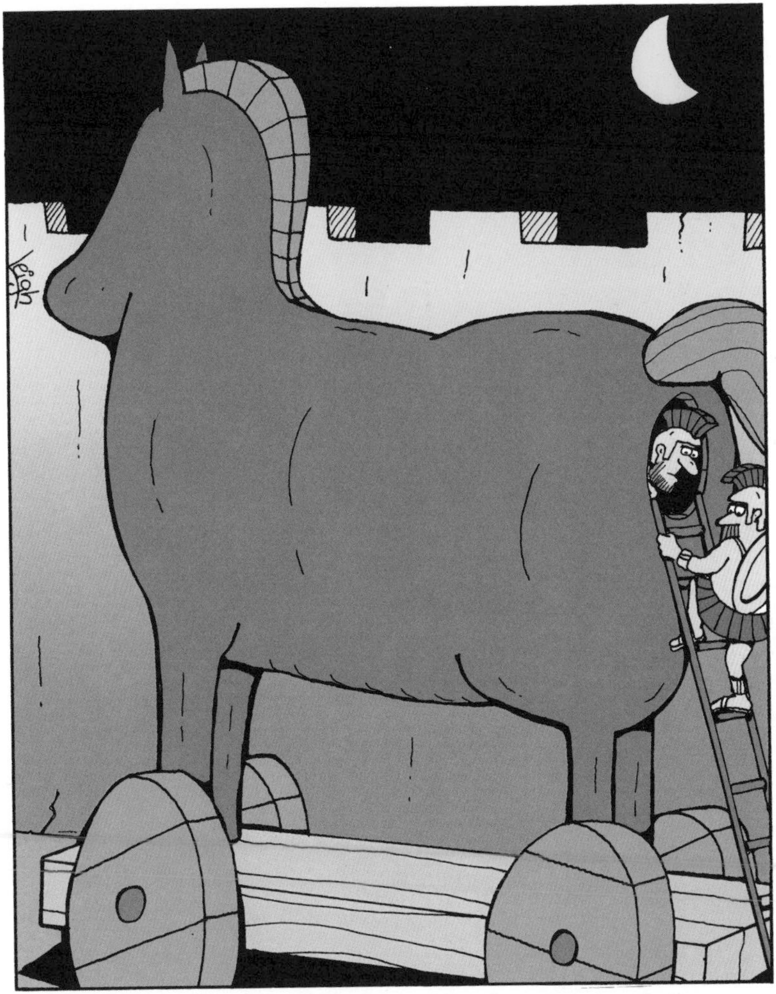
Leigh

In what is now considered an almost legendary classic offensive, the Greeks came from behind to win.

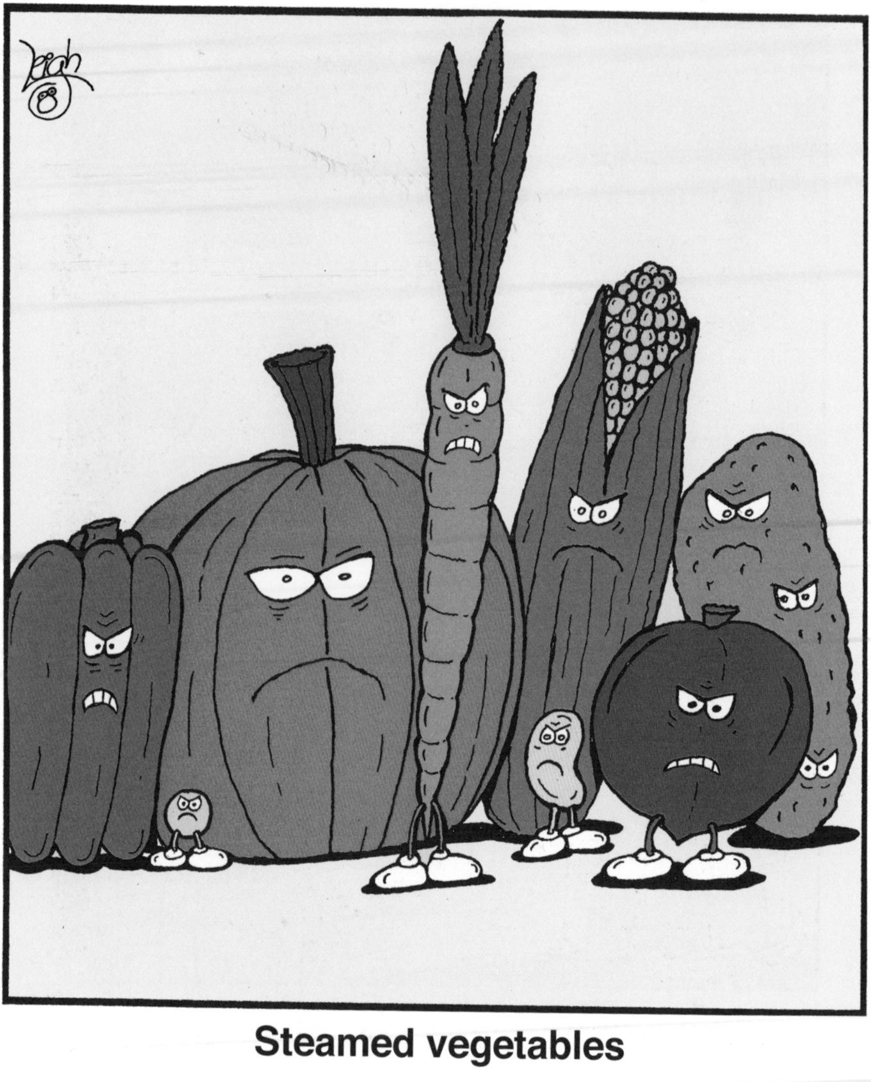
Leigh

Steamed vegetables

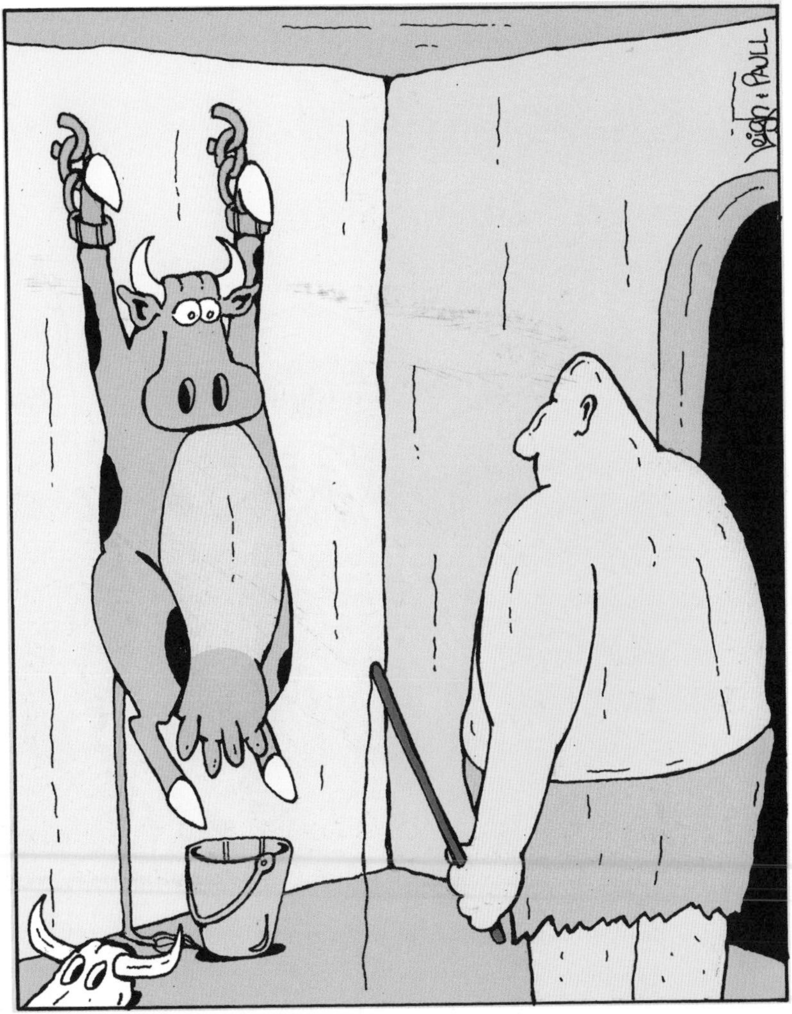
Vaughn Paull

The horrible truth behind whipped cream

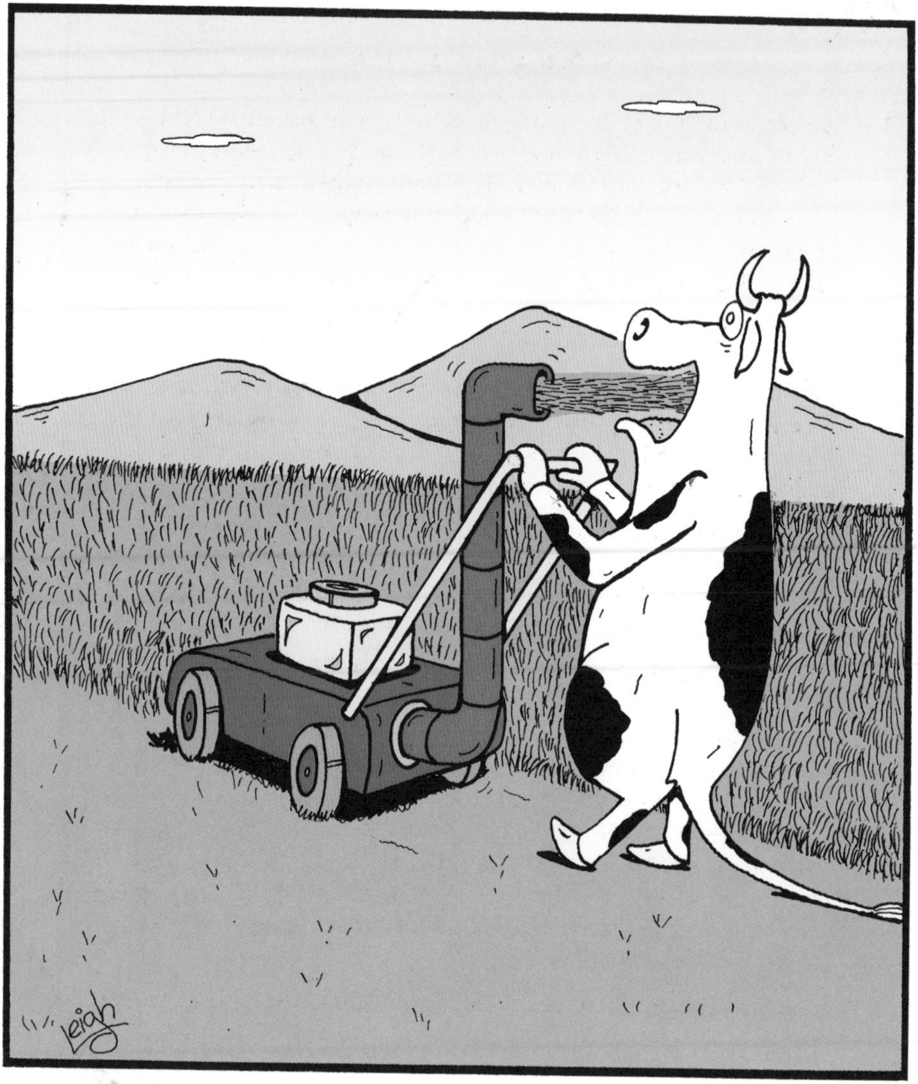
leigh